POPULAR PERFORMANCE
PLAYS OF CANADA

CHAMPLAIN COLLEGE

Popular Performance Plays Of Canada, Volume 1

MARIAN M. WILSON, EDITOR

A THE DONNELLYS
a drama with music
by Peter Colley

B A WIFE IN THE HAND
a farce
by Jack H. Crisp

C HOARSE MUSE
a musical play~
book & lyrics by
Paddy Campbell
music by
Wm. Skolnik

D PUT ON THE SPOT/WHEN EVERYBODY CARES
two children's plays
by Beth McMaster

E WHAT GLORIOUS TIMES THEY HAD ~ NELLIE McCLUNG
a satire
by Diane Grant
and Company

We would like to express our gratitude to The Canada Council and the Ontario Arts Council for their support.

POPULAR PERFORMANCE PLAYS OF CANADA, VOLUME 1
© **Copyright 1976 by Simon & Pierre Publishing Company Limited**
All rights reserved

ISBN 0-88924-044-2
1 2 3 4 5/79 78 77 76
Simon & Pierre Publishing Company Limited, Order Department
P.O.Box 280 Adelaide Street Postal Station
Toronto, Ontario, Canada M5C 2J4

PREFACE

This volume introduces a new illustrated series of Canadian plays — plays which have had outstanding success in their regions, and which are now being made available for reading, study, or production throughout Canada.

We feel there is an ever increasing need to develop Canadian talent. Amateur theatre groups are continuing to build audiences for touring companies. Educational institutions are expanding their theatre arts programs, and providing a workshop environment for students to gain practical experience. Professional theatre has reached a new level of national awareness — and national pride.

The plays included in this volume were selected from forty-eight scripts which we considered. We are proud of the range of theatrical style which they represent, and of the success each has achieved in original production by such diverse theatres as Montreal International Theatre (La Poudrière), Peterborough Theatre Guild, Redlight Theatre (Toronto), Theatre London (Grand Theatre and National Arts Centre) and Alberta Theatre Projects (Calgary).

Whether you are reading the plays for general interest, for study, or with an eye to future production, we hope you will share our enthusiasm for the ever-improving quality of Canadian playwriting. We have endeavoured in our format to match this quality, and to give these plays the attention and recognition we feel they deserve.

Marian M. Wilson
General Editor

<table>
<tr><td>Associate
Editor</td><td>Ron Cameron graduated from the University of Western Ontario in 1966 with a B.A. He then studied at the Banff School of Fine Arts, and in 1970 he graduated from the Guildhall School of Music and Drama in London (England) with his A.G.S.M. in Speech and Drama. In 1971, he received his Diploma of Education from the University of London, and returned to Canada to teach English and Theatre Arts at Riverdale Collegiate Institute in Toronto. Ron undertook to adapt and direct James Reaney's ONE-MAN MASQUE, as Riverdale Collegiate's Drama Club entry into the 1972 Ontario Collegiate Drama Festival. His adaptation, renamed MASQUE, won at the preliminary level and was first runner-up in the Ontario finals.</td></tr>
</table>

Pursuing a career as a director, Ron travelled to the Arts & Culture Centre in St. John's, Newfoundland, to direct LEAVING HOME by David French. He has also adjudicated for the Ontario Collegiate Drama Festival for four years and has directed many community theatre group under the auspices of Theatre Ontario's training program.

Currently, Ron is head of Drama at Sheridan College.

Associate Editor — **Roy Higgins** started his career backstage at the Crest Theatre in Toronto. After some minor roles as an actor in Canada and the United States, he decided that his main talent was in directing. Between the decision and the execution were many years of hard work, which Roy used to become an expert lighting man, make-up man, stage manager, and ultimately technical director.

His directing abilities were utilized as Artistic Director with the Belleville Theatre Guild's Pinnacle Playhouse, the Orono Youtheatre, and Playwrights' Workshop in Montreal.

He has directed McGill University's Red & White Revue and numerous other musicals.

Credits

General Editor Marian M. Wilson
Associate Editors Ron Cameron, Roy Higgins
Designer Catherine P. Wilson
Typesetter Joyce M. Wilson
Copy Editors Ron Cameron, Joyce M. Wilson
Printed and bound in Canada by
The Hunter Rose Company, Toronto, Ontario
Jacket Photos Courtesy of the Picture Collection,
Fine Arts Department, Metropolitan Toronto
Central Library

4

THE DONNELLYS

a drama with music

by Peter Colley

We would like to express our gratitude to The Canada Council and the Ontario Arts Council for their support.

Marian M. Wilson, Publisher

THE DONNELLYS
© **Copyright 1974 by Peter Colley**
All rights reserved

ISBN 0-88924-058-2
1 2 3 4 5/79 78 77 76
Simon & Pierre Publishing Company Limited, Order Department
P.O.Box 280 Adelaide Street Postal Station
Toronto, Ontario, Canada M5C 2J4

Author

Peter Colley comes from England where his grandparents managed several music halls. He himself did not enter this field until he was studying for his B.A. at the University of Sheffield. At that time, he started writing, directing and acting in various comedy revues. His first play THE SAGA OF REGIN was produced at the Drama Studio, Sheffield, in 1971.

Since then, Mr. Colley has played many major roles in his career: Felix Ungar in THE ODD COUPLE, Henry Higgins in MY FAIR LADY, Sir Andrew Aguecheek in TWELFTH NIGHT, and Fagin in OLIVER, to name but a few. He also played Grouchy Ryder in the original production of THE DONNELLYS.

Coming to Canada originally as an actor with Theatre London, he wrote a short play called THE BOX which played at Theatre London's Mini-Theatre. This led to a commission to write THE DONNELLYS for Theatre London's main stage.

THE DONNELLYS turned out to be the most successful play in the theatre's seventy-year history, and many thousands were turned away at the doors. A 1976 revival ran for three weeks at the National Arts Centre in Ottawa, and also played to capacity houses in London.

Mr. Colley's next play YOU'LL GET USED TO IT . . . THE WAR SHOW opened to rave reviews in London, and later moved to a very successful run in Toronto. He also wrote Theatre London's high school touring play in 1975, and was commissioned by the University of Western Ontario to work on their 1978 University Centennial project.

Composer

Berthold Carrière, who wrote the music for THE DONNELLYS, is an experienced composer and musical director.

For three seasons at Theatre London, he was musical director for all productions. Subsequently, he became musical director for Stratford Festival's touring productions of THE TEMPEST and HAMLET. He is now Director of Music for drama at the Stratford Festival.

Among other plays, Mr. Carrière has created scores for THE IMAGIN-ARY INVALID, ST. JOAN, DEATH OF A SALESMAN and THE DONNELLYS, and is currently writing music for a production in early 1977 at Theatre London, entitled ALICE THROUGH THE LOOKING GLASS.

A3

Original cast

Whiteboy, Jim Toohey, Vigilante, Meredith — Greg Brandt
Tim Mulligan — Wayne Burnett
Jim Donnelly — Tom Celli
Whiteboy, Constable, Wedding Party, Grouchy Ryder — Peter Colley
Johannah Donnelly — Patricia Collins
Father Connolly, Vigilante — Robert Cooper
Gossip, Sewing Bee, Wedding Party, Vigilante — Diane Cuthbert
Settler, Barman, McLaughlin — Art Fidler
Jim Donnelly Jr., Wedding Party, Pat Quigly — Tim Grantham
Sewing Bee, Wedding Party, Mrs. Whelan, Vigilante — Caroline Guerin
Gossip, Wedding Party, Vigilante — Darcia Hiltz
Jennie Donnelly, Wedding Party — Karna Ivey
Gossip, Sewing Bee, Wedding Party, Vigilante — Alicia Jeffery
Will Donnelly — David G. Marriage
Gossip, Sewing Bee, Wedding Party, Bridget Donnelly — Shelley Matthews
Settler, Patrick Donnelly, Vigilante, Wedding Party, Johnny O'Connor — Tom McCamus
Priest, Carswell, John Donnelly, Vigilante — Rick Prevett
Gossip, Sewing Bee, Wedding Party, Vigilante — Dace Reimanis
Whiteboy, Farrell, Flanagan, Vigilante, John Purtell — Jim Schaefer
Whiteboy, Tom Donnelly, Railway Guard, Vigilante, Will Casey — Tom Stebing
Whiteboy, Settler, Bob Donnelly, Vigilante, Wedding Party, Ed Ryan — Claude R. Tessier
James Carroll — David Wallett
Irving, Judge, Michael Donnelly — David Wasse
Settler, Thomson, Wedding Party, Mike Madigan, Vigilante — Cecil Wilson

Original production

The original production of THE DONNELLYS opened in 1974 at Theatre London, London, Ontario.
Directed by Heinar Piller
Original Music Composed by Berthold Carrière
Set Designed by Antonin Dimitrov
Lighting Designed by David Wallett
Costumes Designed by Olga Dimitrov

Dedication

The author, Peter Colley, wishes to dedicate this book to Heinar Piller.

A4

The memory of the Donnellys dies hard. In the many years of retelling, it has drifted into the realm of legend. In south-western Ontario, it is certainly the greatest of the folk-legends and has inspired many writers. The legend has painted the Donnellys very black indeed, although recent evidence indicates that they could not possibly have committed all the crimes of which they were accused. Since the massacre took place in 1880, it is very difficult to say what is factual and what is the product of too many bar-room raconteurs. However, this much is fact: in the early hours of February 4th, 1880, the townspeople of Lucan, Ontario rose up against the Donnelly family and murdered as many of them as they could find. That night saw the destruction of Jim and Johannah Donnelly (the parents of the seven Donnelly boys), Tom and John their sons, and their niece Bridget. After the Vigilante Committee had brutally murdered the family, it proceeded to burn the Donnelly farmstead to the ground, and even many of the bones were stolen by souvenir-hunters.

In death, the Donnellys assumed proportions which they had not even managed to attain in life, and the arguments about the justification of the killing rage on even today. We will never know for sure. This play does not claim to be the exact truth; simply a dramatic representation of the way it may have occurred, using as much of the available information as possible. In fact, some of the events and dialogue are taken directly from newspapers and court records of the time. Whichever way you look at it, however, the story of the Donnelly family will continue to intrigue writers and entertain the public for many years to come.

Additional
background

Books
THE DONNELLYS MUST DIE by Orlo Miller
THE BLACK DONNELLYS (The True Story of Canada's Most Barbaric Feud) by Thomas P. Kelley
VENGEANCE OF THE BLACK DONNELLYS by Thomas P. Kelley
Article
"The Canadian Magazine", an article on the Donnellys by Frank Rasky (March 16, 1974)
Plays
THEM DONNELLYS by The Company of Theatre Passe-Muraille, originally presented in 1973
BOYS, YOU HAVE DONE ENOUGH TONIGHT by Hugh Graham, originally presented by Trent University, Peterborough, Ontario, in 1974
HANDCUFFS — THE DONNELLYS, Part 1; ST. NICHOLAS HOTEL — THE DONNELLYS, Part 2; STICKS AND STONES — THE DONNELLYS, Part 3 —— a trilogy by James Reaney, originally presented by the Tarragon Theatre, Toronto, Ontario, from 1973 to 1975

A5

Cast of characters

Jim Donnelly — Father of the family. Stubborn and quick-tempered when provoked, but hard-working and reasonable most of the time.

Johannah Donnelly — Jim's wife. A very strong, practical woman. Once she makes up her mind, she forges forward with great determination. She has the strength of will to raise her large family single-handedly when necessary, and remains loyal to her husband through all his misfortunes.

Will Donnelly — Second son of Jim Donnelly. The leader of the Donnelly boys. Has a noticeable limp from a crippled foot. He is not big, but is aggressive and fairly well educated.

Tim Mulligan — Eternally drunk Irishman. Wears a tatty coat and hat. Has a small shoulder bag with bottle of whisky sticking out. Provides narration and comic relief.

Joe Carswell — Rather ostentatiously dressed landowner. Has fur trim on his jacket and sports a silver walking cane. However, rather spineless when challenged.

Pat Farrell — A thick-set Irish troublemaker. Loud and aggressive — these characteristics increase in direct relationship to the amount of alcohol he consumes.

Aemilius Irving, Q.C. — Plays all of the judges throughout the play, as well as his own character. Typical stiff representation of justice.

Martin McLaughlin — Friend of Will Donnelly. A scholarly man who is perturbed by the tough life-style of Will and his brothers. He becomes a magistrate, and is fairly easily convinced that the Donnellys are the cause of Lucan's problems.

Father Connolly — Local priest. He is naive and very quick to believe the things he is told. He is dragged into the Donnelly story rather unwittingly, and although he helped form the Vigilante Committee, it paid little heed to him.

James Carroll — A roughneck and bully. He is tough and he knows it. He is not totally without feeling, but considers himself a bit of a local hero in waging war against the Donnellys.

Toohey — Local farmer. Hates the Donnellys.

Flanagan — Owner of local stageline.

Thompson — Grumpy old man.

Jim Feeheeley — A young friend of Tom Donnelly.

Pat Quigly — A hanger-on in Carroll's gang, although he secretly befriends the Donnellys.

Purtell — An extremely slow-witted but brutal member of the Vigilante Committee.

Madigan — Member of Vigilante Committee.

Will Casey — An ex-magistrate and member of the Vigilante Committee.

Grouchy Ryder — A farmer who has become very embittered by several attacks on his property. Also partial to the bottle.

A6

Ed Ryan — Member of the Vigilante Committee.

Elliot — A Protestant friend of Jim Donnelly.

Janet — Local lady. She is very pregnant and rather slow-witted.

Agnes — Local lady. Old and crotchety.

Dora — Local lady. Strong-minded. Doesn't believe gossip.

Annie — Local lady. Doesn't like the Donnellys, and believes everything she hears.

Johnny O'Connor — A young boy (12 years old). He was the only eye-witness to the massacre.

Bridget — Niece of the Donnellys.

Assorted — Priests, barmen, constables, Donnelly boys, reporters, street vendors.

General setting   Although part of the opening action takes place in Ireland, most of the play is set in various locations in and around Lucan, Ontario.

Time   Between 1844 and 1881

A7

Act one *The play opens with a low, ominous, rumbling sound. It is the sound of a cluster of notes on a large church organ. It begins softly and builds towards a crescendo. The house lights fade, and the sound of wind is added. A picture fades into view on the screen. It is a film of a large tree standing gauntly against the sky-line of a barren, wintery field. Beside it is a man. He walks towards the camera with a pronounced limp. As he gets nearer the camera, his scarf blowing in the icy wind, an expression of deep hatred can be seen on his face. At the beginning of the film, a sad and haunting tune takes over from the sound of the wind and the organ. As the music progresses, the man's face fills the screen — finally, all that is left is the man's eyes staring accusingly at the audience. The man is William Donnelly. (If the film is not used, a slide of the Donnelly grave is shown with the figure of a man silhouetted against the screen. A spot picks out his face, and his eyes stare accusingly at the audience. The man is William Donnelly.) Suddenly, the stage lights come on to reveal the company. Everyone is in black with no distinguishing costumes.*

(Mulligan enters wearing a dirty overcoat and battered hat.)

Mulligan:

Back in 1880, there was hatred in the air.
The bloody feuds of Ireland had found a foothold there.
The angry roar of horses hooves were echoing the sound.
This night we'll put the Donnellys full six feet underground.

(Slide 1 — map of Lucan and London.)

All *(sing)*:

Forty men went riding, though hundreds more knew why.
Forty men went shouting, "The Donnellys must die!"
And when the night was over and the murdering was through,
A silence came to Lucan town that death could not undo.
Come follow us one hundred years
And we'll take you back to Lucan town and the Black Donnellys.

(Slide 2 — map of Ireland and England.)

Mulligan: The curse of old Ireland, they called it.

(The following lines are done by individuals in the company.)

One: Three hundred years of hate.

A9

Two: The beginning:

Three: Cromwell came to Ireland.

All: And there was us.

Four: Shannons,

Five: O'Haras,

Six: Kellys.

Seven: Catholics and Irish.

All: And them:

Eight: Blakes,

Nine: Walkers,

Ten: Deschamps.

Eleven: Protestants and English.

Twelve: Three hundred years of hate.

All *(sing)*:

> Hate was there in plenty and murderers two score;
> We'll never get the Donnellys on this side of the law.
> But the one they hated most of all still stands alive and tall:
> Will Donnelly by fate survives to prosecute them all.
>
> It's autumn now, summer's gone and justice must be done,
> But the heat of mankind's hatred won't fade beside the sun,
> And if you scream for justice, just stop and think awhile:
> How can a man of law demand to put a town on trial?

Irving: Gentlemen of the jury, you have been called here to pass judgment on one of the foulest and blackest crimes which has ever blighted the history of the Dominion — the culmination of a long and bitter feud that has made Biddulph Township a byword for lawlessness and violence. Why did the so-called "honest" citizens of Biddulph leave the comfort of their homes that cold February night, and attempt to annihilate an entire family? *(Slide 3 — a map of the*

A10

Tipperary area) Mr. William Donnelly, your parents were Irish, were they not?

Will Donnelly: Yes, sir, they came from Tipperary.

Elliot *(to Jim Donnelly)*: That's a fine mare, Jim. But mind the Whiteboys don't find out you're selling it to a Protestant.

Jim Donnelly: The Devil take them! Those bully-boys will not be telling me who I can sell my horses to.

Whiteboy 2: Jim Donnelly was over at Elliot's yesterday. Sold him that chestnut mare.

Whiteboy 1: Elliot?

Whiteboy 2: Aye . . . a Protestant.

(Slide 4 — neutral — blue colour.)

Will Donnelly *(to Irving)*: They said we was associating with Protestants.

Irving: They?

Will Donnelly: The Whiteboys. They were a secret society in Ireland, got together to put the fear of God into the Protestant landlords . . . and any Catholics who had dealings with them.

Whiteboy 1: Sold a horse to a Protestant, eh? Maybe we should pay him a visit? Get up the rest of the boys.

(Slide 5 — the words "Tipperary 1844". Whiteboys 1 and 2 go off to the back of the set to put hats and jackets on, then join four other Whiteboys. Other members of the company set a table and chairs in centre stage. Johannah is sitting working when Jim enters with some firewood.)

Jim Donnelly: Johannah . . . I just seen lanterns coming up from the village . . . half a dozen maybe.

(Slide 6 — warm colour — red.)

Johannah: Coming our way?

A11

Jim Donnelly: Aye . . . looks like it.

Johannah: It's a bit late for anyone to be calling. You don't think they're here about the mare?

Jim Donnelly: I don't know . . . it's possible. Well, if it's trouble they're after, I'll give them their due — and more. *(Knocking at door)* Mind your words now, Johannah. *(More knocking — Jim opens the door to several men)* Well, hello boys . . . Pat . . . Bill . . . come on in.

Men: Evening . . . Jim . . . Johannah.

Jim Donnelly: Well, now . . . it's nice to see you. How are you all? *(Mumblings of "fine" and "alright" from the group, followed by an uncomfortable silence)* Well, what can I do for you? Would you care for a jar?

Whiteboy 1: No thank you, Jim, we're on business.

Jim Donnelly: Business?

Whiteboy 1: We're after a few words with you . . . alone. *(He indicates Johannah.)*

Johannah: What's Jim's business is mine.

Whiteboy 2: Aye, but this is men's talk.

Jim Donnelly: Get on with it.

Whiteboy 2: We're not out to cause trouble, Jim. It's nothing more than some help we're after.

Whiteboy 1: There's a job needs doing for the Whiteboys.

Jim Donnelly: Then get a Whiteboy to do it.

Whiteboy 1: Well, that's what we've come about, Jim. You're Catholic. . . . You're one of us. But you've displayed a kind of . . . how would you say . . .

Whiteboy 2: Reluctance.

Whiteboy 1: Aye, that's a nice word . . . reluctance. You've displayed

A12

a kind of reluctance to join. It's not gone unnoticed.

Johannah: Just because he's not after murdering people in their beds.

Whiteboy 2: Not just people. English murderers and Protestant land-lords are the ones that don't sleep easy. Which is bringing me to another point. Seems there's talk going round that you've been doing business with Protestants. Well, now, I wasn't after believing it myself. It's unheard of, I said, an honest Catholic associating with Protestant bastards. I'd shake hands with the Devil himself the day Jim Donnelly would stoop that low. Donnelly's a good man, I said, let's go ask him. *(Pause)* Well, Jim?

Jim Donnelly: I do business with a lot of people. I don't ask them all which church they go to.

Whiteboy 1: Is it true, Jim?

Jim Donnelly: How the hell should I know?

Whiteboy 1: Do you do business with Protestants?

Jim Donnelly: And what if I do?

Whiteboy 1: I want an answer, Donnelly.

Jim Donnelly: Yes, goddamn it! I do, and I'll do business with who the hell I like!

(Pause.)

Whiteboy 1: I'd rather you hadn't said that, Donnelly. *(Pause)* Well . . . I can't help you now.

(They grab Jim, and a fracas results with Johannah coming to help him, biting and scratching.)

Whiteboy 2: Get a-hold of that bastard she-bitch!

(They drag Johannah to one side where she is held by two men.)

Whiteboy 1: You're cutting your own throat, Donnelly. If you associate with scum, you become scum. Being Catholic won't save you. Remember what happened to the Nangles and the Courceys.

A13

If you want to live in peace, you must come with us and do as you're damn well told. You're too pig-headed by half. See this, Donnelly? *(He shows him a piece of paper.)*

Jim Donnelly: What the hell's that?

Whiteboy 1: It's the Whiteboy's oath, and I want to hear you swear allegiance to it. Read him the oath.

Whiteboy 2: On your knees, and with your hand on the Good Book, you must swear:

(Slide 7 — a cold colour — dark green. The lights dim on the centre stage, and the figures placed around the set appear in silhouette. The oath is spoken in a conspiratorial whisper reinforced by tape-recorded whisperings.)

Voice: One!

All: That I will, at any hour, whether by night or day, perform without fail or inquiry such commands as my superiors may lay upon me.

Voice: Two!

All: I also declare that I will not admit or propose a Protestant or heretic as a member of our fraternal society, knowing him to be such.

Voice: Three!

All: That I will always give preference in dealing to those who are attached to our national cause, and that I will not deal with a Protestant or heretic — so long as I can deal with one of my own faith on equal terms.

Voice: Four!

All: That I will not give evidence in any court of law or justice against a brother, but aid him in his defence by any means in my power.

(Lights change back. Slide 8 — warm colour — red.)

Whiteboy 1: Get on your knees, Donnelly, and swear.

A14

Jim Donnelly: I will not.

(Silence.)

Whiteboy 1: You've had this coming for a long while.

(They beat him up, and leave him on the floor.)

Johannah: You cowardly bastards! You're like a pack of rats.

Whiteboy 1: You must come with us, Donnelly. Come with us, or we'll call you Blackfoot.

Jim Donnelly: Call me what you like!

Whiteboy 1: You're a fool. You're doing the same as Walker did. You remember Walker?

Whiteboy 3: He had dealings with the English tyrants. He's dead now, but before he died he took a bath in a barrel of thorns.

Whiteboy 2: And had his lying tongue cut out.

Whiteboy 1: Remember, Donnelly?

Jim Donnelly: Get out. Get out of here.

Whiteboy 1: Alright, leave him alone. *(He motions to the others, and they draw back)* Look around you, Donnelly. See the eyes that are watching you? Recognize what you see? That's hate you're looking at. You'll be seeing that look again, because you're a Blackfoot, and it'll follow you as sure as your own shadow. And no matter how far you run, you'll have to keep looking over your shoulder — and eyes like these will be watching you, until one night you'll pay your debt in blood. Remember, Donnelly, Ireland never forgets its enemies.

(They leave. Jim and Johannah look at each other in silence. The mood is reinforced by a music bridge.)

Johannah: Did they hurt you bad?

Jim Donnelly: Those bastards don't frighten me. I could beat the hide off any of them.

A15

Johannah: There's too many of them, Jim. You can't be fighting them all. We're best out of all this.

Jim Donnelly: What, and have it said that I ran away? I'd never give them the satisfaction.

Johannah: You know how often we've talked about Canada. In Canada there's farmland . . . a future, and a chance to do something with it. What have we got here? We'll never be able to have our own land. The potato crops have failed for the last two years, and now there's talk of another rebellion. There'll be another blood bath like the '98. The old-timers are shaking their heads because they remember, but the young ones don't listen to them any more. God, how soon they forget the senselessness of it all! Can't you see, Jim, even without the Whiteboys, we've got a dog's chance in hell.

Jim Donnelly: Damn your eyes, Johannah, but I know you're right. *(Pause)* And being right's a man's job, so keep your mouth shut. *(He moves thoughtfully and sits down)* How would you like to go to Canada?

Johannah: Canada?

Jim Donnelly: Aye, Canada.

Johannah: Seems like a good idea.

Jim Donnelly: Good? It's a great idea. I'm glad I thought of it.

(Slide 9 — collage of ship's sails and masts. The musical introduction to the sea-crossing song begins as the slide of a ship's sails appears on the screen. As the members of the company sing, they circle the set, picking up luggage and putting on costumes as they go, making their way to the central playing area which becomes the deck of a ship.)

All *(sing)*:
> Today we shall ride
> On a bright Irish tide,
> And bid fond farewells to the blarney,
> Where Orange and Green
> Are no longer seen,
> A place where no landlords can harm ye.

This is the story that always is told
By all who would come to the land of the bold.
Whether Cornish or Nordic, whether English or Swiss,
If Canada's bad, it's much better than this.

(The deck is full of people watching the harbour as the ship pulls away. Among them are Jim and Johannah, Johannah holding a baby in her arms, and Tim Mulligan, an old and continually drunk Irishman.)

Mulligan: Farewell, Ireland! Farewell, me dear old country. Bugger you, Ireland! What do you think I'm leaving for?

Priest: Mr. Mulligan, are you drinking?

Mulligan: I'm not drinking. I'm drunk.

Man 2 *(sings)*:
A storm came and blew
For a good week or two,
And the women and kids were all crying.
Ship's fever was rife
To add to our strife
And many a man was near dying.

Priest: . . . And may the Lord accept the souls of these humble people, whose dreams ended before they had a chance to begin.

Man 1: There's another one down with cholera. That's sixty in all.

Man 2: The lookout then cried
That land he espied.
And for joy all the lassies were weeping.

Lookout: Land ho!

Priest *(spoken over music)*: Look at this beautiful land, my friends. This will be our heaven on earth.

Mulligan *(drunk again — looks out)*: So this is our heaven? *(Doesn't like what he sees)* Bloody hell!

All *(sing)*:
This is the story that always is told
By all who would come to the land of the bold.

Whether Cornish or Nordic, of low rank or birth,
The sea don't compare with a nice piece of earth.

At Grosse Isle we stopped
And anchor was dropped,
Then we took to the river for Kingston.
From there down to York
On a ship like a cork,
Where we left for a town they call London.

(Slide 10 — London in the 1840's.)

Mulligan: Bit of a nerve calling this London. There's bugger all here. What's this . . . Ridout Street. Nothing. York Street . . . aha! McGregor's Tavern! I feel at home already. *(He stumbles off.)*

All *(sing)*:
This is the story that always is told
By all who would come to the land of the bold.
Whether wildwood or forest, there's nothing so grand
In all of God's heaven as your own piece of land.

(By now, the ship has been rearranged to show people waiting at a stagecoach station, with Jim and Johannah sitting on their luggage, looking rather tired.)

Jim Donnelly: A piece of land. That's what we need. We're farm people . . . there's nothing for us in London.

Johannah: Get a job for a while . . . just until we get up the money. It's not a bad wage clearing the land.

Jim Donnelly: What . . . come all the way to Canada and then end up clearing someone else's land. I'm not working for another landlord, and that's final! *(Changes his mood)* I hear there's plenty of land up in the Queen's bush around Biddulph Township. It's scarce fourteen miles north on the Proof Line.

Johannah: Who'll be owning it?

Jim Donnelly: Absentee landlords. If you clear the land, you can lay claim to it. Squatter's rights, they call it.

Johannah: Jim, what if someone brings the law in?

A19

Jim Donnelly: Aah . . . the owner probably doesn't live within a hundred miles, and even if he does, what the hell . . . it's not right for a man to have land and not use it. Yup . . . I reckon that's what we'll do. *(Slide 11 — open sky and clouds. The music starts, and Jim and Johannah pick up their luggage while the company forms a long procession. As a line of immigrants loaded with their belongings, they circle the stage, each group finding a piece of land and exiting, until Jim and Johannah are left. They find some land they like and stop. Several men appear around them and close in, as an inquisitive crowd with some newcomers. There is some tension in the air)* I was wondering if you knew who'd be owning this land?

Man 1: That's Joe Carswell's land, but he never uses it. He's got a plot on the other side of the township.

Jim Donnelly: That's good land. It should be cleared.

Man 2: Go see Mr. Carswell. He'll likely sell it to you.

Jim Donnelly: Yeah . . . I may do that. I'm Jim Donnelly, this is my wife Johannah. *(They touch their hats to her)* We're from County Tipperary.

Man 4: Tipperary! Well, I'll be . . . .

Man 3: You'll really be at home here. Half of Lucan's from Tipperary.

Man 1: Donnelly, eh? Would I be right in supposing you're . . . er . . . Catholic?

Jim Donnelly: That's right.

Man 1: Well, now, that's even better. There's too many bloody Protestants here, anyway.

Man 3: Yes, you'll be really at home here, all right. When Jim Hodgins settled the township some ten years back, he brought Protestants, Catholics and bastard Blackfeet with him . . . and then he wonders why everyone's fighting.

Jim Donnelly: Fighting . . . eh?

Man 2: If you're planning to stay, mind who you neighbour with. Just down the Roman line, there's Keefes and Feeheeleys. Bad sorts.

A20

I'd give 'em a wide berth, if I were you.

Man 4: I've heard of the Donnellys before. You weren't Whiteboys, by any chance?

Jim Donnelly: No.

Man 4: Oh. *(Pause)* It must have been someone else. Yeah . . . . Good day to you both.

(They all say, "good day" and exit, a few of them casting suspicious looks back at the Donnellys.)

Johannah: Jim, you don't think they'll find out?

Jim Donnelly: We're thousands of miles from Tipperary. We'll be alright.

Johannah: I've a feeling we're a lot closer than you think. Can't we find somewhere else?

Jim Donnelly: We've been travelling for over four months, and here's a fine piece of land. I'm a farmer, not a gypsy. Come on, let's get to work.

(The company enters with axes, spades, hammers, spinning wheels, butter churns, and mimes various activities, such as digging and knocking in fence posts. This is done during the song. Slide 12 — sunset.)

All *(sing)*:
> Hewing and chopping and pulling a plough,
> Digging and sowing and milking cows,
> We'll clear this land, though God knows how,
> Way down in Lucan town.
>
> There's stumps to be pulled and trees to be burned,
> Barns to be built and earth to be turned.
> If we clear this land, it'll sure be earned,
> Way down in Lucan town.

(The company ends in a frozen tableau, with Jim Donnelly sitting centre stage sharpening an axe. Mulligan sits on the side of the stage and casually addresses the audience.)

A21

Mulligan: Well, that's how it all began, near as I can say. Mind you, I could have told them trouble was coming, but, of course, nobody bothered to ask. Not that them Donnellys were particularly bad folk — well, no more than any of those farmers were, and believe me, there are no saints in this little tale — but I had the feeling trouble would follow them around. I mean, stealing someone's land . . . it's not the best way to start. I remember when Carswell found out. *(He laughs)* He wasn't over pleased, I can tell you. He was a funny little man — wouldn't say "boo" to a goose ordinarily, but when he heard about having squatters on his land, he got madder than a hornet, and not knowing what sort of man Jim Donnelly was, he went stomping across in a mighty rage.

(Jim is working as Carswell enters.)

Carswell: Are you Jim Donnelly? Eh? Are you the guy who's squatting on my land?

Jim Donnelly *(stands and absolutely dwarfs him)*: Yup!

Carswell *(his nerve giving way)*: Oh . . . well . . . did you know that this was my land?

Jim Donnelly: Yup!

Carswell: Oh . . . did you not think that I . . . er . . . may . . . er . . . need it?

Jim Donnelly: No.

Carswell: Oh . . . ! Well, I do.

Jim Donnelly: What for?

Carswell: I beg your pardon?

Jim Donnelly: What do you need it for? You've got a plot of land already, and you've not even begun to clear this one. Doesn't look to me as though you need it.

Carswell: Now, look here, this is my land. It doesn't matter whether I need it. It's mine . . . I own it.

Jim Donnelly: Well, I'm here and I ain't moving. What are you going

A22

to do about it?

Carswell: I'm afraid you have no alternative but to buy the land, and I couldn't possibly part with it for less than $200.

Jim Donnelly *(angrily)*: What?

Carswell *(frightened)*: What am I saying? $150.

Jim Donnelly *(grabs him)*: Look, Carswell . . . .

Carswell: $140?

Jim Donnelly: Get this into your stupid head . . . .

Carswell: $135?

Jim Donnelly: I'm not moving off this land!

Carswell: $120?

Jim Donnelly: And I'm not buying it!

Carswell: $100? *(Jim releases him — pause)* $90?

Jim Donnelly: No!

Carswell: I know you're intimidating me to try and make me lower my price, but it won't work. I won't go a penny below $85. *(Jim grabs him by the collar again)* . . . 80 — 76 — 75 — 70 — 69.50? *(Chokes.)*

Jim Donnelly *(still holding him)*: I'll make an arrangement with you. As soon as I earn enough money, I'll pay you for the land. Alright?

Carswell: Never! *(Jim squeezes his throat)* Yes . . . yes . . . good idea!

Jim Donnelly: And you know what'll happen to you if you go running to the law. We understand each other?

Carswell: Yes . . . yes.

Jim Donnelly: Now, get out of here.

(Carswell exits.)

A23

MAP OF THE COUNTY

MIDDLESEX

ONTARIO

SCALE 200 CH.S AN INCH   W.H.GREGOR C.E.

1877.

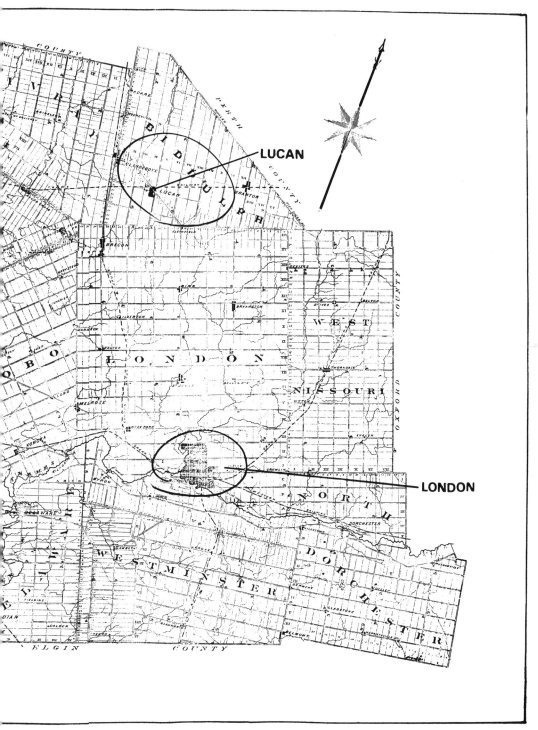

LUCAN

LONDON

(Historical map of 1877)

Mulligan: So Carswell and Donnelly came to an "arrangement" over the land, and quite a few years passed while Jim cleared the land and raised a big family. And it may all have ended there, but for a man called Pat Farrell.

(Pat Farrell enters. He watches as the company sings the first verse while setting up a bar scene. Slide 13 — lantern.)

All *(sing)*:

        Hewing and chopping and pulling a plough,
        Digging and sowing and milking cows,
        We'll clear this land, though God knows how,
        Way down in Lucan town.

(The mood changes during the second verse, as Farrell moves toward centre stage. Donnelly and Farrell eye each other ominously.)

        Months are going, going by,
        Wheat is growing, growing high,
        But someone soon is going to die,
        Way down in Lucan town.

Farrell *(breaks the mood)*: The drinks are on me, boys!

(Suddenly the bar is filled with noise and music.)

Catholic 1: Right, lads, I'm going to sing a song.

Mulligan: Why . . . what have we done to you?

Catholic 1: Less of your lip, Mulligan.

Protestant 1: You can't sing.

Catholic 1: Sure I can bloody sing!

Protestant 1: Someone put birdseed in your beer? Come on, then, what are you going to sing?

Catholic 1: "The Wearing o' the Green."

Protestant 1: That's a damned Catholic song.

Catholic 1: So what, shithead!

A26

Protestant 1: I'll show you so bloody what!

(As Protestant 1 goes for Catholic 1, Farrell steps in on the side of The Catholic. The Protestant 1 stops. Mulligan, not having seen this, rants on.)

Mulligan: A fight! Get 'em, boys! A left poke in the ribs, a right kick to the balls, and you're away!

(Farrell picks up Mulligan.)

Farrell: Would you be after a fight, you stinking Protestant?

Mulligan: Oh no . . . I love the Pope, I love him. *(Farrell puts him down)* It's Catholics I can't stand. *(He dashes out of Farrell's reach.)*

Farrell: You'd better keep out of my way, Mulligan. *(They settle down for a moment. Carswell enters)* Well, if it isn't Mr. Carswell. Let me buy you a drink.

Carswell: Thank you, Pat, but . . . .

Farrell: An ale for Mr. Carswell, Jack. I've been wanting to talk to you. Word's going round you've got a Blackfoot squatting on your land.

Carswell: A Blackfoot? Oh, you mean Mr. Donnelly?

Farrell: They say he just marched in without so much as a "by your leave". Now that's Black Irish for you.

Carswell: Black Irish?

Farrell: Blackfoot, Mr. Carswell. A treacherous lot. You'll never get him off the land, you know.

Carswell: But we've come to an arrangement. He says he'll buy it, when he gets the money.

Farrell: Buy it! Mr. Carswell, you know damned well he'll never buy that land.

Carswell: But he refuses to leave. What can I do?

A27

Farrell: Sell the land.

Carswell: Sell the land? But who'd buy land with squatters on it?

Farrell: Someone who doesn't give a tinker's damn about that blow-hard Donnelly.

Protestant 1: Hey, listen to that. Farrell reckons he can get Jim Donnelly off Carswell's land!

Farrell: I could beat him — and a dozen like him.

Protestant 1: I'd like to be there to see it.

Farrell: You'll see it soon enough. What about it, Mr. Carswell?

Carswell: I'd gladly sell it to you, but do you really think you can get them off the land?

Farrell: Just leave that to me. There's not a Blackfoot this side of hell would stay on that land after I'm finished with him.

Carswell: Well, if you're really serious, the land is yours — and I wish you the best of luck.

Barman: Alright, gentlemen. Time, please.

Mulligan: But, I've only just started!

Barman: That's your lot, boys.

Mulligan: I ain't moving. I'm staying here 'til I get drunk. Call this stuff whisky? I drank stronger stuff from my mother's breast.

Catholic 2: I wouldn't take that, Jack. *(To barman)* Why don't you chuck him out?

Mulligan: I'd like to see you try. *(The barman casually picks him up and throws him out. Mulligan gets up, drunkenly trying to regain his dignity)* To hell with you! I've been thrown out of better bars than this. *(Slide 14 — night sky, moon and clouds. The company laughs at him and exits, striking the set for the bar. Mulligan is left alone on stage. He exits singing)*
    Four-and-twenty virgins went up to Inverness,

And when the ball was over there were four-and-twenty less,
Singing balls to your partner . . . .

(Fade out. The next part of the song has a sombre and ominous quality. During it, Farrell enters and surveys the scene for a moment)

Months are going, going by,
Hate is growing, growing high.
And someone soon is going to die,
Way down in Lucan town.

(At the end of the song, Farrell walks across the stage and bangs on the ground with his foot. Slide 15 — sunset. Jim Donnelly enters.)

Farrell: Jim Donnelly?

Jim Donnelly: Yeah. And who might you be?

Farrell: The name's Pat Farrell.

Jim Donnelly: Good day to you, Mr. Farrell. What business do you have with me?

Farrell: I've come to inform you that you're trespassing.

Jim Donnelly: Well, I reckon you'd just better go back and check your information, mister.

Farrell: There's nothing wrong with my information. You don't own this land.

Jim Donnelly: That's right, I don't, but I've got an arrangement with Mr. Carswell . . . .

Farrell: But none with me. I'm the owner of this land, Donnelly.

Jim Donnelly: Now look here, mister whatever-your-name-is. I don't know what little game you think you're playing, but Mr. Carswell is the owner of this land, and I've got first option on buying it.

Farrell: Like to see the deeds, Donnelly? Nice and legal.

(Jim takes the documents and looks at them.)

A29

Jim Donnelly: I ain't too good at reading. I'm thinking this is some kind of trick.

Farrell: You'll find out soon enough. I want you off this land, and soon. It's the law . . . .

(Enter Johannah.)

Johannah: What's up, Jim?

Jim Donnelly: This son-of-a-bitch says he owns this land.

Farrell: I've come to inform you and your family that you're trespassing on my land.

Jim Donnelly: He says he's bought this land from Carswell.

Farrell: You haven't got a leg to stand on, Donnelly! I want you off this land in ten days.

Jim Donnelly: Ten days . . . ! You think I'd leave a piece of land in ten days that took me ten years to clear? See across to those trees, and back to that barn? Good open land. When we got here, it was forest, and every tree and stump I cleared with my own hands. My hands got mighty strong clearing this land. Strong enough to break your goddamned neck, Farrell!

Farrell: Fine talk for a Blackfoot, Donnelly.

Johannah: You're going to wish that you never said that, mister!

Jim Donnelly: Fetch the kids, Johannah. I want them to see what happens to anyone who calls us Blackfeet.

Johannah *(calls offstage)*: Boys . . . come and see your father have some fun.

(The boys and Mulligan enter with adlibs such as —)

Will Donnelly: Hey . . . Dad's going to beat the piss out of someone!

(A short but ferocious fight ensues in which Jim gets the better of Farrell and knocks him down. As Farrell staggers away, he shouts obscenities at Jim.)

A30

The Village of Lucan

was incorporated as a village in 1872, when Robert H. O'Neil was elected Reeve, and D. McRobert, William Porte, H. B. Quarry, and A. Goodacre, Councillors. S. C. Hersey is Clerk of the village.

In 1873, R. H. O'Neil was re-elected Reeve; in 1874, Thomas Dwight, and since then, H. H Hutchins. The population is about 1,100, and the assessed value, $148,230.

Lucan was at first called Marystown, but when a post-office was opened here, about fifteen years ago, it was called Lucan. Among the first inhabitants were R. H. O'Neil, B. Stanley, William Stanley, Robert McLean, William Porte (now postmaster), M. Connigan, Robert Fox, and John Farr.

Lucan was a place of very little importance until the Grand Trunk Railway was opened, since which time its growth has been extremely rapid, and its increase in wealth wonderful. It is neat and substantial in appearance, being built mostly of white brick, and contains, besides many mercantile establishments, two steam grist-mills, a flax scutching mill, foundry and saw mill.

The energy and enterprise displayed by the inhabitants of Lucan have earned for it the high degree of prosperity which it enjoys. The welfare of the place has of late been imperilled by the unfortunate exhibitions of malice, which have lately culminated in incendiary fires, which have created a great deal of distrust, and checked for a time the progress of the village.

(Historical synopsis circa 1878)

Farrell: Make the most of it, Donnelly. You won't laugh so loud in the law courts.

(The Donnelly boys jeer at him. A spot falls on a judge on a higher level. The Donnellys and Farrell turn to listen.)

Judge: The case of Farrell v̶ in the matter of Lot 18 of the 6th Concession of the Huron Tract. The bench has decided to award twenty-five acres to James Donnelly and twenty-five acres to Patrick Farrell.

(Judge exits.)

Farrell: Damnation!

Jim Donnelly: It could have been worse.

Johannah: The front field looks so narrow now. It's good land that was nothing but wild woods a few years back. It was our sweat that gave the soil its life. What Farrell did was nothing but a cheap trick.

Jim Donnelly: What's done is done. We can't change it.

Farrell: Donnelly, you haven't heard the last of this.

(Slide 16 — inside of a barn wall. The band strikes up a lively jig led by a fiddler. Part of the company dances and the other stands around drinking and talking. Two factions become apparent, each centred around Pat Farrell and Jim Donnelly. The music ends and the dancers settle for a moment.)

Mulligan: Pat Farrell had a big mouth, and it didn't take long for all of Lucan to know he would have used Jim's guts for garters. Everyone knew it was just a matter of time.

(Farrell is drunk and surrounded by several men, also drinking.)

Farrell: The only reason he put me down was because I never expected a Blackfoot to have the guts to fight. The next time, boys . . . .

Mulligan: Well, the next time was a barn-raising bee one Saturday night. No one thought it would turn out the way it did, but even though I'd had a belly full of whisky, I knew it was the beginning

A32

of the end. *(Getting drunker)* Well, really it was the end of the beginning, or around the middle of the beginning of the end . . . but still pretty close to the start of the middle of the beginning, in fact . . . I ought to shut up. Give us a tune, will you?

(The fiddler breaks into a tune and everyone starts dancing again. But, it soon becomes obvious that Farrell is spoiling for a fight, and Jim is trying to control his anger.)

Farrell: Are my eyes deceiving me, Davey, or does that man look uncommon like a thief?

Man 1: How's that?

Farrell: I said, that man's got an evil look in his eye. It's the look of a Blackfoot land-thief, if I'm not mistaken.

Man 1: Come on, Pat . . . you've had enough of that whisky.

(Farrell pushes him away angrily.)

Johannah: Take no notice of him, Jim. He's drunk and sore about you getting half the land.

Jim Donnelly: I've been listening to that big mouth for over an hour. If he carries on much longer, I'll fix it so he can't speak for a month.

Johannah: You've drunk too much yourself, Jim, so there's no point in fighting.

Farrell: Hey, Jack, I hear you got some bad weeds on your land.

Man 2 *(still dancing)*: Sure, Pat, but I cut them down.

Farrell: Well, I got weeds on my land. I got twenty-five acres with weeds all over it. You reckon I should cut them down, Jack?

Man 2: I reckon you oughta stop grousing and have a good time.

Farrell: Ah, you bastards wouldn't feel so good if you'd been robbed of your land by a sneak thief.

Jim Donnelly: Just one more crack, Farrell, and you'd better be ready to answer for it.

A33

Farrell: Go to hell, Donnelly! *(They go for each other, but their friends grab them. The fiddle player falters momentarily, but then starts to play even louder. Jim and Farrell are brought back to their respective areas. The company dances another gay jig. Jim turns his back on Farrell. At first Farrell remains silent, but as the dance progresses he becomes increasingly argumentative, although his friends try to calm him down. Eventually he shouts at them, although obviously loud enough for Jim to hear)* What the hell do you care? No bastard Blackfoot has stolen your land!

(Jim's patience is exhausted. He slams his jug down and turns on Farrell. For a moment there is a deathly silence, Then comes the low rumbling of a cluster of organ notes similar to that heard at the beginning of the play. It will build in volume throughout the rest of the fight.)

Jim Donnelly: All right, Farrell. I'll whip you to the edge of the grave for that!

(Farrell has an axe which he throws at Jim. It misses. They begin to fight, although they are obviously too drunk to fight well.)

Woman 1: Drag them apart or they'll kill themselves!

Woman 2: They're too drunk to hurt each other. Let them be.

Woman 3: They were spoiling for a fight. Let them get it over with.

(Jim gets knocked flat after quite a struggle. Near his hand is a hand-spike. Farrell rushes towards him. Jim poises to hit Farrell with the handspike. Everybody freezes. The organ sound stops dead. The lights on the main scene turn deep red as a light comes up on a higher level to reveal Johannah. Slide 17 — Farrell's face showing an expression of terror as he sees the handspike about to hit him.)

Johannah: It was morning again. A single bird was singing, unseen. The early sun threw a handful of diamonds on the wet grass, and blood on the clouds at the edge of the day. Farrell's blood. *(Slide 18 — Farrell is hit. He grasps his head in his hands. Jim hits Farrell and, at the same moment, the crowd closes in. The effect is like stopping and starting a movie, but the movement only lasts about one second, then everyone freezes in a new pose)* He'd remember that dream, that same dream frozen cold. A handspike frozen in his fist, a white finger pointing into the darkness. Now, it was pointing at him. *(Slide 19 — Farrell is still holding his head, but blood is oozing down his face. Jim drops the handspike and, seeing what he has done, runs away. Again the crowd moves in closer and freezes)* We want you, Donnelly. We want you. The dew won't wash the blood away. *(Slide 20 — Farrell's face and hands are a mass of blood. Farrell falls to the floor, the crowd moves closer, and Jim runs up towards a higher level. All freeze)* Second spring. The sheets are cold beside me as I lie in bed, watching the cool brightness of the dawn dapple the walls. Somewhere, Jim is hiding and dreaming. *(Slide 21 — Farrell's body lying on the floor. The crowd closes in again. Jim reaches a place up on a higher level and stops. Everyone freezes again)* Seeing Farrell's blood in the morning sky. It'll be two years soon. That's a long nightmare, Jim. A long time to be running.

Jim Donnelly: I keep waking up like it just happened.

Johannah: The linen gently folded like a sea of snow.

Man 1: Farrell's dead!

(The crowd moves slowly back from the body. Some take the body off, the rest form little groups around the stage. There is a music bridge. A single light comes up on a constable. Slide 22 — a dark colour — blue.)

Constable: He then ran away from the scene of the crime, m'Lord, and we have not as yet managed to apprehend him.

Jim Donnelly: God, how the damp gets in your bones. I pray for the morning and the sun to drive out the damp and the dreams. Sometimes it's a grey cloudy day with a fine rain hanging in the air. Those are the worst. I'll crawl towards a barn and hide there for a while. But not too long . . . got to keep moving.

Johannah: On cold nights when there's a strong wind blowing and driving the rain, I'll look into the black outside and wonder where you are. Suddenly, a flash of lightning silhouettes the trees at the end of the far field. Is that where you're hiding tonight? I'll put three candles in the window. There's no one here except your children, Jim. The law will not be out on a night like this. *(Sound of thunder)* The summer of '57 quickly lost itself in the fall, and the winter cooled the air of the murder. So, during the cold weather, Jim slept in the barn most of the time. The months were going so slow that I scarce believed it when another summer had passed.

A35

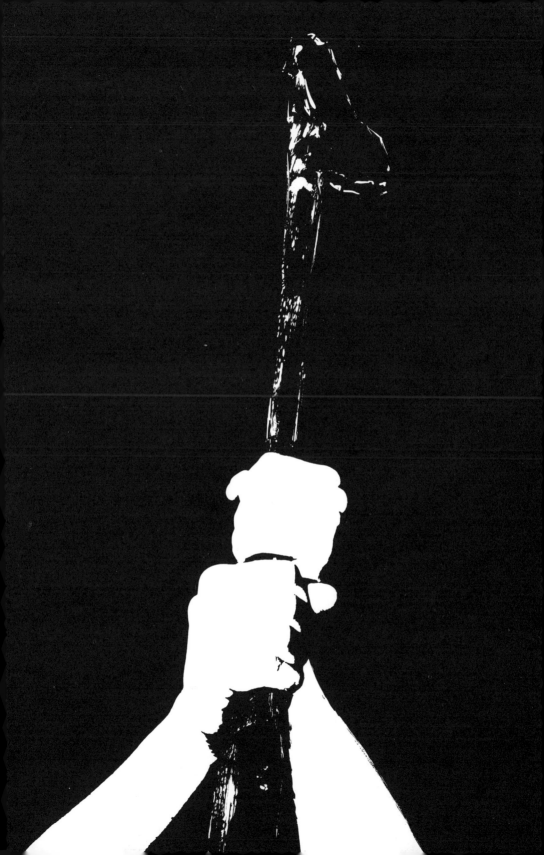

(The cast stands haphazardly on stage, while Jim and the constable play a bizarre game of hide-and-seek amongst them.)

Woman 1: Constable! I saw Jim Donnelly down by the swamp.

(The constable moves and Jim takes up another position.)

Man 1: He'll be in his barn tonight. Watch the candles she puts in the window.

(Hide-and-seek again.)

Constable: Come on, Donnelly. Give yourself up.

Woman 2: He's still around, constable. Johannah's had a baby . . . and a girl this time, thank the Lord.

Constable: Where is he, Mrs. Donnelly?

Johannah: I don't know.

Constable: I suppose that child was a divine conception, then?

Johannah: Did your ma never tell you, constable, but it takes a while for the calf to drop. It's nine months since I've seen him.

Constable: Damn your impertinence! He'll get more than nine months when I find him.

Woman 3: Constable! Over by the trees . . . look!

(The constable moves, but Jim dodges him.)

Constable: Why is it there's not a Protestant in town ever sets eyes on him . . . only Catholics. I thought he was Catholic as well.

Woman 4: Aye . . . a Black one. Watch the shadows, constable.

(The constable thinks he sees him, but Jim dodges again.)

Constable: Winter will be here soon, Donnelly. They say you're black against the snow. *(Pause)* I can wait. *(He rests.)*

Jim Donnelly: It's my second winter, and the cold is deeper than

A38

before. Farrell's body is not half so cold as mine. He's got six feet of earth and a coffin to keep him warm. How many times have I cursed that headful of whisky fumes?

(Johannah looks at him. They have been far apart on the stage. They move towards each other . . . meeting in the centre of the highest level.)

Johannah: You can't go on running forever, Jim.

(They embrace, then Jim walks slowly toward the constable. The actors form a line past which Jim must walk. They watch him with hatred.)

Man 1: A man is walking.

Man 2: Walking down the Roman line.

Man 3: A man with blood on his hands.

Man 4: The first blood was yours, Donnelly . . . the last will be ours.

Woman 1: Jim Donnelly's walking into town.

Woman 2: Two years tiredness lines his face.

Woman 3: Two years in fields and woods.

Woman 4: For two years we have waited. Two long years. Look over your shoulder, Donnelly . . . look into our eyes. Recognize what you see?

(At the end of the line, the constable waits for him. Jim puts his hands out, and the constable puts the handcuffs on him.)

Mulligan: And that, as they say, was that. They'd got him well and truly by the short and curlies. And I saw the whole thing, as I'd been into town for a quick drink and was having a rest in my favorite gutter when it happened. Oh boy . . . I thought to myself. There's gonna be some fun now.

(A single voice sings while the company regroups.)

Voice: They took away Jim Donnelly to face a murder trial.

A40

For the killing of Pat Farrell he'll be jailed for quite a while.
Though sudden death in a drunken brawl is not a murder true,
The Catholic men of Lucan town know well what they must do.

(A judge enters.)

Judge: Will the foreman of the jury please stand? *(Man 2 stands up)*
How do you find the defendant on the charge of murder?

Man 2: Guilty, m'Lord.

Judge: James Donnelly of the Township of Biddulph, you have been
found guilty of the murder of Patrick Farrell on the 27th day of June,
eighteen hundred and fifty-seven. *(He puts on a black patch and a
murmur of disbelief runs through the crowd)* It is the verdict of this
court that you be taken from here to the jail at Goderich in the
County of Huron, there to be hanged by the neck until death. And
may the Lord have mercy on your soul.

*(Johannah turns and faces upstage. The company speaks in unison.
The constable takes Jim Donnelly away.)*

All:　　Take Donnelly and hang him by the neck 'til he is dead.
For taking Farrell's life away, we'll see your body bled.
So you've a wife and children, all needing to be fed,
You should have thought of that before you struck Pat Farrell
dead.

(They turn their backs on the audience. Johannah turns forward.)

Johannah: Jim! Jim! *(Pause)* There was nothing left but silence, and
then, slowly, came the intrusion of sounds. Far away at the end of a
tunnel. The distant echo of voices saying things I couldn't hear. Mur-
murs of people growing loud and then soft, and all I could think about
was Jim. Oh my God, oh my God . . . they're taking him away. They'll
steal the breath from his body and throw him into the cold ground.
To be hanged by the neck until death. The words run through me, my
bones freeze as brittle as chalk and there is nowhere to hide. Nowhere
to hide. *(She keeps repeating this as her children approach her from
a distance. Slide 23 — gallows)* No!

Will Donnelly: Are you alright, mother?

Johannah: It's not over yet, boys. We'll fight this . . . we'll keep

A41

fighting right until they pull the trap. If there's the smallest chance of saving him, we'll take it. We'll get up a petition . . . yes . . . we'll get a petition pleading for clemency . . . I'll take it to the Governor General . . . he's coming to Goderich soon . . . and we'll win . . . we'll win. God give me strength.

(The actors fill the stage, standing motionless while Johannah goes to them with a long scroll. Some sign it, others turn their backs on her and exit. William speaks from a separate area.)

Will Donnelly: I'll never forget that petition. I was thirteen at the time. Mother worked so hard, she was out from sun-up to sundown. She knocked on every farmhouse and store her tired feet could find.

Johannah: The killing was an accident.

Will Donnelly: She stopped people on the roads and in the fields.

Johannah: It was manslaughter, not murder.

Will Donnelly: Some signed, some didn't.

Johannah: I've seven boys and a baby girl need feeding.

Will Donnelly: But, the execution was getting closer, and still she didn't think the list was long enough.

Johannah: Farrell threw the axe at him first. It was self-defence.

Will Donnelly: So one Sunday, she put us in our best clothes, scrubbed our ragamuffin faces, and stood us outside the church.

Johannah: Will you sign this, please?

Will Donnelly: There was Jim, my elder brother who was seventeen, and me, John, Pat, Michael, Bob and Tom. Tom was the youngest, being only five. Of course, that's not counting little Jennie, but she was just a babe in arms. I was standing there trying to stop the wind blowing my hair our of place, and watching all those faces going past. I watched their eyes. Heenans, Thompsons, Ryans, Ryders. I watched Ryders real close. Quiglys, Tooheys, Glendennings, Madigans, Mahers . . . I never forgot any of those faces . . . ever. *(Pause)* It was before sun-up that mother left to go to Goderich that day. I was the only one that saw her go. There, in the grey half-light of a misty April

A42

morning, I watched her get into the buggy and head off towards Lucan, to catch the early coach to Goderich.

(Will watches her leave as if through a window. The others join him at the window and all watch. Then they settle down on one side of the stage to wait. The following dialogue echoes from all corners of the stage, distant and surreal.)

One: Words . . . .

Two: Rolling over the barren ground.

Three: Blown across the wasteland.

One: Words.

Four: Words in the wind.

Five: A handspike frozen cold.

Six: Pointing into the night.

Four: And nowhere to hide, nowhere to hide.

Seven: To be hanged by the neck.

Eight: By the neck until death.

Nine: Until death.

Johannah: Jim! Jim!

One: The lighting silhouettes the trees by the far field.

Two: The damp and the dreams.

Three: Soft folds in the blue sky.

Four: And blood on the clouds by the edge of the day.

Five: A bird sang, unseen.

Six: A long time to be running.

A43

Seven: A long time.

Eight: A long time.

Nine: A long time.

(These words echo for a while, then fade as the music fades. The music indicates the passage of time, as the focus shifts to the boys who are waiting. This can be an improvised scene in mime. For example, they may see someone and rush to the window, only to find it isn't her. They relax. Build the tension of waiting. Finally, they see her coming. They all tense up and look at one another. There is the sound of a buggy pulling up. A silence. Then, Mrs. Donnelly enters.)

Johannah: It's a reprieve.

(A moment's silence, and then they all jump around whooping for joy. They fall silent as Jim Donnelly appears under guard and in chains. He says farewell to the children, and finally Johannah. He tries to put his arms around her, but finds he can't. He kisses her goodbye, then exits with his guard. There is the sound of a train pulling out of a station, and they all wave goodbye. They slowly move back and sit as if spending an evening at home. Mrs. Donnelly sews and the children read or play with games. Slide 24 — warm colour — red.)

Will Donnelly: So we began to wait. The sentence had been changed to seven years at Kingston Prison, and there wasn't much we could do but put on a brave face and sit it out. It was hard work, and we all began to grow up fast. We closed the ranks as we had done before, and learned that by being close we were safe. So, we kept ourselves to ourselves as much as we could. There was something growing around us — we knew it was there. It frightened us — always did — but we never showed it. The first of seven winters was coming up. We had to keep working.

(This is a mime and music scene to cover the seven years during which Jim Donnelly was away in prison. During the song, the company acts out various farming scenes.)

A44

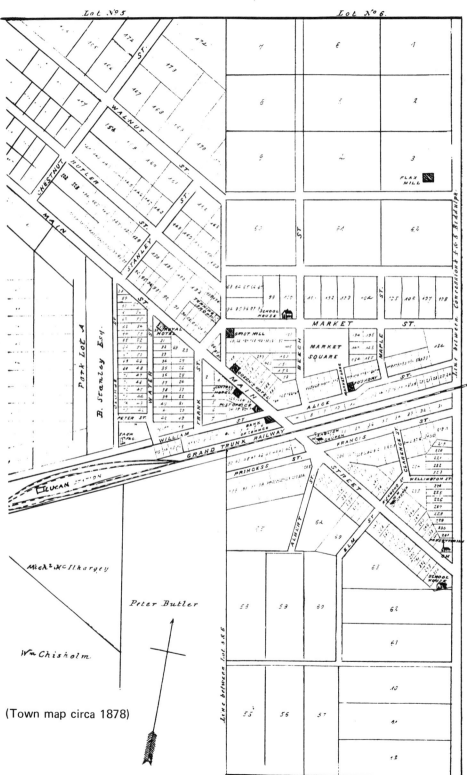

Village of LUCAN

SCALE 500 FT AN INCH.

Drawn by Jno Rogers.

Farm Lot No 27 CON IV.

(Town map circa 1878)

Johannah *(sings)*:
> When the snows have dusted starlight
> On the autumn's faded leaves,
> And the winter winds are blowing half a gale,
> Those cold days just recall
> The coldest of them all
> The day they took my Jim to jail.
>
> One year going
> Kids are growing
> Winds are blowing cold
> Seeds for sowing
> Money owing
> And young men getting bold
> Arms are stronger
> Memories longer
> Yes, boys, you're growing old.

Patrick Donnelly *(ten years old)*: Father never meant to kill that man, did he?

Johannah: No, Patrick. It was done in the fury of a moment. But the law says someone's got to pay. *(She sings)*
> Three years going
> Kids are growing
> Yes, boys — you're growing old.

Boy 1: Hey, cripple!

Boy 2: It's wee Willy Donnelly and his gammy foot.

Boy 1: Where are you going, cripple? Looking for your father?

Boy 2: You'll not find him here.

Will Donnelly: You little bastards! I'll tan your hides.

Boy 1: You'll have to catch us first.

(He chases them. They dodge away.)

Boy 2: What's your father doing now? Killing men at Kingston prison?

(They scatter again. He catches one with the help of one of his brothers. William unclasps his belt and gives him a beating.)

Will Donnelly: This is a special present from the Donnellys. And when you go squealing to your folks, tell them that's what will happen to anyone who thinks we can't look after ourselves while our father's away.

(Several voices offstage sing the chorus while the dialogue goes on at the same time.)

Voices *(sing)*:
  Five years going
  Winds are blowing cold
  Seeds for sowing
  Money owing
  And young men getting bold
  Arms are stronger
  Memories longer
  Yes, boys, you're growing old.

Jennie: What does Papa look like?

Johannah: Well . . . he's a big, strong man with dark hair and . . . .

Jennie: Does he look like Will or Pat or John?

Johannah *(laughs)*: He looks a bit like all of them, to tell the truth.

Jennie: When's he coming home?

Johannah: Just two more years, pet.

Jennie: Two years is an awful long time.

Johannah: Aye . . . it's an awful long time. *(Fade up last lines of "Five Years Going" chorus. Will and his brother return to centre stage)* Boys, boys! You've been fighting again!

Will Donnelly: We had to, mother. They were saying bad things about Pa.

A47

Johannah: They may be saying bad things about Pa, but they'll be saying worse things about us. I think I'm raising devils instead of sons. I wish to heaven your father was here.

Voices: Seven years going
             Kids are growing
             Yes, boys . . . you're growing old.

(There is the sound of a key in a lock and a prison door opening. Johannah and the kids react.)

Johannah: Seven years gone. Your father's coming home.

(Johannah lines the kids up and makes sure they're smart. Jim enters. He greets them all one by one and tries to guess their names. This can be an improvised scene.)

Jim Donnelly: Boys . . . ! I never believed you'd get so big in seven years. You've all worked hard . . . I'm proud of you.

Johannah: There's a lot of people glad you're back, Jim.

Jim Donnelly: Aye, and there's a lot who wish I wasn't. But, they'll think twice about tampering with me, now my boys are getting big. Just look at the size of them!

Will Donnelly: There's no one in Biddulph dares push us around. I never been beat yet.

John Donnelly: Just listen to him, will you? I'm as good a fighter as you any day.

Will Donnelly: Are you, hell!

Jim Donnelly: Boys . . . don't be fighting yourselves. There's plenty of people to fight without turning on your brothers.

Johannah: Come inside, Jim, and rest. You must be tired.

Jim Donnelly: Not yet, Johannah. I want to walk around my fields. Twenty-one years ago we stood here and looked out into the bush, and dreamed of a good life. For a long time, I'd forgotten what that felt like . . . now, I remember. Come with me.

A48

(Jim and Johannah exit. Mulligan enters.)

Mulligan: Jim Donnelly was back. The year was 1866.

Will Donnelly: So, you reckon you can beat me, eh?

John Donnelly: I reckon so.

Will Donnelly: Well . . . you know what that means.

(They take off their coats and begin a lively scrap. The rest of the Donnelly boys cheer them on excitedly, as it is obviously a friendly fight. They freeze during Mulligan's speech.)

Mulligan: 1867, and James Donnelly pistol-whipped Constable Kennedy. *(Fight starts again)* 1869, and Tom Donnelly bit Constable Berryman's nose off in a fight. *(Fight starts again)* 1871, and Will buys a stagecoach line. The seven deadly sons, and Will was still the leader.

(Will gets John in a grip and John gives in. Will is congratulated by the others. Martin McLaughlin enters.)

Pat Donnelly: Hey . . . it's Martin McLaughlin!

Will Donnelly: Hello, Martin. How are you?

McLaughlin: Fine, Will. What the hell have you been doing?

Will Donnelly: Oh, just a friendly scrap with my brother. If you ever want a good fight, Martin, you know where to come.

McLaughlin: Fighting's not my line of business, Will.

Pat Donnelly *(sarcastically)*: His "line of business" is school work.

Will Donnelly: There's nothing wrong with that, Pat. You could do with a bit yourself.

James Donnelly *(mocking)*: We'll have to watch our words, boys. Our Will is a learned man. Remember that love letter he sent to Maggie Thompson? "Oh, me darling Maggie, I love your heavenly face, your angelic disposition . . . . "

A49

John Donnelly: And your big tits.

Will Donnelly: You bastard! *(He chases John as the boys scream with laughter.)*

James Donnelly: Oh, it was written in such a beautiful scholarly hand.

Will Donnelly: Another crack from you and you'll feel my beautiful scholarly hand on your jaw. Clear off, you lot, me and Martin is in need of an intelligent discussion.

James Donnelly: Come on, boys, Let's go chase some of Grouchy Ryder's cows.

(They exit.)

Will Donnelly: Don't mind them, Martin, they're good lads when they want to be. *(He notices a worried look on McLaughlin's face)* What's up? You look troubled.

McLaughlin: Will . . . I came up because . . . well, I thought I'd better tell you something I heard in town. They're saying it was one of your boys that robbed the post office at Granton last week.

Will Donnelly: Is that right? Well, if one of my brothers stole that, the bastard's keeping it to himself.

McLaughlin: They're also laying the burning of Maher's barn at your door.

Will Donnelly: For chrissakes! None of us were in on that.

McLaughlin: I just thought I'd better warn you . . . they're laying a lot of things on you.

Will Donnelly: You don't believe them, do you, Martin?

McLaughlin: Believe them? Of course not.

Will Donnelly: It wasn't our boys, Martin, you must believe that.

McLaughlin: I do, Will. But the rest of the town isn't so sure.

Will Donnelly: To hell with the rest of the town! There's a lot of

A51

people been mighty jealous of me since I got my stage line.

McLaughlin: How's that going, Will?

Will Donnelly: Damned well! I'll have Flannagan's off the road in a year, no trouble. You're not doing too bad yourself. I hear you're going to be our next magistrate.

McLaughlin: Yes . . . chances are pretty good now.

Will Donnelly: That's what learning does for you. You'll be a good one too, Martin.

McLaughlin: I'm going to do my best for the people of Lucan.

Will Donnelly: I'm sure you will. Come on, let's drink to the people of Lucan. I've got a bottle of whisky needs finishing. I stole it out of old man Thompson's shed last Monday.

McLaughlin: You stole it! I heard he keeps a closer count of his whisky bottles than he does of his own children.

Will Donnelly: I know, but I got Maggie to help me.

McLaughlin: Maggie! You really are sweet on Maggie Thompson!

Will Donnelly: She's a fine girl.

McLaughlin: Oh boy . . . if old man Thompson finds out, there'll be trouble.

Will Donnelly: Nothing I can't handle. Come on. Let's drink to it.

(They exit. Slide 25 — inside a church. Three women enter, chattering to themselves, and sit down.)

Annie: Come on, girls . . . I promised Father Connolly we'd have a parcel ready for Ireland by Friday.

Janet: I've nearly finished this one.

(Janet is obviously very pregnant. She holds up a sweater. It is a very tatty piece of work with big holes in it.)

A52

Agnes: Isn't that nice?

Annie: That'll help someone back home.

Agnes: We're not exactly sitting pretty ourselves. I mean, they've got a famine — and we've got the Donnellys. I'm not sure who's better off.

(Dora enters.)

Dora: I'm sorry I'm late, girls. My Henry got blind drunk at the McLeans again, and I had to drag him home.

Annie: Men . . . they're not worth the bother.

Agnes: That's easy enough said, but where would we be without them? I'd like to see you protect yourself against the Donnellys.

Dora: I'd like to see Henry protect me against the Donnellys.

Janet: I know . . . it's terrible, isn't it? All these goings on. My Albert says they're a wicked bunch.

Annie: He's right. They'd steal anything that wasn't nailed down.

Dora: That's a lot of nonsense. They're wild, but no worse than a dozen others.

Janet: Well, I don't know. I just leave it to Albert. But he says all them barn-burnings are being done by him and his sons.

Agnes: My father says the same. After all, it's got a lot worse since Jim Donnelly got back from prison. I think it would have been better if they'd hanged him, rather than letting a murderer back on the streets.

Dora: There's fights every Saturday night that could end in someone getting killed, just the same as the fight Farrell and Donnelly were in. It was a drunken brawl, not a murder. And wasn't it the Donnellys that looked after Farrell's young son ever since the killing?

Annie: That was the least they could do, I think. Don't you think so, Janet?

Janet: Oh, I don't know . . . I just leave it to Albert.

A53

Dora: Well, I think that there's a lot of people in this town committing crimes, just because they know that the Donnellys will get the blame.

Janet: Well, I must admit they've always been very nice to me, but my boys say they throw their weight around a bit. They're all very strong, you know, and my Albert says . . . .

Agnes: That William is the worst of the bunch . . . that affair with Maggie Thompson. Fancy trying to take her by force.

Janet: Albert says they beat old Thompson up.

Dora: That's what Thompson said, but I saw him the morning after — and he didn't have a scratch on him!

Janet: Oh, I don't know anything about it. I just . . . .

Dora: Leave it to Albert.

Janet: Well, he knows about these things.

Dora *(sarcastically)*: Oh . . . I'm sure he does.

Agnes: Isn't it terrible . . . all we seem to talk about nowadays is them Donnellys.

Janet: Well, I must be going. *(She gets up.)*

Annie: Oh, by the way . . . when's the baby due?

Janet: August.

Agnes: How many's that?

Janet: Six. Four boys and a girl — so far.

Dora: Another mouth to feed!

Annie: Going to have any more?

Janet: I'm not sure right now.

Dora: I'm sure you will. Just leave it to Albert.

A55

(Tim Mulligan staggers in singing.)

Mulligan:
> There once was a plumber called Lee,
> Who was plumbing his girl by the sea.
> Said the girl, "Stop your plumbing
> There's someone coming!"
> Said the plumber, still plumbing, "It's me!"

(He roars with laughter. The ladies are shocked. He sees them) Oh, begging your pardon, ladies.

Agnes: I think we'd better be going.

(They begin to exit.)

Mulligan: Just a minute, ladies. *(He gets his pipe out)* Do you have a match?

Dora: Yes . . . your face and a horse's arse.

(Slide 26 — dark colour — blue.)

Mulligan: Jasus . . . she's a sharp one. *(All the ladies exit. Mulligan staggers around for a moment, and then as an afterthought says —)* Would you be after a kiss then? *(He sits down and takes a swig from a bottle)* It was the very worst time in Lucan. The very worst. There was fires and robbings like you wouldn't believe. It was a time when decent folks lived in fear of night, because you never knew what was waiting for you in the shadows.

(Lighting effects of flames in distance. Sound — the clamour of an alarm bell. Mr. Toohey enters with a woman and an old man, as if helping them out of a burning house. He rushes towards the fire again, but the constable stops him.)

Toohey: Christ! Just look at it. The whole house gone. The whole damn thing! Those bastards!

Constable: I'm afraid we'll not save it, Mr. Toohey.

Toohey: Of course you won't. Those bastards know how to set a good fire.

Constable: Have you any idea who may have done this?

A56

Toohey: Have I an idea . . . ? Christ! I know who set the damned fire. Those bloody Donnellys.

(McLaughlin enters.)

McLaughlin: I got here as soon as I heard, Constable. Is there any chance of saving it?

Constable: I'm afraid not, sir.

McLaughlin: I'm sorry about this, Mr. Toohey.

Toohey: You're sorry, are you? Well, that's great, but it's no bloody good to me! Call yourselves the law! What the hell's the use of the law in this godforsaken town?

Constable: He believes it was the Donnellys, Mr. McLaughlin.

Toohey: My barns went two months ago, and now my farmhouse. You don't need to tell me who did it. I sold two of my best thoroughbreds to Flannagan's stage line last week. That bastard Will Donnelly wanted them, but I told him I'd never sell good horses to a Blackfoot. There you see the result.

All (sing):
> Burn, burn,
> Cut and burn,
> The night is long
> When it's your turn.
>
> They cleared the land with axe and fire,
> They made the earth their home.
> Their flames became a funeral pyre,
> The seeds of death were sown.

Flannagan: My name's Flannagan — I own the stage line. I was driving down to London last week when the Donnelly coach comes up behind me . . . driving hard . . . shouting for room to pass. Well, I whipped up the horses so we're both going at a pace, and that damn fool Will tries to pass . . . to knock me off the road. I held my ground . . . and Will's screaming and hollering . . . but God must'a been watching, 'cos it's him that goes flying into the ditch . . . and he knows he's beat fair and square. (Pause) Yesterday, I awoke and found all the tongues cut out of my horses, and my coach chopped to firewood. I had to shoot all my horses . . . they were screaming in agony. Have you ever heard a horse scream? It's not a pretty sound . . . the blood was gushing out of their mouths. I'd only bought the horses a few days before from Mr. Toohey. That's the kind of people those Donnellys are.

All *(sing)*:

> Burn, burn,
> Cut and burn,
> The night is long
> When it's your turn.
>
> The night is dark, the clouds are deep,
> A twig snaps in the breeze.
> A farmer jumps, throws off his sleep
> And curses those Black Donnellys.

Pat Donnelly *(goes to Will)*: Will . ... I just come from Andy Keefe's. A couple of Ryder's boys took him for a walk in a barrel of thorns . . . and on our account, too.

Will Donnelly: That's a damned Whiteboy trick . . . but why on our account, Pat?

Pat Donnelly: They was saying we burned Toohey's barn, and he says he was at our place that night and none of us was out . . . and they says he's a liar and was probably in on it, too . . . and dragged him out and . . . .

Will Donnelly: Boys . . . this account needs settling. If the Devil likes to dance in flames, then the Ryders will feel well at home tonight.

John Donnelly: Will . . . is there no other way?

Will Donnelly: Those Ryder boys could club their grandmother to death in the constable's office, and we'd get blamed for it. Let's give them something real to complain about.

All *(sing)*:

> Burn, burn,
> Cut and burn,
> The night is long
> When it's your turn.

A58

Coach 1880

No one sleeps in Lucan town
No one sleeps
No one sleeps
No one sleeps in Lucan town.

Thompson: I want to see some action against them Donnellys. That young pup Will Donnelly came to my house to try and steal my daughter away, after I'd told him I'd be seen dead before I'd have a Donnelly in the family. He came with his brothers, threatened me with a gun and beat me up.

Man 1: My cows got poisoned.

Man 2: My barns burned.

Man 3: I was beaten up and robbed.

Man 4: The London Free Press 1877 . . . matters have now reached such a crisis in Lucan that nobody thinks of going out at night without a revolver, and a person who goes on another person's property after dark goes at the risk of his life. For, if the owner happens to be a nervous man, he may shoot first, and make inquiries afterwards.

(Father Connolly enters.)

Woman 1: Help us.

Woman 2: Help us, Father Connolly.

Woman 3: There are bad people in this town, Father Connolly.

Woman 1: They are Catholic, Father . . . .

Woman 3: But their friends are Protestants and Orangemen.

Father Connolly: I cannot condemn a man for how he chooses his friends.

Man 1: But worse . . . they kill and burn.

Man 2: And burn and steal . . . .

Man 3: And steal and kill.

A60

Man 4: We live in terror. They are devils, Father.

Man 5: They are the scourge of the township.

Man 6: Rotten to the core.

Man 7: They cut out the tongues of Watson's horses.

Man 8: And when they wouldn't die . . . .

Man 9: Slit their throats.

Father Connolly: But what proof do you have?

Woman 1: I was told.

Woman 2: I was told.

Woman 3: Here in Biddulph, we know these things.

Father Connolly: But the law, what of the law?

Woman 3: Biddulph is beyond the law.

Woman 1: Speak against them, and your horses are killed.

Woman 2: Your homes are burned.

Woman 3: Biddulph is beyond the law.

(Martin McLaughlin moves to Father Connolly.)

McLaughlin: Father Connolly, we need your help. We must form a vigilante committee.

(The stage grows very dark and there is the sound of thunder. After the thunder, the slow and mournful tolling of a bell.)

Johannah: That's the saddest sound I ever heard, Jim. It's giving me a terrible fear, deep to my stomach.

Jim Donnelly: Johannah, our eldest son is dead.

Johannah: How did he die?

A61

Man 1: James Donnelly was shot while trying to fire the McLean's Hotel.

Man 2: A bullet in the groin.

Woman 1: Lead poisoning.

Woman 2: Gunshot wounds.

Man 3: He was knifed in a fight.

Woman 3: Shot by a fire-watcher.

Man 1: A pistol ball in the stomach.

Jim Donnelly: The doctor said it was appendicitis.

Men *(1, 2, 3)*: One down,

Women *(1, 2, 3)*: And six to go.

(Everyone kneels.)

All: Our Father, who art in heaven, give us this day our daily bread, and forgive us our trespasses, except that they be Donnellys.

McLaughlin: Father Connolly, we must form a vigilante committee.

Father Connolly: From what I have seen, I think you are right. We must band together to protect ourselves and maintain peace. It is my duty to keep the peace within my flock. We must find out who are the perpetrators of these crimes.

McLaughlin: The Donnellys, Father. You need look no further.

Father Connolly: You seem very certain.

All: We are, Father.

(The company forms a large circle on the set with Father Connolly in centre stage.)

A62

All *(sing)*:

> We're only honest farmers,
> And we've no mind to kill.
> But if our homes are threatened,
> Then, by Christ, we will.
>
> Of all the thieves in Canada
> This family's the worst.
> Before they come to murder us
> We'll go and kill them first.
>
> And mothers tell their children
> To bolt their windows tight,
> For the Devil and the Donnellys
> Are riding past tonight.

McLaughlin: We need a leader. Someone who does not fear the Donnellys. I believe we have a man. I also have reason to believe that he will be the next constable of Lucan.

All: You may condemn our actions
And say they caused much pain.
But if you'd lived in Lucan town
You would have done the same.

(James Carroll enters from upstage, and slowly moves towards Connolly. He is a big roughneck, dressed in common labourer's clothes.)

> And so the men of Lucan town
> Knew well what must be done.
> We'll stand and fight the Donnellys
> We'll make the bastards run.
>
> We found a fierce leader
> Who all would come to hear
> They called him . . . .

James Carroll *(extending his hand to Connolly)*: James Carroll. I'll drive them out of Lucan . . . or see them buried here.

(Curtain.)

A63

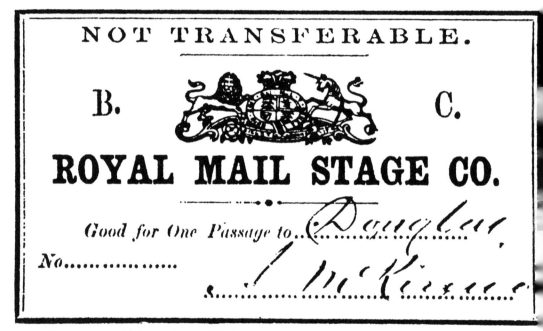

NOT TRANSFERABLE.

B.   C.

ROYAL MAIL STAGE CO.

Good for One Passage to....Douglas

No................

s.....J. McKinne

(Canadian stage coach ticket circa 1880's)

Act two *Tableau as the end of Act one. Also onstage are Jim, Johannah and Will Donnelly.*

Father Connolly: An oath must be taken. *(He goes to each man and woman onstage with a book which they sign. He is accompanied by Carroll. As Connolly reads out each section of the oath, the company repeats it)* We the undersigned —

All: We the undersigned,

Father Connolly: Roman Catholics

All: Roman Catholics

Father Connolly: Of Saint Patrick's

All: Of Saint Patrick's

Father Connolly: Of Biddulph

All: Of Biddulph

Father Connolly: Solemnly pledge ourselves

All: Solemnly pledge ourselves

(They reach Jim Feeheeley. He hesitates.)

Carroll: Jim Feeheeley. Why will you not sign?

Feeheeley: Tom's my best friend. I will not swear against him.

(Carroll grabs Feeheeley in an arm hold. Father Connolly goes on with the book. He pretends not to see what Carroll is doing.)

Father Connolly: Pledge ourselves to aid

All: Pledge ourselves to aid

Father Connolly: Our spiritual director

All: Our spiritual director

Father Connolly: And parish priest

A65

All: And parish priest

Feeheeley: Aaagh! You'll break my arm, Carroll!

Carroll: You'll help the committee when the time comes.

Father Connolly: In the discovery and putting down

All: In the discovery and putting down

Father Connolly: Of crime in this mission.

All: Of crime in this mission.

Feeheeley: I'll do as you say, Carroll.

Father Connolly: So help me God.

All: So help me God.

Will Donnelly: They've got up some kind of committee, and there's talk of an oath.

Jim Donnelly: Aye . . . and they've made that bully-boy Carroll the constable. There's method in all this.

Carroll: Why haven't you signed the oath, Mulligan?

Mulligan: Oh . . . well, I can't read, so I don't know what it's about.

Carroll: I'll read it to you.

Mulligan: Oh . . . oh. I can feel one of my deaf spells coming on.

McLaughlin: Let him be, Carroll. He's not important.

(During the signing, some people sign and some don't. Carroll takes careful note of each. This divides the group up into Carroll's cronies and the rest. At the end of the scene, those who signed gather around Carroll, and the rest exit.)

All: We solemnly pledge ourselves to aid our parish priest in the putting down of crimes committed by — *(overlap — "the rest")* unknown parties — unknown parties — unknown parties — *("Carroll's cronies")* the Don-

A66

nellys — the Donnellys —

Johannah: Why must we stay in Biddulph? Why must we stay in a town that hates us?

Jim Donnelly: There's thirty years work in this land. We can't pack up and start again. All this will pass.

(Jim and Johannah exit. Carroll and his cronies lounge about in the background, like a gang looking for trouble. Mulligan moves downstage.)

Mulligan: Committees, oaths and God knows what else! I might as well have stayed in Tipperary. Myself . . . I'm staying well out of this. I have a feeling this deaf spell is going to last quite a while. There's too many strange things going on for my liking. *(He notices the gang and decides that it's time to exit. Carroll blocks his way)* Ah . . . evening there, constable. Lovely night for a walk. *(Pause)* Waiting for someone, are you?

Carroll: That's right . . . for a friend of the committee.

Mulligan: Well . . . I'll leave you to it.

Carroll: You're a friend of the committee, aren't you, Mulligan?

Mulligan: Me? Why, sure . . . you know me . . . everybody's friend.

Carroll: Everybody's?

Mulligan: Well, not everybody. Look, I have to be going . . . pubs are open. 'Bye!

Carroll: There was a party at the Donnellys' Saturday last. I was wondering if you were there.

Mulligan: Sure, if I can remember where the hell a party was, it wasn't worth going to.

Carroll: Have you been hobnobbing with the Donnellys?

Mulligan: I've always said, Carroll, I'd rather die than be buried near a Donnelly.

Carroll: Just give me a straight answer . . . were you at that party?

A67

Mulligan: I swear by the holy bones of King Billy's horse I don't remember a thing.

(Carroll sees a bottle in Mulligan's pocket and takes it out.)

Carroll: Where did you get this from? Looks expensive.

Mulligan: Ah, no, no . . . that's turpentine. For cleaning me boots.

Carroll: Smells like whisky.

Mulligan: It's rot-gut. The very worst . . . my word of honour.

Carroll: Smells pretty good to me. *(Swigs it)* Mmmm! What do you think, Pat? *(Hands it to Quigly.)*

Mulligan: It burns holes in iron, I tell you.

Quigly *(drinks)*: That's good stuff. The kind the Donnellys would drink.

(Hogan grabs it.)

Hogan: I'll tell you if it's good whisky. *(He takes a large swig.)*

Mulligan: Sure it's whisky, but it's mixed with castor oil.

(Hogan stops abruptly and spits it out.)

Hogan: What?

Mulligan: Well, it tastes rotten, but it gives you a better run for your money. *(Someone else grabs the bottle, drinks, and passes it along to Carroll. Mulligan goes after it)* Take me life if you must, but I need me whisky!

(Carroll suddenly grabs Mulligan viciously.)

Carroll: Alright, you dirty little scum! Think you're clever with your smart-ass jokes, and your bad memory. You were at the Donnellys' Saturday night, and if you don't tell us who was there, we'll cut your nose right down the middle. *(He gets out a knife.)*

Mulligan: Don't cut me, Carroll. I don't know nuthin'!

A68

Carroll: Names, Mulligan . . . names!

Mulligan: In the name of heaven! I was blind drunk.

Carroll: You're a lying pig. *(He is about to cut him.)*

Mulligan: I don't know nuthin' . . . I don't know nuthin' . . . ask him *(pointing at Hogan)* . . . he was there!

(Carroll puts Mulligan down. Mulligan rushes out terrified, the others look at Hogan.)

Hogan: Come on, now. You wouldn't believe an old drunk like him. *(Silence)* Wasn't it me that beat up John Donnelly at that donnybrook down at the Queen's?

Quigly: You never did, Hogan.

Hogan: I did so . . . you ask anyone who was there.

Purtell: I've heard Pat Donnelly's a friend of yours.

Hogan: That's a damned lie. I hate Pat Donnelly . . . I hate all the Donnellys . . . *(sensing that they don't believe him)* I hate them . . . Carroll . . . I hate them!

(Carroll makes a sign to Madigan and a couple of others, and they exit.)

Carroll: That's alright, Hogan — I believe you . . . we all believe you . . . right, lads?

((The others agree, and Madigan enters.)

Madigan: Hey, look what we found.

(They bring on a barrel.)

Carroll: Now, that's a fine barrel . . . but, as constable, I must say it looks uncommon like the barrel we just passed in McCullough's front yard.

Madigan: Sure looks the same, don't it? But this one just fell off a wagon.

A69

Carroll: Well, I know you're an honest man, Mike, so I'll take your word. Anyway, McCullough's a Protestant, so he ain't covered by the law . . . and we need it more than him.

Hogan: Hey . . . we going to do the barrel of thorns trick? We going to find ourselves a Donnelly?

Carroll: Something like that. Come on, boys, let's fill her up. *(They all grab thorns and branches and put them in the barrel)* Looks pretty good. Like to see a Donnelly in there, eh, Hogan?

Hogan: Sure would, Carroll . . . that's where they belong.

Carroll: And all the Blackfeet should be in there, too, right?

Hogan: Right.

Carroll: And all the friends of Donnellys?

Hogan: Right.

Carroll: And all the people who sneak off and neighbour with Donnellys behind our backs?

(Hogan is beginning to realize something strange is going on and begins to get nervous.)

Hogan *(pause)*: Right.

Carroll: Now, I'm a bit worried about this barrel. I don't think it's big enough for a Donnelly or a Donnelly-lover. Would you mind getting in it to check it out?

Hogan *(frightened)*: It looks big enough to me, Carroll.

Carroll: Well, I really need someone in it to judge properly. Just for a moment, now.

(The others grab him and put him in the barrel.)

Hogan: Please . . . please . . . .

Carroll: Now, don't be getting so upset, Hogan. Like I said, this barrel can only hurt Donnellys or Donnelly-lovers. I know some

A71

people have been saying you're neighbouring with the Donnellys . . . .

Hogan: No, Carroll . . . not me . . . I promise . . . .

Carroll: So, we'll just roll you around a bit, and if the thorns hurt you, then we'll know you've been neighbouring with the Donnellys. If they don't, then we know that God and the Pope are watching over you.

Hogan: Nooooooo!

(They begin to roll him around in the barrel, and Hogan screams in pain. The others enjoy this and shout with delight. They lay the barrel on its side and Hogan tries to crawl out. Carroll stands on Hogan's hand.)

Carroll: This town, Hogan, is very much like that barrel of thorns you were just in. It ain't comfortable to live in no more. And we both know who the thorns are, don't we? And when you cut thorns, you use a sharp knife. Stay away from them, Hogan, or you'll get cut too . . . understand me? *(Hogan nods)* Now run along.

(He runs off to the jeers of the gang. A spot comes up on McLaughlin.)

McLaughlin: Carroll! *(Carroll draws his hat in mock reverence)* For the last time, Carroll. Do you have to use such crude methods?

Carroll: You should join in the fun sometime.

(A spot comes up on Father Connolly.)

Father Connolly: Carroll, I don't approve of the way you're handling this.

Carroll: Christ!

Father Connolly: When we made you constable . . . .

Carroll: You made me constable to put down the Donnellys. I've got Pat, John and Will Donnelly up for assault, and Tom for arson, and I sure as hell didn't get them from pussy-footing around like McLaughlin.

Father Connolly: I cannot approve of your methods. You must remember that we are doing this for the good of the people. We

A72

must not usurp the authority given to us by God. Our object is to eliminate fear — not create it.

Carroll *(mocking)*: Yes, Father, I shall remember that.

Father Connolly: Remember, my son.

(The spot fades on Father Connolly.)

Carroll: Goddamned priest!

McLaughlin: Carroll . . . have you got hold of James Keefe yet?

Carroll: No, he's next.

McLaughlin: I also want you to get your hands on Will Farrell, but I warn you, he'll be tough.

Carroll: Farrell. That name's familiar. Didn't the old man murder a Farrell, and then get a reprieve?

McLaughlin: Yes . . . this Will Farrell's his son. The Donnellys looked after him ever since the murder, and now he's as bad as they are.

Carroll: They looked after him, eh? I confess I'm surprised. I wouldn't have thought they'd have it in them.

McLaughlin: Never mind that. We've got business to do. There's a good chance of arresting some of the Donnelly brothers tonight. I've got the warrants here.

Carroll: The case is strong enough?

McLaughlin: It's strong enough.

Carroll: Where will I find them?

McLaughlin: There's a wedding today, and the reception will be at Fitzhenry's Hotel this evening. They'll be there.

(Slide 27 — Fitzhenry's Hotel. The scene becomes a wedding reception in its later and more rowdy stages. There is much noise and singing. John and Will Donnelly are there with Will Farrell. A very drunk man with a pint mug of beer in his hand climbs on a table or level.)

A73

Man *(drunk — sings)*:
> Let's drink to he
> Who is no more free
> No more free
> No more free.

(Everyone joins in.)

All *(sing)*:
> Let's drink to he
> Who is no more free
> No more free-i-oh . . .

(At the last line, they all take a swig from their glasses. The drunk takes his beer, and while someone lies down on the ground, he pours it down the second man's throat from on top of the table. The drunk sings as he does this.)

Man *(drunk — sings)*:
> Open your gob
> And let liquor run in
> Liquor run in
> Liquor run in.

(Everyone joins in.)

All *(sing)*:
> Open your gob
> And let liquor run in
> Liquor run in-i-oh . . .

(Everyone takes another swig as Carroll and two deputies enter. Carroll fires a shot in the air. Everyone freezes.)

Jim Donnelly: What's up, Carroll?

Carroll: I have warrants for the arrest of John Donnelly, William Donnelly and William Farrell.

Jim Donnelly: Ah, come on, Carroll. It's a party . . . have a few drinks first.

(Carroll pushes him out of the way. He looks at Will Donnelly.)

A74

Carroll: Let's go, Donnelly.

Will Donnelly: So you managed to buy yourself some more witnesses, Carroll?

Carroll: You three! Move!

Will Donnelly: If you want us, Carroll, you know what to do.

(Carroll is covered by his deputies, and moves warily towards Will Donnelly with handcuffs. Will holds his hands out for him. Just as he is about to put them on, Will hits him. A struggle ensues, but the deputies cannot shoot for fear of hitting Carroll. Will Farrell pulls out a gun and shoots a deputy in the stomach. Farrell runs for it. But the Donnellys are taken off their guard by the shot and are caught. The stage clears as people chase Farrell and take off the Donnellys, leaving Carroll. A spot comes up on Father Connolly. Slide 28 — Courthouse.)

Carroll: We've got them, Father Connolly! We took them at Fitzhenry's Hotel.

(A judge enters.)

Judge: Before I pass sentence, I would like to say a few words regarding this case against the Donnellys. From the evidence, it seems that they have been infected with the spirit that is the bane of the neighbourhood of Lucan. Now, I have no doubt they can be generous, warmhearted, and would make good friends. But, there is no doubt they make bad enemies. At the same time, I must say to the prosecution that the number of times you have dragged this family into court with just a modicum of evidence is a gross waste of the court's time. For resisting arrest, I sentence you to six months hard labour. Take them away.

(The judge exits.)

Carroll: Damnation! Minimum bloody sentence!

Father Connolly: It is disappointing, but we must have faith in the will of God. In his will is our peace.

Carroll: "Peace" . . . for six months, and what then? Back where we bloody well began. Look, Connolly, you know damned well . . . .

A76

Father Connolly: No! We must keep within the law.

Carroll: The law! What the hell's the good of a law that doesn't know a murderer or a thief when it sees one? We risk our goddamned lives bringing the bastards in, and all the law does is give them a few months inside and a pat on the arse. You'll be screaming for the law when they come to murder you in your bed one night, and a fat lot of good it'll do you.

Father Connolly: I'll not consent to it!

Carroll: I've got over forty vigilantes waiting, and they'll not wait forever.

Father Connolly: We must learn to wait.

(Around them in the shadows there are people. A single spot picks out the judge.)

Judge: The Queen versus Thomas Donnelly.

Man 1: Arson.

Judge: The Queen versus William Donnelly, John Donnelly, William Farrell, James Keefe, William Denby.

Men *(1, 2)*: Assault.

Judge: The Queen versus William Farrell.

Men *(1, 2, 3)*: Shooting with intent to kill.

Judge: The Queen versus William and John Donnelly.

Men *(1, 2, 3, 4)*: Assault.

Judge: The Queen versus James Donnelly.

Men *(1, 2, 3, 4, 5)*: Shooting with intent to kill.

Judge: John Donnelly.

Men *(1, 2, 3, 4, 5, 6)*: Assault.

A77

Judge: Thomas and James Donnelly.

Men *(1, 2, 3, 4, 5, 6, 7)*: Arson.

Judge: Thomas Donnelly.

Men *(1, 2, 3, 4, 5, 6, 7, 8)*: Larceny.

Judge: James and William Donnelly.

Men *(1, 2, 3, 4, 5, 6, 7, 8, 9)*: Assault.

Judge: James and Patrick Donnelly.

Men *(1, 2, 3, 4, 5, 6, 7, 8, 9, 10)*: Assault.

Father Connolly: We must learn to wait.

(Jim and Johannah enter as the others recede. Slide 29 — cold colour blue.)

Jim Donnelly: It's a sad day when a father sees his sons dragged into the courts like this.

Johannah: The charges are rigged, Jim. You know that.

Jim Donnelly: It doesn't make it a hell of a lot easier. Why are they using us like this?

Johannah: They won't rest until we leave.

(Pause.)

Jim Donnelly: I know, Johannah. I guess we've both known it for a long time. I'm too tired, Johannah. I'm getting old, and I'm too tired to fight, and too tired to run. *(Pause)* I've got a feeling deep in the pit of my stomach. It's like there's a rat gnawing at my innards. They're in my dreams as well. I find myself looking into the darkness, and all around there's these eyes watching me. Everywhere . . . everywhere I look. Hundreds of fat black rats . . . whispering and chattering and staring. Eyes full of hatred, and teeth dripping with disease. You can feel their hatred like hot spit burning your face. And all the little bastards are waiting. Waiting for the right time.

Johannah: It's only a dream, Jim.

Jim Donnelly: No, Johannah . . . I get the same feeling when I walk into town. I look into people's eyes and see the same thing, Johannah . . . I see the same goddamned thing!

(The stage is still surrounded by people in the shadows. They whisper without moving.)

All: Waiting
        'Til the time is right,
        Waiting
        Shadows in the night,
        Waiting.

Jim Donnelly: Christ! You think I can't feel it? You think I don't know what you're all thinking?

Johannah: Calm down, Jim . . . I never seen you so shaken up.

Jim Donnelly: Can't you see it? One by one they've stopped talking to us. One by one they've stopped coming around.

Johannah: You're just imagining things, Jim. We've still got a few good friends left.

Jim Donnelly: But how much longer, Johannah? How much longer until they're all gone?

All: Watching
        'Til the time is right,
        Watching
        Shadows in the night,
        Watching.

Jim Donnelly: They'd like to break us. They'd like to see us grovel. But we won't . . . we won't.

All: Waiting
        'Til the time is right,
        Waiting
        Shadows in the night,
        Waiting.

(Company exits. Jim moves to a table where he writes a letter in a slow and painful hand.)

Jim Donnelly: January 12th, 1880. Mr. Meredith: Sir — On the 15th of last month, Pat Ryder's barns were burned. All the vigilante committee at once pointed to my family as the ones that done it. Ryder found out that all my boys were at a wedding that night. He at once arrested me and my wife on suspicion. The trial has been postponed four different times, and although we are ready for trial at any time, they examined a lot of witnesses but can't find anything against us. Ryder swore that we lived neighbours to each other for thirty years and never had any difference, and had no reason for arresting us, only that we are blamed for everything. They are using us worse than mad dogs. They had the first trial in Lucan, and then adjourned to Granton simply to advertise us. I want you to handle the case on our behalf, and if there is any chance for damages, I want you to attack them at once, as they will never let us alone until some of them are made an example of. There is not the slightest cause for our arrest, and it seems hard to see a man and a woman over sixty years of age dragged around as laughing stocks. Yours truly, James Donnelly, Sr.

(Jim exits. Slide 30 — a small lighted window at night. It is the schoolroom where the vigilantes meet. The door creaks open, and a man enters with a limp. He talks in whispers with another man.)

Madigan: Looks like we're early.

Toohey *(entering)*: Brrrr . . . it's cold.

Madigan: He did say eight-thirty?

Toohey: Yeah. *(Pause)* Hey, what are we whispering for?

Madigan: I dunno. Hey . . . you got any whisky left?

(Toohey hands him a jar of whisky and they both drink. John Purtell enters. He is a large and rather stupid individual.)

Purtell: Hello, boys.

Madigan: Hello, John.

Purtell: You got a jar, eh?

VILLAGE OF LUCAN.

NAME.	LOCATION.	Date of Settlement.	NATIVITY.	POST OFFICE.	BUSINESS.
Armitage, J. R.....	Main St...........	1840	Canada	Lucan.	Merchant.
Atkinson, T. T.....	do	1873	do	do	Carpenter.
Cann, L...........	do	1861	do	do	Books & Stationery.
Cain, John F.......	do	1860	do	do	Proprietor "Royal Hotel."
Farrell, John.......	do	1829	do	do	Druggist.
Gibson, S..........	William St........	1867	do	do	Proprietor Planing Mills.
Gear, George.......	Main St...........	1872	England	do	House Decorator.
Hutchins, W. H....	do	1863	Canada	do	Merchant & Reeve.
Hogg & Piefer.....		1876		do	Mfrs of Flax.
Haskett, W........	Market St........	1859	do	do	Farmer and Mill Owner.
Hersey, S. C.	Princess St.......	1862	do	do	Grain Merchant.
Lotz, Rev. H. B....	Pastoral Residence.	1876	U. States......	do	Roman Catholic Priest.
MacDiarmid W....	William St........	1872	Canada	do	Barrister.
McLean, R........	Main St...........	1844	Ireland	Lucan	Proprietor Central Hotel.
McFalls, R........	do	1854	Canada	do	" Queen's Hotel.
McCosh, J. D......	do	1861	do	do	Merchant.
Matheson, William..	do	1870	Scotland	do	Watchmaker & Jeweler.
McBride, William...		1873	Canada	do	Carpenter & Joiner.
Orme, J. W........	do	1855	do	do	Groceries, Flour, Feed, &c.
Reid & Chisholm...				do	Butchers & Drovers.
Shoebottom Bros..	William St........	1843	Scotland......	do	Livery & Pat. Spring Mfrs.
Thomas, J. E.......	Main St..........	1876	U. States......	do	Manager Bank of Commerce.
Tom, James K.....	William St........	1875	Canada	do	Job Printer.
Walker, William....	do	1863	do	do	Prop. Walker House & Stage Line.
Watts, J. C........	Main St...........	1868	England	do	Tinsmith & Stoves.

(Prominent citizens of the community circa 1878)

Madigan: Want some?

Purtell: Sure. *(Takes a swig)* Hey . . . you know who I saw in town today? I saw Will Donnelly in town, and I says to him . . . I said, "Hey, there goes Will Donnelly!" An' I laughed at him, an' all my friends laughed at him. How 'bout that, eh?

Toohey: What did he say to that?

Purtell: He said, "Christ, is you's ever imbecilic." Whassat mean, eh?

Toohey: It means you're stupid.

Purtell: Oh.

(William Casey enters. He is a gentleman farmer.)

Casey: Good evening, Jim, Mike, and, er . . . .

Madigan: John.

Casey: Yes . . . John Purtell, of course. Well, how are you all? Damned cold, eh? He always chooses the coldest nights for his meetings.

Toohey: You reckon it'll be about Ryder's barn?

Casey: Without a doubt.

Madigan: You were a magistrate, Will. What do you think?

Casey: It'll never stick, I'm afraid.

Purtell: You mean he said I was stupid?

(Grouchy Ryder and Ed Ryan enter. They are both drunk.)

Ryder: *(sings to the tune of "Wild Colonial Boy")*:
     I am a wild colonial boy
     And Grouchy is my name,
     I was born and reared in Ireland
     At a place called Castlemaine.
Greetings to you all, boys . . . I smell blood in the air tonight.

A82

Casey: Aye . . . and I smell whisky. Can you never stay sober, Ryder? It's an important meeting.

Ryder: Ah, magistrate . . . *(bows mockingly)* . . . no . . . ex-magistrate. Come to see that justice is done. Or perhaps your pockets are a-jingle with Donnelly silver.

(Suddenly tempers flare . . . they almost go for each other, but the others stop them.)

Toohey: Hold it, Grouchy. Take it easy! You boys been drinking?

Ryder: Sure we've been drinking, and do you want to know why we've been drinking? Tell him, Ed.

Ryan: You all know Grouchy's Sal, don't you?

Toohey: Sure, she's a fine mare.

Ryder: She's dead, boys. And I thought the Donnellys burning down my barn last week was bad enough. You know, I saw them do it. I saw them with my own eyes. And the court asks for evidence. Evidence! Christ . . . I saw them!

Ryan: And now they killed Sal. She broke her leg in a hole in the field over by the tracks.

Ryder: There was never a hole there before. I worked that field for thirty years, and there was never a hole there. Those bastard Donnellys put it there. And now they killed my best mare.

Purtell: You mean he said I was stupid?

Ryder: What are you talking about?

Toohey: Don't mind him, Grouchy.

Ryder: They're going to pay. Those bastards are going to pay, by Christ. They'll pay for burning my barn and killing my Sal. I'll make them pay for everything!

Casey: Not in the law courts they won't, Mr. Ryder.

Ryder: You bastard lawyers with all your "education". What the hell

A83

Dudley Witney

do you know about justice? Pieces of paper and fancy words, that's all.

Toohey: Now cut it out, Grouchy! Will Casey is a friend of the committee. He wants to help us.

(Pat Quigly and several others enter.)

Ryder: Welcome, Pat, and all the rest of you. Welcome to our monthly parlour game. *(He laughs)* That's all this is, you know.

Quigly: Aye . . . I'm inclined to agree with you about that.

Ryder: You're a good man, Pat. Hey . . . let me tell you how it is. Now farmers like us . . . we're trained to use a pick and an axe . . . and once you've learned, you never forget. A constable . . . he's trained to use a gun and a club . . . and once he's learned, he never forgets. It's the same with your magistrates like McLaughlin and Casey here. They're trained to use the law and fancy words — and once they've learned, they never forget . . . right, Will? *(During this speech McLaughlin has entered)* And that's all we're going to get tonight, same as every other time.

McLaughlin: Thanks for the introduction, Grouchy.

Ryder: Oh, Christ.

Quigly: There's more'n a grain of truth in what he says, McLaughlin.

McLaughlin: Why weren't you at the trial this afternoon, Ryder?

Ryder: I was too drunk, damn you.

McLaughlin: For God's sake . . . it was your brother's barn that was burned. We could have used your evidence.

Madigan: How did it go, McLaughlin?

McLaughlin *(avoiding the question)*: Where's Carroll? He's late.

Toohey: I ain't seen him awhile, Mr. McLaughlin.

McLaughlin: Shall we start without him? *(General assent)* Very well. I have just come from the law courts. The case against the Donnellys for the burning of Mr. Ryder's barn is on the verge of falling through.

A85

(Angry shouts from the crowd) Order . . . order, please! I admit that our efforts are continually being frustrated, but the process of the law requires evidence which no one is prepared to give. But, how do you expect people to come forward, if even you — the members of the committee — refuse to go to the trial?

Ryan: What's the point . . . they'd get off anyway.

McLaughlin: If we get the evidence, the law will put them away . . . I guarantee it!

Quigly: Sure, we'll give evidence . . . and get burned out for our troubles.

McLaughlin: I know it's difficult, but the law does work . . . we just got John Donnelly six months . . . .

Ryder: Six months! That means he'll be back with us before you can say barn-burning twice.

McLaughlin: We are doing our best to put the Donnellys behind bars, but while the law . . . .

Ryan: Bugger the law!

(Shouting and assent from crowd.)

McLaughlin: Please . . . let's have some order in here.

(Carroll enters. The crowd falls silent.)

Ryan: Hey . . . it's big, bad Carroll! The man who'd run the Donnellys out of town. You're doing a great bloody job, ain't you?

Carroll: Keep your mouth shut. *(He walks around the room looking at the men)* I suppose our lawyer here has told you about what happened at the law courts today.

McLaughlin: It can't be helped, Carroll. There's just not enough evidence.

Carroll: And how much longer do you intend to go on messing around with the law?

A86

McLaughlin: Look, Carroll . . . the next time . . . .

Carroll: No! No more "next times", McLaughlin!

(Suddenly McLaughlin realizes what Carroll is thinking.)

McLaughlin: I know perfectly well what you want and I absolutely refuse. It would be stupid and dangerous.

Carroll: Well, I reckon that's up to the committee to decide. *(General assent)* Call the vote, McLaughlin.

(Shouts of assent from the crowd.)

McLaughlin: You're crazy! For God's sake . . . do you know what you're asking?

Carroll: Just call the vote.

McLaughlin: We can't vote on that. If Father Connolly . . . .

(Shouts from the crowd.)

Ryder: To hell with Father Connolly! Christ . . . you'd think the sun shines out of Father Connolly's arse. Father Connolly ain't got barns and livestock to lose.

Carroll: That's right, McLaughlin. People like you and Father Connolly can afford to wait. You're not farmers like the rest of the committee. You ain't going to wake up one morning and find a full year's harvest in ashes. You've never lost a thing at their hands.

Madigan: That's true, McLaughlin . . . they've never touched you.

Purtell: And Will Donnelly said I was stupid.

Toohey: Shut up, Purtell.

Carroll: You ain't got nothing to lose, McLaughlin, so you don't mind waiting. But these men have.

Ryder: Yeah . . . we've had enough of talking. Let's vote on it.

McLaughlin: No . . . it's out of the question. There's too much risk

A87

involved. We must learn how to . . . .

(Shouting from the crowd.)

Carroll: McLaughlin . . . we want to vote! You are the chairman of this committee. Call the vote.

McLaughlin: Please be patient.

(The crowd starts a slow handclap.)

Carroll: You know what they want, McLaughlin.

McLaughlin: I don't like it Carroll.

Carroll: I don't think you've got much choice.

McLaughlin: Very well. Silence, please. Silence. You all know the issue. All those in favour say "aye". *(A unanimous "aye")* All those against. *(There is silence)* They're all yours, Carroll.

Carroll: We must keep absolute secrecy, for one word in the wrong ear could ruin us. We shall meet here in three days at the same time, and I will tell you how it will be done . . . and when.

(From the very back of the stage voices can be heard. The men pick up their lanterns, leave the schoolroom, and join the backstage chorus.)

All *(sing)*:
> Forty men went riding,
> Riding, riding.
> Forty men went riding
> Down the Roman line.

(Figures, dressed in black and muffled up, appear at the back of the set during the song. They have clubs and sticks. They circle the stage in sinister silhouettes)

> We met late in a schoolhouse
> Along the Roman line,
> Jim Carroll said, "Just wait, lads,
> 'Til I give you the sign."
> With silent eyes we watched him,
> With clubs fixed in our hands.

Forty men went riding,
Riding, riding.
Forty men went riding
Down the Roman line.

(They fade into the shadows as Jim and Will enter. Slide 31 — night sky.)

Jim Donnelly: Are you sure you won't stop with us tonight, Will?

Will Donnelly: Not tonight. Big Charlie threw a shoe today. I've got to fix it by morning.

Jim Donnelly: Well, keep your eyes open when you ride home.

Will Donnelly: I always do, but it's a very quiet night. I was over at Keefe's Tavern earlier. You've never seen it so quiet.

Jim Donnelly: It's a strange day altogether. I was in town today, and there was scarce a man would look me in the eye. They look down at their feet and scuttle past, but when they think you're not looking, they stare at you. I don't like it. I wouldn't be surprised if Carroll and his cronies haven't been hatching a plot.

Will Donnelly: A plot? We've been living with a plot for forty years, father. It's no different today than it ever was.

Jim Donnelly: I don't know. There's a look in people's eyes different to what I've seen before.

Will Donnelly: It's just your imagination.

Jim Donnelly: Maybe. *(He shrugs)* Look at the sky, Will.

Will Donnelly: Clear. It's a grand night.

Jim Donnelly: Reminds me of the two years I spent on the run.

Will Donnelly: You still think about that?

Jim Donnelly: No. I hadn't thought about it in ages.

Will Donnelly: It must be a strange night if it gets you nostalgic. Is it because of the trial at Granton tomorrow?

Jim Donnelly: No . . . that doesn't worry me. There's not a scrap of evidence in that arson charge that isn't perjured. They'll never make it stick. What worries me is that most of our enemies are beginning to realize that their damned lies never hold water in court.

Will Donnelly: Why does that worry you?

Jim Donnelly: Because they may try something else.

Will Donnelly: Never. That bunch of gutless bastards would never have the nerve. You worry too much, father. By the way, do you want me to come over and look after the animals while you're away at Granton?

Jim Donnelly: Thank you, Will, but that young O'Connor boy is coming round to stay with us tonight.

Will Donnelly: Good. Well, the best of luck tomorrow. I'll see you after the trial.

Jim Donnelly: Right. Goodnight.

Will Donnelly: Goodnight.

(The vigilantes sing.)

All: Forty men went riding,
            Riding, riding.
            Forty men went riding
            Down the Roman line.

(At the end of the song, the low, rumbling organ sound begins. The vigilantes move stealthily into their positions around the set. They wait, poised to spring. The centre of the stage becomes the living room of the Donnelly farm. It is empty. Carroll enters with a lantern. Slide 32 — cold colour — blue.)

Carroll *(calls out)*: Donnelly!

(There is a moment's silence, and Jim's voice is heard offstage.)

Jim Donnelly: Who is it?

Carroll: James Carroll. The constable.

A91

(Jim comes onstage in his nightshirt. He is very sleepy.)

Jim Donnelly: What are you arresting me for now?

Carroll: I've got another charge against you.

(There is a silence while Jim, very annoyed, puts on his boots. Carroll sneaks up to another door and looks in. It is Tom Donnelly's bedroom. He enters and a moment later comes out, dragging behind him a drowsy Tom whom he has handcuffed.)

Tom Donnelly: What the hell?

Jim Donnelly: What's up, Tom? Are you handcuffed?

Tom Donnelly: Yes. He thinks he's smart.

(Jim snorts and heads for the bedroom.)

Carroll: Where do you think you're going?

Jim Donnelly: I'm going to get my coat.

(Carroll follows him to the bedroom door. Johannah enters.)

Johannah: What's going on?

Tom Donnelly: It's Carroll with another charge against us.

Johannah: Holy Jesus? Will we never have any peace? *(Shouts)* Bridget, get up and stoke the fire!

Jim Donnelly: Alright, Carroll . . . now read your warrant.

Carroll: There's plenty of time for that.

(Suddenly the vigilantes jump down from their positions. The organ sound has built into a powerful crescendo. There is a moment's pause — the vigilantes poised, the Donnellys shocked — then Carroll gives the first blow. Suddenly, everything is bedlam. Sticks and fists pounding, screams of terror and roars of rage. A movie projection appears on the screen. It is a collage of faces, the camera zooming in on expressions of fear and hatred. If slides are used, show actors faces in black and white. Slide 33 — faces. John Purtell chases Bridget up-

A93

stairs with an axe. Bridget is followed by Johnny O'Connor, who has been in the bedroom of Jim Donnelly. As O'Connor reaches the top of the stairs, everything freezes. Irving appears at a higher level. Johnny O'Connor is about twelve years old.)

Irving: Johnny O'Connor. What were you doing in the early hours of February the fourth, 1880?

O'Connor: I was staying at the house of the Donnellys.

Irving: As the only surviving witness of the massacre, I hope you realize the importance of the accuracy of your testimony.

O'Connor: Yes, sir.

Irving: Who else was in the house that night?

O'Connor: There was Mr. and Mrs. Donnelly, and Tom and Bridget. Bridget was their niece, they said. Just come from Ireland.

Irving: You say that James Donnelly, Senior, went to the bedroom to get his coat, and you handed it to him?

O'Connor: Yes, sir.

Irving: Did you see anyone else?

O'Connor: I saw James Carroll, the constable, standing in the doorway.

Irving: What happened after the other men entered?

O'Connor: I ran to the top of the stairs after Bridget Donnelly, but she closed the door in my face, so I ran downstairs and hid under the bed.

Irving: Did you recognize any of the men?

O'Connor: Yes, sir.

Irving: What happened next?

O'Connor: Someone smashed the light. It was difficult to see.

(There is the sound of breaking glass and the scene dims, so that only

A94

shadows can be seen. Chaos suddenly bursts out again. The movie or slide collage starts again — similar to the first. John Purtell runs up the stairs and grabs Bridget who is screaming with fear. He has an axe.)

Purtell: You bitch! I'm going to slash you to pieces, you bitch!

(Tom Donnelly manages to chop his way through the oncoming crowd and knocks several of them down. He reaches the door and forces his way outside. Several men follow him. Bridget has been dragged down the stairs, and John Purtell smashes her with his axe, screaming like a maniac. Meanwhile, Jim and Johannah are being clubbed in a corner. Jim is the first to fall. They turn their attention to Johannah. One of them grabs a red hot poker and the others hold Johannah down.)

Ryder: Let's hear the bitch sizzle!

(He rams the poker up her crotch, and she screams terribly. They throw her on the floor and continue to club her. Tom is dragged in by several men. This can be a dummy made to resemble the actor playing Tom so that he can be decapitated. He is beaten up and bloody. Finally, he is thrown on the floor. A man is poised with a spade. Everybody freezes.)

Irving: What was the last thing that happened during the fight?

O'Connor: Tom was the last to die, I think. They were doing terrible things to him. They chopped his head off with a spade.

(The spade comes down on Tom's head with a thump and decapitates him. The body twitches, and then is still. The movie or slide projection fades into blood running down a white background. There is silence, except for the heavy breathing of the vigilantes. As they survey the scene of their night's work, a feeling of horror and disgust begins to run through the group. Carroll senses it . . . .)

Carroll: Don't just stand there, for chrissake! We have work to do. Who has the oil?

Madigan *(still shocked)*: It's here.

Carroll: Get on with it then. Burn this place to the ground! Come on . . . move! *(Madigan throws the oil around and simulates setting it alight. A lot of the group are still stunned)* We're going to Will

A95

Dudley Witney

Donnelly's next, and I'll beat the hell out of anyone who plays chicken on me now. Let's get out of here. *(The men pull themselves together and leave as the music begins. The music is the theme of "Forty Men Went Riding". The bodies still remain on the stage, as the stage fills with smoke and the sound of flames. This fades as if receding into the distance, and the scene becomes moonlight outside Will Donnelly's house. The vigilantes poise on one side of the stage, three rifles aimed at a door. Carroll shouts —)* Fire . . . fire! *(Silence)* Open up! There's a fire!

(A light appears in a window. Slowly the door opens and a figure is silhouetted in the doorway.)

John Donnelly: What do you . . . .

(Three guns go off. He goes flying backwards and collapses.)

Man 1: We've got him, boys, we've got him!

McLaughlin: Come on, let's go. Our work is done.

(The vigilantes exit and Will Donnelly comes running out.)

Will Donnelly: My God! It's John! They've killed my brother!

(They freeze. Suddenly, there is a loud hammering. It is Johnny O'Connor at the Whalen's house. This scene takes place in a separate area so that the bodies can remain on stage. A light goes on and Mrs. Whalen appears. The hammering is quite frantic. Slide 34 — red.)

Mrs. Whalen: Who is it?

O'Connor: It's Johnny O'Connor.

Mr. Whalen *(entering)*: What's the matter?

Mrs. Whalen: It's the O'Connor boy.

Mr. Whalen: What are you doing up at this hour?

O'Connor: I'm froze, Mr. Whalen.

Mrs. Whalen: Where on earth are your shoes?

A97

O'Connor: I had to leave them at the Donnelly's. Don't you have a coat or something? I'm frozen.

Mr. Whalen: What do you mean you had to leave them at the Donnellys? What happened?

O'Connor: The Donnelly house is on fire.

Mr. Whalen: You're dreaming, boy.

O'Connor: A lot of men came in and beat them up with sticks. I think they're all killed.

Mr. Whalen: They're what?

Mrs. Whalen: Do you know what you're saying boy?

O'Connor: They're all killed and Carroll the constable was there.

(Mr. and Mrs. Whalen look at each other.)

Mrs. Whalen: Now you don't say anything more about it. We don't want to be brought into this.

Mr. Whalen: The missus is right, boy. You'd better be mighty careful of what you say. They'll be dragging you in front of a court if something really has happened.

O'Connor: Well, go over and see. Call up your boys and tell them to put the fire out.

Mrs. Whalen: I don't like the sound of this. You say Carroll was there, boy?

O'Connor: That's right. And I saw Ryder and Purtell, as well.

Mrs. Whalen: The committee was out tonight.

(Mr. Whalen grabs Johnny O'Connor.)

Mr. Whalen: What happened? What did they do?

O'Connor: They killed them all, Tom and Bridget and Mrs. Donnelly and the old man. They're all dead.

A98

Mr. Whalen *(looks out)*: Holy Christ! It's done at last!

(They exit. The bodies of the four Donnellys killed at the farm are lying downstage in the same positions as when they were murdered, and the body of John Donnelly with Will is in the same position as at the end of the earlier scene. During the song Will moves in among the dead bodies and looks at them. Standing around the stage are the men of the vigilante committee. They are facing the audience.)

All *(sing)*:

> We're only honest farmers
> And we've no mind to kill,
> But if our homes are threatened
> Then, by Christ, we will.
>
> A brighter dawn is breaking
> Though red has tinged the sky.
> We've left our hate behind us
> Where crimson ashes lie.

(Sound effect like alarm bell indicates sudden clamour and confusion. Rushing everywhere on stage are reporters, frantically asking questions. During this, newspaper vendors rush on shouting the headlines. Men begin to take the bodies off on stretchers. Mulligan enters and looks around to see what is going on. Slide 35 — newspaper.)

Vendor 1: Biddulph horror! Family massacred!

(Slide 36 — newspaper.)

Vendor 2: Horrible tragedy at Lucan! Result of a family feud!

Vendor 3: Family who terrorized district, murdered by neighbours!

(Slide 37 — newspaper.)

Reporter 1: I'm from the London Free Press. Can you tell me about this feud?

Man 1: Feud? What feud?

(Slide 38 — newspaper.)

Reporter 2: I'm from the Toronto Globe. Did you know the Donnellys?

A99

Mulligan: Well, Tom was about seven feet tall and just about as broad. If he didn't like a man's looks, he'd change them — permanently.

(Slide 39 — newspaper.)

Reporter 3: London Advertiser. Who do you think did the killing?

Man 3: If it were known, it will be found that the murderers are the most respectable men in the township, good farmers and honest men. But they had to do it — there was no other way.

(Slide 40 — neutral colour — green. At a higher level there is a burst of riotous laughter, and a light comes up to reveal McLaughlin, Ryder and three other men blind drunk. During this scene, the last of the bodies are removed slowly. McLaughlin is stunned and doesn't join in the celebration. The other men sing "Honest Farmers", but raucously out of tune.)

Men: We're only honest farmers
        And we've no mind to kill
        But if our homes are threatened
        Then, by Christ, we will.

Ryder: Did you see how they got the old woman? *(Laughs)* With a poker up her . . . . *(Indicates it.)*

(Everyone laughs.)

Purtell: Did you hear that there weren't enough of the bodies left after the burning, so they put them all in one coffin. *(The others laugh)* That's right . . . the old man, the old woman, Tom and Bridget . . . all in one coffin. *(More laughter)* And John had one all to himself.

Ryder: Listen to this, everybody! "There does not appear to be much sympathy for the murdered family, on account of the strong feeling that existed against them."

Toohey: You think that's good? How about this one? "Little can be heard in condemnation of the murderers, while such expressions as, 'It's about time they were cleaned out' can be heard by many of the townsfolk." *(They laugh)* We'll be heroes yet!

Purtell: Did you see how Jim here cut Tom's head off with a spade?

A100

(They all laugh) He couldn't find his axe, so the silly bugger used a spade!

(They laugh at him again.)

Ryder: We oughta call him "Spadey".

(They all applaud and bang their glasses on the table shouting, "Spadey, Spadey.")

Toohey: I've got a good one from the Globe in Toronto: "The Donnellys had the unenviable reputation of being the terrors of the township."

Ryder *(splitting himself with laughter)*: Terrors of the township! Oh . . . that's a good one. *(They both rock with laughter. Ryder gets up with difficulty)* I propose a toast. Fill her up. *(The glasses are filled)* I propose a toast to those dear departed friends who cannot be with us today. The terrors of this township!

McLaughlin: Long live the terrors of the township!

(They burst into laughter again and drink their toast. Ryder drains his bottle.)

Ryder: Come on, boys . . . let's get some more whisky. *(They move down from their higher level to centre stage, from which the bodies have been removed. A man enters)* Josh . . . a great night for a celebration! *(The man turns his back on them and stands motionless. A lady enters)* Good evening to you, Beth. *(She turns her back on them)* For chrissake! We're only drunk. *(Four more people enter and turn away from them — all remaining motionless on stage)* Talk to us, you bastards! Ah . . . to hell with you all. Let's go down to Keefe's Tavern.

(They exit. Will and Mulligan are still in the background.)

Will Donnelly: Mulligan! At the Central Hotel last week, you were heard saying you saw a meeting of the vigilante committee. Who did you see there?

One: I saw nothing.

Two: I heard nothing.

A101

Three: I know nothing.

Four: I saw nothing.

Five: I heard nothing.

Six: I know nothing.

Will Donnelly: You must have seen something. Something that can be used as evidence.

Mulligan: There's nothing I can tell you, Will. I'm sorry, but . . . .

One: I saw nothing.

Two: I heard nothing.

Three: I know nothing.

Four: I saw nothing.

Five: I heard nothing.

Six: I know nothing.

Will Donnelly: Why won't you help me . . . why the hell won't any-body help me?

Mulligan: I can't help you. Nobody can help. All you got left is the law! Good luck!

(Slide 41 — inside church. There is a silence and the Kyrie begins. During the Kyrie, the congregation files in and two coffins are carried to centre stage. Father Connolly is on a higher level, as if in a pulpit.)

Father Connolly: I urge you all to pray for the souls of the departed, and I feel certain that this most dreadful act had been the result of midnight walking, drinking and carousing.

(A light falls on Irving, changing the pulpit to the witness box.)

Irving: Father Connolly, why did you instigate the vigilance committee?

Father Connolly: I did not instigate it. It was already in existence

A103

Irving: But you proposed the signing of an oath.

Father Connolly: It was my intention to make sure that its activities were beneficial.

Irving: Did you mean by that the elimination of the Donnellys?

Father Connolly: No, sir. I did not.

Irving: And yet you asked your parishioners to, and I quote, "solemnly pledge ourselves to aid our spiritual director and parish priest in the discovery and putting down of crime in our mission."

Father Connolly: I did not mention the Donnellys.

Irving: And yet you are said to have cursed them from the pulpit.

Father Connolly: That is not true.

Irving: But you did speak out against them.

Father Connolly: I never mentioned them by name.

Irving: It is said that you refused to confess John Donnelly, not long before his death.

Father Connolly: I refused to confess him, because I thought that he intended to confess to an untruth, in order to free his brother and implicate others.

Irving: Don't you think that this is a rather presumptuous attitude for a priest? *(Father Connolly is silent)* What did he do when you told him that?

Father Connolly: He went away.

Irving: So you sent him to his death unshriven?

Father Connolly: But I never meant . . . I never meant it to be like this . . . . *(The light fades on Irving, and Father Connolly is back in the pulpit. A bell tolls)* Today is one of the saddest days of my life. Here are the last earthly remains of five souls whose deaths at the hands of murderers have been a great shock to us all. *(He is overcome with emotion)* A great shock. It may be said that I was not in friend-

A104

ship with the family. That is not true. I was in friendship with the old people, but the young people I did not know much. Particularly with the old woman I was friendly. For two hours she was in my office on Christmas eve giving me the history of her whole life in Biddulph. She received the sacrament, and the last words she spoke to me as she went away were, "Father Connolly, I am going to get not only my boys, but all the Biddulph boys to reform." Who would have thought it would have come to this! *(Silence)* I can't say any more.

(The scene freezes in a tableau. A light comes up on Tim Mulligan. Slide 42 — a cold colour — blue.)

Mulligan: A pretty little picture, isn't it? Father Connolly bawling his eyes out on the coffins. The good citizens of Biddulph sitting quietly through the whole thing, with their hands clenched in prayer and their hearts clenched in hate. There was more than a few in that house of God that day wishing them eternal torment between the lines of the Lord's Prayer. And, of course, Will — his face straight and unmoved. I don't know a man ever saw him smile after the murder — or show anything, come to that. Revenge was all he wanted, but now it was him who had to fight with the tangled web of the law. He wasn't used to fighting that way. Poor bastard. And so there came the trial — for all that it was worth.

Judge: The jury will now retire to consider its verdict.

All *(sing)*:
> The words have all been spoken,
> Our story's almost done.
> But the legend of the Donnellys
> Has only just begun.
>
> But the facts are soon forgotten
> As you watch a legend grow,
> And the truth of all that happened
> I guess we'll never know.

Judge: How do you find the defendants on the charge of murder?

Foreman: Not guilty, Your Honour.

A105

(The band begins a slow, sombre introduction to "Months Are Going".)

All *(sing)*:

> Months are going, going by,
> Wheat is growing, growing high,
> But someone soon is going to die,
> Way down in Lucan town.

Will Donnelly: The work of a lifetime. Memories crumbled in ashes that blow and settle on the snow. Soon they will be lost to the earth, lost in the land they created and that created them. It's all over. I'm too tired to fight any more.

(He breaks down and exits.)

All *(sing)*:

> The words have all been spoken
> Our story's almost done.
> But the legend of the Donnellys
> Has only just begun.
>
> Kids huddle by the fireside
> Amid a winter's gale,
> And grand-folks talk in whispered tones
> About this fearful tale.
>
> And mothers tell their children
> To bolt their windows tight,
> For the Devil and the Donnellys
> Are riding past tonight.
>
> For the facts are soon forgotten
> As you watch a legend grow.
> And the truth of all that happened
> I guess we'll never know.
>
> Follow us . . . one hundred years,
> And we'll take you back to Lucan town . . . .

(The final line is incomplete and the sound of a man whistling takes over. The accompanying music fades away just leaving the whistling alone. Meanwhile, a movie projection appears. It is the same as the opening sequence, except that Will is walking away from the camera.

A106

By the time the whistling ends, Will is far away on the skyline. The sound of an icy winter wind takes over from the whistling, as the movie fades out leaving only darkness and the sound of the wind. Alternatively, the silhouette of Will Donnelly can walk in front of the screen, then exit. Curtain.)

The end

Photo credits A1 *(The Company)*
(left to right) A16 *(Karna Ivey, Diane Cuthbert)*

A39 *(Robert Cooper, Greg Brandt, Peter Colley, David G. Marriage, Art Fidler, Tom Stebing, David Wasse, Claude R. Tessier, Tim Grantham, Cecil Wilson)*

A50 *(Tom Celli, Peter Colley)*

A70 *(Art Fidler, David Wallett, Cecil Wilson, Jim Schaefer, Tom Stebing, Rick Prevett)*

A75 *(David Wallett, Cecil Wilson)*

A89 *(Pat Collins, Tom Celli)*

A92 *(The Company)*

A107 *(Jim Schaefer, Tom Celli)*

Photographs by Jim Hockings.

Additional A8, A54, A61, A64, A84, A96, A102 *(Courtesy of the Picture*
credits *Collection, Fine Arts Department, Metropolitan Toronto Central Library, Toronto, Ontario)*

A24–A25, A31, A45, A81 *(Courtesy of the Historical Atlas of Middlesex County, Ontario, as compiled by H.R.Page and Company, Toronto, Ontario, in 1878. It was edited by Mika Silk Screening Limited of Belleville, Ontario, and printed by Maracle Press, Oshawa, Ontario, in 1972)*

Sources of research material The author wishes to acknowledge the following sources for his research into the Donnelly family:
"The Donnellys Must Die" by Orlo Miller; published by Macmillan Company of Canada Limited, Toronto, Ontario.
"The Black Donnellys (The True Story of Canada's Most Barbaric Feud)" by Thomas P. Kelley; published by Modern Canadian Library Ink, Toronto, Ontario.
"The London Free Press", London, Ontario.
"The Globe", Toronto, Ontario.
Various legal documents of the period.

Original music Original music composed for THE DONNELLYS is available from Berthold Carrière, c/o Simon & Pierre Publishing Company Limited, Toronto, Ontario.

Technical effects A combination of sound tapes, slides and film projections was used in the original production. Sound effects and slides are available on a rental basis from Simon & Pierre Publishing Company Limited, Toronto. The film projections can be omitted if desired, but were used by Theatre London to heighten certain dramatic moments.
Projection one — at the opening of the play as described in the text.
Projection two — a burning barn in the sequence with Toohey and his family in Act one.
Projection three — a collage of faces during the massacre in Act two.
Projection four — blood running down a white screen after Tom's head is severed in Act two.
Projection five: — at the closing of the play as described in the text.

Costumes There were really no definable costumes. Everyone wore a basic black outfit and various nondescript hats and jackets were added. Mulligan had a large, dirty trench coat.

The design for the original production of THE DONNELLYS, as
shown opposite, used a series of ramps and risers. This created a
variety of levels in staging, as well as flexibility and speed in scene
changing. The numbers 1 to 13 indicate thirteen detachable masking
pieces.

Props *The following props were used in the original production, although*
not all are mentioned in the text.

Shawls	Bundles
Aprons	Stools
Assorted jackets	Barrel
Petition	Wash basket
Pencil	Harness
Warrants	Butter churn
Newspapers	Tray
Oath	Beer mugs
Land deed	Mulligan's whisky bottle
Paper	Jugs
Pen	Lanterns
Ink	Handcuffs
Axes	Oil can
File	Logs
Rope	Planks
Mallets	Thorns
Spades	Stretchers
Fake spade	Blanket
Fake hatchet	Two coffins
Soft clubs	Mulligan's knapsack
Two revolvers	Luggage
Shot gun	Trunks
Poker	Fire bell
Cane	Funeral bell
Handspike	Dummy
Manacles	Baby

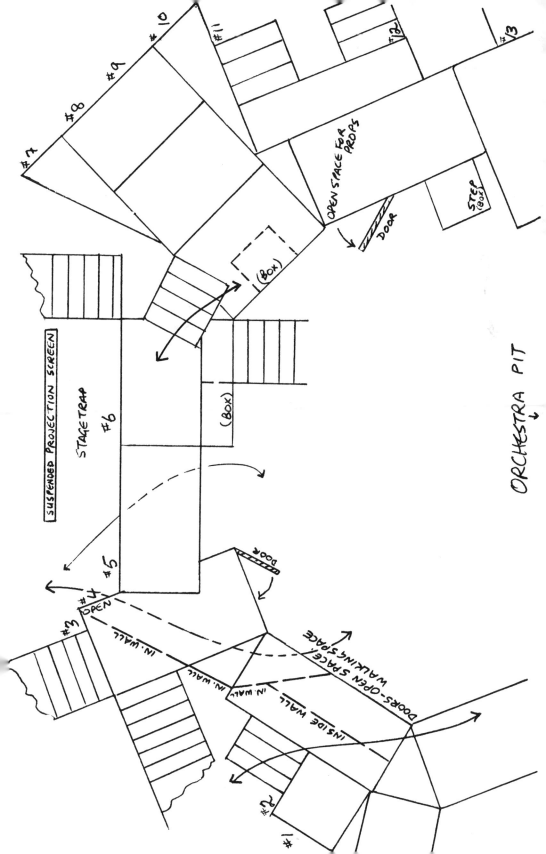

A WIFE IN THE HAND

a farce

by Jack H. Crisp

We would like to express our gratitude to The Canada Council and the Ontario Arts Council for their support.

Marian M. Wilson, Publisher

ISBN 0-88924-046-9
1 2 3 4 5/79 78 77 76
Simon & Pierre Publishing Company Limited, Order Department
P.O.Box 280 Adelaide Street Postal Station
Toronto, Ontario, Canada M5C 2J4

Author  **Jack H. Crisp** probably inherited his interest in the theatre from his parents, both of whom worked in professional theatre in Britain. As a result, Mr. Crisp spent much of his childhood assisting in many phases of theatre production. After the war, he worked with several theatre companies in London and, for a year, as assistant to one of Britain's foremost theatre directors.

Mr. Crisp came to Canada in 1949, and shortly afterwards was given the opportunity to direct the MRT production of VISIT TO A SMALL PLANET. It was an instant success and proved to be the forerunner of several more Crisp-directed MRT hits.

In 1961, Jeanine Beaubien invited Mr. Crisp to direct PRUDENCE SPURNS A WAGER. Since then, he has directed over thirty plays at La Poudrière and has become the company's unofficial resident playwright/director. Mr. Crisp has written several successful plays, six of which were presented by the CBC. His first stage play, MURDER, MY LOVE opened at La Poudrière in 1968 for a scheduled three week run and was held over five weeks. This was followed by A WIFE IN THE HAND which again was written for The Montreal International Theatre with specific actors in mind. The production achieved a record-breaking 121 performances. The German language version was successfully presented in 1969 and the French language version is currently being prepared.

Mr. Crisp's other successful plays include THAT SPRING THING (1969), PLAN A LITTLE MURDER (1973), LOVE THY NEIGHBOUR (1973), and WHO'S HOOME? (1975), all of which were presented at La Poudrière in Montreal.

Mr. Crisp lives with his wife and four children in Montreal, where he somehow divides his time between the two careers of advertising and theatre.

B3

Original	Susan Roberts — Jeannine Beaubien, jr.
cast	Liz Foster — Eileen Clifford
	Lydia Henderson — Jeanine Beaubien
	James Henderson — Len Watt
	Jeff Gordon — Bert Adkins
	Valerie Scott — Michèle Chicoine
	Norman Drummond — Scott Savage

Original production

The original production of A WIFE IN THE HAND opened on Wednesday, July 3, 1968, at La Poudrière, Montreal International Theatre, Montreal, Quebec, produced by Jeanine Beaubien.
Directed by Jack H. Crisp
Set Design by Guy Beauregard
Lighting by Marcel Duplessis
Choreography by Jeff Henry
Stage Manager Normand Gamache

Play background

A WIFE IN THE HAND was first staged by the English section of Montreal International Theatre, and premiered at the International Theatre at HemisFair '68. This important event, which was held in San Antonio, Texas, on June 21, 1968, brought considerable praise to the production.

Following its run at HemisFair, the production transferred to La Poudrière on St. Helen's Island in Montreal, Quebec, where it ran for 121 performances — again to considerable critical and popular acclaim.

Subsequently, the play was translated into German (as BESSER DIE EIGENE FRAU IN DER HAND) by Walter Roome. The German-language production, adapted by Fred Doederlein and directed by Eva Lynn, played in the same Montreal theatre.

Susan Roberts — Young, married and in her middle twenties. She's attractive and bright, ready for fun.

Liz Foster — Perhaps about forty. She's single and very smart. A career type who'd prefer to be a housewife. She's Lydia's literary agent —— and her friend.

Lydia Henderson — In her early forties. She's a spare-time very successful novelist, and a full-time wife to James, to whom she is devoted.

James Henderson — About fifty. He's all business; has just been appointed President of Universal Trust. Business requires that he take a close look at youth, and he likes what he sees!

Jeff Gordon — A bachelor in his late twenties. Loves life, and girls! He is James' nephew and works for him, too. He is good at his job.

Valerie Scott — An airline hostess. She is fun and can handle men of any age. A swinger.

Norman Drummond — A celebrated syndicated columnist with two sets of standards — one for others, one for himself. He is a bachelor in his late forties.

General setting Act one, scene one takes place in the upstairs den of the Henderson home on a Friday evening in the summertime. The balance of the action takes place at Jeff's cottage, "Lookout", which is a comfortable year-round home overlooking a lake in the Laurentians. (See Set Design, pages B126–B127)

Time Present.

Act one, scene one — Early Friday evening
Act one, scene two — Later the same evening
Act two — 9:25 a.m. Saturday morning
Act three, scene one — 4:30 p.m. the same afternoon
Act three, scene two — 8:30 p.m. the same evening

Act one
Scene one *This scene is an inset. It is the attic "den" which serves as Lydia's workroom. The entrance door is down left. Against the left wall, there is a sofa with an end table in front. Against the right wall, there is a small desk with a chair on each side. Down left, next to and below the door, is a small arm chair.*

At rise, the room is in complete disorder. The end table is covered with a wide variety of dirty dishes. There is a dress pattern on the floor. Pieces of material are on the floor and on the chair down left. The table is covered with galley proofs and with typed sheets of paper. The general impression is that of an untidy, busy workroom.

Susan is lying on the sofa. She is apparently wearing something made from the same material scattered around the room although we can hardly see her, her face being covered by a popular magazine she is reading. Liz is sitting on the upstage chair of the desk. She is reading one of the typed sheets of paper. Offstage we hear the frantic clatter of a typewriter. CUE 1 — sound. After a few minutes the typewriter stops.

Lydia *(off)*: Damn! Damn!

(The typewriter starts up again.)

Susan: Damn! Damn! Continued next week. *(She throws magazine on the floor)* Why don't they mark "in two parts" more clearly!

CUE 2 — sound — the typewriter starts up again.

Liz: What did you say?

Susan: They should mark "first of two parts" more clearly.

(Lydia enters quickly and crosses to Liz. She is wearing a housedress and looks a little harried and unglamourous.)

Lydia: Here, Liz. Mark this sheet "insert G". I've already marked the proof. *(She hands a typed sheet and a proof to Liz)* There's only one more.

Liz: Don't rush so. I've plenty of time.

Lydia: You have, Liz, but I haven't. James will be home any

B7

moment now and he's liable to come up and see this mess.

(Lydia starts toward the door.)

Susan: What's all the panic? Isn't this another adventure of Chickie Dickie and Fuzzy Tail?

Lydia: No, dear, it isn't.

Susan: I thought you said you wouldn't write any more sex stories. Only last week you said . . . .

Lydia: This isn't a new story. I'm correcting the proofs of the last one I wrote . . . .

Liz: We must have it this weekend, Susan. It goes to press on Monday.

Susan: Well, Mum, I hope your stories are never published in two parts. It only aggravates the readers.

Lydia: Why? What's the difference?

Susan: I've just read a "part one". There she was, falling for his line of "free love" and it's continued next week. I'll probably never know what happens.

Lydia: Well, dear, you know what usually happens.

Susan: Yes. That's probably why they call us the weaker sex. We're weaker in the head.

Lydia: The weaker sex is the stronger sex because of the weakness of the stronger sex for the weaker sex.

Liz: I'm glad you write more coherently than that. You sound like another Kinsey report!

Lydia: The Kinsey report proved just one thing——

Lydia & Liz: Women like to talk!

Susan: Well, I'd still like to know how that story comes out.

Lydia: If you must find out, you'll just have to wait 'til

B8

next week's issue.

(Lydia rushes off.)

Susan: Wait! Oh, I'm so sick of that word. *(She stands up and we see that she's pregnant — and wearing a pinned-together maternity dress)* I always seem to be waiting.

CUE 3 — sound — the typewriter starts up again.

Liz: But you've only just started. You know what's really the matter, don't you?

Susan: It's not Bob.

Liz: Of course it is. Susan, why not be sensible and go home?

Susan: I can't, Liz, not after the way Bob behaved. I'm never going home. *(Sits)* I'd love to go home.

Liz: Well, then, go home. I'll drive you over as soon as Lydia's finished. You'll feel so much better.

Susan: Oh, I can't. Bob will be so mad with me. He . . . he doesn't love me.

Liz: Of course he does. Lydia told me that she telephoned him and that he was terribly concerned.

Susan: Well, then why didn't he come over, apologize and beg me to go home?

Liz: He is worried about you. Why let a lovers' quarrel come between you? Remember, he's never been a father before. He's nervous and edgy too. That's why you had a fight. He acted the way he did just because he does love you.

Susan: Well, throwing your pregnant wife out of the house is a hell of a funny way of showing your love.

Liz: Men do strange things. My mother told me that my father ran up to the nurse and said, "Well, am I a mother or a father?"

(They both laugh.)

B9

Susan: All I said was, "When I get bigger, will you paint my toenails?"

Liz: Paint your toenails?

Susan *(stands up)*: Sure — I won't be able to reach them. All my life I've felt naked unless my toenails were painted. *(Looks down)* Hell! I won't be able to see them.

CUE 4 — sound — the typewriter stops.

Liz: Well, I'm sure when the time comes, Bob will do a really fine job — provided you're there, of course.

(Lydia enters and crosses to Liz.)

Lydia: Here's "insert H" and that finishes it. That's the last Shelby Sherbrooke story. Now please, please Liz . . . pack it up. It would be awful if James found out I was Shelby Sherbrooke now that I'm not.

Susan: Mum, you should have told him years ago.

Liz *(gathering up the papers)*: If we weren't such good friends, I'd try talking you into one more. I hate to see all the money stop.

Lydia: Spoken like a true agent. Anyway, Liz, I'll continue with Chickee Dickie and Fuzzy Tail — that'll be something.

Liz: Sure. And the Shelby Sherbrooke royalties will continue to come in for another couple of years. Sex won't go out of style.

Lydia: And I don't need to approve the cover, Liz. You do it. Just see that it has a beautiful girl on the cover . . . and no cover on the girl.

Liz: I wonder if James will ever realize that his appointment made such a difference to my income.

Lydia: But Liz, you do see that now he's been made president, I couldn't possibly continue with Shelby Sherbrooke.

Susan: But, Mum, why did you start . . . you're not the sort of person who thinks about sex.

B10

Lydia *(to Liz)*: Why is it that children believe their parents know nothing of sex? *(To Susan)* How do you think you got here?

Susan: You told me you found me under a cabbage.

Lydia: Haven't you ever wondered where I learned all the things I told you not to do?

Susan: No. I thought you got the ideas from T.V.

Liz: Shelby Sherbrooke started a long time ago, Susan.

Lydia: I wrote lots of things. Then, one day — just for fun — I wrote a . . . well . . . a sex novel.

Liz: "Holy Bedlock".

Lydia: Liz sold it. It was a best seller . . . I used my dead uncle's name, and told James that I had a legacy from Uncle Shelby. In those days we needed the money.

Susan: But Daddy has always understood . . . why not tell him . . . .

Lydia: If you had written ten best selling novels — full of sex — could you tell Bob you'd written them?

Susan: Sure. I'd write about him.

Lydia: That's what I mean.

Susan: You mean you wrote about . . . ?

Liz *(has looked over papers, puts them in briefcase)*: Well. There it is. Finished and put away.

Susan: I think I'll re-read all the Shelby Sherbrooke novels.

Lydia: Whatever for?

Susan: Every girl should learn all she can about her father.

Lydia: Well, there are many sexier books on the market.

Susan: Maybe. But they're not about Daddy.

Lydia: Well, I hope not.

Liz: If you like, I'll help you to tidy up.

Susan: I'll help too. *(Struggles to her feet.)*

Lydia *(to Susan)*: Why don't you take that thing off?

Susan: I'm trying to get used to what it will feel like.

Lydia: Well, believe me, you'll get all you can take of it without starting now.

(Susan lifts the maternity top off. We see that she has a pillow tied by a belt to her stomach.)

Liz: Well, that's a relief. I was beginning to wonder if you were carrying an elephant — I mean, two months!

(Susan takes off pillow.)

Lydia: Susan, I do think you should go home. James will be here any minute now and he'll have so much on his mind tonight — you know he's meeting Mr. Drummond tomorrow.

Susan: Yes. I shouldn't give Daddy my problems at a time like this.

Lydia: It's so exciting. *(Turning to Liz)* I hope I get the chance to meet Mr. Drummond. Imagine! Norman Drummond in person. I guess when he does an article on you, you've really made it.

Liz: Yes. And James deserves it. He's worked so hard. Oh . . . just think . . . president of Universal Trust — and "Man of the Year".

(Liz crosses to end table and places dishes on tray.)

Susan: And two-ninths a grandfather. *(Rises)* Alright Liz, I'll take you up on your offer of the drive. Dad won't want a two-hundred-pound seal around.

Lydia: A what?

Susan: That's what Bob said . . . . Ohhhh, I get so mad when I think about it. I only asked him — when I get big — if he'd postpone reading

his sports page and paint my toenails for me. He . . . he just said . . .
you'll probably feel like a two-hundred-pound seal . . . I . . . I told
him that seals don't belong in houses . . . .

(Liz and Lydia exchange an amused look.)

Liz: Susan! He meant it as a joke.

(Liz exits with tray.)

Lydia: Oh, Susan, don't get yourself so worked up. When I telephoned
Bob, he was so relieved that you were here and that you were alright.

Susan: Just the same, he'll be mad with me when I get home.

Lydia: No, he won't. He'll be full of apologies and love.

Susan: Don't count on it. I dented the front of the car.

Liz: Well, the dishes are all out. What next?

Susan: I'll . . . I'll put them in the washer.

(Susan exits.)

Lydia *(looking after Susan)*: When you're young, everything seems
so important.

Liz: Yes. I guess it's the young people who make us feel old. It's a
wonder we don't resent them.

Lydia: Well, don't worry — we'll get our own back. They'll grow
up and worry about their children. They always do. *(Lydia picks
up Susan's belt and sits on sofa)* Maybe you were right when you
avoided getting married.

Liz: Avoided? *(Laughs)* Oh, you're a real friend. *(Lights cigarette.)*

Lydia: You could have married lots of men.

Liz: Not after Enjay. Dear old Enjay. *(Fondly)* I wonder where he
is now. *(Sharply)* The deceiving louse!

Lydia: You give yourself away. You still love him, don't you?

B13

Liz: I really don't know. I loved him then. We're probably two different people now.

Lydia: You should find someone else.

Liz: It would have been easier if we'd argued — or finished it. But he simply didn't call me anymore. He just moved from the hotel and disappeared.

Lydia: Still, the way you speak of him — well . . . he must have been someone special.

Liz: He was. He's the sort of man who'd always remember your birthday — but never your age.

Lydia *(rises and crosses to desk — places belt in drawer)*: Well, now's the time for you to get back into the ball game.

Liz: Oh, I usually made a hit with men . . . and I could get to first base alright. I just never made a home run.

(Susan enters.)

Susan: Daddy's here. He's coming upstairs.

(The women whirl about, finishing tidying up. Liz and Susan sit on sofa. Lydia sits on upstage chair, as James enters.)

(James is dressed in a very formal business suit. He is carrying a large number of boxes containing clothes from a men's store.)

James: Hullo. Hullo. Hullo. How are we all?

Lydia: Oh, fine dear. What've you got?

James: Oh. Just been shopping. Getting a few things for tomorrow. Clothes! I don't like them personally, but I need them to impress Drummond.

Lydia: But you've plenty of clothes — anyway James, you'll impress Drummond — the clothes don't matter — it's the man!

James: It's not as easy as that, dear. When Norman Drummond writes an article on a . . . a personality . . . he does so on his terms . . . on the clear understanding that he'll write the story, good or bad — just as he sees it.

Lydia: You mean he'll go rattling the skeletons in our closets?

James: Oh, don't worry. I certainly don't have any skeletons.

Liz *(with a loud gay laugh)*: James wouldn't even have any closets! *(Everyone looks at Liz — Liz stops laughing)* . . . or anything to hide, would you, James?

James: Er — that's right. Norman Drummond's article could be a big asset and of vital importance to the company this year. It could also be a disaster.

Susan: But, Daddy. I thought Mr. Drummond wanted to write the article.

James: Oh, he does. And he will. But on his own terms. *(Rises)* He's very outspoken. *(Moves down right)* And he believes that Universal Trust should have a young, aggressive president! You see, there are far more people in the world today who are under thirty than over it. Therefore, we must gear ourselves to the younger attitude. It's the masses who buy, who select, who vote. And those masses are now under thirty.

Lydia: Well, dear, I don't understand. Are you planning to get younger?

James: The key is in what Victor Hugo said, "Forty is the old age of youth. Fifty is the youth of old age." You see, it's not how old you are. It's how you are old.

Lydia: I still don't understand.

James: Well, here's the plan. I'm not bringing Mr. Drummond here. He's going to Jeff's cottage. You see, Drummond's weakness is fishing. So Jeff will take him to all the good spots — just to soften him up. Since Jeff can also talk about the company, we should get the desired story over. But, to make certain, I bought myself a few brighter, younger sports clothes.

Lydia: Well, am I going up with you? Or what time should I arrive?

B15

James: Oh yes! Well dear. I don't know if it's altogether necessary for you to come at all. I mean, if you're having a Chickie Dickie and Fuzzy Tail session . . . . My, I'd certainly like a drink. What about you, dear? Liz? Sue?

Lydia: Double gin.

Liz: A gin, please.

Susan: Double milk.

James: Er . . . yes. Gin, gin, milk. Stay right there.

(James exits.)

(For six beats there is a complete silence on stage while the women look straight ahead.)

Lydia: Well. Someone say something.

Susan: What goes on at Jeff's cottage? *(Rises and crosses to desk)* I mean, he's a pretty wild bachelor, isn't he?

Lydia: Do you suppose they're trying to win Drummond over by having a Chickie Dickie and Fuzzy Tail session of their own?

Liz: Maybe James has reached that dangerous age. I think that's how I lost Enjay — not realizing the attraction of youth. They say a man is only as old as he feels, and James seems to be feeling like a two year old.

Lydia: Two-year-old what . . . stallion . . . or egg?

Susan: Look, we're not being fair. Why should we suspect Daddy, just because he's going to the cottage with Jeff, doesn't want us along, and has bought some new clothes?

Lydia: Well, we've heard the case for the prosecution. Now what about the defence?

Liz: Why not telephone Jeff? See what he might say?

Lydia: Oh, I couldn't. It would be like spying. I certainly trust James more than that.

B16

Susan: Well, I'd like to phone. I haven't spoken to Jeff in ages.

(She goes to the telephone and dials. Lydia and Liz rush over to her. She holds the earpiece in front, so that they can all listen. CUE 5 — sound — on speaker we hear ringing. Then receiver is lifted and a sensual dance beat is heard.)

Valerie *(on speaker)*: Hullooooo . . . .

Susan: Er . . . hullo. Could I speak with Jeff, please?

Valerie *(on speaker)*: Jeff? . . . Who is this, honey?

Susan: Just let me speak with Jeff.

Valerie *(on speaker)*: Well, I can't very well let you do that unless you identify yourself first.

Susan: My name is Susan.

Valerie *(on speaker — giggles)*: Stop it. Stop it, Jeff!

Jeff *(speaker)*: Is it a man? Is it my uncle?

Valerie *(speaker)*: Oh noooo.

Jeff *(speaker)*: A woman?

Valerie *(speaker)*: It's a girl.

Jeff *(speaker)*: A girl? It's a wrong number. I don't know any girls.

Valerie *(speaker)*: You're a wrong number.

Susan: I'm his cousin. Please put him on.

Valerie *(on speaker — laughs)*: Oh, I am honey . . . I am.

(CUE 6 — sound — the line goes dead. Susan hangs up. Liz and Lydia exchange a look. Liz gives a short forced laugh. Lydia turns and goes to her chair. Liz and Susan take their seats as James enters carrying tray with drinks.)

James: Here, let's have a little drink and discuss my business trip.

B18

(James distributes the drinks.)

Lydia: Thank you.

Liz: Thank you.

Susan: Thanks.

James: Well, I must say you're all very quiet on the eve of my big day. What's the matter with you?

Lydia *(pulling herself together)*: Oh. We're excited for you. We were just talking and wondering about tomorrow.

James *(pleased)*: Were you?

Liz: Yes. What you'd be doing.

Susan: You're sure you don't want Mum to go with you?

James: Well, I just don't think it's really necessary — you know, Lydia, it'll just be man talk — business and cigars.

Lydia: Are you going to eat cigars?

James: Jeff will cook the fish he catches. And he can make a mean salad.

Lydia: Why does Jeff live out there in the cottage? It's such a long drive to the office everyday.

James: The cottage is useful. Whenever we have a big deal to clinch, we do it at "Lookout".

Liz: "Lookout!" What an interesting name.

James: Yes. It has a terrific view. You can really get a clear perspective up there.

Susan: That's a good name for it. Perspective!

Lydia *(to Liz)*: I wonder what else gets clinched there — apart from business deals.

B19

James: I'm not sure I understand, Lydia. Of course, Jeff often uses the company apartment in town during the week. That's why we get to use his cottage some weekends.

Lydia *(to Liz)*: Apartments and cottages. It's wonderful how the men manage things.

James: Oh, it's all deductible. Business reasons. You understand.

Lydia: Yes. Yes, I do. James, is there some other reason why I shouldn't come this weekend?

Susan: I would have thought that an article on you would be incomplete without Mum.

James: And you'd be right. One evening next week, Lydia and I will take Drummond to dinner. *(To Lydia)* That'll give you time to fix up a little, and by then I should have already won him over.

Lydia: Fix up a little?

James: I told you, Drummond has this youth fixation. *(Rises — crosses down)* That's why I bought all those clothes and things. But I certainly don't expect you to go to all that bother.

Lydia *(rises)*: You mean I look too old for you?

James: Of course not. But why buy a lot of smart things for just one day? This time tomorrow the meeting will be all over.

Lydia: Sure, and there's plenty of wear left in my dresses!

James: I don't understand why you're making such a point of all this. Why are you getting mad? I've always aimed to please you.

Lydia *(crossing to him)*: Well, you should take time out and get some more target practice.

James: But Lydia, I love you. You know that! I love you just as you are. I love all of your lovely qualities, but . . . .

Lydia: . . . But?

James: Well, now don't misunderstand . . . but . . . for the sake of the

B20

company — when you meet Drummond, you should do something a little different to your hair.

Lydia *(upset, but controlling it)*: My hair . . . I see . . . what about my clothes?

James: That's a good idea — get something a little sharper.

Lydia: Sharper?

James: Well, yes. Your clothes are proper and fitting. Jeff says that they shouldn't be either.

Lydia: Oh! Jeff says! And what do you say?

James: Well, for Drummond, he's probably right.

Lydia *(boiling inwardly)*: New hair . . . new clothes . . . how about my face?

James: Oh, the face is fine . . . perhaps a touch more make-up here and there.

Lydia *(bursting)*: Hair. Face. Clothes. You should just get a new wife. A young one!

(Lydia runs off door left.)

James: Why can't women be business-like?

(James crosses to follow Lydia but Liz stops him.)

Liz: No, James. Let me. You'll only make it worse.

James: Well, tell her that I love her just as she is. I'm only concerned about the impression she makes on others!

Liz: How is it that some men can manage large corporations, yet fail to understand their families?

James: Well, what on earth did I say that was so wrong?

Liz: I'm sure that if Lydia asked you to bring home some mood music, you'd get her "music to iron by" or "music to cook by."

(Liz exits door left.)

James: Can you explain why everyone is turning on me?

Susan: I'm afraid not, Dad. It would be like trying to follow the plot in alphabet soup.

James: Look, Sue. Do me a favour and put these things in my room. I've got to think.

(He picks up boxes and piles them on Susan.)

Susan: You could have made everyone happy by inviting Mum to "Lookout".

James: But this is business . . . she'd try to help . . . she'd meddle . . . women in business . . . well, women!

Susan *(with boxes in her arms)*: What's wrong with women?

James: Lots of things. They're like blotters. They soak it all in and get it backwards.

(Susan exits left.)

(James goes to telephone and dials. CUE 7 — sound. We hear ring—ring—ring on speaker. Then we hear some music with a latin beat, followed by Jeff's voice.)

Jeff *(speaker)*: Hullo.

James: That you, Jeff?

Jeff *(speaker)*: Yes. How are you, uncle?

James: Call me James, not uncle. I don't want everyone to think that you got your position in the company because of our relationship.

Jeff *(speaker)*: I got it because you need me. I'm a live wire.

James: Well, a lot of live wires would be dead if it weren't for their connections. *(Thinks about what he said — laughs)* Say, that was funny. Did you get it? A lot of live wires would . . . .

B22

Jeff *(speaker — forced laugh)*: Sure. Sure. Very funny. You must have got the sense of humour with the new clothes. You did get the clothes, didn't you?

James *(doesn't quite know how to handle the situation)*: Yes. Yes, I got them. Look, Jeff, is everything set for tomorrow? I'll arrive about nine. Drummond should arrive at nine-thirty . . . . What's that music?

Jeff *(speaker)*: Oh, I took a job home — I'm . . . I'm working on it. The music helps.

James: Well, you've got to be fresh in the morning. I'd suggest you turn in now.

Jeff *(speaker)*: Oh, I can't yet. I haven't done enough work.

James: Well, why don't you sleep on it?

Jeff *(speaker — laughs)*: That's a good idea. I'll take your advice.

James *(he laughs too)*: Good. Good. *(A thought occurs to him)* Say, you're not . . . er . . . not fooling around up there, are you?

Jeff *(speaker)*: No, uncle, I'm not fooling.

James *(very much the man of the world)*: Good, because I wouldn't want you to forget that I'm your superior. I'm the man who controls your future, who signs your cheques — and you know how I feel about things like that . . . I like to be invited.

(They both roar with laughter.)

Jeff *(speaker — through the laughter)*: See you in the morning.

James *(pleased at his wit)*: Sure . . . see you.

(CUE 8 — sound. James hangs up the telephone. He stands thinking for a moment and starts to dial again when Lydia enters. James hangs up.)

Lydia: Oh, don't let me interrupt. Was it a personal call?

James: No. No. I was going to call Jeff. It's vital that everything be

B23

right for tomorrow — I think I'll just run up to the cottage and check for myself.

Lydia: Tonight?

James: Yes. It'll only take a couple of hours — and it would put my mind at rest. But Lydia — please, I am sorry. If an apology is required, you have it.

Lydia: It's alright. Liz explained it to me and I've thought about it. As always, you're right. I'll see to it. Subject is closed.

James: I knew you'd see it properly as soon as you thought about it. You're so dependable.

Lydia: So square!

(Liz enters — Lydia picks up her drink from desk then crosses down.)

James: Thanks, Liz. I'm . . . I'm just going to run up to the cottage — I may as well take my clothes up . . . Jeff's up there getting ready on his own. He took a project with him, and wants me to help with it. I won't be long.

Lydia: You're going to help Jeff with his project?

James: Oh, sure. I'm always willing to help the boys. I don't expect them to keep their projects to themselves just because I'm president. Goodbye.

(James exits door left.)

Liz: Well! He's getting very bold, isn't he? Oh, Lydia, I am sorry. I never thought it would happen to . . . . *(A new thought)* James! Of all people.

Lydia: Well, I'm not going to weigh the facts with my thumb on the scale.

Liz: If I were you I'd put my foot on it.

Lydia: No. No, Liz . . . we'll do better than that.

Liz: Ohhhh — tell me. I love intrigue.

B25

Lydia: We'll say nothing to James — or anyone — but right now we'll go shopping. Shopping like we've never done before — then — tomorrow . . . .

CUE 1 — lighting

Lydia & Liz: Lookout!

(They both laugh, delighted at their plan as the lights fade and curtain goes down. CUE 9 — sound.)

Act one
Scene two
The inset has been removed and we now see an expensively furnished family room. In the stage right wall there is a long window through which we can see a balcony, tree tops, and sky, indicating that we are somewhere high up, away from the city. This is Jeff's place, "Lookout". The large front door is located upstage of the window in the right wall. The room is divided into two areas by a change in the floor level. The downstage looks like a comfortable living room, while the upstage area, which is raised two steps, serves as an office or work area. In the centre of the upstage wall there is an archway which leads off left to the bedrooms, bathroom and the rest of the house. The stage right wall contains in the living room area a large, practical fireplace and further downstage, a swing door to the kitchen.

The general impression conveyed by the room is warm, bright and comfortable — a nice place in which to relax during summer or winter.

CUE 2 — lighting

The "office" is furnished with an office-type desk and chair and two small easy chairs. The living room contains two sofas, a record player, a coffee table, an end table, a small drinks table and two small chairs.

CUE 10 — sound. Music fades in — a number with a swinging sensual beat. The curtain rises to reveal Valerie dancing, back to audience, swinging to the rhythm of the music, all by herself. After a moment, Jeff enters from the upstage alcove. He sees Valerie, crosses to the phonograph and lowers the volume. CUE 11 — sound. He then joins Valerie and dances with her guiding her to the sofa — centre left. As they reach the sofa, he tries to take her down, but she turns so that he sits on sofa by himself, and she continues to dance.

Valerie: Don't be in such a hurry. I'm thirsty. *(Jeff lies down on the* *sofa. CUE 3 — lighting — all the lights go low. Valerie looks around the room)* What happened?

Jeff: Come on over here. You'll tire yourself out.

Valerie: No, I won't. I'm young. I'm fit — and I'm thirsty.

Jeff: Okay. You win. *(Sits up.)*

CUE 4 — lighting

(The lights return to full brightness. Valerie stops dancing to look at the lights.)

Valerie: Something's wrong with your power supply. Or I've had too much to drink.

Jeff *(rising and crossing to kitchen)*: My power supply is just great — I'll get you something for the thirst.

(Jeff exits.)

(Valerie dances over to sofa. Stops. Looks at lamps then at sofa. Sits sofa. Bounces up and down to beat of the music. Stands up and sits down. Lies down.)

CUE 5 — lighting

(Lamps dim, so she sits up quickly.)

CUE 6 — lighting

(Lamps return to normal. She looks around then slowly, with a loud "Whee", she lies down.)

CUE 7 — lighting

(Lamps dim — Jeff enters with a bottle of champagne.)

Jeff: Ah. That's right. Let's have a rest.

CUE 8 — lighting

(Valerie leaps to her feet — lights return to normal. She starts dancing.)

B27

Valerie: Just trying the sofa. Love that music.

Jeff: So do I, but right now, let's have a drink and relax. Where's your glass?

Valerie: Up there on the desk. Is that another bottle?

Jeff *(crosses up for glass)*: Uh huh.

Valerie: Wow! We must be squiffed. A whole bottle and nothing to eat.

Jeff *(crossing back to sofa)*: They say that champagne makes you feel sophisticated — and you're not squiffed as long as you can say it.

Valerie: They also say it makes you see double and feel single.

(Jeff pours two drinks.)

Jeff: They're wrong. It makes me feel very married.

Valerie *(to Jeff)*: Wow! You can say the word!

Jeff: You're not squiffed. You're foxy. Here's your drink. *(Valerie dances over and takes her glass)* And for heaven's sake stop wiggling.

(She stops, standing close to him.)

Valerie *(toasting)*: To Jeff. A young man in a hurry.

Jeff *(toasting)*: To Valerie. The reason for the hurry.

Valerie *(sitting sofa — getting quite tipsy)*: Tell the truth now. You lied when you told me you were having a party here, didn't you?

Jeff *(sitting beside her)*: Certainly not. We're having a party, aren't we?

Valerie: Some party! Where's the food?

Jeff: I'll get you some in a minute. I'm an excellent cook. You're very beautiful.

Valerie: Are you flattering me because you hope that I'll sleep with you? *(Finishes her drink, puts glass on table.)*

Jeff *(chokes on his drink)*: You're about as subtle as a . . . .

Valerie: Well, what are you? Inviting me up here to a party — telling me there'll be other people here. Filling me up with champagne — not giving me any food . . . .

Jeff: Well, of course I'm attracted to you. You're beautiful and fun to be with — but I'm not the wolf you think I am. *(Refills the glasses.)*

Valerie *(lies back full length on the sofa — CUE 9 — lighting — the lights dim)*: No? Then who installed the trick lighting?

Jeff: That's not trick lighting.

Valerie: Oh!

(Jeff quickly sits down beside Valerie.)

Jeff: It's a modern convenience. *(He lifts her to sitting position. CUE 10 — lighting. Lights up. Puts his arms around her and kisses her. After a moment, she puts her arms around his neck and participates. After a couple of beats, his hand starts feeling around her back — then her side — then her other side. He's feeling for a zipper or buttons. There aren't any. His search ceases to be subtle. It becomes frantic. Then pushes her back flat — Cue 11 — lighting. Lights dim)* What the hell are you wearing?

Valerie *(laughing)*: It's not equipped with any modern conveniences.

Jeff *(his frustration turns to laughter)*: Well, there's a lot to be said in favour of old things. Let's have another drink.

(She hands him her glass and sits up.)

CUE 12 — lighting

(Lights come up. She takes the glass.)

Valerie: I don't know if I should.

Jeff: Sure you should. But you're right about me. I guess I am a wolf.

B29

Valerie: Really? *(Downs her drink and puts glass on table.)*

Jeff: Yes. I grew up to be the kind of kid my mother didn't want me to associate with.

(They laugh.)

Valerie: Well, I'm pleased to be associating with you. Give me a kiss. *(He kisses her — formally)* Thank you.

(She hiccups — obviously tipsy now.)

Jeff: You know — you're very nice! But you sure do confuse me. One minute you're fighting me off — the next you're asking me to kiss you . . . then you're coy . . . then you're talking about sleeping with me . . . you . . . you wear a dress that won't come off . . . .

Valerie: Women used to be laced into corsets at one time.

Jeff: Well, that's an encouraging thought. I mean, people have always managed, haven't they? *(Refills her glass.)*

Valerie: Ohhhh, I guess so. *(Takes glass.)*

Jeff: You guess so? Of course they have.

Valerie: When they wanted to.

Jeff: Well, I want to.

Valerie: When they both wanted to.

Jeff: Oh, Valerie — dear Valerie — you're driving me nuts.

(She drains her glass, puts it on table and leans back on the sofa, looking at Jeff, trying to focus.)

Valerie: That's because you don't understand women.

Jeff: Oh, yes I do. As a bachelor, I know much more about women than a married man does. All bachelors do. If they didn't, they'd be married too.

Valerie: Do you know you've mentioned the word marriage twice in the last few minutes?

Jeff *(alarmed)*: I did? *(Pause)* Thanks for warning me.

Valerie: Do you like me?

Jeff: Very much.

(He refills her glass — she does not take the glass.)

Valerie: How much?

Jeff: Oh, very, very, very much.

Valerie: Enough to do something for me?

Jeff: Oh yes — yes.

Valerie: You're not just saying that?

Jeff: No. No, of course not.

Valerie: Then Jeff. Please, Jeff. Get me something to eat.

Jeff: Sure. Sure . . . .

Valerie: I'm hungry!

Jeff *(puts his arms about her)*: So am I.

Valerie: Jeff — I'm hungry for food!

Jeff: I know. I know.

Valerie: Why do you keep saying everything twice?

Jeff: I do? I do? Er — I mean, do I? I don't know if it's the champagne or you, but I'm sure getting mixed up.

Valerie: Maybe if we both had something to eat, we could get . . . unmixed?

Jeff *(rises — moves to fireplace)*: Oh, Val. Stop that. You're making me feel like a kid on my first date.

Valerie: Why, what did I say? *(Sits up, picks up glass and downs the drink.)*

Jeff *(moves toward her)*: It's not what you say . . . it's the way you say it.

Valerie *(rises, holding empty glass)*: Oh, don't be so tense and serious, Jeff. Let's . . . let's have something to eat and then . . . then we can . . . relax . . . .

Jeff *(moves away)*: You're doing it again.

Valerie *(moves down centre — sways a little)*: Would you like me to get us something to eat?

Jeff: Do you cook?

Valerie: I can make breakfast. Juice, toast and coffee.

Jeff: Huh!

Valerie: And right now that sounds like a banquet.

Jeff *(holds up his hands)*: Okay. I surrender. You win! *(He moves close to her and puts arms around her)* We only have tonight — I'll have to get you home and get back here myself before eight in the morning. My uncle needs this place tomorrow — for business. Now, how we spend the time is up to you — we'll eat — or we'll dance — or we'll go for a drive — or we'll just relax. You name it . . . .

Valerie: And what about after tonight . . . all the other tomorrows? Hic!

Jeff: You're switching gears on me again. *(Breaks clinch — moves to kitchen doorway)* I'll . . . I'll make us something to eat.

Valerie: Well, since you're being so nice, while you're doing that, I'll change into something more . . . comfortable.

(She backs upstage toward centre doorway.)

Jeff: That's a good idea.

Valerie: Could I have another drink? *(Puts empty glass on phono.)*

B33

(Jeff crosses with bottle and hands it to her.)

Jeff: Here. Drink and be merry.

Valerie: Where do I change?

Jeff: In my room. *(Moving up to the alcove)* Second door on the left . . . .

Valerie: You don't mind being compromised?

(She heads to archway in a wide sweeping circle.)

Jeff: Er — the bathroom is first on the left.

Valerie: Thank you. Call if you need any help.

(Jeff kisses her.)

Jeff: Yes. You too.

(Valerie exits. Jeff watches her go, rubs hands in anticipation and crosses down to kitchen as front door opens and James enters, carrying a large suitcase.)

James: Hullo. Hullo. Hullo. How are you, Jeff?

Jeff *(stunned)*: Uncle . . . James . . . I . . . I thought you were coming out in the morning.

(Jeff crosses up to meet James.)

James: Yes. I was. Then I thought that if you were working tonight, I should get out and help.

(He removes raincoat, hands it to Jeff and crosses down to sofa.)

Jeff: Oh. Oh, thanks.

(Puts raincoat on phono and follows James to centre.)

James: Whew! The valley is sinking, Jeff. It gets to be more of a climb every year.

B34

Jeff: Er . . . yes . . . it . . . it seems like it.

James: How about a scotch? *(Sits sofa.)*

CUE 13 — lighting

(Lights dim — Jeff moves towards kitchen door.)

Jeff: Sure. Good idea.

James: What's the matter with the lights? *(Sits up. CUE 14 — lighting. Lights return to normal)* Oh. Must be the power supply! *(Leans back. CUE 15 — lighting. Lights dim. He sits up. CUE 16 — lighting. Lights return to normal)* Well, isn't that strange? Do you realize, Jeff, that the the lights change according to where you put your weight on this sofa?

Jeff: Er, yes, I know. I must have it fixed.

(Valerie sails in through the alcove, sweeps down — unseen by James — picks up her glass and exits.)

James: I wouldn't. If ever you had a girl up here, it might be convenient.

Jeff: Good idea!

James: But I shouldn't have to tell you that! However, Jeff, I don't want any silly business this weekend.

Jeff: Of course not.

(Moves centre, glancing anxiously at archway.)

James: And in the morning, I'll get here before Drummond. Then I'll talk with him, and then suggest that you show him where the fish are biting.

Jeff *(moves down right)*: Yes, well, James, I'm not sure how they're biting right now. Maybe we could take him for a drive?

James *(rises)*: What do you mean, "not sure" — you've been here every minute you could because the catches are so good. Or so you said.

Jeff: That's right. So long as the moon is right.

B35

James *(moving down to Jeff)*: Well, damn well see that it's right tomorrow. What the hell have you been catching anyway?

Jeff: I'll . . . I'll do my best . . . but maybe we should buy a few fish just in case.

James: Drummond doesn't want bought fish!

Jeff: Ah . . . but he need never know the difference.

James: It's completely unethical. Arrange it right away. Now, how about a drink? *(Crosses back to sofa.)*

Jeff: Would you like water?

James: I said a drink, not a wash. I'd like a scotch.

Jeff *(up to sofa)*: Yes. Well, I'm afraid we're out of scotch. The only thing here is champagne.

James: Champagne? What happened to the liquor?

Jeff: I don't know. Maybe someone broke in and stole it.

James: Oh. Were there signs of a break-in?

Jeff: I . . . er . . . I didn't see any — but there's no lock on the front door.

James: Did you look for any?

Jeff: No. Of course not.

James: Then what the hell are we discussing break-ins for?

Jeff: I agree. Let's change the subject.

James *(looks at Jeff — very hard)*: Under the circumstances, you'd better go into town tonight! You can get liquor from the apartment — and buy the fish you want.

Jeff: Oh, but I couldn't . . . .

James *(sits sofa)*: Of course you can. Don't argue. This is an emergency.

I'll stay here and meet Drummond.

Jeff: But that wouldn't do at all . . . .

James: What alternative do you suggest?

Jeff *(pause — glance at archway)*: Well, I'll stay here. You could go and get the . . . .

James: I know nothing about fish. You must go! Furthermore, the stores will close at nine, so I suggest you leave right now.

Jeff: Right now?

James *(rises)*: Yes, right now — and I'll turn in early. *(He moves Jeff to the front door)* I'll tidy up in the morning — because tomorrow I must be "charged with energy" — or at least, give that impression.

Jeff: Well . . . I'll . . . I'll be out first thing.

James: Yes, don't be late. Goodnight.

Jeff: Goodnight. *(CUE 17 — lighting. Jeff exits front door. James closes door — moves up for his suitcase. The door opens and Jeff re-enters laughing)* Er, James?

James: Yes?

Jeff: I just remembered. I — I left something here.

James: Well, it'd better be important because you're losing time.

Jeff: Yes. I think it is — it — it — er, might be in your way.

James: In my way? Oh! Your project! Well, right now it's more important that you get the things for tomorrow. So let me help you out. Show me your project and I'll do it for you.

Jeff: Oh, no, no . . . it . . . it can probably wait.

James: You know, for a minute, I thought you were going to come up with some damn silly statement that had nothing to do with business.

B37

Jeff: Who, me? Of course not.

James: Well, you'd better get along. If there were a drink around I'd offer you one for the road. But we can't afford to drink company champagne, can we?

Jeff: No. Oh no.

(Jeff exits fast. James walks to archway, then stops and crosses down to sofa right. He picks up telephone and dials. CUE 12 — sound.)

Lydia *(on speaker)*: Hello?

James: Hullo, dear, it's James.

Lydia: Is everything alright?

James: Oh yes. Only Jeff forgot a couple of details . . . . *(The front door opens very quietly and Jeff tiptoes in and crosses quickly to the archway and exits)* Liquor and fish. So he's going into town tonight, and I'm afraid I have to stay here . . . hullo . . . are you still there?

Lydia: Yes, James. I'm listening.

James: Good.

Lydia: I'm listening to the music.

James: Oh, Jeff plays it all the time.

(Jeff appears pulling Valerie. She is wearing a long negligee. As Jeff comes on stage he lets go of her hand and crosses to front door. Valerie, very intoxicated, heads downstage towards James who, facing the audience, does not see the action. Jeff spots Valerie and grabs her hand just in time to turn her toward the front door. Valerie collapses into the chair by the front door. Jeff opens front door and reaches to help Valerie to her feet as she folds forward, head down, hands on the floor. Glancing at James, Jeff frantically tries to lift Valerie but cannot do so. He quickly covers her over with James' raincoat, and exits as James finishes his telephone call.)

Lydia: James, don't do anything silly, will you?

B38

James: What do you mean? Me! Silly? Oh, the music. That's not my taste, *(laughs)* although for Drummond tomorrow, I'll pretend I like it, if I have to.

Lydia: James, are you alone?

James: I just told you, Jeff has gone into town.

Lydia: Is there anyone else there?

James: Of course not . . . . Oh, how sweet. Don't be silly, dear . . . there hasn't been anyone here all day. There's no one for miles.

Lydia: Goodnight, James.

James: Goodnight. *(He hangs up the telephone and crosses to kitchen and exits. Valerie sits up, drops raincoat to floor, then staggers down to sofa left and stretches out.)*

CUE 18 — lighting

(Lights go dim. Front door opens. Jeff enters quickly expecting to find Valerie on the chair. He looks around, then quickly crosses up and exits through alcove as James enters with glass of water — crosses up, picks up suitcase, then exits into alcove. A moment later, Jeff rushes on through archway, glancing behind him. He's in a panic. He looks around room, hears a sound and quickly exits front door — slamming door behind him. James enters at a run through the archway, stops as he sees raincoat, picks up raincoat and throws it on chair. He crosses to front door, quickly opens it, looks out, slowly closes it and takes step back. He then jumps forward, swings door open, closes it and moves downstage — not taking his eyes off the door — removes his jacket and places it on Valerie. In her sleep she reaches down and pulls it up to cover her. James sits on arm and removes shoes, then quickly crosses up to front door and opens it — closes it. He switches off remaining source of light.)

CUE 19 — lighting

(The room is now very dimly lighted. James switches off phono. CUE 13 — sound. He crosses down centre and watching front door, starts to remove his pants as . . . the curtain goes down. CUE 14 — sound.)

CUE 20 — lighting

B39

Act two   *9:25 the following morning.*

The scene is exactly the same as the night before. CUE 21 — lighting. Bright sunlight can be seen through the cracks of the drawn curtains. CUE 15 — sound. The chatter of birds can be heard. James is asleep on sofa right, and Valerie is sleeping on sofa left. After twenty seconds or so, James turns over, then sits up quickly and looks at his watch.

James: Hell! Nine twenty-five!

(He bounds to his feet, stands gathering his wits, pulls his pants on, then exits to kitchen.)

(A couple of beats later, there is a knock at the front door. Valerie turns over. The knock is repeated. Valerie sits up, then holds her head. The knocking becomes more insistent.)

Valerie *(looking at door)*: Shhhh!

(The knocking comes again. Valerie gets to her feet, grabs for her head again — a hangover — then totters up to the door, barefooted under her hostess gown.)

Valerie: I'm coming. Hold your horses! *(Opens the door.)*

CUE 22 — lighting

(Norman Drummond stands there. He has a small travel bag.)

Drummond: Good morning. This is "Lookout", isn't it?

Valerie: Yes. Yes, I guess so. Please don't shout. My head is splitting.

Drummond: Oh! I am sorry. *(Takes out small notebook and pencil)* Do you often have headaches?

Valerie: Are you a doctor — or something?

Drummond: No. I'm not . . . I'm Norman Drummond.

Valerie: I've heard the name.

Drummond: Well, may I come in?

B42

(Valerie moves back into the room.)

Valerie: I . . . I suppose. Please come in — and close the door. The light is very bright . . . .

CUE 23 — lighting

(Drummond closes the door. James enters carrying a glass of fizzing Alka Seltzer. He stops in surprise when he sees Norman and Valerie. Then crosses up to meet them.)

James: Good morning. I didn't hear you come in.

Drummond: Mr. Henderson? James Henderson?

James: Yes. And, of course, you're Drummond.

Drummond: That's right, Norman Drummond.

(They shake hands.)

James *(looking at Valerie)*: And this is? *(Shakes Valerie's hand)*

(Valerie has been eyeing the seltzer. She now takes it and drinks it down.)

Drummond: I know. I can guess. Mrs. Henderson! *(Takes Valerie's hand and shakes it.)*

James: Mrs. Henderson . . . ?

Drummond *(looking at Valerie)*: Mrs. Henderson!

Valerie *(looks at James)*: God! I must look awful! Where's the john — er — the bathroom?

(James, slightly stunned, indicates the archway and Valerie quickly exits.)

Drummond *(short laugh)*: Ah! That's a good quality. A sense of humour.

James *(forced laugh)*: Er . . . yes . . . . *(He looks from the archway to Drummond and presumes that he's being tested or is perhaps the*

B43

butt of a joke . . . so he expands — laughs loudly) Oh, yes . . . .
Of course, very funny.

(He puts his arm over Drummond's shoulder and moves him down-stage to the sofa — left.)

Drummond *(writes in his book — laughs)*: There's nothing I like better than a good joke. A man . . . a president . . . will find a sense of humour a big help.

James: Yes. Yes. Of course. I've always loved to laugh.

Drummond: Yes, so have I. *(Stops laughing)* But not always first thing in the morning.

(They sit.)

James *(still laughing)*: No . . . . No . . . not *(stops laughing)* not too early in the day.

Drummond: I seem to be sitting on your wife's shoes.

(He hands Valerie's shoes to James who looks at them blankly. Then James looks from the shoes to Drummond and back, and suddenly bursts into laughter.)

James: Sitting on my wife's . . . my wife's . . . shoes . . . that's . . . that's priceless.

Drummond *(laughing again)*: Yes . . . . Yes . . . . It's also . . . it's *(stops laughing)* it's damned uncomfortable!

James *(still laughing)*: Yes . . . . Yes . . . . *(Stops laughing — very concerned)* It must be!

(James holds shoe out with heel up in the air.)

Drummond: I'm glad they don't have pointed heels this year.

James: The designs are different every year.

Drummond: No. Women's styles change — their designs don't.

James *(laughs)*: I must remember that one.

B44

Drummond *(seriously)*: I was serious.

James: Oh! Er — are these, er . . . *(indicates alcove with his head)* . . . her shoes?

Drummond: Is this a quiz?

James: I . . . I don't know . . . .

(He goes to put shoes on the coffee table, but when Drummond suddenly yells, he snatches them back.)

Drummond: Yaaaahhh! Don't ever put shoes on a table!

James *(nerves shattered)*: It's . . . it's only a little table.

Drummond: It is a table.

James: Yes. Yes I suppose so.

Drummond: Place your shoes upon the table,
             And you'll find in bed that you're unable.

(James looks at him for a couple of beats — deadpan.)

James *(seriously)*: What's the rest of it?

Drummond: Isn't that bad enough?

(James gets up and crosses to end table, downstage sofa right. He goes to put shoes on the table, thinks better of it and puts them on downstage end of sofa.)

James: I have the distinct feeling that this is going to be one of those days that shouldn't happen to a man.

(James crosses to window and draws curtains open.)

CUE 24 — lighting

Drummond: Nonsense. It's starting out perfectly.

James: Well, I'm glad you think so, but you see I overslept . . . probably because I was dreaming such a lot.

B45

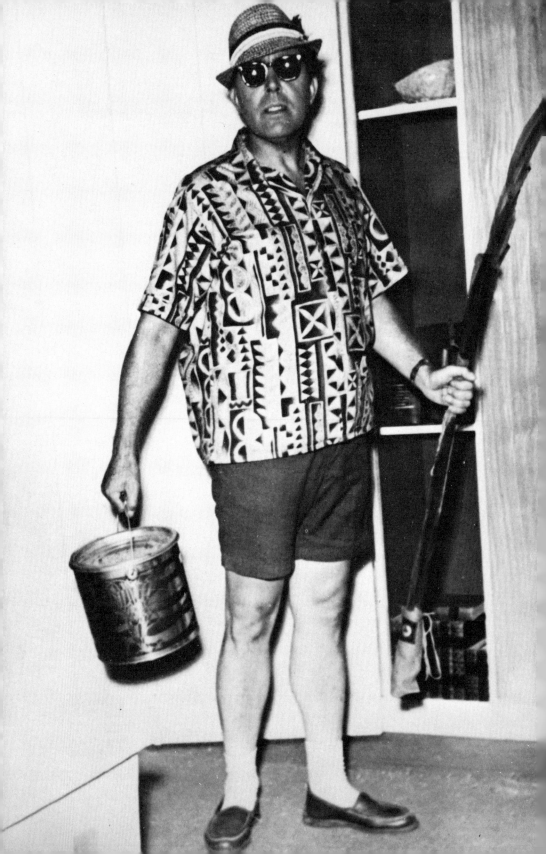

Drummond: Oh! What did you dream?

James *(remembering)*: Perfume! I was in a women's barracks . . . or a dormitory . . . or a harem or something.

Drummond: A brothel, perhaps. *(He starts to write.)*

James: Good heavens — no! *(Crosses quickly to Drummond)* Stop writing — erase it.

Drummond: Once a word has been spoken, it can never be erased from memory. That was our agreement, you know. I will write the article, making it a factual report for my readers in seven countries, who have come to recognize my words as being unbiased — honest and fair. You must appreciate that I can't commit the lie of omission. *(Looks at James)* You don't want me to lie, do you?

James: No!

Drummond *(writing again)*: Brothel! What do you want then?

James: A coffee. *(Crossing to kitchen door)* Then, if I don't feel any better, I'll cut my throat.

Drummond: Are you happily married?

James *(stops at kitchen door — turns)*: You're right. I won't cut my throat.

Drummond: Good. It's a rule of mine that the happily married man is an efficient dependable man.

James: Oh? Are *(looks at archway)* . . . are you married?

Drummond: No. I'm the exception that proves the rule!

James *(crossing to sofa right)*: That surprises me. I mean, that a man who's as well known as you are, hasn't married.

Drummond: I travel a great deal. I haven't had time for marriage.

James: That's poor justification. *(Sits sofa right.)*

Drummond: Well, as far as I'm personally concerned, the only

B47

thoroughly justifiable marriage I can think of — is the one that produced me.

(They both laugh.)

James: You mean, you haven't made the same mistake once.

(They laugh again.)

Drummond: Seriously now. Tell me about your wife. The fact that you're happily married is a plus. It counts for five points. The fact that she's so young and gorgeous counts for another ten . . . . With a wife like that you'd never run around . . . that could get you twenty more. Furthermore, her youth and her intimate conversations will provide you with a link and understanding with the young people of today . . . .

James: Excuse me. Who the hell are you talking about?

Drummond: Your wife. *(Indicates archway, then starts writing again.)*

James *(it dawns on him — indicates archway)*: My wife?

Drummond: Of course. That was some dream you had.

James *(moving up towards archway)*: I was hoping that I was still having it.

(Drummond starts writing again.)

Drummond: Perhaps we should leave our interview 'til later on. It's a perfect morning for fishing.

James *(moving down left)*: Yes, well, the company marketing manager, Jeff Gordon, is our fishing expert. He's due here now — in fact he's late . . . .

Drummond *(looks at his book)*: Yes. He's your nephew!

James *(surprised realization)*: Oh, yes. So he is. *(Forced laugh. The door bursts open, and Jeff comes in carrying a cardboard carton filled with bottles of liquor)* Speak of the devil!

(Jeff puts the box on the floor and comes downstage.)

B48

Jeff: Good morning, uncle . . . er . . . James.

James: Hullo nephew! Mr. Drummond, this is Jeff.

Drummond: Company marketing manager — nephew — and the man who knows where the fish are.

James: Aren't you going to write that down?

(They shake hands.)

Jeff: Pleased to meet you.

Drummond: How do you do? It just shows you the power of thought association. I could swear that I smell fish.

(Jeff quickly puts his hands in his pockets.)

Jeff: Perhaps it's my after-shave.

(Offers his cheek — Drummond sniffs.)

Drummond: No. *(He sniffs his right hand)* Hell's bells, it's my hand!

(James moves down left.)

Jeff *(moving down right)*: Oh, no. Probably the air around here. It's sometimes quite fishy.

James *(turning to Jeff)*: That's the most truthful thing you've said in twenty-four hours.

Jeff: Well, Mr. Drummond. When would you like to fish?

James: Why not go now? It'll give me a chance to get cleaned up.

Jeff: Sure, and the fish will still be there.

Drummond *(puzzled)*: Do they know we're coming?

Jeff: Now's a good time to catch them. *(Looking at James)* Like some people, they're slower witted in the morning.

(James throws a quick look at Jeff — who smiles back.)

Drummond: Aren't you coming?

James: Er — not yet. Maybe later. Golf is my favourite sport.

Drummond: Hmm — golfers don't have to show anything to prove their claims . . . . Well, I brought my fishing clothes, so if I could just change, we could leave in a couple of minutes.

Jeff: Sure. I'll show you where to change.

(Jeff leads Drummond up to archway and off.)

Drummond: I left all my tackle in my car.

Jeff: That's the red convertible?

Drummond: Yes.

Jeff: We'll get it . . . it's on our way.

Drummond: Nice place you have here . . . .

(They are now out of sight. James sits sofa right and starts to put on his shoes. Jeff quickly re-enters.)

Jeff: How did it go?

James: Where the hell have you been? You were supposed to be here at eight. I thought you'd wake me this morning.

Jeff: I couldn't buy the fish until eight.

James: The supermarkets were open last night.

Jeff: Not frozen fish! Live fish! I can't fool Drummond with a frozen fillet.

James: Well, where are the fish?

Jeff: I put them in two ponds.

James *(rises)*: You let them loose? They won't hang around waiting for you, you idiot!

Jeff: Well, it was the only way! *(Moves down left)* You set up the fishing deal, not me! I could have told you that there hasn't been a fish around here for thirty years!

James *(moving down centre)*: Oh! Then what the hell have you been catching? . . . . *(Groans)* Don't answer that. Who the hell is she?

Jeff *(brightly)*: Oh! You met Val. Her name's Valerie Scott. Is she still around?

James *(foreboding)*: Very much so.

Jeff: She's a doll. Valerie Scott is an airline hostess. She's really "the hostess with the mostess"! I'm not sure yet . . . but I just might bring her into the family.

James: You already have!

Jeff *(moving in to James)*: I what? . . . Oh, no! You don't mean? . . . Uncle, what were you doing with her when Drummond arrived?

James: Was that the project I told you to sleep on?

Jeff: Straight from the shoulder — yeah!

James: Instead of speaking straight from the shoulder, why not try a little higher up?

Jeff: Well, you weren't supposed to come here last night — if you'd have stuck to schedule, everything would have worked out.

James: Okay, Jeff. I accept that. But let's get this straight. For today, Valerie whatever-her-name-is is supposed to be my wife — a happily married wife. *(Moving down right)* Heaven knows, it's not my idea — but the alternative to that would make a best selling article for Drummond, and we'd change from Universal Trust to International Mistrust. Do you read me?

Jeff *(taken aback)*: Sure. Sure — it'll be fine — just for the day. *(Pause)* But uncle — don't carry the game of mothers and fathers too far . . . .

(Drummond enters wearing shorts, a multi-coloured sports shirt, sunglasses and small straw hat with a large feather.)

B51

Drummond: I'm ready for the fish.

James *(looking at him)*: And I'm sure they'll bite!

Jeff *(moving to door)*: So am I. Come on, Mr. Drummond.

Drummond: If we're to be fishing buddies . . . call me Norman.

Jeff: Sure, Normie. *(He picks up his fishing rod and pail.)*

Drummond: See you later, James.

(Jeff and Drummond exit.)

James: Yeah. *(Below his breath)* Much later. *(He watches them go, closes front door, then goes to archway and calls)* Alright, "Miss Hostess with the mostess", come in here. I want to talk to you. *(Moves down to living room area — calls louder)* The flight's about to take off. Get in here.

(Valerie appears in archway in bra and half slip. She's now quite sober.)

Valerie: Good morning. This is your hostess, Valerie Scott. On behalf of Captain Bligh and the crew, I'd like to welcome you all aboard.

James: Alright, alright . . . very funny . . . .

(He crosses up to her — she crosses her arms to cover her bust.)

Valerie: Don't come any closer.

James: You've nothing to be nervous about. I've a daughter bigger than you.

Valerie: Bigger?

James: Yes . . . she's pregnant.

Valerie: Married?

James: That wasn't very nice.

Valerie: Well, you weren't very nice yelling at me like that.

B52

James: Well, I know how long you girls can take getting dressed.

Valerie: I had to powder my nose . . . .

James: That's usually a poor substitute for washing your face.

Valerie: Look. I'm not your daughter, and I don't work for you. I can't think of one good reason why I have to put up with your bad manners.

James: Oh, you can't? *(Thinks)* Neither can I.

Valerie: And you're not in the best position to discuss washing faces — unless, of course, you're growing a beard.

James: Alright. I apologize. Now, let's tackle the problem sensibly. *(He moves into living room.)*

Valerie: Is Jeff here?

(She follows him down. James moves to sofa left and sits.)

James: He's taken Drummond fishing. He'll be back in three or four hours. Look, Valerie, Drummond is writing an article on me and my company. Because he found both of us here, he's concluded that you're my wife.

(Valerie sits on right arm of sofa left.)

Valerie: Your wife! What a nerve!

James: Well, I'm grateful he did! The alternative would probably put me out of business.

Valerie: But your wife might not like it.

James: My wife would . . . . Oh God! Lydia! *(Rises.)*

Valerie: Why not telephone her and tell her what's happened?

James *(thinking)*: Were you here all night?

Valerie: Yes — and all evening.

B53

James: And you slept in Jeff's room?

Valerie: Certainly not. I slept in here. Well, I passed out in here — on this sofa.

James: All night?

Valerie: Of course!

James: Oh! I'm dead! I'm finished! *(Crosses right to window.)*

Valerie: It's not that bad.

James: I slept on that sofa!

Valerie *(rises)*: In the room — with me?

James: Not with you!

Valerie *(moves toward James)*: Together?

James *(defensively)*: It's purely circumstantial — you know that.

Valerie: But, do I? *(Sits sofa left.)*

James: What are you saying?

Valerie: Well, you keep bemoaning your fate. But what about me? In here with an old man. I'm ruined!

James *(crosses centre — pulls in his stomach)*: I'm not old!

Valerie: This is not the time to make those claims.

James: Well, what do you suggest?

Valerie: I think we'd better tell everyone the truth.

James *(crosses down — speaking pleasantly to imaginary person)*: Oh, sure! We spent the night alone here — on separate sofas. We each didn't know the other was here, until an outsider arrived and introduced us to each other.

Valerie *(glumly)*: Well, it's the truth.

B54

James: We're the only people in the world who'll ever know it . . . .

Valerie: There has to be some way out.

James *(pause)*: Of course, there is. When Drummond leaves this evening, the problem is over. *(Moves up to her)* Until then, we must let him think you're my wife. Can you cook?

Valerie: I had a course at high school. I can make shepherd's pie and instant pudding.

James: You'll have to do better tonight. You'll also have to charm Drummond and convince him that we're very happy. He's crazy about happy marriages.

Valerie: Why not telephone your wife? In case she gets worried — and telephones or comes here.

James: Yes. I will. *(Moves to telephone.)*

Valerie: Will you tell her the truth?

James *(stops — moves back to Valerie)*: Valerie — I'm all for . . . .

Valerie: Better call me Lydia.

James: Lydia. I'm all for truth and honesty, but Lydia would find this as difficult to believe as — anyone else would. *(Moves back to telephone.)*

Valerie: Oh! You've been caught before, huh?

James: No, I haven't. But explanations are a waste of time. Your friends don't need them and your enemies won't believe them. Now, would you mind going and getting dressed?

Valerie: Sure. *(Rises)* If I bother you this way. *(Crosses and stands close to him)* What would you like me to wear, husband?

James: Nothing too sexy. Lydia is always very reserved.

Valerie: My. You are high strung.

James: Perhaps. *(Her presence disturbs him a little)* But not because

B55

of you. A lot depends on Drummond today. Now get some clothes on and I'll telephone.

Valerie: Could I get dressed after you call?

James: Get dressed!

(Valerie exits — James dials. CUE 16 — sound.)

Woman *(speaker)*: Hello?

James: Hullo, Mrs. Carter, could I speak with Lydia, please?

Woman *(speaker)*: She's out right now, Mr. Henderson.

James: Do you know where I could reach her?

Woman *(speaker)*: I think so. She left a number. It's 434-1111.

James: Four, three, four. Eleven, eleven.

Valerie *(off)*: Oh husband, dear!

James *(hoarse shout)*: I'm on the telephone. Shut up.

Woman *(speaker)*: Shut what, sir?

James: Not shut, cut! I said, "Cut off". I thought we'd been cut off.

Valerie *(calling from off)*: That's not a very happily married way of speaking, dear.

James: Thank you, Mrs. Carter.

(James hangs up quickly — Valerie enters.)

Valerie: Would you zip me up, please?

(James is dialing.)

James: Don't put ideas into my head! Four, three, four — eleven, eleven.

(We hear ringing on speaker.)

B56

Voice *(speaker)*: Good morning, "Lady Beautiful".

James: Lady what?

Voice *(speaker)*: "Lady Beautiful." Can we help you?

James: I'd like to speak to my wife, Lydia Henderson. Is she there?

Voice *(speaker)*: She certainly is. One moment and I'll connect you.

(Valerie moves over with her back to James. He tries to pull zipper with one hand and fails. He hands the telephone receiver to Valerie and works with two hands.)

Valerie: If this bothers you, let me know.

James: Zipping doesn't bother me. You bother me.

Valerie *(quietly)*: Want me to leave?

James: Now you're here, you'll stay here!

Valerie: Ohhhh! You're so strong and authoritative. Do you dominate your women?

James: I don't have any women!

Valerie: How nice! Look, what should I call you? I can't keep saying "husband dear".

James: James.

Valerie: Jimmie?

James: James will do.

Valerie: Jim?

James *(working at the zipper)*: Listen, Valerie. We have a problem — now be a good girl and pitch in, will you? I need your help, not your gags.

Valerie: I'll help. I think I might get to like it.

B57

James: Now hold still. I've got it. *(Struggles with the zipper.)*

Voice *(speaker)*: Hello.

James: Yes! Ah, cleared it. *(Zips up)* There!

Valerie: Good, because I can hear a little voice on this phone.

James: Oh, hell! I forgot.

(He snatches the receiver pushing Valerie down right.)

James *(heartily)*: Hello, darling!

Voice *(speaker)*: Hello?

James *(heartily)*: You sound great this morning.

Voice *(speaker)*: This is not Mrs. Henderson!

James: Not . . . who is it?

Voice *(speaker)*: "Lady Beautiful", Mr. Henderson. *(James closes his eyes and mentally counts to regain control)* Mr. Henderson?

James *(through clenched teeth)*: Yes.

Voice *(speaker)*: Your wife came in here very early this morning. She's already left.

James: Thank you, Lady Bountiful. *(CUE 17 — sound. He hangs up.)* I can't locate her. Well, suppose you tidy this room while I clean up.

Valerie: Oh, sure! *(James crosses up to alcove and exits. Valerie looks around. She straightens the cushions on sofa right, picks up one pillow, puts the things on the coffee table on the floor, then dusts the coffee table with the cushion. She fluffs up the cushion and replaces it on the sofa. She runs to other sofa and repeats the same action on all furniture. She folds blanket and stuffs it under drinks table. She empties all ashtrays into one ashtray, crosses up, opens door and throws contents on Jeff, who is standing there)* Oh, sorry!

Jeff: That's alright. Val, I just wanted to see you alone — to apologize.

B58

Valerie *(moving in — up centre)*: I should think so, leaving me sleeping with another man.

Jeff *(following her)*: I didn't . . . . Oh! You didn't!

Valerie: You should have awakened me.

Jeff: I tried.

Valerie: Why aren't you with what's-his-name?

Jeff: He's busy fishing — but I've got to get back. But first, Val, tell me you'll stay later — when the others leave.

Valerie *(teasing)*: You forget — I'm your aunt.

Jeff: Oh! Cut it out. It's important!

Valerie: Well, maybe you need a "man-to-man" talk with your uncle.

Jeff: Oh, hell!

(He turns and exits. Valerie goes quickly to the door.)

Valerie *(calling)*: Jeff! I'm a very sympathetic aunt.

(Jeff comes back and kisses her quickly and goes. Valerie crosses down and flops on sofa left.)

(James enters at a trot. He is wearing a brightly coloured T-shirt and tennis shoes. He trots downstage, the picture of youthful athletic health, past the windows to downstage right, then turns and sees Valerie. He stops.)

James: Oh! I heard voices. *(Winded)* Thought they were back.

Valerie: No. I'm here . . . all alone.

James *(slowly looks her over — he likes what he sees)*: I'm feeling a lot better about things. *(Crosses up and sits next to her)* If you co-operate, this might work out very well.

Valerie: Co-operate?

B59

James: Yes. You know — the happily married thing — for Drummond's sake.

Valerie: You'll get nothing out of it?

James: Well, perhaps we both will. I mean, I didn't make the situation but so long as we're in it . . . . *(Puts arm around her.)*

Valerie: I suppose in a minute you'll put your hand on my knee . . . . *(He pulls his hand back — disarmingly)* In a fatherly way, of course!

James: I guess I asked for that — but you know what they say — a man is young as long as he looks.

Valerie: Anyone over thirty looks old to me.

(James rises — moves a little right.)

James: You certainly know how to put a man in his place.

Valerie: It's a protective mechanism. Most girls develop one.

James *(moves back)*: Yes, I suppose you have to. *(Sits again)* Otherwise, everyone would be taking advantage.

Valerie: Some would try.

James *(his arm goes around her again)*: So, quite naturally, you have to discourage.

Valerie: Yes. It's worse with old men. I mean, all that flab — yuk!

James *(his arm comes back and he sits up)*: Some old men, as you call them, have no flab. *(Strikes his stomach.)*

Valerie: No, you look quite chipper. I think your after-shave braced you up.

James *(his arm goes back and he offers his cheek)*: Oh! You noticed my after-shave? Do you like it?

Valerie: Mmmmmmmmmm. Smells like Tame.

James: Well, I wouldn't exactly put it in that category.

(He's very close to her now.)

Valerie: Oh, do you put things into categories and groups too . . . . So do I.

James *(right close)*: That's something else we have in common.

Valerie: Yes. In my mind . . . well, I put men into categories.

James: Tell me about it . . . .

Valerie: . . . Into two main groups. They're either young and broke . . . .

James: Or . . . .

Valerie: . . . Old and bent!

(The mood is gone. James rises, moves away left, and turns.)

James: Valerie, I apologize. I guess I deserved that. My only excuse is that you have an irresistible quality. I've only found it in one other woman — Lydia.

Valerie *(rises — moves to James)*: That's the nicest thing you could have said.

(She goes right up to James and kisses him on the cheek as the front door opens and Drummond enters carrying two fishing rods. Jeff limps in after him carrying a pail.)

Drummond: We're back! What a charming scene of togetherness. I must make a note of that. *(He does so.)*

Valerie: I often give him a kiss before I leave the room. I like kissing.

James *(flustered — crosses to centre)*: Why are you back so soon?

Jeff *(grimly, as he moves down right of centre)*: Are we interrupting something?

Valerie *(gay)*: Course not. We don't mind who sees us, do we, James?

Drummond *(moving down right, in front of window)*: That's the idea! We had a tremendous morning too. Just put in the rods and pulled them out. Like picking apples. We caught twenty-three!

James: Twenty-three?

Jeff *(to James)*: One got away.

(They laugh.)

Drummond: Then Jeff turned his ankle, so we came back.

(Jeff remembers and starts to limp.)

Valerie *(to Jeff)*: Let's put the fish in the kitchen.

(Jeff limps down towards kitchen. Unseen by the others, Lydia sweeps in through the open door. She puts a small suitcase down and then poses. She makes quite a picture dressed in an extraordinary outfit. She has a hat with an enormous brim, and a summer dress that belongs in Vogue, but was never seriously intended to be worn.)

Drummond *(to James)*: That's right. And perhaps we can prevail upon Mrs. Henderson to serve them later on.

(Valerie puts her arms around James and kisses him on the cheek.)

Lydia: I'd be delighted!

(They all turn and see Lydia posed on the raised section. They freeze — each with a different expression. James does a 'take' and peers — realizing that it is Lydia. He puts his arms on Valerie's waist.

James: You see, Jeff, it goes like this . . . .

(He starts to "dum-de-dum" to the tune of "Jealousy" and tries to demonstrate a tango, but gets into a hopeless mess. Valerie doesn't move her feet.)

Drummond: Well, isn't anyone going to introduce us? *(Moves up toward Lydia.)*

James: Er, yes. Yes, of course. It is you, isn't it? *(He crosses up to Lydia and looks her in the eye. Valerie moves over to Jeff, down left. Pause)* What's happened to you? You're late. You should have

B62

been here sooner. *(Laughs)* Mr. Drummond arrived earlier and met me . . . and . . . and of course . . . Jeff! He's been fishing with Jeff . . . and he . . . he met Lydia . . . my wife!

Lydia: Oh. He did! Well, I have something to say about that . . . .

James *(laughs)*: I knew you would! I just knew you would. *(To Jeff)* Didn't I tell you that Valerie would have something to say? *(He puts his arm around Lydia)* Good old dependable Valerie.

Drummond *(moving up to join Valerie and James)*: James, you should never refer to a woman as being "old dependable" — especially such a young, young, lovely lady as . . . Valerie? That'll cost you five points. *(He marks it down.)*

Lydia *(now focuses on Drummond)*: Thank you for the compliment — but I'm not what you call "young, young" . . . just young. *(Looks at James.)*

Drummond: I'll not press the point because I wouldn't want to risk being misunderstood.

James: How would we misunderstand?

Drummond: Not you, James — Valerie. You see, when a man compliments a woman on her youthful appearance, it's usually because she's past it.

Lydia: And is that what you meant?

Drummond *(suggestively)*: No, I don't think you're past anything!

Lydia *(enjoying it)*: James. Please introduce me properly to Mr. Drummond.

James: Er . . . yes, dear . . . dear, Valerie . . . er, Valerie . . . Valerie . . . . *(Looks to Jeff and Valerie for help.)*

Jeff & Valerie: Scott!

James: Valerie Scott, this is the Norman Drummond.

Drummond *(kissing her hand)*: I'm very pleased to meet you, Valerie. Do you work for James?

B63

Lydia: Yes. I have for years.

James: She's my airline *(laughs)* . . . my . . . er, hostess . . . . *(Laughs)* What am I saying? She's my girl Friday.

Lydia: He means that I do everything for him.

Drummond: Even on Saturdays?

(Drummond and Lydia laugh — James joins in and waves to the others to laugh it up — they do.)

James *(heartily)*: Well. Now that Valerie's here we can all relax. *(Switch of mood. He means it)* I need a drink!

Jeff: Good idea. I'll set up the drinks table.

(He crosses to the carton by the door and takes carton to drinks' table. He lifts out bottles.)

Valerie: I'll take the fish to the kitchen.

(She does so and hurriedly exits to kitchen.)

Drummond: Well, if you'll excuse me I'd like to wash. I've been fishing. Er, Valerie — you won't go away, will you?

Lydia: No. I intend to stay right here and referee.

Drummond: Good.

(He exits to alcove.)

James: I must go and find . . . . *(Heads for kitchen.)*

Lydia: James!

James: . . . Some glasses? *(He stops down left of centre.)*

Lydia: I want a word with you.

James: Well, first take off that ridiculous hat. *(Moving back to Lydia)* I refuse to discuss anything with anyone when I can't see their head.

Jeff: I'll get the glasses! *(He moves toward kitchen door.)*

Lydia: You too!

(Both men stand looking as guilty as possible.)

Lydia: I would like to know what is going on here . . . .

James *(false heartiness)*: Is that really you? What's the disguise for?

(She removes her hat and crosses down right of centre. James waves to Jeff indicating that he should brighten up the conversation.)

Lydia: . . . I'd like to know what kind of business is sometimes discussed here!

Jeff *(getting James' message)* : Oh — all sorts. You look terrific!

(James closes the front door and moves down centre.)

Lydia: Male or female business?

Jeff: Lyd — er, Valerie. Surely you're not suggesting that James would have anything to do with a woman.

Lydia: And what do you think I am?

Jeff: I mean, other women! James is the epitome of business. He's not the type who would ever think of sex.

James *(a beat — then James turns to Jeff)*: Where in hell did you get that idea?

Jeff: You talk business morning, noon and night.

James: Not all night!

Lydia: He behaves differently with me than he does with you, Jeff.

Jeff *(looks at James)*: Thank God!

James: Amen!

Lydia: If you boys don't give me some answers — the right answers —
B66

I'm going to blow this meeting sky high!

Jeff: We can't explain now. But it's all completely innocent. It started with a misunderstanding.

James: You've never doubted me before . . . .

Lydia: Is that any reason for me to go on being stupid?

James: Yes . . . . No! No. Look, I love you — only you! *(Lydia weakens a little)* I've done nothing to be ashamed of, I wouldn't . . . .

Jeff: He couldn't.

James *(looking at Jeff)*: I could! *(Looking at Lydia)* I wouldn't . . . . I'm . . . I'm too . . . too . . . .

Jeff: . . . Much of a stuffed shirt!

James *(to Jeff)*: Look, will you shut up? I don't need your help. *(To Lydia)* I'm too sophisticated.

Lydia: Sophisticated people can do almost anything without feeling guilty!

Jeff: See! You should listen to me.

James *(grimly)*: You can be replaced.

Lydia: I'd like to know where, why and how you got my replacement.

Jeff: I got her . . . and James only picked up where . . . .

James *(to Jeff)*: Shut up! *(To Lydia)* She's not your replacement!

Lydia: Then why the charade? *(Pause)* Will you introduce me to Drummond properly?

James: I can't . . . well, not just now . . . but I will . . . sometime.

Jeff: No. No, Lydia. If Drummond knew you and James were married, he'd think James was playing around . . . .

James *(to Jeff — through clenched teeth — with a forced laugh)*: Don't

B67

be such an idiot! *(To Lydia, laughing gaily)* Why would Drummond think such a thing?

Jeff *(to James)*: He would! Because he caught you and . . . . Oh! *(He's stopped cold by a look from James)* . . . Er . . . *(looks at Lydia)* . . . because Drummond has an active imagination.

Lydia: So have I! An active temper, too.

James: Please, Lydia, I know this looks unusual . . . .

Lydia: You mean, it isn't unusual?

James: No! No . . . it's very unusual. Very unusual!

Lydia: Just tell me one thing — where did you spend the night?

James *(pause — thinks)*: Here. Right here on that sofa.

Lydia: And Miss Kissy Kissy sex pants — where did she spend the night?

James: Well . . . well, I didn't see her . . . .

Lydia: Is that the truth?

James: Lydia, I swear to you that I first saw her this morning . . . when I first saw Drummond, I thought she was with him, but it seems she's a close friend of Jeff's.

Jeff: Just friend. We haven't had the chance to get close yet.

Lydia: You mean this charade is because you didn't want Drummond to get a poor opinion of Jeff?

James *(grabbing at straws)*: That's right!

Jeff: Sure! James wants to keep the record straight. *(Smiling)* I'm a mixed-up type.

(He crosses left to fireplace — takes cigarette from mantle.)

James: But, Lydia, we'll have to play this thing through — for the sake of the company. You do see that, Lydia?

B68

(Pause.)

Lydia: Very well, James. I'll be Valerie. But it could be difficult. I think Mr. Drummond likes me.

(She picks up her hat from the downstage end table at sofa right, then crosses up and sits sofa left.)

James *(follows Lydia — sits sofa left, to the right of Lydia)*: Of course he does. You're . . . you're beautiful. But don't worry, Drummond meets plenty of beautiful women. I mean . . . he's hardly likely to make a pass *(laughs)* or anything.

Lydia: You don't think so?

James: Of course not! What would he do that for?

Lydia: Well, he might just do it because he's male and I'm female.

James *(discounting the possibility)*: Nooo! Oh, he likes you alright — but not — well, not that way!

Lydia: Well, try not to make it sound so impossible. It might happen.

James *(laughs)*: Yes, but why would he want to . . . .

Lydia: Well, you do, James!

James: Yes . . . well, I'm different, and anyway I know you.

Lydia: Learning to know people can be fun. Remember?

Jeff *(positively)*: That's the best part — er — *(Long pause)* I'll get the glasses.

(Jeff exits quickly to kitchen.)

James: You see what a problem Jeff is? *(Rises — moves down right.)*

Lydia: How does Drummond take to him?

James: All right, I think — but I hope that no questions come up about his marital status or prospects.

B69

Lydia: Well, James, don't worry — now I'm here I'll be pleased to help.

James: Good. But don't meddle with business. You might try distracting Drummond a little — but — well, act your age — I mean, don't behave foolishly . . . .

Lydia: Well — not that my efforts will amount to much. For you, James, I'll try, and don't worry . . . I will act my age.

(Drummond enters. He has changed from his fishing shirt and shorts into the outfit in which he arrived.)

Drummond: Hello, hello. Is James questioning your age? *(Crosses down right of sofa left.)*

Lydia: No. My behaviour.

(Drummond takes out book and writes.)

Drummond: You surprise me, James. There are some subjects that should never be discussed with a woman. Like behaviour and age.

James: I was only generalizing.

Lydia: Oh, I don't mind.

Drummond: But you should! *(Crosses to sofa — sits right of Lydia)* Just because you work for a man is no reason for him to forget the male and female boundaries.

James: Oh, I never forget female boundaries.

(A look from Lydia silences him.)

Lydia *(to Drummond)*: I really don't mind discussing anything — even my age. For instance, how old do you think I am?

Drummond: I . . . I don't know.

Lydia: But you must have some idea.

Drummond *(pause — he looks at her, sizing her up)*: I have several ideas. But I'd hate to guess ten years younger — because of your

B70

looks — ten years older — because of your charm and poise.

Lydia: Thank you for the compliment. Are you married, Mr. Drummond?

Drummond *(suggestively)*: No. Up to now, I've never really found a kindred spirit. How about you?

Lydia: I was. Up to quite recently. But I've been released. My husband has another wife.

Drummond: Wonderful — the — er — the field is clear then?

James: Er, more or less . . . . *(Rises.)*

Drummond *(to Lydia)*: That's a beautiful brooch you're wearing. *(He touches Lydia's lapel)* Very modern.

Lydia: Thank you. I bought it myself. I wanted it modern so that people would think that someone cared for me recently.

James: God! I need a drink. *(Breaks down right)* I wonder what Jeff is doing?

Drummond *(taking out book)*: What about Jeff? Is he married?

James *(absent-mindedly)*: Not exactly.

Drummond: What does that mean?

James *(trying to recover)*: Well — he's . . . he's committed . . . .

Drummond: Engaged?

James *(forceful)*: Um — well . . . more than that. I mean, married men are the most efficient, didn't you say?

Drummond: Yes, they are. But how can he be more than engaged and less than married?

(James is looking dismayed at the situation he's got himself into.)

Lydia: Yes. I'd like to hear that explained too.

B71

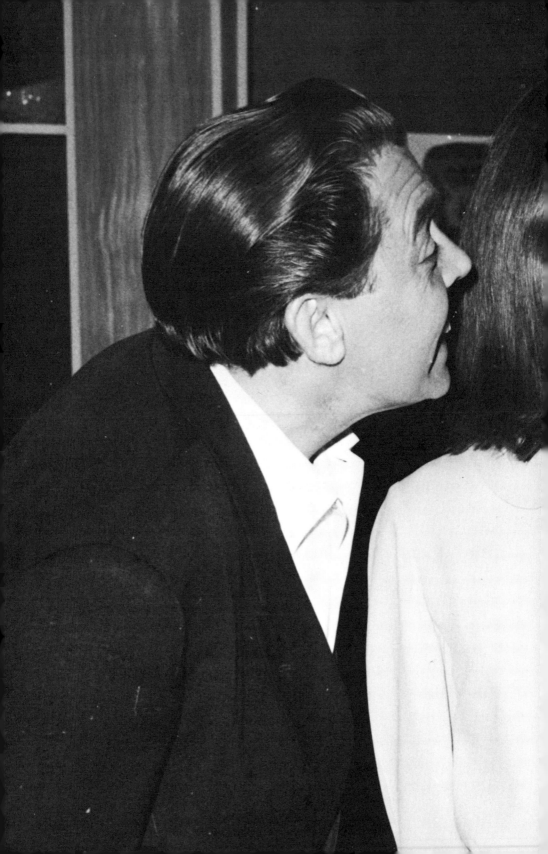

(Enter Jeff with glasses.)

Jeff: Sorry I was so long. Lydia had trouble with the fish. *(Crosses to drinks' table as James, grateful for the interruption, takes a break down right)* Let's all have a drink.

Drummond: Jeff, where do you live?

Jeff *(moves down right to end of sofa left)*: I've two places. I live here, and in an apartment in town.

Drummond: Two homes, ah ha! *(He writes)* And do you come here in winter?

Jeff: Yes. For she-ing! *(Looks at James.)*

Drummond: And summer?

Jeff: Same reason. The apartment's for work, and "Lookout" for love. What would you like to drink . . . Valerie?

Lydia: Oh, I don't really . . . .

James: She'll have a gin and bitter orange.

Drummond: And what does your wife drink, James?

James *(calls)*: Lydia, what would you like to drink?

Jeff: She'll have a gin and bitter orange too. *(They all look at him)* She just told me.

(Jeff retreats by moving to drinks' table and pours drinks.)

Drummond: Then I may as well have the same.

Jeff: So will I.

James *(grimly)*: I'll have scotch and water. A double.

Lydia: I think I'd like a double too, Jeff.

James: Valerie, you must stay sober!

B74

Lydia: I wish you wouldn't say "must". It makes me feel "won't" all over.

James *(to Jeff)*: Make hers a single.

Lydia: But you're having a double.

James: I need a double! I feel like having a double.

Lydia *(to Drummond)*: Some men feel younger when they have doubles.

James: Yes — and what's wrong with a man feeling his oats?

Lydia: Nothing. So long as he doesn't try to sow them!

(They all laugh, except James who goes deadpan and sits sofa right.)

James: Let's all have doubles.

Drummond: I must say that you've kept in good shape for your age, James. Do you belong to a club — or take exercise?

Lydia: He skips! Skips potatoes, skips desserts and skips doubles!

Jeff: Yes, when you reach the metallic age — you know silver in your hair and gold in your teeth, you have to be careful. *(Laughs.)*

(Jeff gives Lydia, then Drummond, their drinks. Then crosses back to drinks' table for James' scotch and his own drink.)

James *(to Jeff)*: 'Specially if you start out with lead in your pants.

(Jeff gives James his drink.)

Drummond: Do I detect a little animosity? I hope so. It usually supplies the best material for an article.

James: Animosity? No. No — just our friendly ribbing.

Drummond: Then perhaps we should start some controversial subjects.

Lydia: Well, I believe we should legalize gambling.

B75

James: We already have. It's just a question of knowing the differences.

Drummond: Are you a gambling man, James?

Jeff: President of a trust company? A gambler? He's pulling your leg! *(Crosses to chair down right, and sits.)*

James: What's gambling? If you bet on a horse . . . well, I don't do that. But, if I bet four no trumps — that's entertainment, and when I bet that GTE will go up four points — that's business.

Lydia: Well, Mr. Drummond, surely it depends upon your terms of reference. It's a gamble when a man crosses the street. A bigger gamble when a man marries — and a bigger gamble when a man deceives his wife.

(James chokes on his drink.)

Drummond: A happily married man — a truly happily married, like James here, has no need to tell lies.

Lydia: Oh, yes. You can tell how happy he is.

(James smiles.)

Drummond: Yes. I've seen it for myself. Why, when I arrived this morning, Lydia struggled up from the sofa to let me in. Now, how many happily married couples spend the night on the sofa . . . with a bottle of champagne?

(James is now looking, with fixed dismay, directly at Jeff.)

Lydia: Well, I'd like you to answer that one, James!

(When nothing comes from Jeff, James gives a forced laugh.)

James *(to Drummond)*: Is that what you thought . . . ? You really thought that . . . that Val . . . that Lydia and I . . . that's what you thought! *(Laugh . . . laugh . . . laugh. To Jeff)* Hear that, Jeff? *(Rises — crosses down to Jeff.)*

Jeff *(laughs)*: Yes . . . what do you know? He thinks . . . . *(Rises.)*

James: Yes, he really thinks . . . .

B76

Lydia: We both do!

James *(laughs louder)*: They both do!

Jeff *(laughing louder)*: Yes, both of them.

James: They both think . . . .

Jeff *(still laughing)*: Yes. Isn't is ridiculous? They . . . they really do.

James *(stops laughing)*: Well, explain it to them, for me. *(Returns to sofa right, and sits.)*

Jeff: Me? *(Moves by window behind sofa right.)*

James: Sure. You're old enough.

Lydia: Yes, Jeff. You explain for James. Then he can explain for you.

Jeff: For me? I wasn't here!

Lydia: No, but Mr. Drummond and I were wondering what James meant when he said you were more than engaged . . . yet less than married, weren't we . . . Norman?

Drummond: Yes . . . yes, we were, Valerie.

James *(rises — grasping at straws)*: I was referring to Va . . . Lyd . . . er . . . .

Jeff: Susan! You meant Susan!

James: That's right, Susan!

Jeff *(laughing)*: Good old Susan! *(Moves down right.)*

James *(laughing)*: Yes, Susan. Quite a girl.

Jeff *(laughing louder)*: More than a girl!

James *(laughing louder)*: That's right. A bit more! Quite a bit more!

(Valerie enters.)

B77

Valerie: What's the joke?

(The men continue to laugh, looking at each other.)

Lydia: Up to now it's a private joke. We're waiting for them to explain it to us.

(Valerie crosses to James.)

Valerie: Oh, James has a terrific sense of humour. *(She kisses him.)*

James: Don't do that! *(Sits on Valerie's shoes, sofa right)* Ow! Your . . . your darn shoes . . . don't you ever wear them? *(He goes to put them on the coffee table.)*

Valerie: Yaaaaah!

(James snatches the shoes back — nerves now completely shattered.)

James: Alright! Alright! I know!

Valerie: Shoes on the table, a brush or a cork
        Is a sure invitation to a big, fat stork!

(She sits upstage end of sofa right.)

James: What? You and Mr. Drummond had better get together!

Drummond: Well, either way it's pretty unnerving!

Lydia: If you'll all excuse me, I'm just going to change. *(Rises — moves up to archway)* I brought something more casual for lounging in. By the time I get back I hope you'll be able to explain, James.

James *(rises)*: Oh, sure, sure. Make yourself comfortable.

Drummond *(crossing up to Lydia)*: Don't be long, Valerie.

Lydia: I just want to improve my appearance a little.

Drummond *(pouring on the charm)*: I can assure you that no improvement is necessary.

Lydia: Thank you, *(looks at James — then Drummond)* Norman.

B78

(Lydia exits through archway.)

Drummond *(to James)*: Now that's what I call a woman. She's got everything.

James: Yes. She has!

Jeff: More than you think . . . . *(A look from James silences him.)*

Drummond: Well — I hope you won't mind if I make a . . . a few advances. I'm very attracted to her.

Jeff *(very enthusiastically)*: Of course, we won't. Go right ahead.

Valerie *(following Jeff's lead)*: Sure. Have fun!

James: You'll be wasting your time. I know her. I have for years.

Drummond: Well, James, if you'll pardon me saying so. Don't think that she won't play on my team just because she didn't play on your team.

James: Dammit! She's on my team!

Drummond: I'll bet you I can score a touchdown, tonight.

James: Any pass you try to make will be intercepted.

Drummond: Well, let's leave it to Valerie, and no interference from the bystanders!

James: Only in case of fouls. You're not stealing any of my staff. So forget it.

Drummond: Perhaps you don't appreciate what you have until you're about to lose it.

Jeff: Yes, James. We can read some people like an open book.

James: Damn pity you can't shut them up as easily.

Drummond: I think you're a clever dog, James. I'll bet you had Valerie come to "Lookout" especially to charm me. Go on — confess!

B79

(The front door bursts open and Susan enters.)

Susan: Oh! Hello.

Drummond: Hi!

Susan: You must be Mr. Drummond. I'm . . . .

Jeff & James *(rise — alarmed)*: Susan!

Susan: Hi!

Drummond: That's wonderful. Now we're all paired off . . . ! *(Susan hands the coat she is carrying in front of her, to Drummond. We see that she's wearing her maternity outfit — and pillow — again. Drummond takes her coat . . . . He sees her size — does a "take")* You're . . . you're Susan?

Susan: Yes. *(To James as she crosses down to sofa left, and sits)* I know you don't like my wearing this and showing so much — but this way I can get a seat in the bus.

Drummond: Now I know what you meant when you said, "more than engaged".

James *(moving up to Drummond)*: Oh, that! . . . I can explain!

Drummond: You realize what it means!

James *(grabbing at straws)*: Yes. Lydia was right. You were wrong!

Drummond: I? . . . Me? . . . Wrong?

James: "Shoes on the table, a brush or a cork,
        Is a sure invitation to a big, fat stork."
(He indicates Susan. Then, desperately to Jeff) Jeff — get us a round of doubles!

CUE 25 — lighting

(The curtain goes down. CUE 18 — sound.)

B80

About 4:30 the same afternoon.

CUE 26 — lighting

The scene is the same except that the room has been tidied. Liz is sitting on the sofa holding a cup of coffee. A briefcase is beside her on the sofa. She is very smartly dressed in "country" clothes. Lydia is pacing towards the window. She is gowned in a gorgeous lounging pyjama outfit bought especially for the occasion. CUE 19 — sound.

Lydia *(angrily)*: Well, now you know everything I know.

Liz: But you've no real proof of anything.

Lydia: What d'you expect, a clinch by clinch account? *(She stands looking out the window)* There were only two people present — and they're both suffering from amnesia.

Liz: Well, you really don't have much to go on.

Lydia: I have enough.

Liz: If you didn't love him so much, you'd give him the benefit of the doubt.

Lydia: I've written so many novels on the subject that all I've left is doubt — and I've plenty of that!

Liz: Any sign of them yet?

Lydia *(looking out of the window)*: No. And that proves something. Why would James suggest they go fishing again? He hates fishing!

Liz: Maybe to butter up Mr. Drummond. You said things weren't going too well.

Lydia: That's an understatement! One look at Susan was enough to make Drummond cancel all the points James had earned.

Liz: Oh, I do hope Mr. Drummond comes back before I leave. *(Looks at her watch)* Heavens, it's four-thirty already. *(She takes a pile of papers out of her briefcase and searches for a particular form)* Ah! Here it is. Sign this and Shelby Sherbrooke is off your hands.

Lydia *(crosses to sofa)*: Where?

Liz: Here! *(Indicates the place. Lydia signs and hands papers to Liz. Liz takes top original and hands copy to Lydia)* This is your copy.

Lydia *(takes copy)*: I wish I knew what to do Liz. I can't let James down, but the position is becoming more difficult every minute. Poor James, falling into the clutches of that airborn witch.

Liz: Maybe it'll get better.

Lydia *(moving down right)*: It'll get worse. When James left with Drummond and Jeff, he looked so flustered. I expect right now he's standing in the water somewhere telling Drummond that I'm married to Jeff and that Valerie's our daughter.

Liz: Yes. And from what you said, Drummond will be writing it all down.

Lydia *(in front of window, behind right sofa)*: And Susan's no help. I actually think she's enjoying it. She's in the kitchen helping Valerie prepare dinner. *(Pause)* Just as well, I suppose! Valerie would probably kiss each fish face . . . . I've never seen anyone who likes to kiss so much . . . . Maybe she has French blood!

Liz *(rises)*: Well, Lydia, keep your cool. I have to go now. I called the meeting so I can't let them down — I must be on time.

Lydia: Oh, I do wish you could stay.

Liz *(crosses to front of sofa right)*: I'd like to. Very much . . . you have no idea how much.

Lydia: Then . . . then come back!

Liz: Come back? This evening?

Lydia: Yes . . . yes, please do . . . and put that new dress on.

Liz: Oh, I'd love to. Then I could meet Mr. Drummond. What's he like?

Lydia: He's a peculiar combination. The type who has the ability of letting other people have his own way.

B83

Liz *(laughs)*: Sounds like almost any man.

Lydia: And when he talks to a woman — on any subject at all — he radiates "bedroom".

Liz *(moving up to front door)*: You sold me! I'll be back — soon as I can. Oh, Lydia. You do look gorgeous — but what a pity you spent all that money for a day like today.

Lydia *(moving to door with Liz)*: Oh, I don't regret it. If I have to fight Kissy Kissy sex pants — or James — or the whole world — I'm glad I'm really dressed for it.

Liz: But it must have cost so much.

Lydia: I'm through with economy . . . and budgets. I'm fed up with spending money without getting any fun out of it.

(Susan enters from kitchen.)

Susan: Anyone like more coffee? Oh. Are you leaving, Liz?

Liz: Yes, but I'll be back.

Lydia: What's Pussy Galore doing?

Susan *(sitting sofa left)*: It's a case of the blind leading the blind. Neither of us knows where anything is in the kitchen — and she was going to serve dinner on individual trays. Imagine!

Lydia *(to Liz)*: She's an airline hostess! She'll probably fasten our seatbelts next.

Liz *(laughs)*: Oh! Tonight will be fun — "Lookout" — see you later.

(She exits through front door.)

Lydia *(calling)*: Hurry back . . . and don't forget to dress. *(Closing door and turning to Susan)* I'm surprised at you helping your father's mistress.

(Lydia crosses down front and puts her copy of the signed paper on end table right.)

B84

Susan: My father's . . . ? That . . . that girl?

Lydia: Look again. That girl has the kind of legs designed for micro-skirts . . . .

Susan: She's got her eye on Jeff.

Lydia *(moving up to Susan)*: So, she's working her way through the family!

Susan: Mum. You've got it all wrong. She hates doing this. Daddy made her.

Lydia *(sits)*: She admitted it?

Susan: She's had nothing to do with Daddy. Look, come and talk to her yourself. *(Rises.)*

Lydia: Do you expect her to tell me the truth?

Susan: Oh, Mum! You've often complained that people only hear what they want to hear. Why not listen with an open mind?

Lydia: Where your father's concerned, I don't have an open mind. I never did have and I won't start now.

Susan *(pulling her mother up)*: Come on, now. You'll see. *(The front door opens. Jeff walks in, leaving door open, crosses to sofa right — flops down)* Hi, Jeff! Where are the others?

Jeff: Drummond picked up a dead fish. It must have been the dead fish. James's been racing around exhibiting his youth, and I've fallen on every rock between here and the lake.

Lydia: I'm glad you boys are having such a nice vacation.

Jeff: This isn't a vacation. It's like six months hard labour compressed into one day. All day out in the damn country. Why, even the air smells! My feet hurt, my chest hurts. I'm pretty sure I've broken my back, and I'm as constipated as hell! *(Flops back on sofa.)*

(We hear James singing, "I love to go a-wandering . . . .")

Lydia: Come on, Susan, let's see about the poor fish in the kitchen.

(James appears in the front doorway as Susan exits to kitchen, followed by Lydia.)

James: Lyd . . . Valerie . . . I'm back . . . hey! *(Lydia has exited — James crosses down centre. To Jeff —)* Is she mad? . . . Very mad?

Jeff: What for? She didn't have to go fishing.

(Drummond enters and closes the door.)

James *(to Drummond)*: That's quite a walk!

Drummond: Just good exercise. I'm pleased to see that you two are not just city types, spending your entire lives wasting away in offices.

James *(strides about)*: Oh, no! To the contrary, we love fresh air. That should be worth some points!

Drummond: Yes. Yes. And as soon as I've cleaned up, we'll start the interview in earnest. My hands smell fishy again!

(Drummond exits alcove — James collapses on sofa left.)

Jeff: What happened to all your bounding energy?

James: Oh, I'm full of it.

Jeff: You're full of it, alright!

James: I'm just resting before the fatigue sets in.

Jeff: Boy, what one does for business! You should pay me more money . . . . Why don't you?

James: Anyone who doesn't receive a raise should ask himself why.

Jeff: I have.

James: And how did you answer yourself?

Jeff: It's because we're related! Any other company would pay me what I'm worth.

James: You'd starve! *(Thinks)* If we paid you what you're worth,

B86

we'd be contravening the minimum wage act.

Jeff: How do you expect to know what I'm worth when you'll never listen to my ideas?

James: I have listened — and I nearly vomited. *(Pause)* As marketing, you're supposed to be in charge of new business.

Jeff: Sure. And I exceed quota every year.

James: But why? . . . Ever ask yourself that question?

Jeff: I don't have to. I plan for increases . . . and get them.

James: Because the economy is going up. Not because of your ideas.

Jeff: Why not be more specific?

James: Easy! What about the crazy notion to set up a ladies' department in each branch. Decorated like . . . like a hotel beauty parlour — all smelling of perfume — and didn't you say, "with love-birds in cages"?

Jeff *(rises)*: It would bring in female business. I know it would.

James: You've got birds on the brain. *(Pause)* You should get married. Then you'd stop thinking about sex.

Jeff: You're negative just because the proposals come from me. If Gerald suggested them, you'd love to exchange ideas.

James *(rises)*: After I've exchanged ideas with you, my mind's a blank.

Jeff: I believe that! I never seem able to get through to you.

James: Maybe if there were more point to your ideas, they'd penetrate!

Jeff: They'd have to be armour piercing.

James: Are you calling me a blockhead?

Jeff: Well, well! I finally drove a point all the way home.

B87

James: Well, now you can damn well drive yourself all the way home — and stay there.

Jeff *(shouts)*: My pleasure! *(Crosses up to front door, opens door, realizes he is home, slams door, and crosses back to sofa and sits)* I am home!

James *(shouts)*: Good! *(Sits.)*

(Drummond enters carrying a large pad of paper and his note book.)

Drummond: My, that air is exhilarating. It fills one with vigour.

James *(sitting up straight)*: Yes, it does.

Drummond *(moving down centre)*: Oh, I thought you were tired; having a rest.

James: No. Jeff and I were wondering how to work off our excess energy. Such a pity there weren't more fish.

Drummond: We must have caught all there were. Twenty-three plus the dead one. Someone must have put them in quite recently.

Jeff: Why do you think that?

Drummond: The water's polluted by that chemical plant. Fish couldn't exist there. The reason we caught all those fish this morning is that they wanted to be caught. They wanted out.

(During the last speech, Valerie enters.)

Valerie: You mean the poor things committed suicide?

James *(rises)*: No. No, of course not . . . dear.

(Valerie looks from James to Jeff to Drummond.)

Valerie: I missed you, darling. *(She kisses James)* You look tired.

Jeff: James was just wondering what to do to work off his excess energy.

Valerie *(to James)*: I'll do whatever you suggest, dear.

B88

Jeff *(a challenge for James)*: Why not dance? You love to dance, don't you, Lydia?

Valerie: Sure!

James *(sits)*: Oh, well that's not much fun for Mr. Drummond. Anyway, he has some questions to ask me now.

Drummond: Oh, they can wait! I'd like to see you dance. You must have strength to burn.

James: I have. I have. *(Rises)* You mustn't judge the company by Jeff. He's just a beginner.

Drummond: But he's younger. Stronger.

James: No! Look at him! *(Jeff straightens up)* It's experience that counts. The ability to pace yourself properly. I can keep going day and night. Used to do the mile in four minutes six.

Jeff: That's not using your head. I do it in forty-four seconds — in my car.

Drummond: Let's have a little contest, if you're both up to it.

James *(crossing up to office area)*: It won't be any contest. I'm ready. What are the rules? *(He starts an exaggerated tango all by himself.)*

Jeff *(struggles to his feet)*: First, we'll need some music. *(Crosses to phonograph.)*

Valerie *(crossing up to James)*: And a partner.

(CUE 20 — sound. Jeff puts on a record with a swinging latin beat.)

Drummond: Jeff, what about your partner? Susan's in no condition . . . .

Jeff *(crossing to kitchen door)*: Maybe Valerie will help out . . . . That'll even up the age factor a little. *(At kitchen door he calls)* Valerie . . . Valerie, care to dance?

(Drummond absent-mindedly picks up Lydia's Shelby Sherbrooke form. He reads it — then pockets it.)

B89

Lydia *(off)*: What? . . . I'm coming . . . .

(James is slowly trying to follow Valerie who is swinging and swaying to the rhythm.)

Drummond: I didn't think either of you had it in you.

Jeff: You may yet be right!

(Lydia enters.)

Lydia: Did you say "dance", Jeff?

Jeff: Yes. It's a contest between James and me. Skill versus dogged persistence.

Lydia: James is going to dance? *(Laughs)* It'll have to be a bunny hop, or a tango.

(They cross up to office area and start to dance.)

Drummond: Right. Let's go! Show a leg, Valerie.

Valerie & Lydia: I'll show two. Anything to oblige.

(After a moment or two, James gets lost in the footwork and gives up.)

James: Hold it! Hold it! That's not fair. That's a foreign number . . . . I can't dance to that stuff.

(Except for James, all continue to dance, enjoying themselves throughout.)

Jeff: Well, I'm fresh out of square dances.

James: You want to exercise everything except discretion.

Lydia: Do you have a waltz?

Valerie: What's that?

Jeff: We're supposed to be having an energy contest. A test in pacing . . . hey! I know! *(CUE 21 — sound. He crosses down to record player*

B90

and puts on a twist) This isn't foreign! *(Crosses back to office area.)*

(James, trapped, tries to follow Valerie. Lydia and Jeff get into full swing. James catches on a little.)

(Susan enters.)

Susan: What's going on?

Drummond: A dance contest.

Susan: It looks like fun. Look at M . . . at Valerie go!

Drummond: I'm watching her . . . closely.

James: Ow! *(He remains in bent over position.)*

Jeff: I win.

James: Help me, you ass!

(Jeff helps James, who walks in 'bent over' fashion, to the sofa. The girls keep dancing. James collapses on sofa left. Jeff flops in chair down left. Both are exhausted. Susan moves up centre and starts to dance.)

Drummond *(worried for Susan)*: Contest is over! It's all over now! Susan . . . Miss . . . Mrs. . . . I don't think you should . . . .

Susan: I'm just getting started.

Lydia: So am I.

Valerie: Where are all the men?

Lydia: Come on, Norman, swing a hip!

Drummond *(reluctantly)*: Oh . . . . Oh very well. Just for a moment.

(He moves up, Lydia takes his hand. They twist around. Drummond suddenly becomes a demon twister and after twenty seconds or so . . . .)

Susan: Oh, dear! *(She keeps twisting)* It's . . . it's loose . . .

B91

Drummond: What's loose?

Lydia: Just her stomach.

Drummond: Just her what? *(He stops, then starts again.)*

(Lydia taps her stomach. Ten seconds later Susan's belt and pillow hit the floor.)

Susan *(still dancing)*: Oh! There it goes! I've lost it.

(Drummond has now stopped dancing. He's looking front, afraid to look anywhere else. The three girls are still dancing.)

Drummond: Lost it?

Susan: Yes. Don't stop. Just kick it out of the way.

Drummond: Oh, no!

(He moves down to sofa right, keeping his eyes averted. He then sits as lights fade.)

CUE 27 — lighting

(Girls are still dancing and music comes up to bridge into next scene. The curtain goes down. CUE 22 — sound.)

**Act three
Scene two**

About 8:30 the same evening.

CUE 28 — lighting

The scene is the same except that the room has been tidied and the front door is open. At curtain, the stage is empty. After a couple of beats, Lydia enters quickly through the front door. She crosses down to the sofa right, and lifts the cushions in turn. She is looking for something. She looks around and under the end table when James enters through the front door. Lydia immediately stops looking.

James: Lydia, what's the matter?

Lydia: Don't speak to me!

B92

James: Why are you so angry? What have you lost?

Lydia: My husband.

James: Did you think I was under the end table?

Lydia *(moving up centre)*: Why don't you keep your jokes for your new wife? She might appreciate them.

James: Lydia, why don't you stop picking on Valerie?

Lydia: What do you mean?

James: When she said the fish will be ready in five or ten minutes, was it necessary for you to say, "What sort of bait are you using? "

Lydia: Then she should stop kissing you.

(He moves down — sits sofa left.)

James: How many times do I have to tell you . . . she's only kissing me for my sake . . . er, our sake.

Lydia *(moving back behind James and sofa)*: Huh! Then why is she enjoying it so much?

James: Because . . . well, dammit, she's kissing me because she loves Jeff.

Lydia: Heaven help you if she ever marries him.

James: Oh, stop it, Lydia. Jeff is playing up to Susan in order to appease Drummond. Valerie is jealous so she plays up to me. I've got to go along with it in order to play up to Drummond. What's wrong with that?

Lydia: No one's playing with me!

James: But you're too sensible for that sort of nonsense . . . you don't like to play . . . look at all of us . . . none of us likes it.

(General laughter is heard off.)

Lydia: Well, I suggest that you stop being martyrs very soon —

B93

otherwise I'm going to stop being a grouch — and join in.

James: Join in . . . who? Oh, Drummond. *(Laughs. Lydia is looking around sofa)* Well, he's just outside on the terrace. Why not try your luck? *(Laughs.)*

Lydia: Are you challenging me?

James: No, of course not. Oh! I don't feel so good. I think the fish has polluted me.

Lydia: It's all your idiotic running around — and the kissing probably tired you out.

James: What on earth are you looking for?

Lydia: Nothing . . . er, a piece of paper. Have you seen it?

James: Paper? Maybe you left it on the terrace . . . .

Lydia: Or with my suitcase . . . . *(Moves up to archway.)*

James: Is that what Drummond meant when he told Jeff that his big scoop was discovering the author? Hell! You don't suppose that he knows my wife writes the Chickie Dickie and Fuzzy Tail stories? We must warn Valerie . . . .

Lydia: I don't think that's the problem.

(Lydia exits up centre.)

James: Then what could . . . . *(He sees that Lydia has gone)* Oh, if only women would stay in their kitchens . . . .

(Valerie enters by front door.)

Valerie: Hi! What's the matter?

James: Nothing. Nothing at all. I was . . . just recovering from dinner.

Valerie *(moving down to sofa right)*: Was it that bad?

James: No. No. It was great . . . the fish was certainly fresh . . . .

Valerie *(sits)*: Oh, I like fish when they're served with the heads off, but Jeff wouldn't let me. Doesn't it bother you when they watch you eating them?

James: You did fine. *(Rises and crosses to her)* Jeff and I certainly appreciate all you are doing.

Valerie: Jeff! Huhh! He doesn't know I'm here.

James: Don't be silly, Valerie. He's putting on a show with Susan — not just for Drummond's benefit. He's trying to find out if you care.

Valerie: Do you think so?

James: I know so — and I, for one, hope he catches you.

Valerie: Oh, you're the nicest man . . . I'd love to join your family.

(She rises, puts her arms around James' neck and kisses him on the mouth — as Lydia enters through archway.)

Lydia: Mouth to mouth resuscitation? *(James and Valerie don't move — they're frozen in position)* You two should enter the Olympics.

(Valerie sags, breaking the kiss.)

James: I think she's fainted!

Lydia: Probably suffocated!

(James moves Valerie to sofa left.)

James: Help me! Get some water or something.

Lydia *(moving down centre, very relaxed)*: If she's fainted, water will only drown her — but I can fix it.

James: How?

Lydia: Well, first, take her pants off.

(Valerie sits bolt upright.)

Valerie: What!

B96

Lydia: See! I fixed it!

James *(moving left)*: That . . . that trick is beneath you . . . Valerie was only trying to show her appreciation . . . .

Lydia: I know it was a low down trick! I shouldn't be such a spoil sport. Well . . . don't worry. I'm about to join the fun.

(She exits through archway.)

Valerie: Oh, dear! She's mad, James. She's really mad. I hope when I'm a wife I'll understand platonic kisses.

James *(crossing and sitting next to Valerie on sofa left)*: You won't, dear. It's a fact of life that a girl understands almost everything about a man until he says, "I do".

(Drummond enters through front door.)

Drummond: Ah! Two lovebirds cooing their "I do's" again. Excuse me. I must wash.

James: Hands smell fishy again?

(Drummond laughs . . . so James laughs.)

Drummond: Matter of fact, they do.

(He exits through archway, laughing.)

James: He's nice. He's well informed. He's interesting. But he sure rubs me the wrong way.

(Susan enters from front door.)

Susan *(hoarse whisper)*: Where is everyone?

Valerie: James and I are just coming out.

James: You go, Valerie. I'll wait for Lydia. *(To Susan)* Your mother's a little upset.

Susan *(moving down centre)*: Well, you'd better come, Val. I'm beginning to enjoy Jeff's performance.

Valerie: Oh! You are!

Susan: Sure. I haven't had so much attention since I was courting. No. That's not true . . . since my honeymoon.

James: Well, you don't look as though you've been ignored.

Susan *(pretending to be shocked)*: Dad! You like to shock people, don't you — coming, Val?

Valerie: I think I'd better . . . . *(She moves up toward front door.)*

James: Take care, Valerie. You're going into fast company.

Valerie: Oh! Terrific!

(She exits front door.)

Susan *(moving up after Valerie)*: Are you coming . . . ? There's a big orange moon, very low down. Oh, I wish Bob were here.

James: Oh! That's all we'd need . . . what is it about a country place that makes everyone think about sex?

(Drummond enters looking very chipper.)

Susan: No T.V.

(Susan exits out front door to terrace — Drummond watches her go.)

Drummond: She's very attractive. I do hope that Jeff plans to do the right thing.

James: Jeff always does the right thing.

Drummond *(moving down and sitting sofa right)*: Well, in view of the evidence, I'd say that's debatable.

James: None of us does the right thing all the time. The important thing is to do it in the end.

Drummond: I'd quote that in the article, but it might be misconstrued.

James: Do you have all the material you need for the article?

B98

Drummond: I think so — except that I find you too modest. No man wins all the acclaim — or earns as much recognition as you have, purely by luck.

James: No? Perhaps not!

Drummond: So what skulduggery did you indulge in?

James: Skulduggery?

Drummond: Sure. Who did you knife in the back, or step on, in your climb to prominence?

James: No one . . . not intentionally or that I know of . . . .

Drummond: Business has changed. It used to be that liars made the best salesmen. Now, the better you are at evading a decision, the higher you get pushed up the ladder of management.

James: Are you really so cynical? Or are you trying to draw me out?

Drummond: What do you think?

James: I don't know. That's why I asked you.

Drummond *(rises and crosses to sofa left — sits next to James)*: I've asked you four questions, and you've avoided answering all of them. You'll make an excellent president!

James: I hope when you put it in the article that you won't put it like that.

Drummond: What sort of a person do you think you are?

James: A fortunate one. I have people I love around me, good health, and a job I enjoy.

Drummond: If all of that were true . . . and there were no more to it, you'd make very dull copy . . . however, there's something you . . . overlooked.

James: Well, shoot! I've nothing to hide.

Drummond *(his trump card)*: Shelby Sherbrooke . . . *(He waves*

Lydia's Shelby Sherbrooke form triumphantly at James — who, of course, doesn't know what it is . . . . Pause) Shelby Sherbrooke!

James: Alright, I confess . . . I've read several Shelby Sherbrooke novels.

Drummond *(laughs)*: Oh! Very good.

James *(laughs without really knowing why)*: Thank you. I . . . I . . . will even confess to feeling a certain affinity . . . .

Drummond *(laughs again)*: Oh, I must write that down. *(He does so . . . laughing)* A certain affinity . . . .

James: Yes. But please don't make too much noise . . . er, Valerie has a . . . a headache.

Drummond: And you don't want your secretary coming in on this joke, huh?

James: Well, she's feeling a little tired . . . you know, it's been a long day . . . .

(Lydia enters dressed to kill. She is "man bait" personified!)

Lydia: Which of you gentlemen has been waiting for me? *(Both men turn and see her. They are speechless — pause for three beats)* What's the matter, haven't you ever seen a lady before?

(Both men leap to their feet.)

James: I . . . I . . . my! I thought you were tired.

Lydia: Tired? No! I'm ready to play.

Drummond *(moving up to Lydia)*: That's . . . that's quite a dress.

James: Yes . . . what there is of it.

Drummond: You must pay her a fortune, James. It really costs to dress like that.

James: It does? Why? . . . There's . . . there's very little dress.

B100

Lydia *(moving down centre)*: You don't pay by the square foot, James. It's not like broadloom or roofing.

James: Well. It shouldn't cost much. You can't do much in it. Hell, if you move, it'll fall down!

Drummond: Yes. Yes!

Lydia: Now whatever made you think thoughts like that, James? What will Mr. Drummond think?

Drummond: Yes. What'll I think?

James: Er . . . Valerie. Why not come slowly over here and sit down? Gently.

Lydia: I'm not the least bit fragile. Want to dance?

James: No! No . . . oh, no!

Lydia: Oh. Are you tired? Pity. I was going to ask you to go down to the cars, and check that all the windows are closed. *(To Drummond)* The dew makes the seats wet. *(To James)* Still, if you've run out of energy, perhaps Mr. Drummond wouldn't mind?

Drummond: It'll be a pleasure.

(Drummond is holding his book, together with Lydia's Shelby Sherbrooke form. Lydia sees the form, and reacts.)

Lydia: Or perhaps we needn't bother. Maybe they won't get too wet.

James *(limbering up)*: They do! It's surprising, but they get soaking wet. Anyway, I'd like the exercise.

Drummond: I'd come with you. But we can't leave Valerie all alone.

James: No. No. Talk to Valerie. She must be tired of talking to young people all day.

(James moves to front door as Drummond and Lydia exchange a look.)

Lydia: Well, James, I doubt whether Mr. Drummond is as old as you are.

B101

James: Huh . . . oh. I didn't mean you were old . . . just that . . . the youngsters are younger.

Drummond: Well, I think young, so don't rush back up the hill. *(He pockets book, form and pen.)*

James: Oh . . . well . . . er, Valerie . . . don't give too many business secrets away. *(Laughs.)*

Lydia: I don't think Mr. Drummond and I will even think about business. *(Laughs — sits sofa left.)*

Drummond: We won't. I promise. So put your mind at rest. *(Laughs — sits next to Lydia.)*

Lydia: I'll conduct myself like you would!

James: Don't do any such thing! *(Laughs)* I don't know what's got into you, Valerie . . . .

Lydia: Well, this dress cost a lot of money. I wouldn't want to waste it . . . . *(Laughs.)*

James: I . . . er . . . I'll try not to be long.

(James plunges out the front door.)

Lydia *(loudly — to Drummond)*: Come and sit closer.

(Drummond does so.)

Drummond: You're very . . . er . . . Valerie . . . er . . . have you had your vacation yet?

Lydia *(amused)*: Why don't we discuss the weather? That's always safe.

(James moves quietly into the doorway and silently waves his arm pointing to Lydia, then to the terrace. She sees him but ignores him.)

Drummond: You're right! Why is it that people can't say exactly what's on their minds . . . ? Instead of fencing around making polite conversation.

B103

Lydia: It's an art we lose when we stop being children. *(Suggestively)* Maybe . . . maybe we should revive it.

Drummond: I might shock you.

(James shakes his fist — Drummond takes Lydia's hand in his.)

Drummond: Valerie . . . I think you're very beautiful . . . .

Lydia: Thank you. Do you like my perfume?

Drummond: Oh yes . . . yes. I'm aware of everything about you. Everything around me.

(Lydia waves James away — unseen by Drummond. James quickly exits.)

Lydia *(in the mood)*: I know what you mean.

Drummond: Do you? I really think you do!

(He puts his hand on her knee — she lifts it off.)

Lydia: Oh, I understand perfectly.

Drummond: Valerie, why don't you leave James?

Lydia: Leave James . . . ? Why? What for?

Drummond: For me! I mean, of course, to work for me.

Lydia *(innocently)*: Is that all you want . . . a secretary?

Drummond *(puts his arm around Lydia's shoulders)*: Oh, Valerie, you'd make a won-der-ful . . . secretary.

Lydia *(primly)*: Now, I suppose, you'll try to kiss me.

Drummond *(a little taken aback)*: Er . . . what do you mean?

Lydia *(direct)*: Well, isn't that the usual routine?

Drummond: Oh, this isn't a routine. I mean it.

Lydia *(pout)*: You mean you don't want to kiss me.

Drummond: Certainly not . . . I mean, certainly . . . oh, Valerie, what are you trying to do to me?

Lydia *(suggestively)*: Well, nothing . . . it's like dancing . . . it's better when the man does the leading.

Drummond: You're very exciting . . . I love the way you walk, the way you stand, the way you sit . . . *(he pulls her back on the sofa — CUE 29 — lighting — the lights dim)* the way you . . . .

Lydia: What happened?

(Drummond is intent on kissing Lydia.)

Drummond: Nothing — nothing!

Lydia *(struggling)*: But the lights are dim.

Drummond: Who cares?

Lydia: Well, something's happened.

Drummond: It hasn't . . . yet!

Lydia: Yet?

(She sits up — he follows up.)

CUE 30 — lighting.

(Lights return to normal.)

Drummond: The lights are alright.

Lydia: Well, they dimmed . . . I'm sorry it . . . it distracted me. I thought someone had come in.

Drummond: I know I'm not much to look at, Valerie, but come with me. I travel a lot. We'd go to Paris, to Milan and to Naples.

Lydia: Oh, I'm sorry, Mr. Drummond, but I couldn't . . . I really couldn't.

B105

Drummond: James?

Lydia *(nods)*: Yes. He does need me. And he . . . he has priority.

Drummond: He doesn't! He has a wife . . . a business . . . he's organized. I'm all alone.

Lydia: Bachelors are never "all alone".

Drummond: Oh, I have friends *(thinks)* . . . a few friends. And I've known some women . . . but not like you, Valerie.

Lydia: But, Mr. Drummond . . . .

Drummond: Call me Norman.

Lydia: Norman sounds so studious.

Drummond: Then call me Enjay.

Lydia: Enjay?

Drummond: It's a nickname. My surname begins with 'J' but I don't like it so I just use Norman Drummond — have for years.

Lydia: What is your name?

Drummond: Promise you'll never tell anyone? *(Lydia nods)* Jelloe.

Lydia: Jello?

Drummond: With an 'E'. J-E-L-L-O-E. Norman Drummond Jelloe.

Lydia: Mr. Jelloe . . . Enjay! Well, what do you know?

Drummond: I know that you're beautiful. That you have charm and personality and . . . and a sort of sparkle that . . . well, it gives me a lift. I think with very little encouragement, I could fall in love with you.

Lydia: Well . . . thank you, Enjay . . . but it's no use. Tell me about yourself.

Drummond: It's no use?

B106

Lydia: No . . . no, I'm already committed.

Drummond: Of course. There's someone else. There has to be.

Lydia *(nods)*: But what about you?

Drummond: I was born when I was very young.

Lydia: Oh, please Enjay, be serious — just for a minute.

Drummond: All right then. I graduated in journalism. Worked on several newspapers. Knew several girls. I nearly married one of them, but then came my big break. An assignment in Europe for a single man. I took the job. I intended to come back to her . . . but . . . well . . . I've been busy.

Lydia: Oh, Enjay, I think that's wonderful. *(Leans back into corner of sofa.)*

Drummond: I'm not going to take no for an answer.

(Drummond leans over Lydia to kiss.)

CUE 31 — lighting

(The lights dim.)

Lydia: Look! Look! The lights! They're doing it again.

Drummond: So they are. *(He goes to kiss her.)*

Lydia: It might be a short circuit . . . I feel heat . . . .

Drummond: It's only me.

Lydia: No! There's a clicking!

Drummond: It's my heart thumping.

Lydia: You must be falling apart!

(Drummond sits up.)

CUE 32 — lighting

B107

(Lights return to normal.)

Drummond: Look. If it'll make you happy, I'll get a checkup on Monday — but right now . . . oh, Valerie, you're so desirable . . . . *(He pushes her down again.)*

CUE 33 — lighting

(Lights dim.)

Lydia: The lights! Ouch! There's something here.

Drummond *(getting carried away)*: Who cares?

Lydia: I do! *(She feels down by the cushions.)*

Drummond: It's a switch! A pressure switch. Every bachelor has one.

Lydia: Well, help me. Here, pull . . . . *(James staggers into the front doorway)* Pull this . . . ah . . . what a relief!

CUE 34 — lighting

(Lights up.)

Drummond: Got it! *(He is holding up a garter belt with nylons attached.)*

James: I closed the windows! *(There is a tableau while they exchange looks. James crosses down)* What the hell are you doing?

Lydia: Well, you can see what we're doing, James. We're testing the sofa.

Drummond: The switch! I thought I had it. I pulled . . . and look what I got! *(Holds up the garter belt.)*

James *(moving down to sofa)*: You'll get a damn sight more . . . .

Lydia: But, James, that isn't mine.

James: Oh, no? *(To Drummond)* I didn't know you wore one.

Drummond: Now, see here —— *(He dumps garter belt on coffee table.)*

B108

James: There are two of you rolling around on the sofa and you come up with . . . with that . . . now, let's guess who it belongs to.

Lydia: You know very well that I haven't worn one for years. *(Rises)* I'll show you what I have on, if you like.

Drummond *(rises — puts his arm around Lydia)*: That's right. Prove it to him!

James *(to Lydia)*: Don't you dare. *(To Drummond)* And take your hand off my wife.

Drummond: Your wife?

James: Yes. My wife!

Drummond *(to Lydia — indicating James)*: You're committed to him?

Lydia: Well, he likes to think so.

Drummond *(to James)*: I thought Lydia was your wife.

James: She is! That's what I'm telling you.

Drummond: I feel as though I've come in in the middle of a movie. *(He sinks to sofa and starts making notes.)*

James: Oh! I've had enough. *(Crosses up to doorway and calls)* Jeff, Susan, Valerie! *(Crossing down again)* We'll get this sorted out once and for all. *(To Lydia)* Straighten your dress and your hair. You look as if you've been wrestling.

Lydia: I was necking . . . for business . . . .

James: What?

Lydia: It was for you . . . for us. I tried not to enjoy it.

Drummond: Speak slower!

James: Where the hell's Jeff? *(Crosses up, opens door and shouts)* Jeff!

(Jeff is right there and shouts back.)

B109

Jeff: Yes!

James: Come in here! How do you expect to get to the top — you're never around.

Jeff: There's a difference between rising to the top and going up in the air . . . !

(James leads Jeff downstage as the two girls appear in doorway. He picks up garter belt.)

James: Who owns this?

Jeff *(taking garter belt and holding it to his waist)*: It doesn't seem to fit me. Is this a game?

James: It was in your sofa.

Lydia: Behind the cushion — the seat cushion.

Jeff: Well, that's what happens when you buy a second hand sofa. Good job you found it. It could be embarrassing. *(He stuffs the garter belt in James' jacket.)*

Valerie *(moving down right)*: Did it come complete with a wolf switch for dimming lights?

Jeff: I can explain all that. I'm a bachelor and I have to live up to a false image . . . . *(Valerie turns away)* Honest, Lydia . . . I . . . I love you.

(Valerie sits in chair, down right.)

Drummond *(to James)*: You don't mind that, eh?

(Susan moves to sofa right, and sits.)

James: Yes! I mind everything.

Drummond: Who does Susan belong to — and who does she love?

Lydia: She belongs to me. I refuse to be left out!

James: She loves Bob.

B110

Drummond: Bob?

Jeff: Er . . . her cat . . . you know Bobcat. *(Laughs.)*

James: Alright, Drummond. You want the truth . . . I'll give it to you. In a way, I ought to thank you because you've shown me what an ass I can be. It all started because I wanted to impress you. Impress you with a youth and vigour that I didn't possess . . . . *(Drummond is busy making notes — James crosses left to Lydia)* Let me introduce you properly . . . Lydia . . . . This is my wife, Lydia . . . I adore her. She's been the only woman in my life for twenty-five years, and in all that time, I've loved her every mood and every expression. She has so filled my heart that there's never been any room for anyone else in any way, shape or form. *(Crosses to Valerie)* And this is Valerie. She really is the mostess. She's the girl who will probably catch Jeff — if he has the rare good sense to move slowly enough to let her. *(Moving back up centre)* As for Jeff — well, you know about him! If I seem to pick on him it's because he has a unique talent . . . an ability to produce ideas that are novel and functional . . . he gets results and remains within budget. But he responds best when he's needled — so I'll go on needling him because his talent deserves every opportunity and encouragement . . . . Finally, let me introduce Susan. *(Moves to sofa right.)*

Drummond: But . . . if Jeff and . . . .

James: Shut up! This is Susan. She's my daughter. Our daughter . . . and soon she's going to make grandparents of us . . . .

Drummond: Ah, but you've overlooked . . . .

James: Shut up! Jeff invited Valerie here last night and through a mix-up in our plans, Valerie stayed the night here. So did I. As impossible as it may seem to you, neither of us knew the other was here until you arrived this morning. *(Moves left to Lydia)* Since then, my little deception has grown and mushroomed out of all proportion, until Lydia believes that I was unfaithful . . . .

Lydia: Oh, James . . . I'm so sorry . . . and so proud of you.

James *(to Lydia)*: Wherever did you get such an inferiority complex? How could you think that I could possibly function without you? Everything I've done is because of you!

B111

Drummond: This story is even better than I hoped for. It's got human interest with a punch.

Lydia: Do you intend to publish it?

Drummond: I certainly do. I couldn't possibly consider deceiving my readers. I take great pride in knowing that I've always published the full story.

(Everyone sits up straight, looking at Drummond — James crosses back up centre to Drummond's right.)

Valerie: I hope I get you on my flight sometime.

Lydia: Er — Valerie . . . how about getting us all another coffee?

Valerie: Oh, sure! *(Rises — moves to kitchen.)*

Jeff: Er — Val . . . I'd like to help!

Valerie: Oh. What do you have in mind? *(Pausing and looking back.)*

Jeff: I'll . . . I'll show you how it's served out of an airplane.

Valerie *(earnestly)*: Would you? I'd be so grateful . . . I really would be.

Jeff: Sure . . . sure I will.

Valerie: Come along, then. *(At door — to Susan)* Sue . . . . Come and chaperone . . . just in case Jeff gets sidetracked.

(Valerie exits — Susan rises.)

Jeff *(crossing to doorway)*: That girl is driving me crazy! *(To Susan)* You're not coming, are you?

Susan *(following)*: Sure. I want to warn her about the high cost of loving.

(Susan exits.)

Jeff: I'm through with sex — er, girls!

B112

(He thinks — then quickly exits, following the girls.)

Lydia: James, I could do with a brandy. It's still on the terrace.

James: All right. But first I'd like to tell you, Mr. Drummond . . . .

Lydia: James . . . tell him after!

James: Oh . . . all right! But no business . . . don't meddle!

(James exits front door.)

Lydia: Now, Enjay — you and I will have a quick little talk . . . .

Drummond: Yes . . . yes . . . anything you say!

Lydia: I'd like to ask you . . . as a favour . . . not to write anything about the mix-up that took place this weekend. Not to mention Valerie or Susan . . . .

Drummond: Oh, but I must . . . .

Lydia: And to make no mention of Shelby Sherbrooke . . . .

(She takes the Shelby Sherbrooke form from Drummond's notebook and proceeds to tear it up.)

Drummond: But that's my real scoop. My readers trust me to tell the truth . . . and I will . . . what are you doing? . . . How did you know? . . . You're . . . of course . . . you're Shelby Sherbrooke.

Lydia: You are, of course, at liberty to write a true factual account on your assessment of James . . . .

Drummond: But I must give the complete story of James . . . he's arrived! He's . . . .

Lydia: And you may certainly not say that. James is not the sort of person who arrives! Going, climbing, working, creating — that's James — that's living. Arriving is the end . . . .

Drummond: I'm sorry, Valerie . . . er, Lydia . . . I'd like to oblige, but my readers expect the truth — and the dirtier the truth, the better they like it.

B113

Lydia: On second thought, you'd better send me the draft for approval before you publish . . . .

Drummond: You just don't understand . . . you're in a squirting match with a skunk.

Lydia: Because if you don't, I'll say that that was my garter belt, and that you attacked me!

(Pause — Drummond looks at her, weighs her up.)

Drummond: You really would, wouldn't you?

Lydia: I'm afraid I would. James has worked too hard to lose it all through a misunderstanding . . . now, what do you say?

(Drummond puts his notes away.)

Drummond: I've been outskunked. I admire you. You're the secret behind James' success! Well, perhaps this way we can stay friends.

Lydia: I hope so. It was fun.

Drummond: I didn't even get a kiss. I'm the type who never gets the girl!

Lydia *(rises)*: Go and pack now. Leave us. On your way out, I'll give you the kiss. I'll be right here — and thank you . . . . Enjay.

Drummond *(rises)*: I shouldn't be so damned nice!

(He moves upstage as James enters.)

James: Drummond, I have just two things to say to you . . . .

Drummond: Oh!

James: First, don't you dare publish anything about today's events — or mention Valerie or Susan.

Drummond: Okay. I'll send you a draft for your approval.

James: If you do . . . I'll take counter action and I'll punch you . . . . What?

B114

Drummond: You can check the copy first . . . .

(Drummond exits through archway.)

Lydia: Oh, James. You were wonderful.

James *(moving down right, pleased with himself)*: Yes. I was. I should have been firm with him earlier . . . . *(Liz enters from doorway)* Just lay it on the line!

Liz: Hello. Have I missed anything?

.ydia: Oh, Liz! Your timing is perfect.

Liz *(moves down in front of sofa left)*: I'm so glad. Tell me what's been happening. *(Sees — and picks up garter belt)* My . . . it's true! Blondes really do have more fun!

Lydia: Er . . . there really isn't time, just now — here . . . come here. *(She guides her to sofa)* Now sit there . . . lean back into the corner.

Liz: What's all this for?

Lydia: A surprise . . . a real fun surprise . . . push back . . . harder . . . .

Liz: How can I push . . . . Oh!

CUE 35 — lighting

(Lights dim.)

Lydia: That's alright. Now just stay there . . . don't move . . . .

(Lydia takes James' hand and goes to front door, pulling door so they are concealed.)

James: What are you doing? What about the brandy?

Lydia: Shhhh! Drink it!

(Drummond comes on and puts bag down — crosses to sofa.)

Drummond: Hi . . . ? Are you there . . . ? *(He sits and moves in close)* Hello beautiful . . . . *(He kisses Liz — it's a long kiss.)*

B115

James: Lydia — poor Liz . . . I've told you not to meddle . . . .

Lydia: Oh, James. I've reunited two lovers. I feel so proud and happy for both of them.

(Lydia moves behind sofa left — between Drummond and Liz — as the kiss breaks.)

CUE 36 — lighting

Drummond: Whew! *(Lights up)* . . . But . . . but you're not . . . . Oh! I'm so sorry.

Liz: That's quite alright. I understand . . . .

Drummond: I do hope that you'll excuse . . . .

Liz: Of course . . . it could happen to anyone . . . .

Lydia *(looking from one to the other — very amused)*: Don't you recognize each other?

Drummond: Oh, we've never met. I would have remembered.

Liz: So would I . . . .

Lydia: But Mr. Drummond . . . Liz . . . Enjay . . . ? *(Full of doubt)* . . . Liz?

James *(moving down to Lydia's side)*: Lydia, when will you learn not to meddle?

(Lydia's hand is up to her mouth as she realizes what she's done. She looks at James as . . . .)

Drummond *(to Liz)*: How do you do?

Liz: Very well. *(She grabs Drummond)* Terrific!

(They go into a big clinch — Lydia looks back, pleased and triumphant — James looks skywards as the lights fade. CUE 37 — lighting. The curtain goes down. CUE 23 — sound.)

The end

B116

Props   Act one, scene one

(Preset)

Two used cups, saucers and plates stacked on end table

Coffee pot, cream jug and plate with sandwich remains on the tray on the desk

Pieces of dress pattern and cut pieces of dress material on the floor and sofa

Four typed sheets of paper on desk (for Liz)

Briefcase beside upstage chair (Liz)

Galley proofs in disarray on desk and on chair (down left)

Two ashtrays — one on end table, one on desk

Popular magazine (i.e. Cosmopolitan) on sofa (for Susan)

Cigarettes and matches on end table

Shopping bag on chair (down left)

Matching slipcover or 'throw' over sofa and chair (down left)

Tray on floor, leaning against telephone table

(Offstage)

Typed sheet (Lydia)

Several boxes and bags containing clothes bought from men's store (James)

Tray with four glasses — two gin and tonic, one scotch, one glass of milk (James)

Act one, scene two

(Strike)

Two side chairs

Shopping bag containing dress pattern and material

B118

Tray with coffee pot, cream jug and plate
Trays and drink glasses
Galley proofs
Briefcase
Wall backing on inset
Remove slipcovers from sofa and chair

(Set)
Sofa (from scene one) into position for sofa (right)
Telephone table and telephone into position for scene two

(Preset prior to Act one, scene one curtain)
Fishing rod and fish pail, behind front door
Two empty champagne glasses — one on the coffee table, one
on desk
Empty champagne bottle on drinks' table
Business papers and ashtray on desk
Bottle opener and ashtray on drinks' table
Cigarettes, ashtray and matches on mantlepiece
Record on phonograph
Selection of record beside, or in, phonograph
Ashtray with cigarettes butts on coffee table
Curtains are drawn, door is closed

(Offstage)
Full bottle of champagne with cork removed (Jeff)
Suitcase and raincoat (James)
Glass of water (James)

Act two
Do not strike anything, action is continuous.
(Set)
Valerie's shoes under or behind right cushion on sofa (left)
Blanket to cover James on sofa (right)

(Offstage)
Small travel bag (personal — Drummond)
Notebook and pencil (personal — Drummond)
Glass of Alka Seltzer (James)
Large cardboard carton containing several bottles of liquor (Jeff)
Fishing rod (Drummond)
Tray with eight glasses (Jeff)
Small suitcase (Lydia)

Act three, scene one
Curtains open, doors closed.
(Strike)
Valerie's shoes (under telephone table)
Five used glasses
Soft drink bottles
Liquor carton
Raincoat (James)
Coat (Susan)

(Set)
Cup of coffee for Liz (sofa left)
Cup of coffee on telephone table
Briefcase for Liz (sofa left)
Garter belt under cushion (sofa left)
Papers, two pink contracts, pen (in briefcase)
Check Records at phono — one Latin beat, one hard rock, plus others

(Offstage)
Coffee pot (Susan)
Large pad of paper (Drummond)

Act three, scene two
Curtains drawn, front door open
(Strike)
Coffee cups
Record jackets, close phonograph

(Set)
Nothing moved or changed.

(Offstage)
Tray with brandy and four glasses, two containing brandy (James)
Travel bag (Drummond)

Costumes **Act one, scene one**
Susan — partially made maternity top; cushion with ties; blouse
and pants
Liz — smart business dress
Lydia — a housedress that has seen better days
James — dark business suit, white shirt, striped tie

Act one, scene two
Valerie — a sensuous, slinky evening dress with no apparent buttons

B120

or zipper; half slip and bra; a long negligee; shoes with heels
Jeff — sports pants, shirt and sports jacket
James — as for scene one, plus raincoat

Act two

James — (from previous scene) shirt and underpants; (from previous scene) pants of business suit; light tan sport pants; light green T-shirt; canvas sports shoes
Valerie — (from previous scene) negligee; half slip and bra; sports dress with zipper down back plus appropriate shoes
Drummond — red sports pants, sports shirt, sports jacket; shorts, bright Hawaiian-type shirt, coloured socks, fishing hat with feather, sunglasses
Jeff — as previous scene, except change of shirt
Lydia — an ultra-feminine flowered dress with a matching wide-brimmed hat; modern brooch on dress
Susan — maternity dress, complete with cushion and ties; light summer coat

Act three, scene one

Lydia — attractive hostess or lounging pyjamas
Liz — smart dress or two-piece outfit
Jeff — change of sports pants and shirt
James — as previous scene, except for change from T-shirt to sports shirt
Drummond — as previous scene, adds ascot
Valerie — as previous scene
Susan — as previous scene

Act three, scene two

Lydia — as previous scene, changes to very sexy, revealing dress
James — sports pants, shirt, ascot, blazer
Valerie — slinky dress from Act one, scene two
Drummond — as previous scene, with ascot
Susan — as previous scene
Jeff — as previous scene
Liz — evening dress and wrap

Lighting The lighting set-up for the original production of A WIFE IN THE HAND at La Poudrière in Montreal was basically very simple. Front of house; on the ceiling bar, four 750-watt lekos and, at each side of the theatre, three 750-watt lekos.

On the first pipe: eight 500-watt fresnels and two 500-watt lekos. On the second pipe: six 500-watt fresnels and two 500-watt lekos. Necessary backing lights were added for doorways and windows.

Since the play is a farce, the aim is to produce a general overall bright, warm light.

Act one, scene one
The area simply requires a general bright, warm light. Apparent source of light is from a wall lamp over the sofa and a small lamp on the desk.
CUE 1 — Lydia and Liz: "Lookout! " Medium fast fade, with curtain

Act one, scene two
The apparent source of light comes from two suspended lamps in front of the window and one suspended lamp over the desk.
CUE 2 — with curtain: lights go up to a bright, warm, even light
CUE 3 — Jeff lies down on sofa: all lights go down to quarter light
CUE 4 — Jeff sits up on sofa: all lights return to original setting
CUE 5 — Valerie lies down on sofa: all lights go down to quarter light
CUE 6 — Valerie sits up on sofa: all light return to original setting
CUE 7 — Valerie lies down on sofa: "Wheee". All lights dim to quarter light
CUE 8 — Valerie leaps to her feet: lights return to normal
CUE 9 — Valerie lies down on sofa: lights dim to quarter light
CUE 10 — Jeff: "It's a modern convenience". He lifts Valerie to a sitting position: lights return to normal
CUE 11 — Jeff pushes Valerie flat on sofa: lights dim to quarter light
CUE 12 — Jeff hands Valerie a glass, she sits up: lights return to normal
CUE 13 — James: "How about a scotch? " Sits sofa: light dim to quarter light
CUE 14 — James: "What's the matter with the lights? " He sits up: lights return to normal
CUE 15 — James: "Oh, must be the power supply! " He leans back: lights dim to quarter light

B122

CUE 16 — James sits up: lights return to normal

CUE 17 — Jeff: "Goodnight". Light outside front door should now be deep blue

CUE 18 — Valerie staggers to sofa and lies down: lights dim to quarter light

CUE 19 — James switches off remaining source of light: reduce to very dim

CUE 20 — fade light with curtain

Act two

CUE 21 — at curtain, light comes up to 60 percent

CUE 22 — Valerie opens front door: bright light from door on Valerie

CUE 23 — Drummond closes door: CUE 22 off

CUE 24 — James draws curtains open: general lighting full up

CUE 25 — James: "Jeff, get us a round of doubles." Fast fade with curtain

Act three, scene one

CUE 26 — with curtain: lights come up to 85 percent

CUE 27 — Drummond: "Oh, no!" Moves to sofa right: medium fast fade with curtain

Act three, scene two

CUE 28 — with curtain: lights up to 75 percent. Outside front door is deep blue

CUE 29 — Drummond pulls Lydia back on sofa: lights dim to quarter light

CUE 30 — Lydia: "Yet?" She sits up: lights return to normal

CUE 31 — Drummond: "I'm not going to take no for an answer." He leans over Lydia: lights dim to quarter light

CUE 32 — Lydia: "You must be falling apart!" Drummond sits up: lights return to normal

CUE 33 — Drummond: ". . . you're so desirable." Lights dim to quarter light

CUE 34 — Lydia: ". . . Ah, what a relief." Lights return to normal

CUE 35 — Liz: "How can I push . . . Oh!" Lights dim to quarter light

CUE 36 — Drummond (after kiss) "Whew!" Lights return to normal

CUE 37 — medium fast fade with curtain

Sound effects The sound effects for the original production at La Poudrière in Montreal were operated by using two 40-watt tape recorders.

Tape recorder A had one speaker at front of house, behind the audience, and one speaker located outside the window (right) of the main set.

Tape recorder B had speakers located downstage, left and right, behind the set, and a non-directional microphone backstage for use by the cast for the "telephone calls".

Act one, scene one
(Tape recorder B, left speaker only)
CUE 1 — with curtain: sound of typewriter for eight seconds
CUE 2 — "Damn! Damn!" Sound of typewriter for five seconds
CUE 3 — Susan: "I always seem to be waiting." Typewriter starts again
CUE 4 — Susan: "Hell! I won't be able to see them." Typewriter stops
CUE 5 — Susan goes to telephone and dials, Lydia and Liz rush over to her. She holds earpiece so that they can all hear. On tape recorder A, from stage speaker, we hear four telephone rings, then dance music with a sensual beat. Valerie and Jeff speak their lines into microphone connected to tape recorder B, which feeds speakers downstage left and right
CUE 6 — Valerie (laughs): "Oh, I am honey, I am." Switch off music and voices
CUE 7 — James goes to telephone and dials. We hear three rings, then dance music with a latin beat (tape recorder A, stage speaker). Jeff speaks into microphone connected to tape recorder B feeding speakers downstage left and right
CUE 8 — James: "Sure . . . see you." He replaces the receiver. Music and microphone off
CUE 9 — with curtain: on tape recorder A — both speakers. Bring in music with a swinging, dancing, sensual beat to serve as a music bridge during strike on scene one inset. Set change should be accomplished in fifty seconds or less

Act one, scene two
CUE 10 — with curtain opening: switch off speaker behind audience
CUE 11 — Jeff crosses to phonograph and lowers volume: lower volume (music runs on)
CUE 12 — James picks up telephone and dials: Lydia speaks into

microphone connected to tape recorder B, feeding downstage speakers left and right

CUE 13 — James switches off the phonograph: stop music on tape recorder A

CUE 14 — start ten minutes of intermission music by switching on tape recorder A and both F.O.H. and backstage speakers

Act two

CUE 15 — fade music with curtain for Act two. Bring in twenty-five seconds of bird chatter on tape recorder B on both speakers

CUE 16 — James dials: woman (could be played by Liz) uses microphone connected to tape recorder B feeding both downstage speakers

CUE 17 — James: "Thank you, Lady Bountiful." Switch off microphone

CUE 18 — with curtain, start ten minutes of intermission music. Use tape recorder A, both speakers

Act three, scene one

CUE 19 — fade music with curtain opening. Switch off F.O.H. speaker

CUE 20 — Jeff puts a record with a swinging latin beat on the phonograph (visual cue — tape recorder A, stage speaker)

CUE 21 — Jeff: "Hey! I know." Jeff switches off the phonograph, replaces the record with a twist record. Cue on tape recorder B, both speakers

CUE 22 — at curtain: bring up volume. Let music serve as interscene thirty second bridge. Fade out with curtain for . . .

Act three, scene two

CUE 23 — on final curtain: replay CUE 20 on tape recorder A, stage speaker during curtain calls. After curtain calls, switch on F.O.H. speaker and let music run to play audience out

Music   The music suggested within the script was appropriate at the time the play was written. In approaching a production, the director is encouraged to select contemporary music which captures the style and spirit of the scene, in order to keep the play as up-to-date as possible.

Set design   The set for Act one, scene one is created by placing an inset in front of the main set construction — this represents the attic den of the Henderson home, which serves as Lydia's workroom. This is illustrated in the set design by the dotted lines.

The balance of the action takes place in Jeff's cottage, "Lookout", which is represented by the solid lines in the diagram opposite. (See photo below)

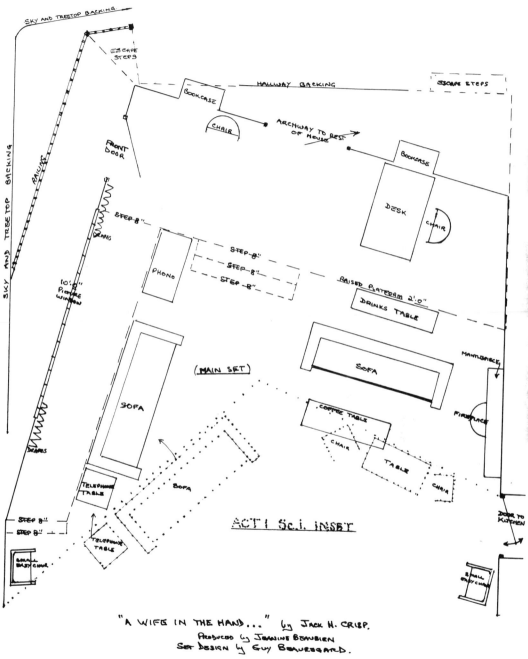

SKY AND TREETOP BACKING.

ESCAPE STEPS

HALLWAY BACKING

ESCAPE STEPS

BOOKCASE

CHAIR

ARCHWAY TO REST OF HOUSE

BOOKCASE

FRONT DOOR

RAILING

DESK

CHAIR

STEP 8"

SKY AND TREE TOP BACKING

DRAPES

STEP 8"

STEP 8"

STEP 8"

PHONO

RAISED PLATFORM 2'.0

10'.0" PICTURE WINDOW

DRINKS TABLE

(MAIN SET)

SOFA

MANTLEPIECE

SOFA

FIREPLACE

DRAPES

COFFEE TABLE

TELEPHONE TABLE

SOFA

CHAIR

TABLE

CHAIR

STEP 8"

DOOR TO KITCHEN

STEP 8"

TELEPHONE TABLE

SMALL EASY CHAIR

ACT I Sc.i. INSET

SMALL EASY CHAIR

"A WIFE IN THE HAND..." by JACK H. CRISP.
PRODUCED by JEANINE BEAUBIEN
SET DESIGN by GUY BEAUREGARD.

HOARSE MUSE

a musical play~
book & lyrics by
Paddy Campbell
music by
Wm. Skolnik

We would like to express our gratitude to The Canada Council and the Ontario Arts Council for their support.

Marian M. Wilson, Publisher

HOARSE MUSE

ISBN 0-88924-047-7
1 2 3 4 5/79 78 77 76
Simon & Pierre Publishing Company Limited, Order Department
P.O.Box 280 Adelaide Street Postal Station
Toronto, Ontario, Canada M5C 2J4

Onions Photography

Author **Paddy Campbell** was born in Lancashire, England in 1944 and grew up in Calgary, Alberta.

She began writing in 1967 after a few years of working as a professional actress, "appearing mostly in bad plays for bored kids, barely paying my dues". Perhaps as a result of this experience, her first plays were for young audiences. They include CHINOOK and TOO MANY KINGS. Some of these plays are still a part of the Canadian theatrical scene and are also produced in Great Britain and the United States.

To date, Miss Campbell has written over twenty plays for all ages. HOARSE MUSE was her first musical and her first collaboration.

After residing briefly in England and other parts of Canada, Miss Campbell has returned to Calgary. She has been married since 1967 and has a daughter, six years old. Although she teaches occasionally for the University of Calgary and still appears infrequently on stage and in television productions, her time is primarily filled with writing. Recently in collaboration with William Skolnik, Miss Campbell wrote UNDER THE ARCH which was a look at western Canadian history through the music hall. At present she is again collaborating with Mr. Skolnik on a new musical, with some gratefully acknowledged assistance from the Canada Council.

Composer **William Skolnik** was born in Montreal in 1950, and raised in Toronto. He studied Voice and Piano at the Royal Conservatory of Music, and Political Science at the University of Toronto, from which he graduated in 1972.

Turning to music as a career, his talents as composer, musical director and musician have brought him into contact with a wide range of theatres across Canada. His works have been performed at The Gryphon Theatre, Barrie, Ontario, Playhouse Holiday, Vancouver, B.C., Calgary's Alberta Theatre Projects, Festival Lennoxville and for a production by the Tarragon Theatre at Toronto's Poor Alex Theatre. In addition, Mr. Skolnik has provided the musical direction for several companies across Canada including the Manitoba Theatre Centre, the Vancouver Playhouse and Theatre London.

Credits Production photographs are by Martin Riehl and Steve Ramsey. Caricature of Bob Edwards courtesy of the Glenbow Museum, Calgary. Special thanks to the Glenbow Museum and Grant MacEwan.

C3

Original
cast

HOARSE MUSE

Mrs. Bucklewhackster, Jury, Salvation Army Major — Georgie Collins
Bertie, Juryman, Hotelman — David J. Dunbar
Paddy Nolan — Brian Gromoff
Peter McGonigle, Friend of Bennett, Frank, Beaverbrook — Stephen Hair
Bob Edwards — Robert Haley
Woman 1, Widowed Mother, Salvation Army Lady, Nurse — Jennifer
Higgin
Mother Fulham, Salvation Army Lady — Linda Kupecek
**Daniel McGillicuddy, Shorty, Gravedigger, A Best Person, Salvation
Army Man, Doctor** — Rafe Macpherson
R.B.Bennett, A Best Person, Judge, Hotelman, Lloyd George —
Alan Robertson
Newsboy, Gravedigger, Smith, Wendell — Glenn Roddie
Kate Edwards, McGonigle's Widow, Salvation Army Lady, Jury —
Leslie Saunders
Clergy, Friend of Bennett, Clerk, Charley, Montague — Alan
Stebbings

Original
production

The original production of HOARSE MUSE opened in 1974 at the
Canmore Opera House, Heritage Park, Calgary, Alberta, commissioned
by Alberta Theatre Projects.
Directed by Douglas Riske
Musical Director William Skolnik
Music Numbers Staged by Bryan Toews
Set & Lighting Designed by George Dexter
Costumes Designed by Jean Englebright

Play
background

*This play background was written by The Honourable Grant
MacEwan (a former Lieutenant-Governor of Alberta) who was the
author of the book "Eye Opener Bob" about Bob Edwards.*

After being voted Alberta's Prize Personality and called the "Mark
Twain" of the West, it is hardly necessary to explain why the memory
of Bob Edwards of Calgary Eye Opener fame should be perpetuated.
Born in Scotland, Bob tested the social climate in various parts of the
world and finally adopted the Alberta frontier and Calgary in particular where he found citizens unusually benevolent in assessing his
unsteady ways.

It was not that even Calgarians understood the man. He was the great
enigma of his time; a professed Conservative in politics, he was essen-
tially a reformer; as one who needled the churchmen, he practised an

admirable charity; he hounded the politicians and then went actively into politics; he did not hide his rather heavy drinking habits, but in the big test which came with the provincial plebiscite of 1915, Bob Edwards stood with the prohibitionists. How could fellow citizens understand such a man?

Arriving in Western Canada in 1894, Bob's first stop was at Wetaskiwin where he found the population to consist of "287 souls and three total abstainers". There he embarked upon the rough seas of journalism, deciding against calling his paper the "Wetaskiwin Bottling Works" because it was sure to be "a corker", and giving it the conventional name of Wetaskiwin Free Lance. After a relatively short stay at Wetaskiwin, the editor tried publishing at various points in the Northwest Territories and came to High River in 1902 where the Eye Opener had its birth in name. But two years later, the editor was moving again, this time to Calgary where the Eye Opener became the Calgary Eye Opener. There, city and editor seemed to accept each other and in spite of many jounalistic indiscretions, the paper's popularity soared until the Calgary Eye Opener had the highest circulation of newspapers published in the West. Subscribers received only one promise, that the paper would be published "semi-occasionally". The subscription price, the editor told his readers, "should be $10 but owing to slight irregularities and an occasional punk issue, we knock off nine".

Except for part of a year, Bob remained in Calgary until his death in 1922. They were exciting years for the city and the Edwards' role was important, furnishing bold criticism of public affairs and a superior brand of entertainment. Offending a few readers, amusing most and enlightening all who cared to be enlightened, his leadership and influence were far greater than most people realized.

⋑⋑⋑⋑⋑⋑⋑⋑⋑⋑⋑⋑⋑⋑⋑⋑⋑⋑⋑⋑⋑⋑⋑⋑

Alas! my roupet Muse is hearse!
Your Honours' hearts wi' grief 'twad pierce,
To see her sitting on her arse
       Low i' the dust,
And scriechin' out prosaic verse,
       An' like to brust!

from "The Author's Earnest Cry and Prayer" to the Scottish Representatives in the House of Commons.

                                        Robert Burns

Cast of characters

Bob Edwards — Creator, editor and only contributor to the Eye Opener, a semi-occasional western newspaper presenting "news" with a blend of fancy, fiction and satire. Edwards is Scottish, soft-spoken, wry and often drunk.

Paddy Nolan — A lawyer, Edwards' best friend, advisor and "Minister of Defence", and drinking pal. Eloquent, Irish, a noted wit, a fervent lawyer given to grandstanding theatrics in the courtroom.

R.B.Bennett — Solicitor for the C.P.R. Ambitious, on the way up (later became Prime Minister and a Viscount). A Methodist, an intellectual, somewhat righteous. A most unfrivolous man.

Daniel McGillicuddy — Edwards' nemesis, editor of another news-paper. A dour, morose, deadly and doom-saying sort, spiteful and self-righteous. He bears the distinction of being the only person who maligned Edwards to the point of a lawsuit for defamation of character.

Mother Fulham — A hefty Irishwoman of unfathomable age who raises and slaughters pigs for a living. She is crusty and unclean, her lifestyle, drinking habits and language always in questionable taste. She is often in trouble, both socially and legally. Edwards and Nolan, for obvious reasons, are her champions.

Rosie — A waitress and sometime proofreader for Edwards. Still young but weary around the edges from a rather bleak life. A practical girl with a clear-eyed approach to life, but one who harbours a secret romanticism and delight in fantasy.

The next four are all fantasy characters who spring from the mind of Bob Edwards. They should all enter from the same place in the same manner. They should have a strong visual costume link that immediately sets them apart from the "real" characters, yet ties them to each other (see costume notes). Their style and delivery is larger than life.

Albert Buzzard-Cholomondeley — pronounced "Chumley". Born and bred in the mischievous mind of Bob Edwards. A remittance man, super English, super phoney, with a core of vulnerability that is Edwards' own, and a gaucheness that makes him endearing. Gullible, exasperating, basically likeable.

Peter McGonigle — Also a creation of Edwards'. A thoroughly dis-reputable and dissolute character. Editor of the Midnapore Gazette and one-time horse thief. A drunken, lurching, leching ruffian always in trouble. His devil-be-damned attitude to life is the envy of many.

Mrs. Bucklewhackster — One of Edwards' most ludicrous creations. She is a composite of the things Edwards most despises. She is rich, phoney, desperately cultured, and mixes only with the "very best people". She is given to throwing elaborate parties that display the overwhelming combination of money and bad taste.

Thomas the Hangman — Edwards' most macabre creation, a mystery man whose face is never seen, whose voice is never heard by anyone other than Edwards. He represents Edwards' dark and horrific fantasies of booze, self-destruction and death. He is very adept at rope tricks.

The following are other characters within the play who comprise the singing and dancing chorus.

The Major — Salvation Army, militant, zealous, dedicated to the cause of prohibition

Wendell — her straight man

Kate Edwards — an afterthought in Edwards' life (his wife)

Shorty — a volatile rancher

A clergyman

A judge — who becomes a fantasy character

A court clerk

A plaintiff

A widowed mother — fantasy character

McGonigle's widow — a fantasy character

Assorted Mounties

Frank — hotelman

Charlie — hotelman

A jury foreman

A gravedigger — fantasy character

A nurse

Four musicians

Party woman

Four musicians

Party people, Salvation Army, jurors

Orchestration   Piano, cello, four-string banjo, drums
Note: A mandolin attachment to give the piano a honky-tonk quality is available through Q.R.S. Music Rolls, Inc., Buffalo, N.Y.

General setting   The play is set in Calgary, Alberta, at a funeral parlour. Within the action of the play, the funeral parlour becomes a bar at the Alberta Hotel, a newspaper office, a society soirée, a jail cell, a courtroom, and a hospital. A play in two acts.

Time   Between 1900 and 1922.

Note   *The following text is a revised version of HOARSE MUSE, developed in 1975 with the help of The Canada Council, and produced by Alberta Theatre Projects.*

C7

"Some people spoil a good story by sticking to the facts."

Robert Chambers Edwards, Calgary, 1864 - 1922
Sketch by R. Randolph Bruce, c. 1904, of Bob Edwards (the founder and editor of the Eye Opener), courtesy of Mrs. G.W.Bureau, Calgary.

Act one   *The entire play takes place at the funeral of Bob Edwards, beginning as the coffin enters flanked by a cortege of Mounties. The events did and did not happen. To the mourners gathered at his funeral, Bob Edwards was many different men: saint, sinner, champion of the common folk, tiresome bleeding heart, a brilliant satirist, a yellow journalist, moral watchdog, moral deficient . . . .*

From his writings, humour emerges as a vehicle for crusade and cause, for delight and doomsaying. He despised phoniness, the misuse of wealth, dishonesty, and yet perhaps because of his own weaknesses he had a large degree of compassion for human failing. His own private hell was a strong predilection for whisky and a continuing obsession with death and its more macabre forms. These terrors hang like a noose over the events in the play.

Inside the funeral parlour, we visit the Alberta Hotel, a society soirée, a jail cell, a courtroom and a hospital, but we never leave the funeral and the coffin is always the most imposing piece of furniture.

The first scene is the dimly lit funeral parlour. Unlit candles are on the piano. From the lectern hangs a silken scroll stating, "Forgive your Enemies; if you have no Enemies, forgive a few of your Friends". On one side of the stage is a set of pews. This is for the "real" characters. On the other side is a raised platform. This is where the fantasy characters assemble. A dias in the centre is draped with a banner reading, "A Thing of Boozey is a Joy Forever". The members of the company enter in silence and take their places. The clergyman enters last and lights the candles. There is an air of expectancy, broken finally by a stage whisper.

On stage on the "real" side are Paddy Nolan, R. B. Bennett, Daniel McGillicuddy, Mother Fulham, Rosie, Kate Edwards. On the other side are Bertie, Mrs. Bucklewhackster and McGonigle.

Bennett *(breaking the silence)*: Well, now, where do you suppose they are?

Nolan: Perhaps they stopped off for a wee drop.

McGillicuddy: Running true to form — damned degenerate.

Mother Fulham: Careful, Daniel, yer horns are showing — an' in this Christian place.

C9

Mrs. Bucklewhackster: Trust that man to be late for his own funeral. Such bad taste.

Bertie: Tut-tut, now, now — mustn't speak ill of the dead. After all, we owe him a great deal.

McGonigle: Speak for yerself. If it wasn't for him, I'd be alive today,

Bertie: Really, McGonigle, you will go on about that, won't you? You have no sense of occasion. None at all.

McGonigle *(to Mrs. Bucklewhackster)*: Care for a little snort while we're waiting?

Mrs. Bucklewhackster: My God.

(A funeral drum roll — the procession arrives.)

Mother Fulham: Stop yer blathering. They're here.

(The coffin enters carried by four Mounties in full dress uniform. The coffin is plain and unadorned, its only outstanding feature being a roll top like an old-fashioned desk. The coffin is placed on the centre dias, the roll-top being downstage.)

Clergyman *(with obvious relief and haste)*: Hymn number one! "Lord, let me keep a straight face."

(All rise and open hymn books. Bertie steps forward into a spotlight and sings.)

Bertie: Lord, let me keep a straight face
in the presence of solemn asses.

Let me not truckle to the high
or bulldoze to the low.

Let me frolic with the jack and the joker
and win the game.

Lead me unto truth and beauty
and tell me her name.

Keep me sane but not too sane.

Let me condemn no man for his grammar
and no woman for her morals,

neither being responsible for either.

Preserve my sense of humour
and values and proportions.

Let me be healthy while I live,
but not live too long.

Which is about all for today, Lord.

Amen.

Clergyman: He whose memory we hallow today was one of the most widely known men in the Dominion of Canada.

McGillicuddy: The great man of today in Canada is made up of one part achievement and nine parts printer's ink!

Clergyman: I doubt if there is anyone in Canada who had more intimate friends.

Mrs. Bucklewhackster: It is well that there is no one without fault, for he would not have a friend in the world!

Clergyman: Or whose loss will have a greater impact on his family.

Rosie: Never judge a man by the opinion his wife has of him. Be fair.

Clergyman: His pen was powerful in defence of those who suffered injustice.

Mother Fulham: Meanwhile, the meek are a long time inheriting the earth.

Clergyman: On many an occasion he had the opportunity of rich reward, if only he would swerve from what he believed.

Bertie: The way of the transgressor is very popular.

Clergyman: But he was always true to his principles.

Bennett: Graft is still graft — even when they call it commission!

Clergyman: Our friend turned his satire on snobbery and tried to make it vanish. His sense of humour helped to banish many a foolish custom, and helped people to gain a correct perspective.

Nolan: People always laugh at the fool things you do, until they discover you're making money out of them!

Clergyman: And although he fought many a private battle within himself . . . .

McGonigle: When a man is driven to drink, he usually has to walk back!

Clergyman: They only served to strengthen his wisdom, his character, and his humility.

Mother Fulham: The water wagon is certainly a more dangerous vehicle than the automobile — at least more people fall off it!

Clergyman: As Robert Chambers Edwards himself observed . . . .

Chorus: While some of us have more ups and downs than others, we'll all be on the dead level sooner or later — like brothers.

(There is a sound. The lights change and a spotlight appears on the coffin. The roll top opens revealing Bob Edwards reclining comfortably. There is enthusiastic applause from the assembled company which rouses him. He climbs out of the coffin and looks around with surprised pleasure.)

Edwards: You're having a funeral, are you? Isn't that fine. I hope it's jolly. *(The piano plays a brief introduction to "Hucksters and Fools")* An orchestra! Must be one of the classy ones.

Nolan: Only the best, Bob.

Edwards: Whose is that whisky voice? Hello, Paddy, my lad. Are you the featured speaker? I hope I'm in time. Mother Fulham! Are you responsible for the decor? I should have known. You always give the best wakes. *(Mrs. Bucklewhackster makes an offended sound at this. Edwards turns and notices her, Bertie, and McGonigle)* Not you lot, too! Hello, McGonigle, you old scoundrel. You're looking

C12

very spruce. I'm flattered. Don't tell me that's McGillicuddy slouching around back there. The Devil gave you time off for bad behavior, did he, Daniel?

Nolan: Bob, we're waiting.

Edwards: Waiting? Now, Paddy, you know the things that come to the man who waits are seldom the things he's waited for. *(Piano plays the introduction again)* That sounds like an introduction.

Nolan: It is, Bob. Go on. It's expected, you know.

Edwards: Don't be a damned fool, Paddy. That Irish whisky's got you pixilated.

Nolan: Just a few words.

Rosie: Keep it simple, Bob.

Edwards: Good old Rosie. Something simple, eh? Well, let's hear that twiddly bit again, lad. *(The introduction is played again and Edwards sings)*

> Hucksters and fools — fair game!
> Ill-gotten fortunes and fame
> A little satire
> Crumbles the empire
> Words have the power to tame.
>
> Though I express some chagrin
> Over a leader's cheap win
> No need for outrage
> Right on the front page
> Cash in the wages of sin.
>
> High class ladies — in society
> Dreary teas and chats
> Comical in desperate propriety
> Feather brains 'neath feathered hats.
>
> Doctors who exploit authority
> Prey on ignorance and fears
> Charlatans who salt away their gain
> In the brine of others' tears.

C13

Libel! Slander! Charges laid
Stop Bob Edwards' lone crusade!

Politicians only pretend to care
Untouched by trials and strife
Empty promises written on the air
Pledging to voters — the good life!

Judges, clergymen — all the pious folk
Righteous and grand
Gain perspective with a little joke
Eye Opener does the sleight-of-hand!

My paper's never humdrum
Too near the knuckle for some
All of the local
Critics are vocal
Your view is always welcome.

Let me frolic with the jack and the joker
And win the game.
Lead me unto truth and to beauty
And tell me her name.

Trust God, it's well that you remember when
you serve,
He will bestow on us the fruits we deserve.
Life has a fine reward — it's only what you
make —
Treat others fairly and you'll get a fair
shake!

Chorus *(repeat)*:
Hucksters and fools — fair game!
Ill-gotten fortunes and fame
A little satire
Crumbles the empire
Words have the power to tame.

Nolan: Well, Bob. How do you like it so far?

Edwards: You know me, Paddy. I always enjoy a good funeral. The
opportunity for a little informal drunk.

C14

Nolan: You must be a bit dry. Come along to the hotel. It's almost lunch time, anyway.

Rosie: Lunch time! My God, I'm late for work!

(There is a musical bridge which clears the stage.)

Edwards: How are they treating you over there, Rosie?

Rosie *(exiting)*: Come on over and find out!

(Edwards moves over to the desk/coffin and takes out an Eye Opener.)

Nolan: Well, what about it, Bob? Are you coming to lunch?

Edwards: Oh, I don't know, Paddy. The old hotel just isn't the same anymore. There's been a distinct deterioration in the class of clientele.

Nolan: What do you mean?

Edwards: I should think with your keen nose for the odour of mendacity you would have noticed it.

Nolan: You mean McGillicuddy.

Edwards: Among others. What's McGillicuddy doing here, Paddy? We don't need another newspaper, especially one espousing more Clifford Sifton liberal doggerel.

Nolan: You know, Bob, rumour has it that Sifton is privately backing the Daily News because he's tired of your insults.

Edwards: You flatter me. And the old rag.

Nolan: Don't pass it off so lightly, Bob. You've made an enemy of McGillicuddy, and a newspaper is a powerful forum.

Edwards: Don't worry, Paddy. McGillicuddy is so busy reforming Calgary I doubt if he even notices my bit of fun. Listen, you go on without me. I packed a lunch today. *(Pulls a flask out of the desk.)*

Nolan: Some of Rosie's hash would do you good.

Edwards: Oh, that C. P. R. hotshot will be there, too. He curdles

C15

the gravy with one sour look.

Nolan: Poor Bennett! You can hardly blame him. You've been printing those pictures of C. P. R. wrecks for weeks.

Edwards: I'd be neglecting my duty if I didn't. It's about time they worried less about profit and more about the safety of the people who ride the damn things.

Nolan: Now, Bob, be fair. Isn't the real reason you're needling Bennett the fact that he won't allow your paper to be sold on the trains?

Edwards *(handing him an Eye Opener)*: Here, Paddy, have a look at today's newspaper. This'll get Bennett for sure.

Nolan *(reading)*: "Another C. P. R. wreck". Bob! This is a picture of Bennett!

Edwards: That should raise his Methodist ire, don't you think? Tell me, Paddy, am I libellous yet?

Nolan: Pretty close.

Edwards: Maybe I will come to lunch, after all.

Nolan: You mean maybe they'll have crow on the menu?

Edwards *(as they exit)*: You know, Paddy, I've just been thinking, if Moses had been a Methodist, we'd probably have a hundred "Thou Shalt Nots" instead of only ten!

(As they exit, part of the parlour becomes the Alberta Hotel. Bar-type music in the background, which continues through the opening of the scene. There are two tables. One is vacant. At the other table are Bennett, McGillicuddy, and Frank, the hotelman. Rosie is wiping the bar — coffin.)

McGillicuddy: I would think, Mr. Bennett, that as one of Calgary's leading citizens, you would be outraged by this ridicule. Have you seen this picture?

Bennett *(not really liking McGillicuddy but conceding his point)*: Yes, Mr. McGillicuddy, I have seen today's Eye Opener, although I

C17

must say it is not my habit to indulge in this scurrilous publication. However, concerned colleagues have brought the article in question to my attention.

(Rosie has been setting drinks on their table — Bennett has a glass of milk. At this point, she leans over McGillicuddy's shoulder and sees the photograph. She bursts out laughing as she leaves them. McGillicuddy stares after her with disgust.)

McGillicuddy: Where I come from, respectable young women do not work in . . . .

Bennett *(hastily cutting him off)*: Rest assured, gentlemen, that the C. P. R. will deal with this severely. We have already struck a counter-blow, so to speak. The ultimate penalty has been imposed on this person who dares to call himself a newspaperman.

(Edwards and Nolan have appeared in the entrance and overhear this speech with amusement.)

Edwards: It is not strictly true that Bennett invented oratory, but doubtless he would have done so had he been there at the time.

Bennett: We have revoked his C. P. R. pass!

(Edwards and Nolan cross to the empty table.)

Nolan: Did you hear that, Bob?

Edwards: What do I need with a pass? Give it to McGillicuddy. He needs an extra one for the hand that's always up his sleeve. I hear you're conducting a survey on the wages of sin, Daniel. Are they keeping up with the cost of living?

McGillicuddy: I warn you, Edwards . . . .

Edwards: Have you inventoried the C. P. R.? They're experts on the subject.

Bennett: Mr. Edwards, this is outrageous! The C. P. R. is a public service, and we have never tried to hide the truth.

Edwards: The truth can be awkward.

C18

Nolan: Patch things up, Bob. Before it goes too far.

Edwards: It already has.

Nolan: Bennett has his pride, too. Give him a way out.

Edwards: He has a way out. Clean up his act.

Bennett: The C. P. R. is the fulfillment of a national dream!

Edwards: It's a national nightmare.

Bennett: All reasonable precautions have been taken.

Edwards: To ensure major profit and minor safety.

Nolan: Perhaps you could put it more diplomatically . . . .

Edwards: Those crossings are a menace!

Bennett: You have yet to prove one substantial case of neglect on the part of the C. P. R.!

(There is an off stage bellow of "Paddy! Where's my lawyer?" Mother Fulham charges on stage.)

Nolan: It's Mother Fulham with blood in her eye.

Bennett: Who is this person?

Nolan: What is it, Mother?

Mother: It's that bleeding train again! Oooh, if I could just get me hands on that wicked trainman!

Bennett: What seems to be the problem, uh, Madam?

Mother *(realizing who he is and losing total control)*: It's my cow! You've run over my cow! My best cow, Nellie, who gave six quarts on an off day, bless her dear departed soul. And you blackguards dare to deny any responsibility!

Edwards: What do you say to that, Mr. Bennett?

C19

Bennett *(ignoring him)*: Most unfortunate but, as a lawyer, I'm sure you will understand, Mr. Nolan, that legally all the C. P. R. is required to do is post a warning: Danger, Stop, Do Not Enter. You will please take note that the C. P. R. has fulfilled its duty in this respect. All the signs have been duly posted. It is most unfortunate that the cow in question appears to have ignored . . . .

Mother: You blathering idiot! Do you think my cow can read?

(There is general laughter.)

Edwards: It's true that most of our tragedies look like comedies to the neighbours.

(Mother Fulham cries bitterly.)

Bennett *(uncomfortably)*: Most distressing . . . an isolated incident, I'm sure. I mean, one cow . . . .

(Shorty rushes in calling for Mr. Nolan.)

Shorty: Mr. Nolan! Mr. Nolan, you've got to do something! It's that damn train again!

Nolan: You surely can't be meaning the Canadian Pacific Railway? Our national dream?

Shorty: Dream be damned! It's a national disgrace! Strewing death and destruction. The damn thing's just run over and killed twenty-one of my best horses. Twenty-one!

Nolan: Well, now, Shorty, what do you want me to do about it?

Shorty: You're a lawyer, ain't ya? I want to sue! I want double value for every one of them horses!

Nolan: I'm sorry, Shorty. I'd like to help, but it is a little awkward.

Shorty: What do you mean?

Nolan: I'm afraid I can't take your case.

Shorty: Why not? Ain't my money as good as anyone else's?

C20

Nolan: No, no, Shorty. It's got nothing to do with money. You see, my friend, in a way, the railroad is right. *(Bennett beams with vindication — Paddy cuts in firmly)* Any horse that can't outrun the C. P. R. deserves to die!

Edwards: Well, Mr. Bennett? Do you have your proof?

Bennett: While it appears on the surface that these two unrelated instances may, in fact, have some tenuous connection . . . .

Edwards: Or do you have to lose another election before you come to your senses?

Bennett: Mr. Edwards, are you suggesting . . . ?

Edwards: The Eye Opener cannot support a dishonest man, even if he is a Conservative!

Nolan: Remember, sir, not all of Bob's readers travel by C. P. R.

Bennett: Gentlemen . . . .

Edwards: Twenty-nine votes kept you out of the Legislature last time, Bennett.

Nolan: That's a pretty pill to swallow, eh?

Mother: Perhaps those voters was influenced — by all them wrecks!

(Musical introduction under Bennett's next lines into the song.)

Bennett: Gentlemen, it's all so simple really. Let me make my position quite clear.
        The C. P. R. wants to be your friend,
        And bring misunderstanding to a
        satisfactory end.
        My venture into politics is something
        quite apart —
        The image of the C. P. R. lies closest
        to my heart.
        Now the C. P. R. is a humane institution . . . .

Shorty: I demand full restitution!

C21

Bennett: Of course, of course, double cash on
every horse!
I must say this bickering fills me
with remorse.
For gentlemen, the C. P. R.'s an awe-
inspiring force!
It spans the land with an iron trail —
a unifying course!
A link to stretch from sea to sea
So Canada can be a family.
Now east and west will soon be brothers!

Edwards: Only those who can pay the fare — to hell with all the
others!

(Dance bridge.)

Bennett: Mr. Edwards, if, just if, I vowed to
do my best
To make those crossings safe for every
creature in the west,
Would you consider laying this absurd
campaign to rest?

Nolan: A judicious sense of timing is vastly underrated. Gentlemen,
a toast! To quarrels settled now!

Mother: I'd be happy with a cow!

Edwards: I'll drink to Richard Bennett, a fellow of the bar!

Mother: To love!

Shorty: And honour! And satisfaction guaranteed!

Nolan: To truth and justice — for even clever cows don't read!

Bennett: To charity and unity, and pray the
profits pick up speed.

All *(toasting)*: And the C! P! R!

*(There is handshaking all round and general bonhomie. Mother Fulham
and Shorty exit together. Frank disappears behind the bar.)*

Bennett *(expansively)*: Come, Mr. Nolan, I'll walk you over to the courthouse.

Nolan: Lovely. I'll drop by later, Bob. *(He and Bennett exit together)* Richard, did I ever tell you about the time that Mother Fulham went to the Orangemen's Ball . . . .

Bennett: No!

Nolan: Dressed in paddy-green, she was, from head to foot . . . .

(McGillicuddy and Edwards are left on opposite sides of the stage. Rosie is busy behind the bar.)

McGillicuddy: Very neat, Mr. Edwards. Very clever.

Edwards *(giving a mock bow)*: Did we tickle your fancy, Daniel? Perhaps that's a little strong. From a brief perusal of your newspaper, I suspect you haven't a fancy. A lot of fie and fight — but no fancy.

McGillicuddy: You're not the only one who can use words, Mr. Edwards, and twist them to suit your own purposes.

Edwards: And just what is your purpose, Daniel?

McGillicuddy: Others are not so gullible. Others see you and your filthy rag for what they really are. Tripe! Drivel. Trecherous and malicious scandal. Instead of trying to strengthen the moral fibre of this community, you indulge its weaknesses and encourage it to laugh at its vices. You stick your nose into business better left to qualified men.

Edwards: Like Clifford Sifton? Or perhaps we're talking about a higher authority?

McGillicuddy: Mark my words, Edwards. You have been warned, and judgment is upon you! *(Rises.)*

Edwards: Surely you're not leaving so soon? You know, Daniel, I really don't think our purposes are so different, just our methods . . . .

McGillicuddy: My purpose is to see you and the Eye Opener out of business. Good day, Mr. Edwards. *(He exits.)*

Edwards: Rosie, may I have another drink, please?

(Rosie brings over a drink and sets it down.)

Rosie: I don't think you should pass it off so lightly, Bob. He means you harm.

Edwards: Nonsense. He's a fanatic. Those kind of people are basically harmless, except to themselves. He'd never get any kind of support for that tirade.

Rosie: He has support. *(There is a pause)* Bob, not everyone looks at life the way you do.

Edwards: God forbid. That would be tedious. I'd have no fun at all.

Rosie: But I don't think you realize how strongly some people react to what you write. It's not just McGillicuddy . . . .

Edwards: Rosie, you're to stop worrying about me. From the looks of you, you have enough to worry about right now. Be a good girl and fetch me another drink.

Rosie: Aren't you putting out a paper tonight?

Edwards: You have no subtlety at all.

Rosie: That's what Rupert says.

Edwards: What do you hear from Rupert? I hear he went back to England.

Rosie: Well, you knew the ranch fell through. He went back to talk his Papa out of some more money. I expect he'll be back any day now — they'll be so glad to get rid of him again, I bet they'd hock the family jewels to send him back to Canada.

Edwards: Poor Rupert. What does he want to do this time?

Rosie: You won't believe it. He wants to open an English gentlemen's riding shop. I reminded him that there are all of half a dozen English gentlemen in Calgary, and they are poor as church mice. He says I am setting obstacles in his way — that it's a wife's duty to support her husband — no matter what madness he tries.

C24

Edwards: And do you believe that, Rosie?

Rosie: I married him, didn't I?

Edwards: Forgive me for prying, but you're a sensible girl, Rosie. Why did you marry him?

Rosie: I guess at my age . . . .

Edwards: You're just a girl.

Rosie: I'm not a girl, Bob Edwards! And in a frontier town, well, I guess I figured that charming manners and a cute accent were enough to base a marriage on!

Edwards: You're not being very kind to yourself — or to Rupert.

Rosie: I guess that does sound awful. He really is sweet and nice — if only he weren't so . . . .

Edwards: Helpless?

Rosie: And English!

Edwards: Let's have another drink. You look as if you could use one, too. Better still, come back to the office with me. I have something for you to proofread for me.

Rosie: At the rate you're going, I won't even be able to read . . . .

Edwards: Humour me. Besides, I seem to have temporarily forgotten where I live.

(They get up to leave.)

Rosie: All right.

Edwards: If we hurry, we'll have time for a nightcap. *(He pulls out a pencil and pad, and starts to write as they walk into the office)* I've had this cooking in my brain for a long time. *(He goes over to the desk/coffin)* Would you mind doing the honours, my dear?

(Rosie reads over his shoulder while he writes.)

C25

Rosie: "A little learning is a dangerous thing, but a lot of ignorance is just as bad."

Edwards: With a certain class of high-bred Englishmen, there is only the twinkle of a star between the glory of a well-wined mess . . . and a shack on a western "raunch"!

(During this speech, Bertie has risen from the trapdoor into a spotlight. By designating a trapdoor for the entrances of the fantasy characters, the author merely wishes to emphasize that these characters do not "enter", conventionally speaking, they "appear". For theatres which are not equipped with traps, these characters may use any entrance to the set which is not used by other characters, accompanied by a dramatic lighting change. They should not, however, enter from the house, as they dwell in the mind of Bob Edwards.)

(There is a general lighting change indicating a fantasy sequence. Bertie is dressed like any Englishman of impeccable taste and limitless fortune in the early 1900's, but entirely in white. All his accessories are the same colour. The general impression is one of ghostly silliness. He carries an umbrella.)

Bertie: "Raunching!" Has rather a thrilling ring to it, don't you think? Well, my dear chaps, it's really quite simple. I mean, there comes a time in every man's life when he must take stock. He must say to himself, "What does it all mean?" There must be more to life than fox hunting and dreary teas at the palace. There's always one's family, of course. They keep expecting one to do something!

Rosie *(laughing)*: Bob, you are wicked. Who is this fellow?

Bertie: I thought you'd never ask! *(He sings in broad music hall style)*
    Now, Mater and Pater are strictly upper
    crust.
    They said, "Albert, my boy, a trip abroad
    is a must.
    Though you are quite useless and lazy as
    can be,
    Perhaps you'll find your niche in life
    out in the colony."

    I'd like to be a rancher, it has a splendid
    ring!
    I know that you need ropes and cows and

all that sort of thing.
With good old British know-how, and what
my Mum calls pluck,
I'll drain my Pater's fortune in a year
with any luck.

Chorus   I'm Albert Buzzard-Cholomondeley *(pronounced "Chumly")*
from Skookingham Hall,
Kicked out of the palace and late of Pall
Mall.
The tenderest shoot on the old family
tree,
My blood's as blue as any royal progeny.

So when you see me coming remember who
I am.
I'm a new breed in the wooly west — a
real remittance man!
I may be green and gullible and shameless
to the core,
For when the cash has all run out, I'll
just write home for more. *(End of chorus)*

Despite some minor flaws, I'm a most
likeable chap,
And though I'll never put the Cholomondely
ranch upon the map,
My Pater's cash will buy us many drinks
to his health,
And you're all invited to the bar to
share Britannia's wealth!

I have a little weakness that's passed
on by my kin,
A strong aversion to hard work, but
surely that's no sin.
The secret of success to which the
Empire testifies:
Make others do the work for you, and be
considered wise!

Repeat
Chorus   I'm Albert Buzzard-Cholomondeley
from Skookingham Hall,
Kicked out of the palace and late of Pall Mall.

C27

The tenderest shoot on the old family
tree,
My blood's as blue as any royal progeny . . . *(continue)*
*(Chorus continues until "just write home for more". Bertie gives an
elaborate bow to the audience, Edwards and Rosie. He expansively
brings out his wallet. It is empty. He makes a great show of embarrassment and turns to Edwards)* I say, old chap, I seem to be temporarily
out of funds. Most embarrassing. Do you think you could . . . ?

Edwards *(handing him a flask)*: Here you are, Bertie, my boy!

Bertie *(drinking)*: Most kind. I'm expecting a cheque any day now.
Well, as they say on the frontier, here's mud in your eyes!

*(He salutes them both and exits drinking. Edwards is quite drunk by
now.)*

Rosie *(amused, but a little sad)*: Poor Bertie.

Edwards: He'll be all right, you'll see. Don't you worry, Rosie.

Rosie: Rupert doesn't drink, you know.

Edwards: Bertie does.

Rosie: Why is it, Bob, that you give all your characters . . . .

Edwards: A booze problem? I don't know, Rosie. It gives us a certain
. . . kinship. Keeps us all on the same squalid level.

Rosie: That's not true.

Edwards: It's a kind of test, you see. After a man has passed through
his baptism of booze, so to speak, he is either ready for big business
or the discard. If he survives, nothing can stop him . . . if he is weak,
he will not survive. Booze has been the great eliminator!

Rosie: You also said once that whisky floats more trouble than it
drowns.

Edwards: I'll drink to that.

Rosie: I must go home — unless you want me to "proofread" anything
else?

C28

Edwards: No.

(He fumbles in his pocket, brings out a ten dollar bill and puts it in Rosie's apron pocket.)

Rosie: What's that for?

Edwards: I forgot to pay for my drinks.

Rosie: I put them on your bill.

Edwards: For the proofreading.

Rosie: Bob . . . .

Edwards: 'Til Rupert gets home . . . buy yourself . . . a new hat.

Rosie (kisses him on the cheek): Good night, Bob. (She starts to exit.)

Edwards: Rosie?

Rosie: Yes?

Edwards: Did I cheer you up, girl?

Rosie: Yes, Bob. Good night.

(She exits. Edwards pours himself another drink, picks up his pencil and pad.)

Edwards: Let's see . . . . (He writes) Mrs. Bucklewhackster of Riverside was hostess at a jolly tea last Wednesday. Autumn foliage brightened the pretty table at which Mrs. Bucklewhackster presided with her usual charming air of embonpoint. Mr. Bucklewhackster staggered in during the proceedings and kicked over the table, falling asleep on the sofa. Mrs. Bucklewhackster was deeply mortified, and says she is through with pink teas for all time.

Disembodied Voice: Edwards! Bob Edwards!

Edwards: Ah, a disembodied voice. Pray identify yourself.

(Peter McGonigle rises out of the trap door. He is dressed scruffily in

C29

unpressed trousers, open-neck shirt, neckerchief, unbuttoned vest and battered cowboy hat and boots — all white. He is unshaven and thoroughly seedy looking.)

McGonigle: You know who I am, you old curmudgeon!

Edwards: Well, I'll be damned. McGonigle, is that you?

McGonigle: Yer damned right it's me!

Edwards: Not possible. You no longer exist. I killed you off in the last paper.

McGonigle: Well, I'm not having it!

Edwards: I'm afraid it's out of your hands, Peter. I gave you birth and I killed you off. It's right here somewhere. Oh yes, *(he reads from a crumpled Eye Opener)* "It is with great regret that we learn of the passing of that great editor of the Midnapore Gazette and one-time horse-thief, Peter McGonigle."

McGonigle: Bullshit!

Edwards: Peter, really! That's one of the very reasons you had to go, but what a way to go! Listen. "While McGonigle was handling an ivory handled revolver, which the bartender of the Nevermore House had accepted from him in lieu of payment for a two-day drunk, the weapon unexpectedly went off, and lodged a bullet in McGonigle's abdomen. He died stretched out on the bar . . . . "

McGonigle: That's crazy!

Edwards: ". . . with his head resting comfortably on the slot machine."

McGonigle: You sadistic bastard! Why did you kill me?

Edwards: It was time, Peter. You were getting entirely out of hand. Besides, my readers were tired of you.

McGonigle: That's a lie! You're just jealous 'cause I'm so popular. I have years of outrageous stories in me yet. *(Slyly)* Do you think that stupid Englishman's going to improve your circulation? That smarmy Bertie!

C30

Edwards: Jealousy will get you nowhere. Bertie has breeding and class, and he's a good man basically . . . .

McGonigle *(sarcastically)*: "Some men are good only because they find it cheaper than being wicked."

Edwards: And don't quote me to me! This is confusing enough.

McGonigle: What about my fans? My friends? My wife?

Edwards: I intend for your good wife to remarry, after a decent period of mourning, of course — in about a week. I think Jimmy the bartender would be a good match. What do you think?

McGonigle: You're not usually so vindictive. What did I ever do to you?

Edwards: Well, there was that awful mess with Lord Strathcona over that telegram he sent you when you were released from jail. He almost sued me for libel.

McGonigle: You wrote that piece! You invented that goddamn telegram. Remember? That trouble served you right for poking fun at a lord of the realm. I was an innocent pawn.

Edwards: You've never been innocent in your life.

McGonigle: You've seen to that. Ah, come on, Edwards, who's going to do all your dirty work with me dead?

Edwards: Don't whine, Peter. It's entirely out of character.

McGonigle: You could dig me up.

Edwards: Think of the upheaval.

McGonigle: Think of the story! The second coming of Peter McGonigle!

Edwards: It has possibilities.

(Edwards picks up pad and pencil. The lights dim. Out of the trap rises a coffin, a gravedigger with a shovel, and McGonigle's widow with a bouquet of dead lilies. She hands the bouquet to McGonigle who climbs into the coffin. The widow raps on the lid of the coffin.)

C31

Widow: Peter! Hey, Pete! Are you in there? *(She notices Edwards)* Oh, doctor, thank God you've come. I've been praying all night!

Edwards *(playing the drunken doctor)*: Really? That's too bad. Aspirin would have been better.

Widow: But you came.

Edwards: I can explain that. The good Lord usually gives us what we deserve rather than what we ask for. Never mind, open your mouth and say, "Ah".

Widow: It's not me. *(Pointing down)* It's him.

Edwards: This is very serious. He's stiff as a board. Oh, inside you mean. *(He takes out a stethoscope, adjusts it. The gravedigger kneels beside him like a nurse assisting in surgery)* Spade! *(He pries open the coffin. The sides fall away revealing McGonigle stretched out stiffly, the lilies on his chest)* As I suspected. An advanced case of death.

Widow: He looks so natural. He hasn't changed a bit. I just know he's still alive and in a trance. That bullet was such a shock to him.

Edwards *(tweaking McGonigle's nose)*: Well, he looks dead as a doormat to me, but then again it may just be a case of flexibilitas cerea. How long has he been dead?

Widow: About six months.

Edwards: Oh, well then, there's no particular hurry. I should like to hold a professional consultation with my fellow physicians over at the bar. I won't be a minute.

Widow: Oh no you don't! You'll be over there all day getting crocked. You stay right here and bring my Peter back to life! You haven't tried sticking a pin in him yet.

Edwards: Quite so. Pin! *(He is handed the pin which he sticks indiscriminately all over McGonigle's body)* As you can see, I've stuck the pin clear through his nose. If he were, as you claim, alive, the motor centres would be excited by reflex reaction. I have no hesitation in pronouncing your husband a dead duck! Madam, he has had the benefit of all modern science. There is nought that I can do. *(The*

widow throws her apron over her head with loud sobs) For you, however, I prescribe two aspirins and a bottle of Johnny Walker.

(The widow takes the bottle and looks from it to the coffin. The penny drops. She swiftly opens the bottle and places it under McGonigle's nose. They all stand in silent observation. McGonigle's nose twitches.)

Widow: Look!

(His mouth drops open suddenly and the widow pours a quantity of whisky down his throat.)

McGonigle: Wow! *(His eyes snap open.)*

Widow: Here, dear. You must be thirsty.

McGonigle: I thought you didn't like me to drink.

Widow *(sobbing)*: Well, dear, after all, it is your birthday.

Edwards: Another triumph for the medical profession!

McGonigle: I'll drink to that!

Edwards *(as himself)*: You're just in time, Pete.

McGonigle: What for?

Edwards: Mrs. Bucklewhackster's party.

McGonigle: I didn't know she was having one.

Edwards: I just decided. You must come. You know how she adores your off-colour humour.

McGonigle: I'll have to change.

Edwards: Nonsense. She wouldn't hear of it. It's a come-as-you-are.

Gravedigger: What about me?

Edwards: Of course! All the very best people will be there!

C34

(The coffin, widow and gravedigger disappear down the trap. Edwards and McGonigle — still carrying the lilies — go to the party. A stuffy, rather stilted dance is playing. There is the sound of forced and mirthless laughter, clinking of tiny glasses, refined accents. The dance is a parody of a minuet. Seen at the party in the opening number are — Bertie, Mother Fulham, Bennett, Rosie, Paddy Nolan, the clergyman, McGonigle, various assorted party ladies.)

Everyone: We're the very best of people,
As you can plainly see.
We're the top of the ladder,
The cream of high society.
We're not wise or clever
Or even very nice,
But such virtues are a bother
And don't cut any ice.

With the very best of people,
Whose greatest claim to fame
Is a pile of lovely money,
An old impressive family name.
The common folk may grumble
And say that we are snobs,
But actually they'd give their souls
To mix with the nobs.

So if you're green with envy
And want to join our bash,
Stick a hyphen in your name,
Pretend that you have lots of cash.
A phoney English accent
Will help you play the part,
And the very best of people,
The beautiful people
Will take you into their heart,
Take you into their heart!

(The dance loses its structure and drifts into general conversational groupings. Edwards wanders vaguely from group to group, writing his "society column".)

Edwards: Charming, simply charming. What a gallimaufry. I must write this up for my society column tomorrow. Let's see now, who's here? *(He takes out pad and pencil)* "A gorgeous creation from Paris,

C35

Saskatchewan, of sequin trimmings and sage and onion stuffing." "A lovely gown of green satin, edged with point d'esprit and old silk, with touches of burlap." I see, "Miss Jessie Marshfield, staying in town for a few days nursing her alleged father, whose addiction to whisky is most distressing to his friends, especially as he seldom has the price." "Maude de Vere of Drumheller arrived in the city this afternoon and will be run out of town tonight. It is a pity Miss de Vere is not a racehorse. She is very fast." And finally, from the cultural community I see, "Miss Annabel Pink de Petticoat, who gave a charming recital at the Palliser Hotel last week. Her interpretation of Beethoven's Moonshine Sonata was scholarly and remarkable for its technique. This charming artiste remained perfectly sober until after the recital. She got excellent notices next day."

(A group of party women crowd around Edwards, fluttering and giggling. Rosie, passing around a tray of drinks, gives him one.)

Party Woman: Oh, Mr. Edwards, I just love your newspaper!

Rosie: He must be slipping.

Party Woman: When does it come out?

Edwards: We like to say semi-occasionally.

(The group titters and dissolves.)

Nolan: Bob, you old rascal, this is quite a party.

Edwards: Glad you're enjoying it, Paddy. We aim to please.

Nolan: But where's our charming hostess?

Edwards: Fortifying herself with a bit of bubbly in the boudoir.

Nolan: It's not like Mrs. B. to forget her manners.

Edwards: Right you are, Paddy.

(There is a spotlight on the trap and Mrs. Bucklewhackster ascends.)

Mrs. Bucklewhackster *(in full regalia)*: Yoo-hoo, everyone! *(She recoils in distaste from McGonigle and his outstretched lilies)* My God! *(To Edwards)* Oh, Mr. Edwards! How divine of you to come!

C36

Edwards: 'Twas divine intervention indeed, Mrs. Bucklewhackster. You see, I'm between drunks so to speak.

Mrs. Bucklewhackster: Why, you naughty boy. I had no idea you were religious.

Edwards: Well, I don't like to spread it around, madam. I find that those who use religion as a cloak in this world have more use for a smoking jacket in the next.

Mrs. Bucklewhackster: You clever fellow! Is that an example of frontier humour?

Mother Fulham (digging Bertie in the ribs): Go on, Sport, you're a betting man, I hear.

Bertie: My good woman, this is really in the worst possible taste.

Mother Fulham (lifting her skirt): Go on now, what'll you bet me that this is the dirtiest leg in town?

Bertie: Oh, very well, I wager ten dollars that that is the dirtiest leg in town.

Mother Fulham: You lose! (She shrieks with laughter) You haven't seen me other one yet! (She lifts the other side of her skirt.)

Edwards: That's frontier humour!

Mrs. Bucklewhackster: Oh, Mr. Nolan, I was simply enchanted to see you at our little theatricals last week. I do so adore "Hamlet", don't you? Did you see our little effort, Mr. Edwards?

Edwards: No, madam, I regret that I did not. But I understand it will prove beyond a shadow of a doubt a long-standing literary argument.

Mrs. Bucklewhackster: How thrilling! What argument?

Edwards: Who really wrote Shakespeare? Shakespeare or Bacon? They're planning to exhume both graves and see which one has turned over most recently.

Mrs. Bucklewhackster: Mr. Edwards, really! (She sweeps away from them, cutting a swath through the crowd and runs into Mother

C37

Fulham, who is staggering away from the hors d'oeuvre table with a gunny sack full of goodies. Mrs. Bucklewhackster shrieks in horror) What are you doing? Who are you, anyway? Who let you in?

Mother Fulham: I was escorted in by my date, Mr. Nolan.

Mrs. Bucklewhackster: Your date!

Edwards: What's going on here?

Nolan: Is something the matter, Mrs. Bucklewhackster? Oh, I see you've already met my friend, Mother Fulham.

Mrs. Bucklewhackster: Your friend, Mr. Nolan, your friend . . . was . . . stealing!

Nolan: Stealing? That's very serious. What's this all about, Mother?

Mother Fulham: She means all them dinky little cakes and things. I thought they were there for folks to help themselves.

Bertie: Most folk, madam, do not bring a gunny sack to a high-class soiree.

Mother Fulham: Well, no one was eating them. Can't say's I blame them neither. I just thought I'd take a little treat home for Sylvester. High-class garbage is really scarce these days.

Mrs. Bucklewhackster: And who, I tremble to ask, is Sylvester?

Mother Fulham: My prize hog.

Mrs. Bucklewhackster: I think I'm going to faint. My imported caviar to a . . . a . . . hog.

Mother Fulham: Gawd! Is that what it is? You could scoop rabbit droppings off the prairie — looks just the same. *(Mrs. Bucklewhackster does faint)* These society women ain't got much stamina. If that's all they eat, it's no bloody wonder.

(Mrs. Bucklewhackster is carried out.)

Nolan: Music please!

C38

Edwards: Quick thinking, Paddy. It'll raise the tone of this whole affair.

(The orchestra starts to play the party music again. Mother Fulham turns and bawls at the musicians.)

Mother Fulham: Gawd! Can't you do better than that? This isn't a wake, it's a party! *(The orchestra starts the jig. Mother Fulham starts to dance)* That's more like it! Come on, Paddy, let's get something out of this evening. To think I could have stayed home with Sylvester. Come on, Rosie, girl. Put some pink in your cheeks. You too, Bob, you need a bit of trimming.

(The four of them dance a jig. The light fades out around them and the party people disperse. The party has become "real". During the jig, Edwards and Rosie drop out, exhausted, and let the two Irishmen finish. At the end of the dance, the morning newspaper is delivered. Rosie goes to pick it up.)

Edwards: Ah, Mother, you always know how to make a party!

Nolan: Is that the paper, then, Rosie? I believe it's time we were getting home, Mother.

(Rosie is standing slightly upstage reading the paper.)

Edwards: Why the frown, Rosie? Oh, it's the Daily News, is it?

Nolan: You surely wouldn't expect Mrs. Bucklewhackster to be taking the Eye Opener?

Edwards: What's the matter, girl? I know it's a hell of a way to start the morning, but it can't be that bad?

Rosie: Oh, Bob . . . .

Edwards: Let's see. *(She hands him the paper)* . . . Just the usual McGillicuddy drivel . . . .

Rosie: Letters column.

Edwards: "Sir, for years now this city has been cursed with a make-believe journalist, one Robert C. Edwards, who has done more harm to the morality of the community, and brought more disgrace upon

C39

the fair name of this city, than all other vile agencies combined."
(As he reads, the lights fade to black leaving a spotlight on his face)
"The police and the magistrate must deal with the output of the
putrid brain of Bob Edwards as they would any other pedlar of
obscene literature, the contents of his disreputable sheet being black-
mail, slander . . . and smut." Signed, "Nemesis".

(Blackout interval.)

Act two   *(Lights come up on the closed coffin. Paddy Nolan enters calling.)*

Nolan: Bob! Where the devil are you? *(He sees the coffin closed)*
Come on, open up. I know you're in there, Bob. You can't hide
away like this.

*(The coffin opens revealing Edwards in an advanced state of
inebriation. During the scene he drinks heavily.)*

Edwards: Paddy, my old friend! How's the wake progressing?

Nolan: Bob, we're not going to let McGillicuddy get away with this.
Let your friends help. We're all behind you, you know.

Edwards: I have a new friend, Paddy. Did you know that? He stands
in front of me.

Nolan: Bob, this is no time for obscure jokes . . . .

Edwards: Let me introduce you to Calgary's newest citizen! *(The
lights change. The trap opens and Thomas slowly rises. He carries
a long noose. During the speech, he uses the rope to illustrate some
of the described activities. Nolan does not see him)* Thomas B.
Prendergast, the popular hangman, has recently arrived from Port
Arthur, Ontario.

Nolan: Bob, will you listen to me? We're going to sue McGillicuddy
for libel.

Edwards: All our best murderers are hanged by Mr. Prendergast. His
jovial methods on the scaffold tend to subdue the terrors of death,
and he does not consider a job well done unless he sends the doomed
wretch to eternity roaring with laughter at one of his merry jests.

C42

Nolan: Bob, you're not listening to me.

Edwards: And you're not listening to me. This is really very funny, Paddy. It will cheer you up. Mr. Prendergast is the inventor of the new knot which fits snugly under the right ear instead of the left. Many murderers seem to prefer it.

Nolan: McGillicuddy will have a summons in his hands by noon tomorrow. I'm itching to take him on.

Edwards: In addition to a fixed salary, Mr. Prendergast receives an honorarium of $50 an execution, with permission to sell small pieces of the rope to curio hunters. The new suit of clothes in which the murderer is hanged is also one of the perquisites of his office, and Mr. Prendergast's wardrobe is said to be second to none.

Nolan: Bob, I think we've got a very strong case for libel, but you'll have to give me the go-ahead.

Edwards: Mr. Prendergast's hobbies, outside of his work, are trap-shooting and rope tricks! Oh, well done, Thomas! *(Thomas bows and stands silently)* Well, what do you think, Paddy? Do you think Thomas will fit in to the upper echelons of Calgary society?

Nolan: This is crazy, Bob! You're retreating from this menace by twisting your hurt into a sick joke! You're trying to say you don't give a damn, but you do. This ridiculous fantasy is unhealthy and just another way of backing down. For God's sake, let's fight this insult where it belongs — in court. I'm trying to tell you we have a case, Bob! It's not just the reputation of the Eye Opener, but McGillicuddy's attacks on your character must be challenged. They are truly libellous.

Edwards *(grabbing a crumpled copy of the Daily News)*: Let's see now, "Born in a brothel, bred on a dung-pile. Character-thief, liar, coward, drunkard and dope-fiend." I wonder where he picked that up?

Nolan: He hasn't a shred of evidence to support any of it. Surely you realize that. I don't understand your reluctance to fight this.

Edwards: Because there's a seed of truth in it.

Nolan: So you drink too much. You've never denied it. My God,

C43

Bob, if we condemmed every man who tends to have one too many, three-quarters of the population would be under judgment, myself included.

Edwards: Do you really think we have a case, Paddy? It would be a slight change of pace for me — to be the outraged instead of the outrageous.

Nolan: You should be outraged. All your friends and readers are.

Edwards: All right, Paddy. We'll take on McGillicuddy.

Nolan: That's the spirit, Bob! I'll set proceedings in motion.

Edwards: I leave it in your hands, Paddy. It's always handy to know the best defence lawyer in the country.

Nolan: This isn't a defence, Bob. It's a prosecution.

(He exits.)

Edwards: Well, Thomas, are you coming to court? No? Not interested in that part, are you, you old rascal? Pretty dry stuff. Let's see if we can't liven things up a bit.

(Lighting change to fantasy sequence. Music parody of pompous courtroom music — perhaps circus overtones. Beginning of trial scene is exaggerated, cartoon-like in style, a bit slapstick. Spectators file in.)

Clerk: All rise! The Honourable Justice Fairplay.

(The judge staggers in obviously drunk. He wears a ridiculously long powdered wig. He carries a bottle of whisky. He cannot find the bench, but is finally guided to his place by the clerk. He makes a show of pulling himself together.)

Judge *(obviously looking for the gavel)*: Where is that damn thing? *(He cannot find it and uses the bottle of whisky instead)* Court is in session! First case!

Clerk: Smith vs. McGonigle. Assault and battery.

Judge: Will the plaintiff please step forward?

C44

(Smith painfully takes his place. He is bruised and battered and has his arm in a sling. McGonigle also lurches to his feet. He is drunk also.)

Nolan: You're the defendant, Peter, not the plaintiff.

(McGonigle bows to the court and falls on his face.)

Judge: Mr. Nolan, I suppose it is too much to hope that you're not defending this creature.

Nolan: It is, Your Honour. I am.

Judge: I suppose you want to cross-examine the plaintiff?

Nolan: I do.

Judge: Proceed.

Nolan: Now, my good fellow. *(He pats the man gently on the arm. The plaintiff screams with pain)* Oh, dear, this is terrible. Strong young fellow like you, cut down in his prime. How did my learned friend so eloquently put it? A flower nipped in the bud.

Plaintiff: It's true, sir, I'm not the man I was.

(There is a general exaggerated murmur from the crowd.)

Nolan: And just what was the man you were? Would you mind telling the court what you did for a living before this alleged attack occurred?

Plaintiff: I worked in the basement of the Alberta Hotel, sir. It was my job to lift the heavy cases of whisky off the top shelf and bring them up to the bar.

Nolan: Oh, an important job, indeed. Almost a community service. Am I to understand, then, that you have lost this prestigious position?

Plaintiff: Yes, sir. Ever since that dirty, sneaking, bad-tempered, horse-thieving McGonigle jumped me for no good . . . .

McGonigle *(jumping up and attacking the plaintiff)*: Why, you snivelling little . . . .

Nolan *(pushing McGonigle back into his seat)*: You surely wouldn't be

C45

referring to my client, would you? That illustrious man of letters, Peter McGonigle?

Plaintiff: Illustrious, hell! Ever since he broke my arm, I can't lift it at all. I can't even lift a glass, let alone a whole case.

(General murmur of sympathy.)

Nolan: I'm sure we are all distressed to hear this. None more than Mr. McGonigle, I know.

Plaintiff: I want compensation. I want damages. That bum should have to pay. I have a widowed mother to support.

Clerk: Exhibit A — widowed mother.

(Widowed mother takes a bow.)

Nolan: It is true, sir, that if you cannot continue in your chosen career, you must be compensated. No one with any compassion disputes this. It is only the degree with which we are concerned. Now, *(Nolan dramatically addresses the court)* could we please have a demonstration of how high you can lift the alleged arm?

(Plaintiff slowly and painfully removes the sling and moves his arm imperceptibly. There is a sympathetic murmur.)

Nolan: My, my, that is not very promising. However, sir, are you sure you are not misleading this court?

Plaintiff: What do you mean?

Nolan *(building dramatically, pulling out the stops)*: I mean, sir, and I suggest to you and this court, that you could never raise that arm, that indeed that arm was always useless, and you kept your job at the Alberta Hotel through a clever illusion! Until you decided to perpetrate this outrageous hoax on the court, manipulating to your own advantage my client's dismal reputation and his unfortunate lapse of memory on the night in question!

Plaintiff: That's not true!

Nolan: I do not believe that you could ever raise that arm!

C46

Plaintiff: I could too!

Nolan *(quickly)*: How high?

Plaintiff *(throwing off his sling and shooting his arm in the air)*: This high!

Widowed Mother: Dummy!

Judge *(banging the whisky bottle)*: Case dismissed! Next case.

Clerk: Buzzard-Cholomondeley vs. the Crown. Drunken and disorderly conduct.

(Bertie approaches the bench with great dignity.)

Judge: Ten dollars and costs.

Bertie: This is most embarrassing. I seem to be temporarily short.

Judge: How about five dollars? Can you pay that?

Bertie: Well, not actually . . . .

Judge: I'll make it two and a half, then.

Bertie: To use the vernacular, Your Honour, I'm flat broke.

Judge: And dry, too, no doubt.

Bertie: Yes, sir.

Judge: Oh, get the hell out of here. Here's two bits for a wee drop!

Bertie: Thank you. Most kind. I've always had implicit faith in the Canadian judicial system.

Judge: Next case!

(The atmosphere of the courtroom changes. The fantasy disappears. Bertie and McGonigle exit. The judge removes his wig. The bottle disappears and is replaced by a real gavel. The style becomes realistic. Edwards enters and sits down next to Nolan. Everyone is sober.)

C47

Clerk: Edwards vs. McGillicuddy. Defamatory libel. Do you swear to tell the truth, the whole truth and nothing but the truth, so help you God?

McGillicuddy *(sings)*:

> Edwards is a coward, a drunkard and a fiend!
> It worries me that no one save myself has ever deemed
> It vital that this journalistic bully be impeached,
> When our standards of morality have crumbled to this leech!
> I hear you out there jeering,
> But truth will get a hearing!
> You think I say these shocking things
> For some warped pleasure that it brings!
>
> His smut sheet is a fraud!
> He deserves the wrath of God
> To smite him as it did the Sodomites.
> For God will punish those
> Who indulge in wicked prose,
> And fate is clear for those hermaphrodites,
> Like the evil Oscar Wilde
> Whose punishment was mild —
> A moral leper lost to Christian hope.
> He deserved to go the way
> As Edwards does, I say,
> Of pistol, poison, razor, or the rope!

(The court is genuinely devastated by McGillicuddy's hatred. Nolan starts his speech sanely and quietly.)

Nolan: May it please the court, I should like to respectfully remind this assembly that it is Daniel McGillicuddy who is on trial here today, not Bob Edwards. I gravely doubt whether there is anyone sitting in this courtroom today knowing Bob Edwards who would recognize his friend in this evil, malevolent tirade. Robert Chambers Edwards — a name, ladies and gentlemen, that brings a smile to the lips and a fondness to the heart — not just here in our city, but all over the country where his newspaper is read. Bob Edwards is a man of the people — not those perfect mythical people with no failings or weaknesses, but people like you and me who need to laugh at ourselves occasionally. Bob's ready humour and gentle satire help us to see ourselves and our sacred cows — our churches, our governments, our courts — in their true perspective — a perspective based on human fallibility. There is not one among us who has not recognized himself, at one time or another, in the pages of the Eye Opener.

McGillicuddy: Bob Edwards is a degenerate scoundrel!

Nolan: Those of us who are fortunate enough to know Bob well, are only too aware of his personal kindnesses and charity. There isn't a down-and-out soul in this town who hasn't had the benefit of Bob's "little something to tide them over" . . . .

McGillicuddy: Your Honour, I object! The issue here is public corruption — not some paltry, imagined do-gooding!

Nolan: Now you might be asking yourselves, ladies and gentlemen, if Bob Edwards is such a fine man, such a well-known and respected journalist, how could anyone dare to say such slanderous things? How could anyone stick his neck out like this? What kind of a man would slander Bob Edwards? Daniel McGillicuddy, that's who! A fellow journalist, a member of the same community, a righteous, upstanding, church-going fellow. A family man. Oh, yes, and very fond of his family is our Daniel . . . and now we come to the crux of the matter. It pains me to bring this up . . . . You see, Daniel has this nephew . . . .

McGillicuddy: I object!

Judge: Mr. McGillicuddy, you are out of order!

Nolan: You are about to see our avenging angel for what he really is!

McGillicuddy: I object!

Nolan: And well you might. I object, too! This shameless charade is just a transparent diversion from your nephew's shame and yours! You see, Daniel's nephew is a sneaky little third-rate poet whom Bob Edwards . . . .

McGillicuddy: I most strongly object!

Judge: Mr. McGillicuddy, sit down. You are charged with a most serious offence. We will hear all the evidence. Proceed, Mr. Nolan.

Nolan: Thank you, Your Honour. I would like to tell you about Daniel's nephew and the real reason for Daniel's hatred — that is, aside from him being a mean, self-righteous, and humourless little

C49

rodent. Daniel's nephew wrote a poem. Esteemed critics from coast to coast acclaimed it as a new literary work of art. Now, Bob Edwards, as you all know, is a man of letters, always ready to encourage new literary talent . . . so he printed nephew's poem. But Bob, being an honest man and a journalist of integrity, thought it only fair to point out to his readers that the poem was written some years ago by E. Pauline Johnson! Awkward for one proud uncle, but unfortunately true. Your righteous fire, McGillicuddy, is the heat of embarrassment!

McGillicuddy: None of this alters the fact that . . . .

Nolan: M'Lord, surely we have heard enough unseemly rhetoric! As honest men, I charge you to find Daniel McGillicuddy guilty of malicious slander and libel!

Judge: Members of the jury, you have heard the charge. You must find the defendant guilty of libel or innocent by reason of justification.

(The members of the jury talk and argue amongst themselves in hushed tones.)

Mother Fulham: Ah, that was a fine speech you made, Paddy.

Nolan: Thank you, Mother, I was just getting warmed up. I could go on for hours now.

Mother Fulham: Well, I don't know's I'd care for that.

Rosie: It'll be fine, Bob. You'll see.

Edwards: I'm very grateful to you, Paddy. You know, I'd forgotten about that poem. Such a little thing.

Judge: Order! Order! Members of the jury, have you reached a verdict?

Jury Foreman: We have, Your Honour. We find the accused guilty of libel. Plea of justification not sustained.

(There is a general relief. Edwards and his friends congratulate each other. Daniel is in a state of high dudgeon.)

Judge: Order, please! What is your recommendation?

Jury Foreman: Well, Your Honour . . . . *(He looks awkwardly at*

C50

Edwards) We, the jury, feel that while Mr. McGillicuddy went to
extremes, he does have some valid points in his objections to some
of the material printed in the Eye Opener. Therefore, we recommend
that the editor of the Eye Opener be cautioned against printing
debasing or immoral articles, and that Mr. McGillicuddy be fined the
minimum for the charge of libel.

*(There is general puzzlement in the courtroom. McGillicuddy rises
with a smirk of satisfaction.)*

Judge: Daniel McGillicuddy, you are fined $100 without costs. Mr.
Edwards, you are warned that the contents of your newpaper contra-
vene the accepted public standards of morality, and you are cautioned
against further breaches of this standard. Case closed.

*(Everyone rises as the judge exits. People start to file out of the
courtroom. Mother Fulham and Rosie say good-bye, leaving
McGillicuddy, Nolan and a very dejected Edwards alone on stage.)*

McGillicuddy: As far as I'm concerned, Edwards, you lost your case.
I consider this a moral victory for all men of decency!

(He exits.)

Edwards: He's right, Paddy.

Nolan: Pay no attention to him, Bob. We won! He was guilty of
libel and the court recognized that — despite those qualifications.

Edwards: It's a rather hollow triumph. I'm not blaming you, Paddy.
You did a fine job for me, but I realized something when the jury
made that statement. There are people who agree with McGillicuddy.

Nolan: In part, Bob. Only in part.

Edwards: Maybe they're right.

Nolan: What?

Edwards: Maybe I have been too outspoken — made fun of things
in the wrong kind of way. You know, I never meant to hurt anyone,
really. You must leave people some dignity, even when you laugh at
them.

C51

Nolan: Some people have too much!

Edwards: From now on, I'm going to run that rag of mine on the straight and narrow.

Nolan: Oh, God! If there's one thing this country doesn't need, it's another dreary, predictable newspaper! How can you be intimidated by that disgusting little vermin!

Edwards: Oh, no, Paddy. I'll still stand by what I believe in, but I guess I'll cut out my little risqué jokes.

Nolan: It's all so harmless, Bob. I think you're taking this far too seriously . . . you're the newspaperman. I guess you know better than I.

Edwards: Ah, many a man who's old enough to know better wishes he was young enough not to!

Nolan: That's more like you. I hate to see you so low.

Edwards: You can't win all the time, Paddy, and if your luck isn't what it should be — well, just put a ''p'' in front of it and start again! *(They do a little soft shoe)*
What if you don't win the race — forget it!
If you're beaten for a place — forget it!

Nolan: And when it came to the test
You were passed by all the rest.

Edwards &
Nolan: If you did your level best — forget it!

Edwards: Never mind Dame Fortune's frown,
Just get up as you went down.

Nolan: There are thousands just like you
With the same hard tasks to do

Edwards &
Nolan: And they're always pulling through — forget it!

(There is a dance bridge. They repeat the second verse in unison.)

Edwards: Paddy, I feel a jag coming on! *(Blackout. Lights come up on Edwards at his desk, drinking and writing. Thomas stands to one side watching)* Well, Thomas, it's been a great bender. I really do appreciate your joi de vivre in my hour of need. You really know how to make a party swing. But, I simply must get to work. *(He writes)* Dear Readers, your editor apologizes for the seven week silence. However, I have not been in the mood for getting out a paper while the celebrated libel suit was pending. We wish to express from this corner our half-hearted sympathy at the recent illness of one Daniel McGillicuddy, but we're sure the old chap will be out in the streets again soon, shaking hands with his numerous creditors. And now, some anxiously awaited news from a fellow whom no one will ever sue for libel — for all the trouble he creates is for himself. Pay attention now, Thomas. This is someone you should meet . . . "Dear Father" . . . . *(Mournful reprise of Bertie's music. Bertie enters in dishevelled state. He has lost his coat, hat, tie, gloves and umbrella. He is furiously writing and wretchedly miserable)* ". . . I often think of dear old Skookingham Hall and all the splendid shooting. The only shooting I have done here has been at craps, a different species of game from grouse or partridge . . . . "

Bertie: About things in this country. The few thousand pounds you gave me to start farming with were duly invested in a farm. In my labours, I had several assistants . . . .

Edwards: "Hiram Walker, Joe Seagram and Johnny Dewar, men of great strength and fiery temperament. In place of me serving as their master . . . ."

Bertie: They soon became mine. I lost my farm and went tending bar for an hotel-keeper, but . . . .

Edwards: "The love of liquor, which I must have inherited from yourself or Grandfather, made me a failure as a bartender, and now . . . ."

Bertie: If only I had a thousand pounds to start afresh! I am at present in the direst distress!

Edwards: "I have had to postpone indefinitely my newspaper venture at Leduc."

Bertie: I am now incarcerated in the Fort Saskatchewan jail awaiting trial due to a most unfortunate accident! *(Thomas takes a definite interest at these words. Bertie begins to confront Edwards directly)*

C53

It's a misunderstanding. The man is dead!

Edwards: Well, it's your own fault, isn't it?

Bertie: No, it's your fault, Edwards! I just wanted to frighten him. You know, like they do with poachers in the old country. My Papa's gamekeeper always fills his gun with salt — gives the blighters a good scare.

Edwards: Sounds fine in principle, Bertie, but didn't your Daddy's gamekeeper ever tell you you're not to use rock salt?

Bertie: Well, I was fresh out of the other kind. I let him have it with both barrels at close range. He's dead!

Edwards: I know. I wrote it that way.

Bertie: You always go too far.

Edwards: It gives the story more pathos.

Bertie: You heartless sod! Here I am, chained to a ring in the floor of this cell — visitors communicating through a megaphone half a mile away. My God, what's to become of me?

Edwards: Be a man, Bertie. If you go into court looking like a whipped puppy, they'll hang you for sure, isn't that right, Thomas? "Albert Buzzard-Cholomondeley, Son of Old Man Cholomondeley, Hanged Today! Strung Up For Foul Murder!"

Bertie: Have you no heart at all, Edwards? It's all a horrible mistake. Think of your Bertie in a murderer's cell. You must do something!

Edwards: You must ask your father for another thousand pounds . . . .

Bertie: Oh, I don't think he'll go for that.

Edwards: . . . to secure the services of that great criminal lawyer, my friend, Paddy Nolan. All the best murderers of the west employ him.

Bertie: Dearest Father, it is essential that I be immediately provided with funds to hire this lawyer. I am the victim of circumstances!

Edwards: A good man gone wrong is just a bad man found out! "Scion

C54

of Old English Family Sent to Kingdom Come! Says He Had No Table Salt!''

Bertie: Dearest Father, cable money at once!

Edwards: ''Buzzard-Cholomondeley, the assassin, in dying speech, attributes his fate to refusal of father to provide funds for lawyer.''

Bertie *(terrified)*: Oh, no! Surely not. Surely he won't refuse! I am lost. *(He is down on his knees, sobbing.)*

Edwards *(somewhat disconcerted that he has gone so far)*: Perhaps Paddy can get you off on a plea of insanity.

(A steady drum beat begins.)

Bertie: Too late. I am doomed!

Edwards: Hold on, Bertie.

Bertie: They're coming for me. It's the Death March!

Edwards: Nonsense, Bertie. It's just a spill-over from one of Mother Fulham's delightful musicales.

Bertie: No one can save me now.

Edwards: Good Lord, Bertie, I think they've come to save us both.

(The lights swing up as Bertie and Thomas disappear. The Salvation Army Band appears, led by the Major. Wendell brings up the rear with a huge drum. They sing.)

Salvation Army Band:
> Are you washed in the blood?
> Are you washed in the blood of the lamb?
> Are your garments spotless, are they white as snow?
> Are you washed in the blood of the lamb?
>
> Are you saved, or depraved?
> Depraved by the vile devil's brew.
> Is your soul besotted, has your liver rotted?
> Has that old demon rum got to you?

Chorus   Sing Glory Hallelujah!
              Lift up those poor drunken souls
              Sing Glory Hallelujah!
              Serve God when you go to the polls!

              Sing Glory Hallelujah!
              Bring prohibition to stay.
              Sing Glory Hallelujah!
              Climb on the wagon today!

              Booze will kill. Yes it will!
              Just as sure as the gun or the knife.
              So repent, you sinners, and we'll all be winners.
              We'll follow the good Christian life!

              Fools will quake, in the wake
              Of the blast from the Almighty's voice!
              Throw away that bottle, pull back on the throttle.
              Give up booze while you still have the choice.
(Repeat chorus.)

(The Army musters on one side of the stage. Frank, the hotelman, enters Bob's office.)

Edwards: Hello there, Frank. Catchy little ditty, don't you think?

Frank: Bunch of tub-thumping do-gooders is what I think. Stirring up a mess of trouble.

Edwards: Now, Frank, the Army does a lot of good work, despite what you may think of its methods.

Frank: They're bad for business.

Edwards: How is the hotel business, Frank?

Frank: Still going strong, but I don't know for how long with all this here prohibitionist talk — which reminds me . . . by the way, Bob . . . .

Edwards: Something I can do for you, Frank?

Frank: Well, I haven't seen you over at the hotel lately. Hope my

C58

bartenders are treating you okay. You're one of my best customers, you know.

Edwards: Your fellows treat me fine, Frank. Some of my best friends are bartenders.

Frank: Some of the other hotel owners are saying you might be influenced by these here prohibitionists. Course, I told them that was a lot of bull! Why, no one likes a drink better than Bob Edwards, I said. He's the last person to be influenced by the ravings of a lunatic fringe, I said. Isn't that right, Bob?

Edwards: I don't know, Frank. Gallons of trouble can come out of a pint flask.

Frank: It'll be a black day for us, you start talking like that!

Edwards: You mean, don't you, Frank, if I start printing like that?

Frank: Well, you do have a certain influence in the community . . . .

Edwards: You make me sick, the lot of you — pretending to be in the business of renting rooms! You're really only interested in the booze trade! And the quality of that snake poison you sell is about the same as the accommodation — not fit for a dog!

Frank: Bob, that's no way to talk to a friend . . . .

Edwards: I don't owe you a thing! I've always paid for my fun.

Frank: Bob, if the prohibitionists win, there'll be no fun for anyone. This town'll be dry as dust!

Edwards: Maybe it'll be good for me to go on the wagon. I'm fed up with the poison you've been passing off, anyway!

Frank: How's the newspaper business, Bob? I mean . . . since the trial and all?

Edwards: You read the Eye Opener, don't you?

Frank: I mean, you could use a little money, couldn't you?

Edwards: I can always use money, Frank.

C59

Frank: I've been authorized to offer you $15,000 if you'll support the hotelmen in the prohibition vote.

Edwards *(incredulous)*: I've never sold the old rag yet and I never will. Good night, Frank!

Frank: Think it over, Bob. Remember, there's more than one way to . . . .

Edwards: Good night, Frank!

(Frank exits angrily colliding with Paddy Nolan.)

Edwards: Paddy, my lad! You're just in time.

Nolan: For what?

Edwards: To join me in a drink. I've just taken a vow of poverty.

Nolan: Good idea, Bob. Prosperity would just spoil you.

Edwards *(toasting)*: Prosperity never spoils a man whom adversity cannot crush. *(The drum begins. The Army is on the march again)* Oh Lord, there they go again!

Nolan: Bob, they're coming here.

Edwards: What?

Nolan: They've stopped right outside your door.

Wendell: See, Major, the light's still on in his office. He must still be there.

Major: Ah, Wendell, when the Devil works overtime, so must we. We must save this unfortunate soul from the demon rum!

Wendell: I'll come too!

Major: No, Wendell, if what's-his-name could face the fiery furnace alone, I can certainly handle Bob Edwards.

Wendell: But it's my turn! I haven't saved anybody yet today.

C60

Major: Don't snivel, Wendell, I know the drum is heavy, but working for the Lord is never easy.

Wendell *(muttering)*: I could've joined the Highlanders and got a swell kilt and everything.

Major: Now, you stay here and pray. Bang the drum or something. *(Calling)* Mr. Edwards! Are you there?

Edwards: I believe so, yes.

Major: May I speak with you?

Nolan: My God, it's the Major herself.

Edwards: Put the bottle away, Paddy, and pull yourself together, for heaven's sake!

Nolan: It must be about the prohibition vote. It goes to the polls tomorrow, you know.

Edwards: Hmm, I wonder what they'll offer me? Come in, Major!

Major: Good evening, Mr. Edwards. Ah, Mr. Nolan, what a surprise. Never mind, I know some of your countrymen are very Christian people. Didn't St. what's-his-name drive out all the drunkards?

Nolan: St. Patrick, madam, drove out all the snakes.

Major: Hallelujah! Now, Mr. Edwards, I've come to plead our cause. Prohibition goes to a vote tomorrow, and I have no doubt that your support would greatly enhance our chances for victory.

Edwards: I'm flattered, Major. You don't think my support would simply strain your credibility?

Major: Now, Mr. Edwards, I know that I can speak plainly. After all, we are all cosmopolites here. *(Sotto voce)* I know that you drink. But, you also have a powerful voice in this city through your newspaper. If you would come out strongly against the evils of whisky . . . .

Nolan: Not Irish whisky, surely?

Edwards: What are you prepared to offer me, Major?

C61

Major: I beg your pardon?

Edwards: Well, the hotelmen offered me $15,000 if I'd take their side. What will you offer?

Major: God does not make bargains, Mr. Edwards!

Edwards: And it's a good thing, too. I won't be bought or sold.

Major: We can, of course, offer you salvation if you renounce the evils of drink . . . .

Edwards *(quickly)*: Tell you what I'll do, Major. I've already told the hotelmen how I feel. I'll write an article in support of prohibition for tomorrow's paper.

Major: Hallelujah! Praise the Lord!

Edwards: If you don't mind, Major, I'd just as soon the good Lord didn't know I was here. It's a matter of principle. You know, if the hotelmen had shot square with me, I'd have supported them. Let's see what you folks can do.

Major: Thank you, Mr. Edwards. Good night, gentlemen!

(She joins her band. They exit triumphantly.)

Nolan: Good heavens, Bob, I hope you know what you're doing.

Edwards: Yes, Paddy, it's time. It's so easy to do the right thing when sin ceases to be a pleasure! *(He reaches for his pad and pencil.)*

Nolan: You're surely not going to be writing prohibition copy now? When you're . . . .

Edwards: Slightly sozzled?

Nolan: You are a little . . . under the weather, Bob.

Edwards: It's the best time, Paddy. You see, booze acts on the human character as developer on a photographic negative. It brings out the light and shadows. It shows up the black spots . . . .

Nolan: I'll leave you to it. See you in the morning.

C62

Edwards: Well, I can't promise that, Paddy, but you will see the Eye Opener. *(Nolan exits. Edwards pours himself another drink and starts to write his article)* Dear Readers, today we weigh the merits of prohibition, and from where your humble editor sits, the hotel-keepers have their elbows on the scale . . . consider the hardships of drink on women and children, innocent victims of the damnable traffic of booze . . . .

(The lights fade out to black. When they rise, it is early morning. Edwards has passed out, stretched out on the desk/coffin. There is a stack of fresh newspapers beside him. Rosie enters in a hurry.)

Rosie: Bob! Are the papers ready? Bob! Wake up! The newsboys are here! And the hotelmen are right behind them. Bob! *(She spots the Eye Opener and snatches up the top copy — she reads)* . . . . "We see a multitude of downcast men, panhandling for dimes on the street, to procure more of the very booze that lost them every job they ever had . . . remember, gentle reader, if your vote will help dash the glass from a drunkard's lips, support the Bill!"

(There is a commotion as the hotelmen arrive, Frank and Charley barge in.)

Frank: Okay, Rosie, where are the papers?

Rosie: This is a private office. You can't barge in here like this!

Charley: We're here on legitimate business.

Frank: We want to buy every single copy of this morning's Eye Opener.

Rosie: Don't be ridiculous! You can't do that.

Frank: It's perfectly legal. We'll pay full retail price.

Rosie: I don't care. Bob wouldn't like it.

Charley: He don't look like he's in any position to care one way or the other.

Rosie: Those papers are going out onto the streets for people to read.

C63

Frank: I'm afraid not, Rosie. *(He tosses a bunch of bills at Edwards)* Pick up the papers, Charley. We bought them fair and square!

(Charley goes to pick up the papers. Rosie moves in front of him. At the same time the Army appears with the Major in the lead. Rosie rushes to meet them.)

Rosie: Major! Mr. Edwards needs your help. The hotelmen are trying to keep the Eye Openers off the streets.

Major: Say no more, Rosie. Come on, Wendell! *(They march into the office, barring the way to Frank and Charley)* Young man, give me those papers!

Frank: Listen, Major, stay out of this. This is none of your business.

Major: If it's the Lord's business, it's my business!

Frank: Look, Major, I don't want to have to use . . . .

Major: You would strike a woman in uniform! That does it! I am the leader of God's army and I am prepared to do battle! Armed with the wrath of . . . .

Charley: Uh, Frank, maybe we'd better . . . .

Frank: Give her the papers, Charley. We'll find another way.

(Charley hands over the papers. Rosie picks up the bills and stuffs them in Frank's hands.)

Major: Thank you, sir. You'll find that God's way is always best.

Frank *(gestures angrily with the bills)*: You'll regret this, Major!

Major *(taking the bills)*: God bless you, sir. All donations gratefully received. Hallelujah! Onward, soldiers!

(They march off with the papers.)

Frank: Come on, Charley, the damage is done. Let's get over to the polling station.

(They exit. Rosie sinks down wearily in the chair and sings.)

Rosie: Wondering, can you say
With any truth that you can rearrange the way
That the world slips by
In a single day . . . ?

Pondering, through the night,
When was the crucial moment that you lost the fight?
And the world slipped by
In a single day.

Tilting at windmills only batters a gentle mind.
Searching out dragons in the lairs of humankind
Is a frustrating game — not worth the strain,
They just remain in rankled slumber, 'til their silent number
Comes up again, kindles again,
Embers of fear that smoulder in all men —
And the dragons win
In a single play.

Comforting to recall
It's only pride that vanishes before you fall . . . .
Why not let it all
Pass away?

Tilting at windmills can abuse a gentle mind.
Searching out dragons in the lairs of humankind
Is a singular game, but all the same
It still remains the only way to keep the dark at bay!

Changes often start
Within the stronghold of a stubborn heart
It's the greatest part
Of another day . . . and the world goes on . . . to another day.

*(At the end of the song, Rosie leaves quietly. The lights dim. The
following scene is only heard, not seen. During the scene, Edwards'
office is transformed into a hospital room. A nurse in uniform walks
in with a blanket and pillows. She puts the pillows underneath Edwards'
head and covers him with a blanket. She fetches a tray with a glass of
juice and several books on it. She places this on the floor and sits down
on the chair. The following scene comes through like snatches of a
dream, as though from a great distance.)*

Charley: Prohibition wins! Sixty thousand for, to forty thousand

C65

against!

Frank: That bloody hypocrite!

Major: Hallelujah!

(Reprise of Army song.)

Band: Are you washed?

Hotelmen: We're washed out!

Band: In the blood?

Hotelmen: It's a drought!

Band: In the soul-cleansing blood of the lamb!
We have been victorious!

Hotelmen: And it's damned inglorious!

Band: Praise the Lord and the Eye Opener man!

(There is a cheer which fades away. Edwards wakes up.)

Edwards: Sounds like a party out there. What's the occasion?

Nurse: The prohibitionists won. You're a popular man, Mr. Edwards.

Edwards: You're very formal today, Rosie. *(He sits up)* You're not Rosie. I seem to remember Rosie being here . . . .

Nurse: You're a little confused, Mr. Edwards.

Edwards: I need a drink. *(He searches around.)*

Nurse: There won't be any drinking for a long time, I'm afraid. Not in here, anyway.

Edwards: Just where is here?

Nurse: You're in a hospital in Banff. You've been very ill, Mr. Edwards. Your friends thought it best that you . . . have a rest for awhile.

C66

Edwards: I've always liked Banff. Is it dry too?

Nurse: The whole province is dry — and about time.

Edwards: Well, then, I suppose I shall be, too.

Nurse: That's the idea. It won't be so bad, really. It's just a question of will-power, isn't it? Pulling oneself up by the bootstraps. I'll leave you now. You just take it easy and you'll be out of here in no time.

(She exits.)

Edwards: There's a lady who's never had a hangover. Let's see now . . . what have we got here to while away the thirsty hours? Hmm, grapefruit juice. I'm not that thirsty yet! God, it's quiet in here. *(He calls)* Where is everyone? *(He listens to the silence)* A little light reading perhaps? *(He examines the books)* "Hansard". That's enough to give anyone the d.t.'s! "Famous Works of Art in the Western World". *(He opens it)* "The Langevin Bridge by Moonlight". "Mayor and the Aldermen in the Altogether". Strong stuff. Ah, Robbie Burns. Someone was thinking . . . . *(He reads)* "Alas! my roupet Muse is hearse! Your Honours' hearts wi' grief 'twad pierce, To see her sitting on her arse Low i' the dust, And scriechin' out prosaic verse, An' like to brust!" . . . You said it, Robbie. I know just how you feel . . . God, I wish there was someone to talk to . . . Rosie or good old Paddy . . . or . . . .

(The lights change to fantasy sequence. There is a difference. It is harsher and more glaring. Bertie appears.)

Bertie: You have your bloody nerve.

Edwards: Hello, Bertie. What are you doing here? I thought I put you in the asylum.

Bertie: Don't change the subject!

Edwards: All right. What was I saying before you so rudely interrupted me?

Bertie: You were reading Robert Burns — badly, I might add, and affecting, in your usual arrogant way, some sort of kinship.

Edwards: You've grown rather pompous since our last meeting, Bertie.

C67

I do feel a kind of kinship. After all, we're both Scots.

Bertie: And there the similiarity ends. Burns was a real writer.

Edwards: Oh. And what am I?

Bertie: A hack. A cheap pretender, labouring forced jokes that no one sees the point of.

Edwards: Dangling participle there, Bertie. That's no way for a fellow with an English education to speak.

Bertie: You manipulate other people's lives!

Edwards: Well, it's true I've manipulated yours, but after all, I did invent you, Bertie. You don't really exist.

Bertie: That gives you a somewhat awkward definition, doesn't it? You're sitting here talking to me.

Edwards: Well, I have to talk to someone. Only those who are insane talk to themselves.

Bertie: Perhaps we'd better not dwell on it.

Edwards: Touchy subject, is it?

Bertie: Now, look here, Edwards, I realize that anything is preferable to being hanged, especially by that grotesque friend of yours, but the thought of spending the rest of my life in the Brandon Asylum was not an alluring one!

Edwards: You escaped, didn't you?

Bertie: In the nick of time, it appears. God knows how long you'll be in here — drying out!

Edwards: That's true. It gets longer every time. I guess I'm not as young as I used to be.

Bertie: How original.

Edwards: It's a humbling experience, Bertie. I'm feeling rather low.

C68

Bertie: Oh, for God's sake, don't get maudlin. If there's one thing I cannot stand, it's a man crying in his cups.

Edwards: I'm not in my cups! Why the hell do you think I'm here?

Bertie: If you're going to be profane, perhaps McGonigle would be more your style.

Edwards: Good old Peter. He'll cheer me up. Where is the old rascal?

Bertie: He's around somewhere. Attacking the nurses, no doubt!

(McGonigle appears.)

McGonigle: Goddamn little prude! You should try it sometime — put some colour in your cheeks. You have all the bloom of a soggy bread pudding.

Edwards: Now, Peter, let's not get personal. How have you been, you old devil?

McGonigle: You should know. I've been meaning to speak to you about that. Things have been pretty bloody dull since you've been holed up in here.

Edwards: Well, I haven't felt much like writing anything lately.

McGonigle: You've gone soft, Edwards.

Edwards: Don't you think it's time you slowed down, Peter?

McGonigle: Don't give me that garbage. You created me to liven things up — and do all the things you never had the courage to do yourself.

Edwards: I don't think that's true.

McGonigle: Sure it is. And you envy me — well, my way with the ladies, anyway.

Bertie: Is that what you call them? God, I need a drink.

McGonigle: Bertie, my boy, that's the first sensible thing I've ever heard you say. Name your poison!

Edwards: You won't find anything in here, Peter.

McGonigle: Where are you hiding the stuff?

Edwards: There's not a drop on the premises.

McGonigle: Come on, you must have a bottle stashed somewhere.

Edwards: I'm beginning to wish I did.

Bertie: Really, Edwards, this is most inhospitable of you. I didn't come all this way for tea, you know!

Edwards: When a man goes on the wagon he really discovers who his friends are.

McGonigle: Well, I can see this is going to be a crashing bore. Come on, Bertie, what do you say we nip over to the Nevermore for a little snort?

Bertie: Well, I don't mind if I do.

Edwards: You're not leaving? Just when it was getting jolly?

McGonigle: Jolly, hell! It's bad enough you going on the wagon without dragging us along!

Bertie: Quite right! I see no need for us to ride the bumpy road to sobriety as well.

Edwards: You don't eh? Well, let me tell you something, both of you! It's time we all dried out. This whole booze thing has gotten entirely out of hand!

Bertie: Speak for yourself, please. We can hold our . . . .

Edwards: What goes for me, goes for you — the pair of you.

McGonigle: How's that?

Edwards: Because I say so!

McGonigle: Now it comes out — just what I suspected all along.

C70

Edwards: What the hell are you talking about?

McGonigle: You've been working out your own problems — through us ever since the beginning.

Bertie: Absolutely right! You despise the upper class because they've never taken you or your little paper seriously — so you make them out to be the fools — through me! Making me the butt of your sick jokes!

Edwards: Now, Bertie . . . .

Bertie: Don't you patronize me! You make sport of my origins because you can't even verify your own. That fancy university you claim to have attended in Scotland doesn't even have a record of your being a student, let alone a graduate! As for your supposed family . . . .

Edwards: I can explain all that.

Bertie: Save it for your biographers — that is, if anyone's ever interested.

McGonigle: Oh, he'll just turn it into a big joke — come out smelling like a rose, or should I say a pansy? Poor old Bob Edwards! Can't even be in the company of a lady without blushing and stammering like a school boy.

Bertie: Unless she's married, of course.

McGonigle: Unless she's safe! Can't take the risk of eligibility, can you, Edwards? So you make old Peter your patsy — let me do the conniving and romancing — not to mention all the skulduggery you don't have the guts for!

Bertie: Just who do you think you are?

McGonigle: Just who are you, Bob Edwards?

Edwards: Well, I know one thing. I'm in control here! You two are nothing without me! I call the shots.

McGonigle: Speaking of which I'm long overdue. Coming, Bertie?

C71

Edwards: Stay where you are!

Bertie: We have a most pressing appointment . . . .

Edwards: You don't leave until I want you to! That's the way it goes — and you're not leaving! You're all there is . . . I need you!

Bertie: How boring.

McGonigle: Most dispiriting.

Bertie *(as they both chuckle)*: Rather good, McGonigle.

Edwards: It's not funny. It's not a joke anymore. Sooner or later you have to face what life really is, don't you see?

Bertie: Perhaps you've taught us too well, Edwards. Isn't this how to lighten one's burden? With a little giggle?

McGonigle *(as he and Bertie exit)*: We'll give your regards to the bartender, Bob.

(Edwards stares after them. He sinks down heavily on the bed. He picks up the tray and studies his reflection.)

Edwards: Well, Bob, looks like there's just you and me left. You're a rum-looking fellow, aren't you? Come on, things aren't so bad. It's true, you're not carrying this particular moment off with much wit and style, but it's your choice, isn't it? Don't get too serious, Bob. Make the people laugh . . . and if they find your weakness and laugh back . . . well, that's the biggest joke of all. What were we laughing at? I seem to have forgotten . . . I'm sure it was very funny . . . . *(He sings.)*

> Hey, jolly man, play me a comedy,
> Sing a cheerful melody. Can't you see
> I'm alone?

> Hey, jolly man, talk with me here awhile
> Maybe you can make me smile,
> Jolly man, jolly man.

> Here in my solitude, my troubled mind
> Falls in a pensive mood.
> Where can I find

C72

My jolly man, who gives such sympathy
To others' tragedy?
Where is he, jolly man?

Hey, jolly man, you know my perfect scheme
Lies in some forgotten dream.
Jolly man, if you can,

Help me to mend again visions of happiness,
You've always been my friend —
Where are you now?

When I am low, guess I depend on you
For a jest to pull me through.
Now you're gone — I go on.

(Near the end of the song Kate has appeared in the doorway.)

Kate: Hello there.

Edwards: Hello. Are you looking for someone?

Kate: I'm looking for Bob Edwards.

Edwards: A remarkable coincidence. I know the fellow well. He's not exactly receiving today.

Kate: Oh, I think he'll see me. I'm Kate.

Edwards: Of course! You're the Love Interest. Are we that close to the end?

Kate: You need taking in hand, Bob Edwards.

Edwards: Clever girl. You knew it was me all along. So you think I need taking in hand. What did you have in mind?

Kate: A quiet wedding, I think. I know you don't like a lot of fuss.

Edwards: You know, a girl should never marry until she is fully competent to support a husband . . . .

Kate: And then she has no business marrying that kind of man.

C73

Edwards: I think we'll make a good team, Katie.

Kate *(sings)*:

> Hey, jolly man, why search the stars above?
> Look more close to home for love
> And you'll see, it will be
>
> Easy to mend again, those visions of happiness.
> I'll always be your friend
> If you'll let me try.
>
> Hey, jolly man, when all the world's passed by,
> There will still be you and I.
> Take my hand, jolly man.

(Edwards and Kate step forward.)

Edwards: A certain newspaperman got married the other day. He is pretty well known, especially to the old-timers, and much sympathy has been expressed for the bride. After receiving the ministrations of his spiritual advisor, the condemned man partook of a hearty break-fast, after which he smoked a cigar with apparent relish. To the last, he stoutly maintained his innocence. At the appointed hour, the good Reverend adjusted the noose, and the distinguished criminal was launched into matrimony!

(The bridal party gathers. There are general congratulations.)

Mrs. Bucklewhackster: Why, Mr. Edwards, you sly fellow! Disguising yourself as a misogynist all these years!

Edwards: Well, Mrs. Bucklewhackster, not all women are as bad as they paint themselves.

(During the flutter of laughter, the members of the company gradually drift into their opening funeral positions. Edwards remains down front, watching as the clergy and the Mounties enter. The candles are lit as Nolan joins Edwards. The mood has changed.)

Nolan: Congratulations, Bob. You finally did it.

Edwards: Yes, Paddy, and none too soon, it appears.

C74

Clergyman: Our late friend, Bob Edwards, had qualities of mind such as are given to few. Had he been more ambitious, his works might have been placed beside the great writers of the world.

Edwards: Pretty heady stuff.

(Nolan leaves him and joins the company in his opening position.)

Clergyman: He often showed to the world the mask of frivolity, yet behind that mask was a reverence for all that was pure and beautiful. We shall never see his like again.

(The Mounties open the coffin. Edwards starts back towards it.)

Nolan: Well, Bob, is there anything else you'd like to say?

Rosie: Keep it simple, Bob.

(Edwards smiles and speaks to the audience. Under his speech the lights slowly fade to a spot on his face. The cello plays a soft reprise of "Jolly Man".)

Edwards: As one journeys through life and the shadows begin to fall eastward, one reaches the solemn conclusion that too much of the world's wisdom is uttered — and too little lived.

(Edwards turns and sits on the edge of the coffin, the company focuses out front. He winks at the audience. Blackout. An instrumental reprise of "Hucksters and Fools" underscores the curtain call.)

The end

Costumes **Bob Edwards** — Neat and presentable always, never eccentric. Grey suit, Christie bowler (not necessarily the height of fashion, but never dowdy).

Paddy Nolan — A large man, considered quite debonaire. Dresses with more flair than Edwards but nothing gaudy. There should be a good colour complement between him and Edwards. They are on stage together throughout the play. Desirable to give impression of considerable bulk.

R.B.Bennett — Considered at this time to be one of Calgary's most eligible bachelors. Dressed with impeccable cut and taste - very conservative.

McGillicuddy — He is small-minded and mean. His clothes may reflect this: dark and narrow cut, nothing colourful or pleasing.

Rosie — A waitress. Poor, but attractive and always dignified. She is still young. Her clothes, although chosen mainly for practicality, reflect a basic femininity and underlying romanticism (could wear a pretty print).

Mother Fulham — Raises and slaughter pigs for a living. She is crusty and unclean. A true eccentric, her clothes are a grab-bag of convenience and reflect her occupation — man's shirt, heavy warm skirt, man's work boots and socks, all old and discarded. For festive occasions, she favours a large paddy-green sash tied around her waist in a huge bow.

Kate Edwards — Very young, pretty. A recent immigrant from Scotland, but doing well for herself. She may wear an outdoor outfit as she appears from outside. Attractive and understated.

Mounties — Full period dress uniform.

Party people — Gay, pretty, somewhat artificial. None of them should compete visually with Mrs. Bucklewhackster.

Judge — Long ridiculous powdered wig for fantasy sequence.

Others — Typical period dress, may be fairly realistic within the concept of the play.

C77

Musicians — Comfortable, casual period dress (like bar-room musicians).

The rest are all mythical beings, different in style and attitude from the rest of the characters, and they should be immediately visually apparent as such. They should all have a strong colour link to each other and every article of their clothing should be in the same chromatic range.

Albert Buzzard-Cholomondeley — A remittance man. Impeccably dressed as a moneyed Englishman of the early 1900's, but absurdly exaggerated and overstated (especially with accessories: ascots, spats, gloves and umbrella). As a fantasy character, he is entirely monochromatic in shades of white.

Mrs. Bucklewhackster — A totally gross exaggeration of the latest fashion — overdrawn, overdressed, entirely too many pearls, pins, feathers. May have a lorgnette. Also monochromatic.

McGonigle — Incredibly seedy. Looks like a dirty cowboy — dishevelled, reeking and untidy. Open-neck shirt, greasy neckerchief, unbuttoned vest, western hat and boots. Monochromatic.

McGonigle's Widow — Exaggerated mourning outfit. Veiled. Apron.

Gravedigger — Unkempt and ghastly, horror-movie type.

Thomas the Hangman — Medieval concept. Monochromatic. Hooded.

Song titles

EDWARDS' PRAYER — Bertie and chorus
HUCKSTERS AND FOOLS — Edwards and chorus
THE C.P.R. WANTS TO BE YOUR FRIEND — Nolan, Mother Fulham, Bennett, Shorty, Edwards
ALBERT BUZZARD-CHOLOMONDELEY — Bertie
WE'RE THE VERY BEST OF PEOPLE — Chorus
McGILLICUDDY'S SONG — McGillicuddy
FORGET IT — Edwards, Nolan
ARE YOU WASHED — Salvation Army Chorus
ROSIE'S SONG — Rosie
JOLLY MAN — Edwards
JOLLY MAN REPRISE — Kate
(Production music available upon application to Simon & Pierre Publishing Company Limited. See Copyright on page C2.)

Sources of research material

Glenbow Museum Archives, Calgary, Alberta (a source of surviving back issues of The Eye Opener).
"Eye Opener Bob" by Grant MacEwan; published by The Institute of Applied Arts Limited, Edmonton, Alberta.
"The Best Of Bob Edwards", edited by Hugh Dempsey; published by Hurtig Publishers, Edmonton, Alberta.
Calgary Herald Archives, Calgary, Alberta.

Props *The play deals roughly with the time period 1900 to 1922. The setting, however, is an isolated frontier town; therefore, set dressing and costume pieces from a slightly earlier period are most authentic. The first production of HOARSE MUSE was set in the 1890's.*

Two plush settees
Four small chairs
Two small round tables
Tiffany lamp
Pair of wall sconces
Chandelier
Coffin/desk of dark varnished wood
Lectern
Candelabra
Candles
Candle lighter
Candle snuffer
Bible
Two hanging banners — one for coffin, one for lectern

For the coffin/desk — small flask, black notebook, pad of paper, pencils, ink pot, straight nib pen, assorted papers, Eye Openers (several), two glasses, three bottles of scotch (one must be Johnny Walker), stethoscope

Rough pine coffin
Spade
Dead lilies
Clerk's folder
Large black book for Judge
Punch bowl
Punch glasses
Four silver trays with crackers and caviar

Bass drum with harness
Drum stick
Pair of cymbals
Tambourine

Two bundled stacks of Eye Openers (dummy)
Gavel

Pillow
Blanket
Copy of Hansard
Art book
Collection of Robert Burns
Copy of The Daily News
Tray
Glass of grapefruit juice
Ashtrays
Corks

Personal props
Edwards –
small notebook
pencil
$10 bill
Nolan —
pocket watch
pipe and matches
tobacco pouch
Bertie —
umbrella (curved handle)
notepad and pencil
wallet
McGonigle —
dead cigar
Mother Fulham —
corn cob pipe
gunny sack
Thomas —
trick rope
Judge —
coin

PUT ON THE SPOT/WHEN EVERYBODY CARES

two children's plays

by Beth McMaster

We would like to express our gratitude to The Canada Council and the Ontario Arts Council for their support.

Marian M. Wilson, Publisher

ISBN 0-88924-045-0
1 2 3 4 5/79 78 77 76
Simon & Pierre Publishing Company Limited, Order Department
P.O.Box 280 Adelaide Street Postal Station
Toronto, Ontario, Canada M5C 2J4

Author   **Beth McMaster** began writing for the theatre in 1969. For several years previous to that she had written for newspapers and magazines and had graduated into the fiction market with her first published children's story in 1965.

Her first play, THE MAGIC RING, was written for Peterborough Theatre Guild, a fast-growing amateur group. Since then, the Guild has produced the premiere production of THE HAUNTED CASTLE; STICK WITH MOLASSES (winner of the 1972 Nova Scotia Drama League Children's Playwriting Contest); ECHO, WHERE ARE YOU?; WHICH WITCH IS WHICH? (a finalist in the 1974 Touring Players' Foundation competition); A FLUMPET, A TRUMPET; and, PUT ON THE SPOT.

Mrs. McMaster's newest play WHEN EVERYBODY CARES, which appears in this volume, won an award in the Ontario Multicultural Theatre Association's National Playwriting Competition in 1976.

Added to this list are four shorter plays written for, and produced by, Peterborough Theatre Guild as entertainment at children's Christmas parties. All four — HAPPY HOLLY, THE DOLL SAID OUCH, STRIPES FOR CHRISTMAS, and HAPPY CHRISTMAS — have been so popular that in all they have been performed 95 times to a total audience in excess of 14,000.

One of the devices Mrs. McMaster uses to keep audience attention in all her plays is participation.

"In my plays I predict how the children will react in a certain instance and what they will say at a particular time. In that way I am treating the audience as a group.

"There are some who would say that I am stifling the child's individual creativity by treating him as part of a group. The type of approach they would use might be to bring a child on stage from the audience and have him actually participate in the play in some way."

Sometimes, that happens on its own in Mrs. McMaster's plays. "We have had children wander onto stage in the middle of a play and take a prop." *(quoted from Peterborough Examiner, Nov/76)*

Mrs. McMaster lives in a country home near Peterborough, Ontario, with her husband and three children.

D3

Artist

Ursula Reid was born in Essen, Germany in 1921 and lived there until she finished the German equivalent of Canadian high school. She continued her education in Berlin where she applied her talents to Art School. There she became a Master-Class-Student whose studies included drawing and painting, illustration, costume design and history.

Upon completion of her student years she taught for a short period at her alma mater. Her teaching career was brought to an abrupt halt by the Second World War during which time she changed her occupation to interpreter for the British Military Government in Essen. The post war years were spent at this job as a sketch artist for a fashion trade paper in Düsseldorf.

In 1951 Ursula emigrated to Canada and came to Toronto.

Her career in Canada began the next year when she was hired by the Canadian Broadcasting Corporation as a costume designer. She was to design costumes for a gamut of productions — from historical and period drama through opera to contemporary pieces.

After two years with the CBC in Toronto, she was transferred to Vancouver, at the request of the Design Director in Vancouver. There, she took on the responsibility for costuming all productions for the Vancouver area.

From Vancouver she moved to Burbank, California to work as a costume designer for the National Broadcasting Corporation. She stayed with them for two years and then moved on to Hollywood to become a sketch artist for 20th Century Fox.

Her next major job came in 1963, following a period of travel and painting in Europe. Ursula became a Costume Designer with the British Broadcasting Corporation in London, England. Her repertoire of costumes expanded dramatically during the thirteen years she worked on the wide variety of BBC productions.

In 1976 Ursula returned to Canada where she wished to resume her career.

Note

The costume sketches executed by Ms. Reid for the two plays PUT ON THE SPOT and WHEN EVERYBODY CARES are suggestions and imaginative ideas. All of the costumes are totally flexible and can be adapted according to materials and budgets available.

D5

PUT ON THE SPOT

Janie — Margaret Maloney

Mother — Una Mellors

Zebediah — Donald Endicott

Zoe — Una Mellors

Lubard — Larry Lewis

Benson — Tim Rowat

Rosy — Julie Hannaford

Calliope — Margaret Maloney

Zoing — Bertye Fremes

Hiram Krupt — David Fraser

Gonda Seed — Monica Palmer

**Original
production**

The original production of PUT ON THE SPOT was in June, 1975 by Peterborough Theatre Guild, Peterborough, Ontario. *Directed and Designed by* Terry Mellors

**Summary of
music credits**

Music for PUT ON THE SPOT was written by **Monica Palmer**, a pianist and former teacher in Peterborough. Mrs. Palmer has written the music and lyrics for several of Beth McMaster's plays. She has also written complete musical shows which have been produced in Peterborough, Ontario.

Lyrics for PUT ON THE SPOT were written by **Terry Mellors**, a professor at Trent University in Peterborough. Professor Mellors directed the original production of "PUT ON THE SPOT".

PUT ON THE SPOT

Janie — a young child (she may become Calliope Cuckoo)

Mother — (she may become Zoe)

Zebediah — the zookeeper

Zoe — the wife of the zookeeper

Lubard Leopard — the leader

Benson Bear — a slow, warm character

Rosy Rabbit — scatterbrained, but sincere

Calliope Cuckoo — a worrier

Zoing — a Dr. Suess-like character ("oi" pronounced as in "coin")

Mayor Hiram Krupt — the villain who may be tall and thin or
short and stout

Commissioner Gonda Seed — the mayor's female accomplice
should contrast in height and weight to Mayor Krupt *(see page D32 for
note regarding the alternative dialogue)*

**General
setting**

PUT ON THE SPOT
The set can be kept simple with minimal set pieces suggesting the
different playing areas.

Time   Present

Notes   A one-act play for children.
Running time of approximately 45 minutes.
Can be performed by senior elementary students.

MAYOR
HIRAM KRUPT   GONDA SEED

The stage is dark. During the overture the cast assembles down centre becoming a closely knit group or 'spot'. Only this 'spot' is lit as the cast sings.

All: Put on the spot, put on the spot.
We're ready to begin, so we've put on the spot.
Put on the spot, put on the spot.
The show's about to start, so we've put on the spot.

(Spot fades to blackout. Exit cast except Janie who moves down centre to main playing level where toy instruments and stuffed animals — each one representative of an animal in the play — are scattered about. Lights up. Janie is playing with the toys. A cuckoo clock — up centre — strikes 8 o'clock. Janie is holding stuffed leopard.)

Janie: Oh, oh, Lubard. You know what that means.

(Enter Mother.)

Mother: Janie, Calliope Cuckoo says it's your bedtime.

Janie: I'm getting my animals ready for the night. Now, Lubard Leopard, you can go in here.

(A section of the ramp from the upper level to the main level opens to become a toy box. The toys are put into it.)

Mother: Here's Rosy Rabbit. I guess we'd better pick these up too, hadn't we? *(She gathers musical instruments.)*

Janie: Put them in the cupboard, Mom. Come on, Benson, in you go.

Mother: The drum and the horn in the animals' cupboard?

Janie: Yes, Mom. So the animals can play them.

Mother: The animals play the instruments, do they?

Janie: Oh, yes, they have a band of their own, just like in my story, and they play the nicest songs.

Mother: What do they play?

D9

Janie: "Balakanoo Waltz" and lots of others, too.

Mother: I'd like to hear them sometime. Now you jump into bed and I'll read your story.

Janie *(jumping into bed)*: Can we have the one about Zoe and Zebediah and the Zoo?

Mother: That's your favorite, isn't it?

Janie: I like it and I like "The Magic Afghan".

Mother: Oh yes, "The Magic Afghan" . . . that's the one about the little boy who told untrue stories.

Janie: But then he got a magic afghan to help him tell the truth. That's what this is. It's a magic afghan.

Mother: It is? Well, then, let's put your magic afghan over you. Do you remember the little verse about telling the truth?

Janie: To tell the truth is best for all,
           The best for you and me,
           As sure as summer follows spring
           And butterflies are free.

Mother: In a nearby place called Balakanoo
           There's what you'd call a most interesting zoo.
           A zoo that's different, a zoo that's unique,
           A zoo you could go to week after week.

           Now here is the man who runs the whole zoo,
           His name's Zebediah — that's Zeb to you,
           Zoe's his wife and she knits all the time,
           Knitting and rocking and singing this rhyme.

(Slow fade. Blackout complete on word "rhyme". Janie exits during blackout. Cuckoo clock is removed. Mother moves down left to Zoe's chair and becomes Zoe. Mother's recorded voice continues with verse right after her voice stops.)

           To tell the truth is best for all,
           The best for you and me,
           As sure as summer follows spring
           And butterflies are free.

(Lights up on Zoe in chair knitting.)

> And the animals come to play at the gate,
> The children are there and can hardly wait
> To hear the sound of the serenade;
> They clap when their favorite songs are played.

(Enter Zeb as stage lights come up.)

Zeb *(blows whistle for animals)*: Alright, gang, let's try out our new number. *(Animals appear from many directions. Lubard pops out of what was toy box. Rosy comes through trap door in upper ramp)* The mayor's coming today to hear the band. *(General excitement among the animals — who, why?)* Yes, Mayor Krupt is coming and I do want the band to sound really good.

Lub: I've heard people say the mayor wants to close the zoo.

Zeb: The mayor wants to close the zoo?

Benson: They say he's going to put an apartment building right here where the zoo is now.

Zeb: Oh no . . . .

Zoe: The mayor won't close the zoo.

Zeb: How do you know, Zoe?

Zoe: I just know he won't.

Rosy: One of my cousins who used to live in Riverside Park has had to move because the mayor had apartments built on the property.

Zeb: Really, Rosy?

Rosy: And finding a new place to live when you have fourteen children isn't easy.

Lub: The mayor says there aren't enough people interested in a zoo.

Benson: Well, we get pretty good crowds here, Lubard.

Zeb: Some days we do.

D11

Zoe: Now that we have the band, the crowds are getting better and better.

Benson: When the word gets around, everyone will want to hear us play.

Zeb: I do hope so, Benson.

Zoe: Why don't you try out your song now, Zebediah? Once the mayor hears it, he'll never consider closing the zoo.

Zeb: Okay, we'll try it. Places. Same as usual. Alright, is everyone here?

Rosy: Yes, I'm here.

Benson: I'm ready.

Lubard: Where's my other drumstick?

Rosy: Here it is silly.

(There is general confusion.)

Zeb: Alright, let's hear the song now — one, two — *(For the Balakanoo Waltz the well-known "Blue Danube" may be used. The band plays it through once and Calliope comes in on the last two beats of each line)* Just a minute. Let's start it again. Try to be a little louder with your "cuckoo", Calliope. Remember, when I point my stick at you, let's hear it loud and clear. Ready? *(They play again. When Zeb signals to Calliope to come in, Calliope says nothing)* Calliope, you missed your cue. Now let's begin again. Ready? *(Calliope is trying to figure out what happened to her voice. The band plays again and at the same spot no "cuckoo")* Calliope!

(Calliope is miming — no voice.)

Rosy: What's the matter, Calliope?

Zeb: Yes, what's the matter?

Lub: You've lost your voice?

Benson: Oh dear, this is serious.

D12

Zeb: Lost your voice? Is that it? You've got laryngitis?

Benson: Say something, Calliope. Try to say something.

Rosy: You mean she can't say anything. She's lost her voice.

Zoe *(moves up from chair)*: Calliope dear, let me see your throat. *(Calliope comes down)* Oh goodness, that looks bad.

Rosy: You must have something to cure it, Zoe. You can cure anything.

Lub: After all she cured your lockjaw, Benson.

Benson: That's right.

Zoe: Fortunately I have. It'll cure it and almost immediately too. It's my special oil of skunk throat gargle. Benson, would you get it for me?

(Calliope starts to run and is grabbed by Zeb. Benson exits.)

Rosy: Run, Calliope, run.

Zeb: Oh no you don't! Stop that, Rosy. *(To Calliope)* You just stay right here. We've got to make that throat better. Don't forget the mayor is coming to hear the band today and if it doesn't play well —

Zoe: Now Zeb, we'll have Calliope's voice back in a minute.

Lub: Zoe, Benson will never find the medicine by himself.

Zoe: You go and help him, Lubard.

(Lubard exits.)

Rosy: Zeb's right, I guess. We need your voice in the band, Calliope.

Zeb: Zoe will fix you up, Calliope.

(Enter Benson and Lubard down left.)

Zoe: Oh, here you are. *(Medicine and spoon ready)* I'll just pour this out. Here now, you take it. *(Calliope squirms and makes faces)* Gargling is very simple. Just watch. There's nothing to it.

D13

(Here you can use the old music hall trick. Zoe takes the medicine, Lubard gargles and Benson spits. Lubard and Benson have, of course, prepared for this when they were off stage.)

Rosy: You see, Calliope.

Benson: It's good for you, Calliope.

Zoe: It'll clear your throat right away. *(Calliope gargles)* That's a good girl.

Zeb: Try to speak now, Calliope. Say something.

(Calliope tries with no results.)

Lub: Say "cuckoo", Calliope.

(Still no results.)

Zoe: That's funny, it usually works so fast.

Zeb: Well, that's the end of the band.

Benson: And likely the end of the zoo.

Rosy: Oh no, not the end of the zoo.

(Enter Zoing, magnifying glass around neck, pouch on side.)

Zoing: Greetings, everyone.

All: Oh hi. Hello . . . .

Zoing: Why all the sadness? I usually get a happy reception here.

Zoe: Calliope has laryngitis and can't "cuckoo" in the band.

Zoing: How very troublesome. I wondered why you weren't practising.

Zeb: Well, now you know.

Zoing: That's a pity, Zebediah. Can't you say anything, Calliope? *(Checks Calliope's throat)* My, you are incapacitated.

D14

Rosy: Zoe gave her some horrible medicine but it didn't do any good.

Zoing: I have my detective kit with me but I fear it doesn't include a voice finder.

Zoe: Thanks anyway for trying to help, Zoing.

Zeb: The band was to perform for Mayor Krupt today. And now we have no "cuckoo".

Lub: I've got an idea. Maybe Zoing could take Calliope's place.

Rosy: Zoing?

Zoing: Who me?

Benson: That sounds like a good idea.

Zoing: But I can't "cuckoo".

Lub: But you can "boing"! So, instead of *(hums Balakanoo March)* cuckoo, cuckoo, the song would go *(hums)* boing, boing — boing, boing.

(Calliope nods.)

Rosy: Hey, I think that sounds great. *(Hums)* Boing, boing — boing, boing.

Zeb: Well, it might sound alright.

Zoe: Of course it will, Zebediah. Why not try it?

Zeb: Would you help us out, Zoing?

Zoing: If I can assist, Zeb, I'd be glad to.

Zeb: Alright, let's try it. Places, everyone.

Lub: Right, Zeb.

Rosy: Sure, Zeb.

Benson: I'm coming, I'm coming.

Zeb *(with baton)*: Now, Calliope, you can play your instrument like you usually do and, Zoing, you come in with "boing" when I point to you.

Zoing: I understand.

(Band plays. Zoing does his part well and the effect is good.)

Zeb: How did that sound, Zoe?

Zoe: It sounded wonderful, Zeb.

Rosy: Weren't we terrific?

Benson: Remarkably good.

(General enthusiasm from all the animals.)

Zoe: I think you should keep Zoing in the band permanently.

Lub: That's a good idea, Zeb.

Rosy: Zoing, you could move right into the zoo.

Benson: I'd be glad to share my quarters with you.

Zoing: How generous of you, Benson.

Zeb: Just a minute, gang. That would be fine with me, but unfortunately I'm not the one to decide who joins the zoo.

Zoing: I know what you mean, Zeb. I'm not an animal and I'm not a person. It's doubtful if everyone would want me in the zoo.

Zeb: That's the problem, Zoing.

Lub: I think you'd be great, Zoing.

Rosy: I want you in the zoo, Zoing.

Benson: I think people would flock to the zoo to see you.

Lub: And the band would play.

JUMPSUIT + TAIL
OF LEOPARD-SPOTS-FUR-
FABRIC. HEAD + EARS CAN BE
FACE-HUGGING, AND FACE
CAN BE MADE-UP SPOTS;
AND FUN-UNDERWEAR.

LUBARD
LEOPARD

Rosy *(excited)*: I can see the billboards . . . . "The world's only zoo with a Zoing."

Benson *(saying as a recitation — each time Benson says a recitation he moves to bandstand to give a performance effect)*:
>We have a rare Zoing in our zoo,
>A Zoing that goes boing right on cue,
>He's not quite a beast
>But a music artiste;
>Do come and see him, he's new.

Zoe: Very good, Benson.

(Applause from animals. Benson bows shyly.)

Zeb: Hold it, everyone. Hold it. It may not work out that Zoing will be allowed to join the zoo.

Lub: But, Zeb, surely the mayor and the parks commissioner will agree . . . .

Rosy: . . . That he would be a super attraction for the zoo.

Zoe: And I have a feeling that what this zoo needs is a Zoing.

(Applause from animals.)

Zeb: Maybe you're right. Let's try that song again. *(Zeb is warming up band as a clanking is heard off stage. Tapping his baton)* Is there an echo in here?

Rosy: Listen . . . .

Zoing: What's that?

Rosy: Could it be . . . could it be . . . .

Zoe: A ghost?

Rosy: A g-g-ghost!

Lub: Sounds like a chain of some sort.

Benson: It must be a heavy one.

D18

(Enter Mayor Krupt with an oversize chain of office hanging to the ground.)

Krupt: Oh—oh—oh——

Zeb: Good morning, Mayor Krupt.

All: Good morning, Mayor Krupt.

Zoe: Was that your chain of office we heard?

Krupt: Oh, this chain is getting me down. *(He hands the chain to Benson to hold)*
> This chain, it's getting me down,
> It means I'm the mayor of the town.
> But it's getting so heavy
> I think I shall levy
> New taxes to pay for a crown.
>
> A crown will draw better respect,
> For the mayor that the people elect.
> Some will bow, some will scrape
> With their mouths all agape,
> And others may well genuflect.
>
> What a treat to have limitless power,
> To make people quake when I glower,
> To close down a zoo
> Just because I want to,
> And put up a great high rise tower.

(Krupt laughs loudly.)

Zoe: You do carry a great weight of responsibility, Mr. Mayor.

Krupt: Yes — and you know I'm the youngest man on council.

Lub: Really? How come?

Krupt: Because all the others are aldermen. *(Animals laugh politely)* What was that ghastly noise I heard as I came in?

Zeb: Oh, we were playing a tune, Mayor Krupt.

D19

Krupt: Standing around playing would be alright if the grounds were spotless, but they're not. *(He picks up gargle bottle which has been left)* I have a buyer interested in the property and I want it cleaned up. *(Hands bottle forcefully to Zeb.)*

Zeb: A buyer?

Krupt: Yes, a buyer.

Zoe: Who wants to buy the zoo property?

Krupt: Me.

Zeb: You?

Krupt: Yes, me. People don't care about a paltry zoo anymore. We need more apartment buildings. I plan to have a huge high rise built here.

Lub: But what will become of us?

Krupt: Well, I can think of a wonderful use for you. I have a special friend who wants a leopard-skin coat in the worst way. *(Lubard cringes. To Benson)* And a bearskin rug would look just right in front of my fireplace. *(To Rosy)* Don't get yourself into a stew, rabbit. Ha, ha. *(To Calliope)* And you . . . you should fit nicely into the town clock. I think every town should have a cuckoo clock. *(Calliope mimes that she has no voice)* What's the matter with her?

Zeb: Calliope has laryngitis.

Krupt: Laryngitis! Well, you'd be no good for a clock. What's more useless than a cuckoo without a voice? But we could, of course, make you into a nice feather hat to go with the leopard-skin coat.

Zoe: Just a minute, Mr. Mayor. You have no right frightening the animals like that.

Zeb: Zoe's right, Mr. Mayor.

Zoe: You won't come in here and close the zoo. There would have to be a bylaw passed.

Krupt: You are right, madam. But if the parks commissioner agrees

D20

when she inspects the zoo . . . .

Zeb: Inspects the zoo?

Krupt: Yes. Commissioner Gonda Seed, that most notable personage, the biggest magnate in the parks business, is coming to inspect the zoo tomorrow.

Rosy: If she's a magnate, will she be attractive?

Lub: Oh, Rosy!

Benson: Commissioner Gonda Seed is coming.

Lub: I know, Benson.

Zoe: And if it passes inspection, we'll be able to stay here?

Krupt: It won't. Commissioner Gonda Seed has very high standards.

Zoing: If I may interject, I would say this is a zoo of very high standards.

Krupt: And who are you?

Rosy: Oh, this is Zoing. He's very good in the band and he wants to join the zoo.

Krupt: A Zoing? A Zoing in a zoo? What's a Zoing?

Benson: Well, he isn't exactly an animal . . . .

Krupt: That's obvious. So why would he be allowed in the zoo? He looks like a . . . submarine with a warped periscope.

Lub: But he's very good in the band.

Zeb: Yes, he's first rate.

Krupt: This is not a music camp. This is a zoo. Now get this Zoing going. *(Turning to Zeb)* And remember we'll be around for inspection tomorrow.

Zoe: And if the commissioner is impressed, the zoo will stay open?

D21

Krupt: The commissioner won't be impressed. I'll make sure of that. *(To Benson re chain of office)* You! Bring that to my car.

(Krupt and Benson exit.)

Zeb: Oh Rosy, take this back. *(He hands Rosy gargle bottle. Rosy exits)* I'm sorry, Zoing. He shouldn't have said those things.

Zoing: I understand, Zeb. I've grown accustomed to it. I don't seem to belong anywhere.

Zoe: You belong here with us, Zoing.

Zeb: The trouble is, this doesn't seem like a very good place for anyone to belong, anymore. I don't think the zoo's going to be around much longer.

(Benson enters.)

Lub: I don't want to become a fur coat.

(Rosy enters.)

Benson: And I don't want to be a rug in front of anyone's fireplace . . . not even the mayor's.

Rosy: You wouldn't eat rabbit stew, would you, Zoe?

Zoe: Never, Rosy, never. And you're not going to become a rabbit stew. *(To Lubard and Benson)* And you won't be a rug, nor you a coat. This zoo is not going to close.

Zeb: How do you know that, Zoe?

Zoe: Because we won't let it.

Zeb: But Zoe, you heard what the mayor said.

Zoe: We'll have this place spotless tomorrow. We'll clean and scrub and polish. Everyone will shampoo and brush his coat. We'll clip the hedges and paint the fences.

Lub: I believe her. Zoe's always right, isn't she?

D22

Zoe: We'll weed the gardens and sweep the walks. We'll practise the band 'til it's perfect. It'll be as if someone had taken a magic wand of perfection and waved it over the whole zoo.

Rosy: Hurray for Zoe.

(Great enthusiasm and applause from animals. Calliope mimes, "But what about my voice?")

Zoe: What about your voice? It'll come back. But for tomorrow we'll let Zoing take your place in the band.

Benson: But if Mayor Krupt sees Zoing here . . . .

Rosy: . . . He'll be as cross as a wolf on a diet.

Zoe: We'll disguise Zoing and make him look like a cuckoo. Calliope can stay out of sight and no one will ever know.

(Zoe exits.)

Zoing: But how can I be made to look like Calliope?

(Zoe enters with feathers and bow.)

Zoe: Here's a special feather duster that's been used for many things. If we just tie it on here like this and this little bow will go here . . . . *(She quickly disguises Zoing.)*

Rosy: Oh super! She's right, Zoing. You do look like Calliope.

Benson: We have a smart Zoing in our zoo,
And that Zoing can become a cuckoo,
He's a talented beast,
Not dumb in the least,
Tomorrow he makes his debut.

(Animals applaud.)

Lub: He's right, Zoing, you look just like Calliope.

Zeb: But what if no one comes to the zoo tomorrow? If the place is empty, they'll close it for sure.

D23

TAIL CAN BE AN OVER-SKIRT, OVER LEOTARD, FEATHERS CAN BE CUT + STUCK ON, FELT, OR BRUSHSTROKES PAINTED ON.

WINGS: CAPE + BEAKED HOOD - HEAD • CUCKOO - EYES SEE - THROUGH

CALLIOPE CUCKOO

Zoe: But it won't be empty. The boys and girls out here will come. *(To audience)* Will you be here when the mayor comes? And will you clap when the band plays? And all pretend that Zoing is Calliope? See Zebediah, everything's going to be fine. These nice people are on our side.

Zeb: I wonder if we can save the zoo after all.

Zoe: Yes, we can. *(To animals)* What do you say?

All: Yes, we can!

Zoe *(to audience)*: And what do you say?

Audience: Yes, we can!

(Blackout. All exit except Zoe who is down left when lights come up on her only.)

Zoe: You know, I feel sure my words have done the trick. The dust and the fur are flying around this zoo. *(Lights are coming up on set to reveal animals busy working. Lubard is filling bathtub from a rain barrel at stage right)* Zebediah's mending fences and oiling hinges. Benson Bear's busy inventing rhymes to honour the occasion. Rosy Rabbit is prettily painting. And Calliope's putting up decorations. *(Lubard is removing his skin)* Zoing is giving things a final going over with the broom and Lubard Leopard has slipped out of his skin and is in his underwear having his Saturday bath on Friday night. Did I say his underwear?

(All except Benson, Lubard and Zoing exit during this speech.)

Lub *(now in tub, is blowing bubbles)*: Take a look at this, Zoing.

Zoing *(as he sweeps)*: That's terrific, Lubard, but why do you bathe in your underwear?

(Benson, oblivious to conversation, is on bandstand.)

Lub: Saves time. I don't have to launder the underwear separately. When I'm clean, it's clean.

Zoing: That sounds sensible.

D25

(Lubard continues to scrub, wrings out his sponge. At this point a pole with a hook comes from stage right and silently removes the skin.)

Lub *(stands, shakes and steps out of tub)*: Now, where did I put my skin? Zoing, did you see my skin?

Zoing: No, I didn't, Lubard.

Lub: It must be here somewhere. Didn't you just sweep this area?

Zoing: I did, but I didn't see a leopard skin.

Lub: Where can it have gone?

Zoing: I don't know, Lubard.

Lub: Well, we've got to find it.

Zoing: Come and we'll get my detective kit. You can borrow my spy glass. I'll use my animal skin detector.

Lub: I can't understand where it could have gone.

(Both exit. Benson comes down centre. Enter Calliope.)

Benson: Oh, hello, Calliope. I thought I heard someone speaking. *(Calliope mimes)* Oh, it wasn't you. You still have no voice. I guess I was imagining things. *(Sits centre. Calliope is at stage right with her back to wings. During Benson's speech a net on a long handle drops over her head and pulls her off)* You know, Calliope, I'm sorry we made you have that horrible gargle, but we only did it because we thought it would do you good. *(Turns and sees Calliope is gone)* Hmmm. I wonder where she went. *(Audience will tell him a net has pulled her off. If they don't, he elicits the information with . . .)* Did anyone see where Calliope went? Caught in a net? You say a net pulled her out that way? Oh no! So many things are happening around here . . . I don't know what I'm going to do. If we all have to leave the zoo, what's going to become of me? Maybe people outside won't understand a slow old bear. *(For this verse he remains seated down centre)*

> Sometimes I'm misunderstood,
> I'd like to succeed if I could,
> But what will I do,

If they close down the zoo?
My future just doesn't look good.

(Blackout. Exit Benson. As lights come up Zoe and Zeb enter.)

Zeb: Zoe, how can you be so calm when you know this may be the last day for this zoo?

Zoe: It won't be, Zeb. I know it won't be. Things will be fine. I walked through the zoo last night and everything and everybody looked splendid. Lubard was just about to have his bath, and Zoing was doing a last minute check on everything.

Zeb: Well, I hope you're right. I think I'll call Lubard and see how things are going.

(Uses whistle to call Lubard.)

Zoe *(sits in chair and knits)*:
       To tell the truth is best for all,
       The best for you and me,
       As sure as summer follows spring,
       And butterflies are free.

(Lubard peeks in from toy chest trap door and catches Zeb's eye.)

Zeb: What are you doing back there?

Zoe: What is it, Lubard?

(Lubard motions Zeb over . . . whispers problem to him and Zeb relays to audience.)

Zeb: You what? Your what was stolen? But who? You don't know? You have nothing but your underwear? You don't look your best in your underwear? I can believe that!

Zoe: What is it, Zebediah?

Zeb: Someone stole Lubard's skin last night while he was bathing.

Zoe: Stole his skin?

Zeb: Yes, he has nothing to wear but his underwear.

D27

Zoe: Only his underwear!

Zeb: I just knew things were going to go wrong.

Zoe: Now, Zeb. Don't get upset. Come on out, Luby. He may not look that bad in his underwear. *(Lubard comes out of box)* He looks that bad.

Zeb: Oh, no!

Lub: I'm sorry, Zeb.

Zoe: You have no idea who took your skin?

Lub: No idea at all. And my skin's not all that's missing.

Zeb: What else is gone?

Lub: You're not going to be happy, Zeb.

Zeb: I'm not happy now, so tell me. *(Enter Zoing backwards with magnifying glass. He is examining the floor as he comes)* What are you doing, Zoing?

Zoing: I'm looking for Lubard's skin.

Lub: Zoing, tell Zeb what else is missing besides my skin.

Zoing: Calliope Cuckoo.

Zeb: Calliope Cuckoo!

Zoe: Calliope's missing?

Lub *(nodding)*: Whoever took my skin has probably birdnapped Calliope.

Zoe: Oh, poor Calliope. And her with a bad throat.

Zeb: Oh, so many problems, I can't think. *(Turning to Lubard)* First, what are we going to do about you?

Lub: I guess I don't look much like a leopard without my spots.

D28

Zeb: That's for sure.

Zoe *(moving to Lubard)*: I know what we'll do Lubard. We'll put some of my afghan pieces on you for spots.

Lub: Your afghan pieces?

Zoe *(demonstrating)*: You see — a few of these and you'll be as good as new.

Lub: Do you really think I'll look better?

Zeb: You have nowhere to go but up.

Zoing: He's right, Lubard. Here, let's try a few more.

Zoe: Put one over here.

Zoing: He needs another one to balance this side.

Zeb: There now. Let me stand back. I think that was a good idea of yours, Zoe.

Zoe: They look great, Lubard! Yes, they do.

Zoing: Lubard, that's marvellous!

Lub: Well, I do feel better.

Zeb: Good. Let's get Zoing into his cuckoo disguise. Mayor Krupt and Commissioner Gonda Seed will be here any minute. If this whole thing works out, it'll be a miracle.

Zoing *(indicating audience)*: I see we have a big crowd today.

Lub: Isn't it wonderful? All these people came to help save the zoo.

Zeb: Come on. Let's get ready for the mayor and commissioner.

Zoe: We'll save the zoo, just wait and see. *(Blackout. Exit all but Zoe. Spot on Zoe in her chair)* Do you know I have a secret I'm going to tell you. Not even Zebediah knows. No one does. Those knitted spots Lubard is wearing, they aren't just ordinary afghan pieces. Oh no. You know how I sing whenever I knit? Well, I found out one day that I'd knitted the song right into the pieces. That's right. I don't know how it happened but the magic of the song is in the spots Lubard is wearing. And you know what the words of the song say —

> To tell the truth is best for all,
> The best for you and me,
> As sure as summer follows spring
> And butterflies are free.

And that's what Lubard is going to have to do . . . tell the truth . . . all the time. As long as he wears those spots he has no choice, he'll have to tell the truth. That's right. It doesn't matter what happens, you can believe everything Lubard says. I do hope these truth spots don't cause him any embarassment. Saying nothing but the truth can be a bit of a problem. Sometimes people don't want to hear the truth about themselves. I have a suspicion about who might have taken Lubard's skin. I am not sure yet but I'm doing a little detective work. I'll let you know when I have some news.

(Blackout. Enter Krupt and Commissioner Gonda Seed with Zeb on ramp upstage. Krupt and Gonda should contrast physically. Ideally he is tall and thin and she is short and fat.)

Zeb: Oh yes, things are going well at the zoo. Of course we have the odd little problem.

Gonda: So the mayor told me.

Zeb: Good crowd we have today, don't you think?

Krupt: I can't understand why all these people would come to a zoo.

Zeb: They like to come to hear the band. It's just about time for the concert. I'll call the animals now. *(He uses whistle.)*

Krupt *(aside to Gonda Seed)*: I guess we have to hear this band, my sweet.

Gonda: Oh well, if it can't be avoided . . . .

Zeb: I'm sure you'll be really impressed with the band, commissioner. Alright, is everyone here? Places everyone. As you can see we have special guests, so let's give them our rendition of "The Balakanoo Waltz". Ready? *(Band plays. If audience doesn't clap, Zeb should encourage them to)* How did you like it, Commissioner Seed?

Gonda: Well, I suppose it was alright, if you like that kind of music. I myself am used to loftier things.

Krupt: Me too, of course.

Zeb: Oh . . . .

Gonda: What is that bird or whatever it is over there?

Zeb *(hesitantly)*: Why, that's our new cuckoo.

Krupt: Cuckoo . . . you can't have a cuckoo . . . I mean, let me talk to that cuckoo. Come here, bird. *(Zoing approaches)* Let's hear you "cuckoo". *(Zoing hesitates)* Come on. Let's hear it. I want to hear you "cuckoo"!

Zoing: Coo — coo — boing!

Gonda: Coo what?

Zoing: Coo boing.

Krupt: Just as I thought. This is no cuckoo. This whole thing is a disguise. *(Jerks feathers off tail.)*

Gonda *(snatches ribbon)*: Well! Such deception! Where is the cuckoo? What is the explanation for this?

Zeb: I'm sorry, Commissioner Seed, but at the moment, our cuckoo is missing.

Gonda: Imagine mislaying a cuckoo. That animal over there. *(Indicates Lubard)* What is that?

Zeb: It's a leopard, Commissioner.

Gonda: That's the strangest looking skin I've ever seen on a leopard. Has he moulted?

Zeb: Well . . . .

Gonda: I've always wanted a leopard-skin coat but not if it's going to look like that. I'd like to have a closer look.

D31

Zeb: Lubard, please come down here.

Benson *(aside)*: Oh, oh.

Rosy: Poor Luby.

Gonda: My, those are weird looking spots.

Lub: So . . . that dress you're wearing is pretty awful too. *(Covers mouth in amazement.)*

Zeb: Lubard!

Gonda: What did you say?

Lub: I said your dress looks dreadful.

Gonda: The nerve of you . . . .

Krupt: Really.

Lub: Well, it matches your hat. They both look like something that came off the trash heap.

Gonda: Oh!

Krupt: Why, you insolent, ill-mannered cat!

(In the following, the dialogue in brackets is suggested as an alternative to be used if Gonda is tall and thin.)

Lub: I suppose when anything built like her needs a new dress, they send out for a tentmaker.
(I suppose when anything as high as that needs makeup, you send out for a flagpole painter.)

Gonda: Oh! Do something with this animal before I strike him.
(Oh! Do something with this animal. A person who has climbed to my social position doesn't have to tolerate such behaviour.)

Lub: I'd better be careful. I'll bet your swing could knock an elephant into the middle of next week!
(I wouldn't throw my nose into the air if I were you. It's high enough as it is.)

D32

BENSON

iG FLOPPY BROWN SWEATER + BAGGY PANTS. FURRY HEAD-HAT, LEAVING FACE
REE FOR TEDDY-MAKEUP. OR A TEDDY-FUR JUMP-SUIT, MITTS + SLIPPERS.

Krupt: Zookeeper, can't you control that animal?

Zeb: Luby, stop that! *(Clamps hand over Lubard's mouth)* I'm sorry, Mayor Krupt. I just can't understand what's got into Lubard. He's usually not like this, commissioner.

Lub *(pulling Zeb's hand away)*: I calls them as I sees them.

Zeb: Lubard! Stop that! Now don't say another word, please!

(Lubard retreats.)

Krupt *(to Gonda)*: My poor Gonda, you see this is what I told you. I said the whole place was out of control. I was right, wasn't I, my sweet one?

Gonda: You were right, Hiram. You were right. *(Getting control of herself)* There is no way this place can remain open. The animals are obviously out of control.

Zeb: But, Commissioner Seed . . . .

Gonda: Never mind the excuses. I've seen enough. A—a—a—thing trying to pass as a cuckoo. And then a leopard who likes to insult people.

Zeb: But, commissioner . . . that's never happened before and . . .

Krupt: And we'll make sure it won't happen again.

Gonda: Let us go right now, Hiram, and have a bylaw passed to close this zoo . . . this despicable institution.

Krupt: Yes, yes, my dear. Such insults to one as flawless as you. *(To Zeb)* I'll be back later.

(Krupt and Gonda exit.)

Zeb: Lubard, how could you . . . ?

Rosy: Why did you say those things, Luby?

Benson: That's not like you, Lubard.

D34

Lub: I don't know. I don't know why I said them.

Zoing: You couldn't blame the commissioner for being so angry.

Lub: Boy, she looked like a battle ship with all guns firing!
(Boy, she looked like forty stories of short circuits!)

Zeb: Lubard, that's enough.

Benson: Look at the problems you've caused for everyone by your thoughtless insults.

Zeb: Lubard, when you're ready to apologize for the things that you've done, you come and tell us. *(Lubard is dejected)* Come on, everyone. We'd better start packing up.

Rosy: Oh no! Come on, Benson.

(All exit but Lubard and Zoing.)

Lub: Oh Zoing, what have I done? I've ruined everything for everybody.

Zoing: You didn't conduct yourself as well as you might have.

Lub: I did a real job of putting my paw in my mouth. And I can't understand it. I'm not usually like that. I just had to tell the truth, and the truth about that lady . . . .

Zoing: . . . Is better left untold.

Lub: But why? Why did I have to say those things? Even if they are true, I know you shouldn't say things like that.

Zoing: Lubard, I'm wondering . . . I have an idea. I'm going to get something from my kit.

(Zoing exits quickly.)

Lub: From your kit? Oh, from your detective kit.

(Zoing re-enters.)

Zoing: Yes, here it is.

D35

Lub: What are you doing, Zoing? Why are you doing that? *(Zoing takes out a stethoscope. He puts it on one spot and then another. He examines spots with a magnifying glass)* What are you doing, Zoing? Do you hear anything? Why are you doing that?

Zoing: Hush, will you!

Lub: Are you trying to find out why I told the truth? What's the matter? Do you know what's wrong? Gee, I hope I haven't got leopard-sy.

(The examination is finished. Zoing turns away looking concerned.)

Zoing: I know why you said all those things.

Lub: You do? Why?

Zoing: Those spots Zoe put on you have a song knitted into them.

Lub: A song knitted into them? What kind of song?

Zoing: It's that truth song Zoe sings while she knits. So with those spots touching you . . . .

Lub: . . . I have to tell the truth! Right?

Zoing: Right.

Lub: Are you sure that's it, Zoing?

Zoing: I'm fairly sure, but we can test it.

Lub: How?

Zoing: Here, give me one of those spots. I'll put it on myself. *(He does.)*

(Zoing looks at Lub and starts to laugh. He laughs and laughs.)

Lub: What's so funny?

Zoing: In that spotted underwear you're the funniest thing I've seen.

Lub: But you said before that I looked fine.

D36

Zoing *(still laughing, he speaks to audience)*: Anybody who says he looks fine needs his eyes examined.

Lub *(jerking spot off Zoing and then starting to rapidly remove his own)*: Let's get these spots off both of us before we ruin a beautiful friendship.

(Enter Zoe.)

Zoe: I just saw Mayor Krupt and Commissioner Seed leaving. They didn't like the band, did they?

Lub: They didn't like the band and they liked even less what they heard after that.

Zoe: Why's that?

Zoing: You didn't tell us you had knitted your song into the afghan squares.

Zoe *(probably to audience)*: Did the truth get Luby into trouble? What did he say?

Lub: I simply compared Commissioner Seed to everything from an elephant to a tent maker's model.
(I simply compared Commissioner Seed to everything from a giraffe to a flagpole.)

Zoe: I'm so sorry, Luby.

Lub: You're not to blame, Zoe. You only wanted to help me out. But I sure ruined everything for the zoo! Commissioner Seed is going to close it. Of course, I'm not much good in a zoo anyway without my skin.

Zoe: I think I know who took your skin, Luby.

Lub: You do? Who?

Zoe: It was Mayor Krupt.

Zoing: Mayor Krupt? How do you know?

Zoe *(pulls from pocket a bit of fur)*: Whose fur does this look like?

D37

Lub: Mine. Why, it's a piece of my coat! Where did you get it?

Zoe: I've been doing a little investigating and I found it by the mayor's car.

Lub: No wonder he wanted to see my spots up close. He couldn't figure out where I got them.

Zoing: He probably has Calliope, too. That's why he was suspicious when he saw me.

Zoe: I think you're right, Zoing.

Lub: Why, that rotten . . . he said he wanted my skin for a coat but I never thought he'd steal it!

Zoe: The problem is going to be to prove that the mayor did steal your skin and birdnap Calliope.

Lub: He'll certainly never admit it.

Zoe: You're right.

Lub *(song)*:
>When you're really on the spot,
>When the situation's hot,
>Then you have to think out carefully what to do.

>We're close to desperation,
>It's a hopeless situation,
>But we've really got to try to save the zoo.

Zoe, Zoing & Lub:
>Put on the spot, put on the spot,
>What do you do when you're put on the spot?

>When you're really on the spot,
>When you're losing all you've got,
>Just sing a song and it will come to you.

>So, let's contemplate again
>The words of our refrain
>For that may tell us what we need to do.

Put on the spot, put on the spot,
That's what you do when you're put on the spot.

Zoe: I've got it!
There's an answer to our plight,
Everything will turn out right
If you can put the spot on Mr. Mayor.

Magic words and magic song,
We know you can't be wrong,
So we'll do it right away . . . that's if we dare.

Zoe, Zoing & Lub:
Put on the spot, put on the spot,
That's what you do when you're put on the spot.

Zoing: I see what you mean, Zoe. When they come back to close the zoo, we'll get one of these spots onto the mayor . . . .

Zoe: Yes.

Lub: Yes . . . and then he'll have to tell the truth!

Zoing: Right! That's it Lubard. If we ask a few careful questions, he'll tell the whole story.

Lub: Oh, boy! *(Pause)* But how do we get a spot onto him?

Zoe: Yes, how?

Zoing: I'll put glue on the back of the spot . . . . *(Indicates.)*

Lub: . . . And you could hold it in your hand like this and slap the mayor on the back and say, "You know, sir, I think you're right. This would be a great place for an apartment". And the spot will stick to him.

Zoing: Yes, the spot will stick to him.

Zoe: That's a splendid idea.

Zoing: Just in case it doesn't, Lubard, you can have a second spot ready and be prepared to do the same thing.

D39

FLUFFY PINK JUMPSUIT,
MAYBE. A RED BOW, BOOTIES
AND MITTS. FURRY BUNNYHEAD
FITTING AROUND FACE, MAKE-UP.
WIRED EARS, WIRED ACROSS
UNDER THE BONNET.

ROSY RABBIT

Lub: Alright! Let's get these spots all gluey so we'll be ready. I can hardly wait to hear that scoundrel admit the whole thing.

Zoe: I'll go and tell Zebediah what's happened. The poor dear must be so upset.

Zoing: Think how upset Calliope must be. *(To audience)* I hope she's alright.

(Blackout. Chair is placed down right. Lights up. Gonda Seed is sitting and Krupt is standing down right. Calliope, nearby, is curled up dejectedly and on a leash.)

Krupt: I'm going to have a nice coaty woaty made for my little spring flower. *(Puts skin around her.)*

Gonda: Oh, really Hiram dear, you do spoil me. And what about that bird? What will you do with her?

Krupt: I was going to put her into the town clock, but since she has no voice, I guess we'll have to think of something else. How would my sweet Gonda like a new feather hat for her pretty little head?

Calliope *(with alarm)*: Cuckoo, cuckoo!

Krupt: Oh, so you've found your voice again, have you? Well, we'll have to decide what's to become of you.

Gonda: Hiram, dear, I think a feather hat sounds lovely.

Krupt: Alright, my little lovebird, You shall have a feather hat.

Calliope: Cuckoo, cuckoo!

Krupt: Quiet you. *(To commissioner)* We'll take this leopard skin and the bird with us, and then we'll stop at the furrier's and at the milliner's after we close the zoo. Come here, you! *(Jerks leash.)*

Gonda: You're so very good to me, Hiram.

Krupt: You're my little sugar wugar. *(To Calliope)* Come on, you!

(Blackout. Enter Lubard and Zoing as lights come up.)

Zoing: I think this should work, Lubard. Have you got the spots?

Lub: Right here, Zoing. They're nice and gluey.

Zoing: Good. Then all is in readiness. Here they come.

(Enter Krupt and Gonda on upstage ramp. Krupt carries the bylaw, rolled up.)

Krupt *(as he enters)*: Alright, we have the zoo closing bylaw ready to post.

Gonda: There's been enough of this mismanagement and insolent behaviour among the animals. Where's the zookeeper?

Lub: Oh, he'll be along shortly.

Krupt *(really noticing Lubard for the first time)*: What are you doing running around in that outfit? It looks like your underwear.

Gonda *(turning in disgust)*: Oh, no!

Lub: It is. You see I have nothing to wear. Someone stole my skin . . . .

Zoing: You wouldn't know anything about Lubard's missing skin, would you, Mr. Mayor?

Krupt: Of course I wouldn't.

Gonda *(to Lubard)*: You won't need a skin now that the zoo's closing.

Krupt: Just think, in a few months this very place will be covered with apartment buildings.

Zoing: This would be a fine place for an apartment, sir.

(Just as Zoing is about to slap the spot on Krupt, he moves to Gonda Seed. Zoing's hand swings around and smacks the spot onto Lubard who has moved in for a closer look. The spot catches Lubard on the side of the face. He removes it with distaste.)

D42

Krupt: And you, my little chickadee . . . I mean, commissioner . . . you will have a penthouse apartment.

Gonda: You are good to me, Hiram.

Lub *(he has collected his thoughts and is moving in with his spot)*: There's certainly lots of money to be made in apartments these days, Mr. Mayor.

(Lubard slaps his spot on and it sticks. The mayor turns to look at him and in so doing turns his back to Gonda Seed.)

Gonda: Oh, Mayor Krupt seems to make money no matter what he does. Oh, oh, what's this? You've got a spot on you.

Krupt: Where?

Gonda: Here. *(She removes it)* There now, you're all handsome again.

Krupt: You take such good care of me, my sweetie pie. Now we'll just post this bylaw, and we'll go on to you-know-where.

Gonda: How sweet you are, Hiram.

(During these speeches Lubard and Zoing have communicated to the audience and to each other that they will now put a spot on a chair and get Krupt to sit on it. Zoing has circled to chair down right and placed spot on it.)

Zoing: Before you begin your business, Mr. Mayor, why don't you sit down and we'll get you a glass of lemonade.

Krupt: A glass of lemonade? That sounds like a good idea.

Zoing: Sit right here then and be comfortable. I'll get it.

Krupt *(about to sit)*: Thank you, my boy.

Gonda: Hiram, don't be ridiculous. *(The word "Hiram" causes him to straighten up)* We have to get you-know-where.

Krupt: Oh yes, my precious. I did promise you, didn't I? We'll just get this bylaw up . . . .

D43

Zoing *(takes bylaw from his hand)*: Perhaps Lubard could put this up for you. You just sit and rest while he does it. You can tell us if it's straight.

Krupt: Oh yes, certainly, yes indeed.

Lub: Sit right here, Mr. Mayor, and I'll look after it.

Krupt: Well, I have had a busy day, and I would like to sit down.

(Krupt is about to sit. Gonda moves quickly to him and grabs his arm.)

Gonda: Come on, Hiram. Who cares if the notice is straight? The bulldozers will be here in a day or so anyway.

Krupt *(as she leads him across left)*: You're right, my dear. Just put it up any way at all. I've got to be going.

Lub: Bulldozers! I happen to know someone who could let you have a bulldozer . . . for . . . .

Krupt: How much?

Lub: Oh nothing, nothing if you'd tell him you know me.

Krupt: Really?

Gonda: Hiram, let us go.

Krupt: Just a minute, my sweet one. This could save me a lot of money.

Lub: If you'd care to sit down we can discuss it.

Gonda: Hiram!

Krupt: Patience, my sweet, patience. Are you sure this is true? *(On the word "true" he sits on the spot.)*

Zoing: I'm sure you'll hear nothing but the truth spoken around here.

Gonda: You can talk business some other time, Hiram.

D44

(Gonda pulls him to his feet and as she does he turns his back to audience so the spot is plainly visible.)

Krupt: Yes, but dear, this is a chance . . . .

Lub: I think now would be a good time to talk business. *(Moves to Krupt and turns him around to face audience.)*

Zoing: Did you take Lubard Leopard's skin?

(The following dialogue must be delivered rapidly.)

Krupt: Yes, I took it. *(Covers mouth in surprise at what he has said.)*

Lub: Did you birdnap Calliope Cuckoo?

Krupt: Yes, I did.

Gonda: Hiram!

Zoing: And where are the cuckoo and the leopard skin now?

Krupt: They're in the car.

Lub: And where's the car?

Krupt: It's parked out front.

Zoing: Where are the keys?

Krupt: Here they are.

Zoing: There, Lubard, go get your skin.

Lub: Right away, Zoing.

(Lubard exits.)

Gonda: Hiram, you fool. Don't say another word.

Krupt: But I have to.

Gonda: Why?

D45

Zoing: Because it's true, Commissioner Seed.

Gonda: But he's never told the truth before. What about my leopard skin?

Krupt: Putting a leopard skin on you would be like trying to cover an elephant with a pocket hankie.
(Putting a leopard skin on you would be like trying to cover a tower with a towel.)

Gonda: Oh!

(Enter Lubard in skin with Calliope.)

Zoing: Calliope, you are safe! You are safe!

Calliope: Cuckoo, cuckoo.

Lub: See . . . she has her voice back.

Zoing: So now, Mr. Mayor, I think the zoo should stay open, don't you?

Krupt: Definitely. It's a fine institution.

Lub: And there's no reason why Zoing can't join the zoo?

Krupt: Of course not.

Gonda: Him? At the zoo? He's too queer looking to be here.

Krupt: If we made that a rule you'd never get in.

Gonda: Hiram! I'm very annoyed with you!

Krupt: Who cares?

Gonda: Why, Hiram, I'd just like to say to you . . . .

Krupt *(to others)*: You know, it's surprising something that full of hot air doesn't just rise into the atmosphere.

Gonda *(whining)*: Oh—h—h. What about my coat? Aren't I your little spring flower?

D46

Krupt: Little spring flower? You look more like somebody's fall pumpkin!
(You look more like one of last season's cat-tails.)

Gonda *(chasing him with umbrella)*: Why, you! When I catch you——

Krupt *(running)*: You won't. You move like a tank . . . slow and heavy.
(You move like a giraffe running through a mudhole.)

Gonda: Oh—h—h—h!

(She chases him off right via ramp. Enter Zeb, Zoe, Rosy and Benson.)

Zeb: What's all the commotion about?

Zoe: Calliope, Calliope, you're back. How's your throat?

Calliope: Cuckoo, cuckoo!

Zoe: Wonderful!

Rosy: And you have your skin back, Luby?

Lub: Yes, and I don't think I'll ever take it off again.

Benson: Not even to bathe?

Lub: Not even to bathe.

Zoing: Zebediah, Mayor Krupt has decided the zoo will stay open.

Zeb: He has?

Rosy: Oh goody, goody, goody.

Zoe: Your plan worked?

Lub: It sure did.

Zoing: The mayor said *(imitating)*, "This zoo is a fine institution".

Lub: He also said Zoing should definitely be included in the zoo.

D47

All: Hurray!

Benson: We now have a Zoing and a zoo:
I'm happy, I hope you are too.
We'll play in our band
And won't it be grand
With sounds such as "boing" and "cuckoo".

(Applause from the others.)

Zeb: Zoe, you said it would all work out. You always seem to know.

Zoe: So now in that place called Balakanoo
All is fine in our favourite zoo.
There is no worry, there's no dismay.
The animal band is here to stay.
(Blackout. Clock begins to "cuckoo" eight times during blackout. Lights up. Janie is sitting up in bed stretching. Mother enters up left.)

Mother: Time to get up, Janie. Did you sleep well?

Janie: Yes, I did and I had . . . *(remembering)* I had a wonderful dream.

Mother: What about?

Janie: About my animals and their instruments in a zoo. I want to see if they had the same dream. Lubard, Benson . . . . *(She lifts lid of toy box and Lubard appears)* Oh hello!

(At the same time, the animals appear from all around and go right into finale song.)

All: Now it's time to close the show,
Wish we didn't have to go,
But plays, like dreams, must always have an end.
Lubard's now got back his coat,
Cuckoo's cured her silent throat,
And there's absolutely nothing to append.
Put out the spot, put out the spot,
The moment has come to put out the spot.
(Cast is back in opening spot formation and only this spot is lit. After the last line, all the cast "blows" and the spot goes out.)
The end

ZEBEDIAH

Set design **PUT ON THE SPOT**

The original play was done on a variety of levels. The highest level, up left, was the bandstand. A ramp of the same level crossed the stage from it to an exit up right. The next level was the main playing area, part of which was lifted to make a bathtub for Lubard. A still lower level at the centre downstage area was Janie's bed. Downstage left, a little higher than the main playing area was Zoe's chair (which was a hanging-type basket chair). About mid-right was Calliope's swing.

Props **PUT ON THE SPOT**

Toy instruments (drum, horn)
Stuffed animals (leopard, rabbit, bear)
Afghan
Story book
Knitting and afghan pieces
Baton and whistle for Zeb
Instruments for animal band
Medicine and spoon
Magnifying glass
Pouch
Chain of office for Mayor Krupt
Feathers and bows
Bathtub
Rainbarrel
Broom, tools, oil can, paint brush, decorations
Sponge
Bubble-making equipment
Pole with hook
Long-handled net
Stethoscope
Piece of fur (leopard)
Glue
Leash
Bylaw (rolled up)
Car keys
Umbrella

Sound effects **PUT ON THE SPOT**

Cuckoo clock
Mother's voice (recorded)

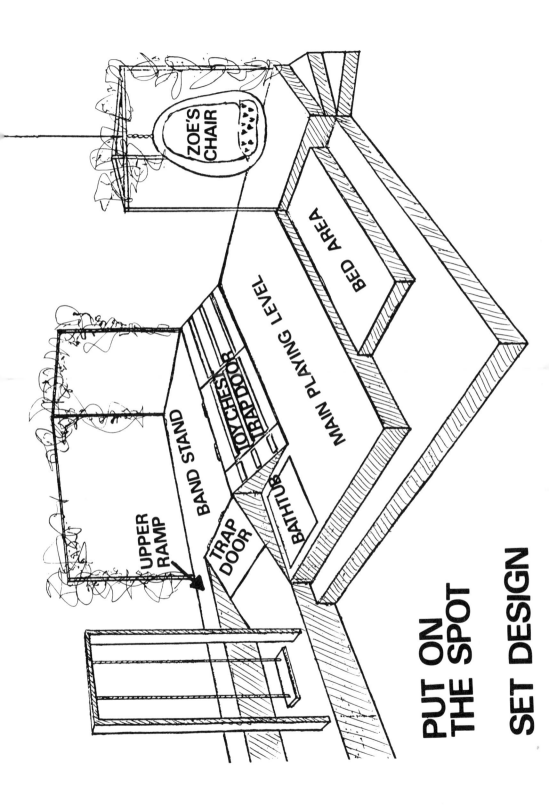

PUT ON
THE SPOT

SET DESIGN

ZOE'S CHAIR

BED AREA

MAIN PLAYING LEVEL

BAND STAND

TOYCHEST
TRAPDOOR

BATHTUB

UPPER
RAMP

TRAP
DOOR

Costumes   **PUT ON THE SPOT**

Janie — Dressed in night attire and then changes into her Calliope Cuckoo costume.

Mother — May wear her Zoe costume as the mother. In the original production, Zoe wore a full-length, scarlet, cotton gown with gold braid trim.

Zebediah — Wears a traditional municipal employee's uniform.

The Animals — May have traditional or imaginative costumes but the toy animals in the opening scene must be in comparable attire.

Zoing — May have an antenna and all sorts of strange colours and combinations of shapes.

Mayor Hiram Krupt — Wears a loud, distasteful suit and bowler hat.

Commissioner Gonda Seed — Wears a dress designed to emphasize her worst features.

Song titles   *PUT ON THE SPOT* — Company
THE BALAKANOO WALTZ (instrumental) — Zeb, Rosy, Benson, Lubard, Calliope
THE BALAKANOO WALTZ (instrumental) — Zeb, Rosy, Benson, Lubard, Zoing
KRUPT'S SONG — Hiram Krupt
THE BALAKANOO WALTZ (instrumental) — Zeb, Rosy, Benson, Lubard, Zoing
FINALE — Company
(Production music available upon application to Simon & Pierre Publishing Company Limited. See Copyright on page D2.)

MAYOR KRUPT

ALTERNATIVE IDEA
WITH STOUTER
BUILD

WHEN EVERYBODY CARES

by Beth McMaster

We would like to express our gratitude to The Canada Council and the Ontario Arts Council for their support.

Marian M. Wilson, Publisher

WHEN EVERYBODY CARES
© Copyright 1976 by Beth McMaster
All rights reserved

Published simultaneously in 1976 in the United States by Books Canada Inc., 33 East Tupper Street, Buffalo, N.Y. 14203.

ISBN 0-88924-045-0
1 2 3 4 5/79 78 77 76
Simon & Pierre Publishing Company Limited, Order Department
P.O.Box 280 Adelaide Street Postal Station
Toronto, Ontario, Canada M5C 2J4

Play background

WHEN EVERYBODY CARES was Beth McMaster's entry in a National Playwriting Competition sponsored by the Ontario Multicultural Theatre Association in 1976.

The contest terms of reference called for a play with "a definite multicultural flavour, emphasizing tolerance and understanding among peoples and races, while instilling pride in one's own heritage, regardless of origin".

WHEN EVERYBODY CARES was awarded third prize.

Cast of characters

WHEN EVERYBODY CARES

Announcer — over forty, easily flustered

Marvin — not too bright, but eager

Leon — a songwriter and singer who plays the guitar; sensitive, but practical

Janet — a friend of Leon's; levelheaded and friendly

Dagmar — Simon's girlfriend

Simon — overbearing and loud

Richard Robot — a robot who is used to being a part of a minority group; mature and pleasant

NOTE: Marvin, Leon, Janet, Dagmar, Simon and Richard are all young people about the same age.

The boys and girls in the opening scene are played by the above characters.

General setting

WHEN EVERYBODY CARES

The action takes place out-of-doors and no particular set is necessary. At least one hiding place in the playing area will help with the staging. Since it is Labor Day, some decorative banners and pennants could be used. These might have a futuristic theme to suggest the 1990 period.

Time 1990

SLINKY +
GLITTERY GEAR

LEON

Ursula

The play begins with recorded band music — the type which might be heard at a fair. The announcer, wearing a garish suit and a hat, enters.

Announcer *(in a barker voice)*: Alrighty folks, I want to say how delighted we are to have such a fine crowd here for our Labor Day celebrations in Fairway City. And look at that weather! Just look at that weather! *(Enter boy)* Have you ever seen such a beautiful day? Your holiday committee has some great activities planned for you. There are games and contests for the young folk . . . . *(The boy taps the announcer to get his attention)* Yes, my boy?

Boy: When do the contests start?

Announcer: Soon, my boy, soon. *(Exit boy)* Now where was I? . . . Oh, yes — *(switching to barker voice)* games and contests for the young folk, and games and contests for the not-so-young folk. There are sack races, wheelbarrow races, relay races, potato races, baton races — *(enter girl on crutches)* foot races, three-legged races, two-legged races and——

(The girl taps the announcer.)

Girl: Are there any one-legged races?

Announcer: Ah . . . ah . . . we'll have one added to the list. *(Exit girl)* Yes . . . now . . . *(again in barker voice)* there are contests for high jumping, pole jumping, broad jumping — *(enter boy with a frog on a leash. The frog jumps by means of an invisible thread, and is hopping along beside the boy)* . . . sideways jumping and jumping over the moon.

(Boy taps the announcer.)

Boy: Are there frog jumping contests?

Announcer: No, there aren't. Now will you get that thing away from here? *(Boy and frog exit)* Now where was I . . . oh yes. *(In barker voice)* In our beard growing contest, there are prizes for the men for long beards, broad beards, new beards, curly beards — *(enter girl with an obviously false beard)* . . . old beards and braided beards.

(Girl taps announcer.)

Girl: Can girls enter the beard contest?

Announcer: Absolutely not. Really! Since women have been liberated you never know what they'll think of next! *(In barker voice)* Then, too, we have an annual favourite, our hobby contest. I've seen stamp collections, model trains — *(enter boy carrying basket with large snake's head coming out through hole in top)* . . . and model planes, macrame and rockets and . . . and . . . . *(He notices the snake.)*

Boy: My hobby is raising boa constrictors.

Announcer: And a fine hobby it is, I'm sure, young man. Now run along . . . . *(Exit boy)* And, of course, the biggest item in our day's events — the Fairway City Centennial Song Contest. By the end of the day, we'll all be humming a brand new tune that will be a salute to 100 years of progress in our city. And the judges of this special song contest will be you — you the people who have come to join this celebration. Your applause is going to decide our centennial song. *(Enter Marvin dressed as magician with appropriate coat and top hat. He carries a case that has legs which fold out to make it into a small table)* That, however, will be the final event of the day. And now to organize the games.

Marvin: Pardon me, sir. I'm Madwick the Magician. I know you'll want to see this wonderful act of magic that I have prepared.

(He drops the table legs and opens his case.)

Announcer: Well, actually, I'm very busy . . . .

Marvin: But this is to be my entry in the hobby contest.

Announcer: I see. Well, the hobby contest will be judged later.

Marvin: Good. That will give me time to practise. Now, if I may just borrow your hat. *(He takes it.)*

Announcer: But . . . but . . . .

(The following is an unsuccessful attempt at the flourish of an accomplished magician.)

Marvin: Now if you will just watch, you will see the most amazing

D60

feat of magic ever done in this city. This is a day of celebration, is it not?

Announcer: Well, I guess . . . .

Marvin: Absolutely! And, of course, no celebration is complete without a cake. Right?

Announcer: A cake?

Marvin: A cake, my dear chap, a cake. So I simply take this hat — this completely empty hat — and into it I will break two eggs.

Announcer: Two eggs into my hat?

Marvin: Relax, my dear chap. We can't make a cake without eggs, can we? *(To audience)* We've got to have eggs for a cake, don't we?

Announcer: But . . . but . . . .

Marvin: Now we'll beat the eggs well, and to them we add some flour . . . .

Announcer: Flour?

Marvin: . . . And some butter and some raisins. Everybody likes raisin cake. Now we stir this up and cover it over with this magic cloth.

Announcer: Oh—h—h, my good hat . . . .

Marvin: I simply wave my wand over it all and say . . . .
　　　　　Abra-ka-dabra,
　　　　　Ali-kazan,
　　　　　Cake will you bake,
　　　　　As fast as you can!
And out of the hat I pull . . . . *(The announcer is leaning over looking into the hat. He obviously sees no cake, only a mess of ingredients)* I pull . . . it didn't work! Funny, I was sure that was how the book said to do it. It didn't work.

Announcer: It obviously didn't work.

Marvin: I can't understand it. Oh well, that's how it goes sometimes.

D61

Here's your hat.

(He puts the hat onto the announcer's head and of course the batter runs down over him.)

Announcer: "Here's your hat!" Is that all you can say? "Here's your hat!" You've ruined my hat with your stupid trick.

Marvin: It's not a stupid trick. It just doesn't work sometimes.

Announcer: You've ruined my hat. You can be sure you're not going to win the hobby contest if I have anything to do with it.

Marvin: You can't say that. That's prejudice. You don't like people from East City, do you?

Announcer: I love people from East City. My mother lives in East City. What I don't like is eggs in my hat and on my head.

(Marvin is gathering up his equipment.)

Marvin: I knew I'd never get a fair chance. You're obviously against certain people. *(To audience)* He's against certain people, isn't he? *(Audience will respond "no")* He is so. I'm going to talk to the officials about this.

(Exit Marvin.)

Announcer: Oh dear, oh dear.

(Enter Leon with his guitar. He wears a green ribbon.)

Leon: Where will the song contest be held?

Announcer: The song contest? We'll hear all the entries separately.

Leon: I have an entry.

Announcer: Well, I hope it's better than the contest entry I just witnessed. You can do your song right here if you want.

Leon: Oh fine, but not 'til after the games?

Announcer: That's right. Now if you'll excuse me, I have a little

D62

cleaning up to do.

(Exit announcer. Enter boy, running.)

Boy: Hey, do we go with those that have a ribbon like ours?

Leon: That's right.

Boy: Have you seen anyone with a red ribbon?

(Enter girl.)

Leon: There's one over there. *(Indicates a direction.)*

(Exit boy.)

Girl: Do you know where the blue ribbons go?

Leon: Right down that way.

(Exit girl. Leon strums on his guitar and in a moment Janet and Richard Robot enter. Both are wearing green ribbons.)

Janet: Hi Leon! I see you're on the green team. So am I.

Leon: Oh great, Janet.

Janet: And so is Richard Robot. I don't think you know him, Leon.

Leon: Hi Richard!

(Richard is costumed as the traditional robot, but moves with the ease of a human, although he is sometimes bothered by a squeak in his joints. Each speech of Richard's begins and ends with a mechanical beep, which he makes with some sort of buzzer or tone device on his person. He may also have a battery operated light on his helmet which comes on when he speaks.)

Richard: Hello, Leon.

Janet: Richard's new in the area.

Richard: We just moved onto Elm Street.

D63

Leon: Oh yeh, into that house where the Chinese family was.

Richard: That's right.

Leon: They certainly didn't stay in this neighbourhood long . . . I mean the Chinese.

Richard: They didn't seem to like it.

Janet: I can understand that. Some people weren't very nice to them.

Richard: That can happen when you're different.

Leon: Yeh, I guess you should know.

Janet: Leon!

Richard: That's alright. I'm used to it, Janet. We were the first family of robots in our last neighbourhood, too.

Janet: It must be hard.

Richard: Sometimes it is. It depends on the people. Anyway, I'm proud to be a robot. We may have our shortcomings, but we've got a lot going for us.

Leon *(strumming guitar)*: Yeh . . . .

Janet: You've written a song for the centennial contest, haven't you, Leon?

Leon: Yeh, but I'm not very happy with it.

Janet: Let's hear it, Leon.

Leon: Okay, it goes like this . . . . *(Sings — Fairway City.)*
       Have you heard, come join the crowd,
       We're having our hundredth birthday party!

       Fairway City, that's for me,
       Fairway City, that's for everybody,
       It's so pretty — Fairway City,
       That's where I hope to spend my next hundred years!

Just one hundred years ago,
Our fair city began to grow,
It started small — but grew up tall,
Now we are proud to be part of it all.

Fairway City, that's for me,
Fairway City, that's for everybody,
It's so pretty — Fairway City,
That's where I hope to spend my next hundred years!

Janet: It's good, Leon.

Richard: Yes, Leon, I think it sounds just fine.

Leon: I'm not really happy with it. It seems to need something else.
Say, Janet, you sing. Why don't you sing along? Maybe an extra voice
will help.

Janet: Sure, Leon. I'd love to.

Leon: You can sing too, Richard, if you want. Here's a copy of the
music. *(Hands one to each)* Let's try the chorus and the first verse.
Ready? Here goes.

All *(reprise — Fairway City)*:
Fairway City, that's for me,
Fairway City, that's for everybody,
It's so pretty — Fairway City,
That's where I hope to spend my next hundred years!

Just one hundred years ago,
Our fair city began to grow,
It started small — but grew up tall,
Now we are proud to be part of it all.

(Richard has a tinny voice and does nothing to improve the song.)

Richard: How does it sound?

Leon: Ah—h—h—h not perfect.

Janet: I think it needs a little more work.

Leon: That's an understatement.

Richard: Well, I'll be glad to help you out, Leon, even if we do have to practise.

Janet: Maybe we should try it again, Leon.

Leon: Well . . . .

Richard: I'm so glad you're including me in the group. It'll be a great way to get to know people.

Janet: Yes . . . .

Leon *(aside)*: It'll be a good way to ruin my reputation as a song-writer.

Janet: Let's try it again, Leon.

Leon: Okay. All ready?

Richard: I'm ready Leon.

Leon: And Richard, could you possibly try to tone your voice down. It seems to be coming through a bit strong.

Richard: Sure, Leon.

All *(reprise — Fairway City)*:
>Fairway City, that's for me,
>Fairway City, that's for everybody,
>It's so pretty — Fairway City,
>That's where I hope to spend my next hundred years!

>Just one hundred years ago,
>Our fair city began to grow,
>It started small . . . .

(The song is interrupted by Marvin who comes running in. He has his magician's equipment with him.)

Marvin: Say folks, I'm glad to see a little gathering here. You lucky people are looking upon Madwick the Magician. I have a trick I'm planning to do for the hobby contest, and I'm going to let you in on a preview.

Janet: Oh, I'd love to see it.

Marvin: I attempted to show the announcer my skill a few minutes ago, but found I was dealing with a completely prejudiced man.

Leon: The announcer is prejudiced?

Richard: In what way?

Marvin: As soon as he found out I was from East City, he said I would never win the contest.

Richard: That hardly sounds fair.

Marvin: Well, you know how some people are. Anyway, I'll do my famous live-rabbit-out-of-the-hat trick. You see this hat? *(He uses his own hat)* Empty. Right? Absolutely empty.

Janet: Yes, I see.

Marvin: Now, into the hat I put this scarf, which as you can see has a rabbit painted on it.

Leon: So I see.

Marvin: I stir it around with this magic spoon. Abra-ka-dabra, ali-kazan . . . and out comes a live rabbit. *(He pulls out a dead plucked chicken.)*

Janet: Oh—h—h.

Marvin: Hm—m—m—m. Something must have gone wrong.

Leon: Ha, ha, ha.

Richard: That's a sick looking rabbit.

Janet: I think you need a little more practice if you hope to win the hobby contest.

Leon: Why don't you take up chicken farming? You seem to have a knack for it.

Marvin: So you've got something against magicians, have you?

D67

Janet: We're only saying your act needs a little polishing. *(To audience)* It does, doesn't it?

(Audience will likely answer "yes".)

Marvin: Oh, don't ask them. They're all against me too. I thought when I saw you with this . . . this robot, that I was dealing with people free of prejudices. I can see I was wrong.

Janet: That's not prejudice. We're just saying you lack the skill of a polished magician.

Marvin: You'll see when the judging comes. I'll be way out front . . . in spite of the fact that everyone's against me. You'll see!

(Exit Marvin.)

Richard: Good luck!

Leon: What a nut!

Janet: That guy's got a real problem.

(Enter Simon and Dagmar. Simon has a sports equipment bag. Both are wearing green ribbons. Dagmar wears a rope belt.)

Simon: Greetings all!

Janet: Hi Simon! Hi Dagmar!

Dagmar: Hi!

Leon: You're both on our team too, eh?

Simon *(as a yell)*: Green, green, we're really keen! We're the top! We're the team!

(All laugh.)

Janet: Simon, Dagmar, this is Richard Robot. He just moved into the empty house on Elm Street.

Dagmar: Oh no!

D68

Simon: You're kidding?

Janet: What's the matter?

Simon: When the Chinks moved out, I thought we had nowhere to go but up, and now look at this!

Leon: Simon!

Janet: That's a dreadful thing to say. I'm sorry, Richard. We do have some ignorant people in this neighbourhood.

Richard: That's alright, Janet.

Dagmar: Gee, you talk funny.

Simon: What can you expect from a misshapen tin can?

Richard: Have you ever known a robot before, Simon?

Simon: Fortunately I've managed to escape up until now.

Dagmar: Your luck's run out.

Richard: I'd suggest you at least give us a chance to prove ourselves.

Simon: Wha'd'y' want to prove?

Janet *(trying to prevent open warfare)*: Come on, fellows. Let's get started. The first game scheduled is hide-and-seek.

Leon: Hide-and-seek?

Janet: Yeh, it's just to fill in 'til they organize the races.

Simon: But hide-and-seek?

Dagmar: Oh, come on. It'll be fun. I'll be "it". Okay?

Simon: Alright. Let's go. Green, green! We're really keen. Watch us now! Watch this team!

Leon *(he has gotten rid of his guitar)*: I'm game. It'll take my mind off my song.

D69

Dagmar: I'm counting.

(Dagmar covers her eyes and the others scatter to hide as she counts. The audience area may be used for hiding. Richard moves in the same direction as Simon. His squeaking is particularly bad.)

Simon: Go somewhere else, creaky joints. You'll give me away.

(Richard turns to go but there isn't time.)

Dagmar: Ready or not you must be caught.

(Dagmar is looking for others and Simon decides to make a run for the goal. He might make it, except that at the same time, Richard, squeaking loudly, also decides to head for the goal and attracts Dagmar's attention. Richard, who is a fast runner, makes it to the goal. Simon is caught.)

Dagmar: You're "it", Simon.

Simon *(to Richard)*: You stupid, creaking tin can. I knew you'd ruin the game. *(Leon and Janet have come out of hiding)* I knew he'd ruin the whole thing.

Richard: I'm sorry. I'll drop out.

Simon: Well, I should hope so.

Janet: Never mind the hide-and-seek. We'll get on to something else.

Simon: What's there to do if he's got to be included?

Dagmar: I can't think of anything a robot can do that's any fun.

Janet: I'm sure there are lots of things.

Richard: What about doing relay races? I can run pretty fast.

Simon: I'll bet. Clunk, clunk. Beep, beep.

Dagmar: Squeak, squeak.

Leon: Let's give him a chance, fellows.

D70

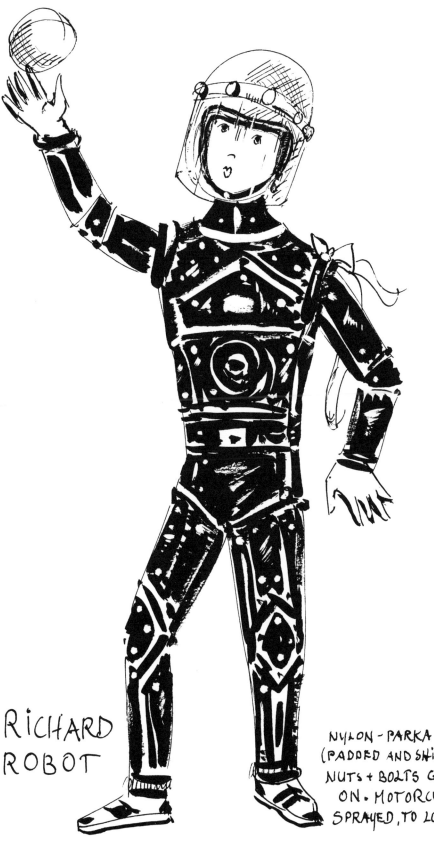

RICHARD
ROBOT

NYLON - PARKA AND PANTS,
(PADDED AND SHINY). JOINTS,
NUTS + BOLTS GLUE-TAPED
ON. MOTORCYCLE-HELMET.
SPRAYED, TO LOOK METALLIC.

Janet: I'll be the starter and the judge. Simon, you and Dagmar can be one team and Leon, you and Richard will be the other. Okay?

Leon *(not very confident)*: Well, I guess . . . .

Richard: I haven't got my track shoes with me.

Simon: There he goes. Trying to weasel out.

Dagmar: He knows a lost cause when he sees one.

Janet: Leon, could you lend Richard a pair of Adidas?

Leon: Yeh, I guess I could. I'll have to get them.

Janet: Good. You get them and I'll get a starting whistle.

Simon: I've got some balls in my equipment bag we can use.

Leon: Come on, Richard.

Janet: We'll be right back.

(Exit Richard, Leon and Janet. Simon is getting the balls out of the equipment bag.)

Dagmar: Listen Simon, you may wish you had that squeaky drum on your team.

Simon: Why?

Dagmar: 'Cause I can't run worth a hoot.

Simon: You can surely run faster than that clunker.

Dagmar: I'm not so sure. He was pretty fast when we were playing hide-and-seek.

Simon: Never mind. I've got an idea that will take care of the whole problem.

(Enter Leon, Richard and Janet. Richard is wearing track shoes. Janet carries baskets.)

D72

Richard *(as they enter)*: The shoes feel fine, Leon.

Leon: We're all set, Simon.

Janet: I've got the whistle. And they said we needed these baskets.

Simon: They must be for the goals. I've got the balls ready.

Janet: I guess we put the baskets out here, do we?

Leon: Yeh. That one could go over there for Simon and Dagmar, and the other one out here for Richard and me.

Dagmar: Here, I'll take one.

Simon: I'll put a red ball in each basket. *(They put the baskets out in the audience area, likely in two different aisles, equidistant from centre stage area. Ad lib conversation — i.e. 'I think this is about right for distance.' 'Does that seem even to you?')* Ready?

Janet & Dagmar: All set. Ready.

Janet: I'm not even sure how to run a relay race.

Simon: Okay. I'll tell you. Here's what we do. Each team gets a blue ball. The first person has to run with the blue ball, drop it into the basket, pick up the red ball and bring it back. He gives it to the next runner and that runner has to leave the red ball in the basket and bring the blue ball back.

Dagmar: So we have to end up with the red ball in the basket and the blue ball here?

Janet: The first team to hand me the blue ball is the winner?

Simon: That's right.

Leon: Okay. Are you ready, Richard?

Richard: All ready.

Janet: Let's have Dagmar and Leon run first for each team. Are you ready? Have you got your blue ball?

D73

Dagmar: All set.

Janet: I'll count down and then blow the whistle to start.

Leon: Fine.

Janet: On your mark . . . five, four, three, two, one. *(Whistle.)*

(Leon and Dagmar race to the two separate baskets, leave the blue ball and bring back the red. Leon should be considerably ahead of Dagmar when they reach the start again so that Richard Robot starts out with a decided lead. Of course there is great cheering from the other member of each team and likely from the audience. Janet tries to remain neutral but is obviously pro Leon and Richard. When Richard reaches the basket, he is unable to drop the red ball in. Simon has put a magnet into the ball and it has stuck to Richard's metal hand. Of course no one knows this, and Leon and Janet are shouting instructions to Richard who struggles to drop the ball and, in fact, is still struggling to get the ball off when Simon wins the race. Richard moves back toward the stage area, the ball still in his hand.)

Dagmar: We won, Simon! We won!

Simon: Of course we won. What did I tell you, robot?

Richard *(to Leon)*: The ball stuck to my hand.

Leon: Oh brother! What a way to lose a race!

Dagmar: I guess you're no better at relays than you are at hide-and-seek.

Simon: Let's go, Dagmar. This dump for tin cans is getting me down.

Dagmar: I'm going to be beeping myself if I don't get away from here.

Simon: We'll leave our latest immigrant for you and Leon. Don't forget to oil him. C'mon Dagmar. I want to get the rocket I'm entering in the hobby contest. Green! Green! The beeper's team! Funniest members I've ever seen!

(Exit Simon and Dagmar laughing, repeating verse, and perhaps doing a simple choreographed step to help with the ridicule.)

D74

Janet: How can they be so mean? I'm sorry, Richard, but most of the neighbourhood is very nice, isn't it, Leon?

Leon: Yeh, I guess so. Listen, I'm not going to be able to stay. I've got to run and do some work on my song.

Janet: But, we won't have a team if you leave.

Leon: Because of certain members, we haven't got much of a team now. See you around.

(Exit Leon.)

Richard: I guess he's really mad at me.

Janet: I'm afraid so.

Richard: I'm really sorry about losing that race. I can't seem to do anything right. Maybe this isn't my kind of neighbourhood.

Janet: Don't say that, Richard. It wasn't your fault.

Richard: I still can't get this ball off my hand.

Janet: Let me see. There must be something holding it.

Richard: Do you see what it is?

Janet: Look! There's something pushed inside the ball.

Richard: What is it?

Janet: It looks like a piece of metal. Let me try to pull it out. It's coming.

(She struggles and finally gets it. The ball comes easily from Richard's hand.)

Richard: There, I can get the ball away from my hand now. What is it?

Janet: I think it's a magnet.

Richard: A magnet! No wonder I couldn't put the ball in the basket.

That's one disadvantage of being a robot. You can really get hung up on magnets.

Janet: I'm going to run and tell Leon what happened.

Richard: Oh don't bother, Janet. If it weren't the magnet, it would be something else. Like my singing. I know he didn't like it either. I'm really not a very good singer.

Janet: Oh don't mind Leon, Richard. He's not usually like that. He's worried about his song. He wants very much to win that contest.

Richard: It's a good song, but I think it needs a stronger beat. The guitar accompaniment just doesn't do it.

Janet: I wonder how it would sound with a drum?

Richard: Hey, do you know what? My beep might be some help here. I did specialized percussion in a band where we used to live.

Janet: What do you mean "specialized percussion"?

Richard: I used my beep. *(He beeps several times.)*

Janet: You can beep whenever you want?

Richard: Oh yes. Beep, beep. Beep, beep.

Janet: Then I think you're right. That would strengthen the beat in the song. *(To audience)* Don't you think that would help? That's just what the song needs. Why don't we suggest it to Leon?

Richard: I doubt if he'd even want to try it.

Janet: Oh, I think he would.

Richard: I'm not so sure.

Janet: I'll tell you what. Why don't you hide over there? When Leon comes back we'll try the song, and you come in with the beep, beep.

Richard: And he won't know it's me doing it?

Janet: Right. *(To audience)* If you like it, will you applaud?

D76

(Audience will confirm support.)

Richard: Well, I don't know . . . .

Janet: If Leon doesn't like it, he'll say so and you can forget about it.

Richard: And if he does, I'll come out and he'll know I'm the one who's done it.

Janet: Exactly.

Richard: Maybe he won't come back at all.

Janet: Relax. If he doesn't, I'll go and find him.

Richard: I hope it works.

Janet: It will. *(To audience)* Won't it? Here come Simon and Dagmar. I'm going to tell Simon what kind of a sport I think he is.

(Enter Simon and Dagmar. Simon has his rocket.)

Dagmar: Squeak, squeak. Beep, beep.

Simon: Well, if it isn't old sardine can. Anybody got a can opener?

Janet: Never mind the nasty remarks, Simon. At least Richard doesn't cheat to win relay races.

Simon: Who cheated?

Richard: You did! You put a magnet in the ball.

Simon: I've never heard of magnets in balls being against the rules in relays. Have you, Dag?

Dagmar: Never heard of such a rule.

Janet: You knew Richard wouldn't be able to put the ball down if there was a magnet in it.

Simon: So? That's his problem. We don't make special rules for robots.

D77

Richard: I'm not asking for special rules . . . only fair play.

Simon: Did the rules seem fair to you, Dag?

Dagmar: Sure did. I didn't find myself sticking to the ball.

Janet: It's no use, Richard. Some people just won't try to see how things are for those who are a little different.

Richard: I think you're right.

Janet: Let's go down to the corner and watch for Leon so we can do the song.

Simon: You mean Leon is letting you sing with him?

Richard: It's not completely decided.

Dagmar: It's not like Leon to throw away a chance to win a contest.

Simon: Maybe he's gone beepers! Ha! Ha! Get it, Dag?

Dagmar: Gone beepers! That's a good one, Simon.

Janet: Come on, Richard. Let's get away from here.

(Exit Janet and Richard. Simon and Dagmar laugh.)

Dagmar: That's a good one you pulled on old squeaky joints, Simon.

Simon: The sooner that creep and his whole rattling family get out of here, the better it'll be for all of us.

(Enter Marvin.)

Marvin: Good afternoon, folks. I'm Madwick the Magician. I'd like to show you one of the famous tricks I'll be doing this afternoon as part of my hobby contest entry.

(He sets up his stand and opens his case.)

Simon: You entering the hobby contest?

Marvin: I most certainly am, and with my natural skill I expect I'll be walking off with the prize.

Simon: Okay. Let's see you perform.

Marvin: Alright. Young lady, if I may have that rope you're wearing around your waist.

Dagmar: What are you going to do with it?

Marvin: I simply need it as a prop to assist me in an amazing feat of magic.

Dagmar: Alright. Here it is.

Marvin: Now, you see this rope? All one piece. I jerk it. I snap it. It cannot be broken. Now, I take my scissors and I cut it in half.

Dagmar: Hey, that's my belt!

Marvin: Relax, my dear.

Simon: Never mind, Dag. I've seen this trick done before. They put it all back together again later.

Dagmar: Oh—h—h . . . .

Marvin: Now, I cut each half of the rope in half again. And now we have four pieces. We drop the four pieces into this magic box and I put the lid on. Now, with a wave of my magic wand, I shall reconstruct the rope which is within the box. Abra-ka-dabra. Ali-kazan. There. Now I open the box and presto, your rope . . . .

(His voice fades as he picks the four pieces out of the box.)

Dagmar: My belt! You've ruined my belt!

Simon: What kind of a trick is that?

Marvin: Hm—m—m. I wonder what went wrong. Here's your belt. *(He hands the pieces to Dagmar.)*

Dagmar: You call this a belt?

Simon: Listen, buddy. I'll show you a different kind of belt if you

D79

don't get Dagmar a new rope.

Marvin: Don't threaten me. I'm not going to fight you. I don't believe in fighting.

Simon: If you don't believe in fighting, you should quit borrowing things for your dumb tricks.

Marvin: I knew I shouldn't have done the trick for you. You're in the hobby contest, aren't you?

Simon: As a matter of fact I am.

Marvin: That's it. You've got a grudge against me 'cause you want to win.

Simon: Well, I'm sure you won't be much competition.

Marvin: Everyone's against me. Everyone!

(Exit Marvin.)

Dagmar: What a dope!

Simon: I'm sorry about your belt.

Dagmar: Oh, it's not important. It was just a piece of rope. It looks like you might have a good chance of winning if that's a sample of the competition. Let's see your rocket work, Simon.

Simon: Okay. Just a sec 'til I get it ready. I have to check this connection.

Dagmar: Does it go high?

Simon: Way up. Here, tie this string around my wrist. It's attached to the rocket so it won't get away on me.

Dagmar: You don't want to lose it.

Simon: I sure don't ! *(She ties the string)* That's it. All set. Oh, oh, the string is tangled around. That's no good. The rocket can't take off at all when it's like that. *(He is trying to free the rocket when suddenly it begins to smoke. A manually operated flashing light inside* *the rocket, shining through coloured celluloid, will give the appearance of an internal fire)* Oh! Oh! It's caught fire! Oh—h—h—h! Get this out of my hand! Quick! Quick! Oh—h—h! *(Dagmar is struggling to free him)* Help! Oh! It's hot! Oh my rocket!

Dagmar: Help! Help! *(Enter Richard and Janet running)* Help! Quick, help us! Quick! Somebody do something!

(Richard puts his hand over the rocket and extinguishes the fire.)

Richard: There. I think that's got it. Are you hurt, Simon?

Dagmar: Did it burn your hand, Simon?

Janet: Let's see, Simon.

Simon: Not badly. Just along this side. Man, that hurts!

Richard: Is your rocket ruined?

Simon: I'll have to have a look at it.

Dagmar: Did you get burned, Richard?

Richard: Me? No.

Dagmar: But you put your hands right over the flames.

Richard: That's the advantage of being a robot. Fire doesn't bother metal hands.

Janet: I'd never thought of that.

Simon: My rocket's okay. A little charred, and some of the wiring burned, but it can be fixed.

Dagmar: Can you see what made it catch fire?

Simon: Yes, it's right here. A fuel leak near the exhaust system.

Dagmar: What a close call!

Simon: It sure was, but it turned out okay.

SIMON AND DAGMAR

LEOTARDS, OR OVERALLS, T-SHIRTS, SOME "ORBIT"-TYPE SIGN ON IT.

Janet: Thanks to you, Richard. Eh, Simon?

Simon: Yeh.

Richard: Glad I was close enough to help.

Dagmar: That was fortunate, Simon.

Simon: Yeh.

Janet: No burns, eh, Richard?

Richard: Robots don't burn, Janet.

Dagmar: They don't?

Richard: That's right.

Simon: Yeh, I suppose they wouldn't — with metal skin and all.

Richard: Oh, we have some unique problems, but we do have some special features that simplify life.

Dagmar: So I'm finding out.

Janet: Now Simon, aren't you sorry about the things you said about Richard?

Simon: I suppose so.

Richard: Wha' d'ya say Simon we get off to a new start?

Simon: Sure, why not?

Dagmar: Richard, I'll bet you don't bruise any more easily than you burn.

Richard: That's right.

Dagmar: How come you didn't punch us when we were saying those nasty things about you?

Richard: I'm not stainless steel, and I hated to get blood all over my suit!

D83

(All laugh.)

Janet: How practical of you! Tell us more about yourself, Richard.

Richard: Alright. I'll do that. *(Song — What Really Counts)*
A robot is like other people,
Although he's different, too.
Come listen to me and I'll tell you why,
A robot is quite different,
But still he's just like you!

There are some things that are different
About a robot's skin,
It doesn't burn and it doesn't wear thin,
But it's warmed by the sun and it keeps bones in!
And although my colour is a little odd, too,
It suits me fine, just as yours suits you,
Yes, we all have skins of our very, very own,
And they suit us both quite well, quite well,
And our skins suit us both quite well.

Now your voice and mine are different,
Our accents aren't the same,
Though my robot voice I have tried to train,
It speaks as it's told by my robot brain.
So the sounds from me and the sounds from you,
Like the songs of the birds are different too!
Yes, it doesn't really matter how our voices sound,
It's the meaning that really counts, that counts,
It's the meaning that really counts!

Another thing that is different,
Is a robot's computer brain,
Which makes some things very simple to do,
Like arithmetic, yes, and spelling too!
And when things get broken, I repair them fast,
And I fix them well, so they really last!
So although they're different, my brains are my own,
To use as best I can, as I can.
To use as best I can.

But although our brains are different,
Our looks and our voices too,
We each have our own special way to live,

Our own ways of sharing what we can give,
And although I don't think the same as you,
My self suits me, just as you suit you.
And together we can share in everything we do,
Now we've found what really matters, yes,
Now we've found what really counts!

Janet: Oh, boy, Richard! Are we lucky to have you in the neighbourhood!

Simon: Yeh, Richard. I guess you're okay.

Richard: Thanks, Simon.

Janet: Will you be able to fix your rocket for the hobby contest, Simon?

Simon: I don't know if I can get it done on time. I haven't much equipment with me.

Richard: Maybe I can help. Being metal, I find electrical connections pretty easy.

Simon: Great, Richard. Can we do it now?

Richard: Until Leon gets here, we can. We've got a little project on when he arrives.

Janet: Shall we let Dagmar and Simon in on our plans Richard?

Richard: Sure thing.

Simon: What's happening?

Janet: I think Richard's 'beep' is just the beat that Leon's song needs. But now Leon's mad at Richard and won't give him a chance.

Richard: So, I'm going to hide and use my beep, beep when Leon and Janet go through the song.

Dagmar: Hey, that sounds great.

Janet: Why don't you stay and listen?

D85

Simon: I'd like to.

Dagmar: Me too.

Janet: You could sit with the boys and girls. They're going to applaud if the song's good, aren't you?

(Audience will confirm support.)

Janet: You can clap with them.

Dagmar: Great idea.

Janet: You'd better get going. Here comes Leon now. Quick hide, Richard.

Simon: Come on, Dag. Let's find a spot.

(Richard hides. Dagmar and Simon go into audience.)

Janet: Richard, are you ready?

Richard: Ready.

Janet *(to audience)*: Are you all set?

Simon & Dagmar: All set.

(Enter Leon.)

Leon: Where's the robot?

Janet: Oh he left, Leon.

Leon: Maybe my luck's changing.

Janet: Why not try the song, Leon? The gang out here can tell us how it sounds.

Leon: Good idea. I hope we get the competition over before Richard arrives back. If we have to do the number with the help of that tinny voice, I may as well forget about my song winning.

Janet: You want me to sing, Leon?

D86

Leon: Definitely, Janet. Don't get the idea I'm down on you. Ready?

Leon & Janet *(Reprise — Fairway City)*:
>Fairway City, that's for me,
>Fairway City, that's for everybody.
>It's so pretty — Fairway City,
>That's where I hope to spend my next hundred years!
>
>Just one hundred years ago,
>Our fair city began to grow,
>It started small — but grew up tall,
>Now we are proud to be part of it all.

(Richard has come in with "beep, beep" at the appropriate spots. Audience applauds.)

Leon: I think it sounded not bad. It seems to have a beat we never got before.

Janet: You liked it?

Leon: Sure did. Didn't you think it sounded good?

Janet: Yes, I did.

Leon: And it sounded as though these folks liked it too. *(Audience approves)* Let's try it again, Janet.

(During the song, Leon is looking around trying to decide where the "beep" is coming from.)

Leon & Janet *(Reprise — Fairway City)*:
>Fairway City, that's for me,
>Fairway City, that's for everybody,
>It's so pretty — Fairway City,
>That's where I hope to spend my next hundred years!

(Audience applauds.)

Leon: It's definitely a brand new beat. Is someone out there doing that? *(Audience will deny responsibility)* Then who? Who's giving it that terrific beat? *(Audience will tell Leon that it is Richard Robot)* You're fooling me. It can't be him. He's not even here.

LEON

ANOTHER IDEA
USING GLITTERY
LEOTARD

Janet: Come on out, Richard. Leon, your beat is definitely a "beep, beep"!

Leon: Richard! Richard Robot! It was you!

Richard: Did you like it, Leon?

Leon: Did I like it? I loved it! It's the making of the song.

Janet: I told you he'd like it, Richard.

Leon: You know, Richard, a guy like you could get a job with any band in the country. Wow! What a talent!

Richard: That's Leon.

(Enter Marvin.)

Marvin: Listen, group, how would you like to see Madwick the Magician do an absolutely fantastic magic trick . . . oh, it's you guys. Well, no sense trying to show you. You're all against me.

Janet: We're not against you, Madwick.

Leon: We just think magic tricks aren't your thing. *(To audience)* Should this guy become a magician?

(Audience will agree with Leon.)

Marvin: But I wanted something for the hobby contest.

Leon: Why in the world did you decide to be a magician?

Marvin: My name's Marvin Madwick — I thought Madwick the Magician sounded good.

Janet: It does — but what good is a clever title if it's not your thing? There must be something else you're interested in.

Richard: Marvin, did you ever try Morse code?

Marvin: No. No . . . I never did.

Richard: Why don't you stick with me? I'll show you how my set

D89

works. It's interesting . . . you might like it.

Marvin: I'd sure like to have a look at it.

Janet: With Richard's help and advice, Marvin, you could likely have your own set and use it for the next hobby show.

Marvin: Say, maybe you're right. *(To audience)* Do you really think I should drop the magic tricks? *(Audience responds.)*

Leon: I agree with them, Marvin. I think I'd try the Morse code.

(Enter announcer carrying applause meter. It is a large self-standing piece with figures on it visible to the audience, and a pointer that moves to the figures.)

Announcer: You're the young man who wanted to enter the song contest?

Leon: That's right, sir.

Announcer: Well, you're the last contestant. The results of all the other entries have been recorded on the applause meter.

Janet: What's the highest so far?

Announcer: The highest is eight, recorded when that group from the south end sang their song.

Leon: Eight, eh? That's pretty high. Well, anyway, I guess we're as ready as we'll ever be. All set, Richard?

Richard: Sure am, Leon.

Marvin: I'll run and sit down here.

(He moves to audience area.)

Leon, Janet & Richard *(Reprise — Fairway City)*:
        Have you heard, come join the crowd,
        We're having our hundredth birthday party . . . !

Fairway City, that's for me,
Fairway City, that's for everybody,
It's so pretty — Fairway City,
That's where I hope to spend my next hundred years!

Just one hundred years ago,
Our fair city began to grow,
It started small — but grew up tall,
Now we are proud to be part of it all.

Fairway City, that's for me,
Fairway City, that's for everybody,
It's so pretty — Fairway City,
That's where I hope to spend my next hundred years!

Our city grew and learned to live,
Our people grew, learned to care and give,
So join us now, we're feeling fine,
Happy birthday for the one hundredth time!

Fairway City, that's for me,
Fairway City, that's for everybody,
It's so pretty — Fairway City,
That's where I hope to spend my next hundred years!
That's where I hope to spend my next hundred years!

(The applause from the audience is led by Simon and Dagmar and Marvin. The announcer is in such a position that he can make the meter register ten which is as high as it goes.)

Announcer: Thank you, folks. Thank you. It seems we have a winner here. You wrote the song, young man?

Leon: That's right, but it really wouldn't have worked if it hadn't been for Richard Robot and, of course, Janet.

Announcer: It's a good song and you have a good group here. I hope you'll keep them together to promote the city for the whole centennial year.

Leon: You can be sure I will.

Announcer: If you'll come over to the main bandstand in a few minutes, the mayor of Fairway City will present the award to you.

Leon: I'll be there, sir.

Announcer: Good.

(Exit announcer.)

Leon: Well, wha' d' ya know!

Richard: Isn't it great, Leon?

Marvin *(returning to stage)*: That sounded terrific, gang!

Janet: You were fabulous, Richard.

Leon: You sure were, Richard. *(He notices Simon and Dagmar)* Hey, I didn't see you out there, Simon. And there's Dagmar. How did you like the song?

(Simon and Dagmar return to stage area.)

Simon: Great, Leon.

Dagmar: With that arrangement, I knew you had to win the contest, Leon. *(Noticing Marvin)* Oh, it's you.

Janet: Oh, this is Marvin Madwick.

Simon: We've already met.

Marvin *(to Dagmar)*: I got a new rope for you. Here it is.

Dagmar: Oh . . . thanks.

Richard: Marvin's giving up magic. He's going to work with me on Morse code.

Simon: That sounds like a break for everybody. C'mon, Richard. Sorry to take Richard away but he's promised to help with my rocket.

(Pulls Richard toward him. During these speeches, Richard is pulled between Simon, Leon and Marvin.)

Leon: You can't take him. As soon as we get the award I want to talk to him about another song I have.

Marvin: He's going to show me Morse code.

Simon: But I need him to make a couple of connections on my rocket.

Leon: I need his beep, beep for my arrangements.

Marvin: He promised to help me.

Simon: But I discovered his talent first.

Leon: But I met him first.

Dagmar: Hey fellows, stop! You're going to pull Richard to pieces.

Janet: He can help us all. He's going to be around for a while, aren't you, Richard?

Richard: I sure am. This has turned out to be a neighbourhood where my metal skin and my "beep, beep" aren't going to make any difference.

Janet: We're glad you moved to our neighbourhood.

Richard: Me too!

All: Hurray for Richard Robot! *(Song — Everyone Matters, When Everybody Cares):*

> Let's all give a hand to our new-found friend!
> Bonjour! Good morning! I hope we meet again.
> He may be different from me and from you,
> But he's like many others who are very different too.
> He's like many others who are very different too.
>
> Let's all pull together as we build the land,
> Let's build a better future with a helping hand!
> The load will be lighter, if everyone shares,
> Everyone matters, when everybody cares!
> Everyone matters, when everybody cares!

(Possibly spoken.)

> Let's all get together, shout the happy sound,

In everyone there's something good, just waiting to be found!
There are things that make a man worthwhile whatever job
he's in,
But it matters not how he looks or talks, or the colour of his
skin!
It matters not how he looks or talks, or the colour of his
skin!

Let's all pull together as we build the land,
Let's build a better future with a helping hand!
The load will be lighter, if everyone shares,
Everyone matters, when everybody cares!
Everyone matters, when everybody cares!

(Optional sing-along.)

Leon *(to audience)*: Why don't you sing along with us? Richard will
call out the words in case you don't know them. Ready, Richard?

Richard: Ready, Leon. Let's all pull together . . . .

(The chorus of the song is taught to the audience.)

The end

MARVIN
MADWICK

Song titles	WHEN EVERYBODY CARES

Song titles   WHEN EVERYBODY CARES

FAIRWAY CITY — Leon
FAIRWAY CITY REPRISE — Leon, Richard, Janet
WHAT REALLY COUNTS — Richard
FAIRWAY CITY REPRISE — Leon, Janet
EVERYONE MATTERS WHEN EVERYBODY CARES — Company
*(Production music available upon application to Simon & Pierre
Publishing Company Limited. See Copyright on page D56.)*

Summary of music credits   Music and lyrics for WHEN EVERYBODY CARES were written by
Dick Beck who is a project engineer with Canadian General Electric
in Peterborough. Besides his score for WHEN EVERYBODY CARES,
Mr. Beck has written the music and lyrics for four Christmas plays
by Beth McMaster. He directed the play HAPPY HOLLY which, at
the 1976 Eastern Ontario Drama League One-Act Festival, received
five awards, including Best Production of a Canadian Play, and a
special adjudicator's award for music and lyrics.

Props   WHEN EVERYBODY CARES

Barker's hat
Crutches
Frog on leash
False beard
Basket with snake's head
A case with legs which open out. At various times, the case contains:
two eggs, flour, butter, raisins, cloth, scarf with a rabbit painted on it,
magic spoon, scissors, magic wand
A top hat containing a dead, plucked chicken
Guitar
Five green ribbons
One red ribbon
One blue ribbon
Sheet music
Sports equipment bag containing two red balls and two blue balls
Two rope belts
Starting whistle
Two baskets
Magnet
Model rocket with flashing light, and piece of string attached
Freestanding applause meter

Sound effects   WHEN EVERYBODY CARES

Recorded band music
Mechanical 'beep' or buzzer sound in Richard Robot's costume

WHAT GLORIOUS TIMES THEY HAD ~ NELLIE McCLUNG

a satire

by Diane Grant and Company

We would like to express our gratitude to The Canada Council and the Ontario Arts Council for their support.

Marian M. Wilson, Publisher

ISBN 0-88924-048-5
1 2 3 4 5/79 78 77 76
Simon & Pierre Publishing Company Limited, Order Department
P.O.Box 280 Adelaide Street Postal Station
Toronto, Ontario, Canada M5C 2J4

Author **Diane Grant** began playwriting at the University of British Columbia in 1961 with a one-act play called FAZAR. She learned stagecraft as an apprentice with Toronto Workshop Productions and has since worked as an actress and director in various theatres throughout Canada. Her last engagement was with the Stratford Festival as Melinda Moorhill in Brecht's TRUMPETS AND DRUMS.

She became interested in playwriting again while directing a documentary about the Toronto Islanders, called I'M HANLAN, I'M DURNAN, HE'S WARD. After completing work on WHAT GLORIOUS TIMES THEY HAD, she again collaborated with Redlight Theatre on a play about the comic strip character, Broom Hilda. She has just finished co-writing a Canadian film script with K.L.B.Feltham called A MILD SENSE OF DISAPPOINTMENT.

Play background **How the play was developed**
WHAT GLORIOUS TIMES THEY HAD began as an idea for a play about the life of Nellie McClung. Diane Grant began research by reading Nellie McClung's novels — thirteen in all — and by acquiring newspaper reports of her activities.

Diane wrote a scenario of chronological events and worked with the cast, scene by scene, improvising and writing. The cast members conducted their own research into their characters and provided new material and ideas.

The play has since been revised and reworked several times.

Credits Production photographs are by Anne Wordsworth.
Photograph of Political Equality League, page E6, appears with special thanks to the Manitoba Archives, Winnipeg, Manitoba.

E3

Original cast   The play WHAT GLORIOUS TIMES THEY HAD was first produced by Redlight Theatre at Bathurst Street United Church,
736 Bathurst Street, Toronto, Ontario on May 8th, 1974 with
the following cast:

Directed by Diane Grant
Musical Accompaniment by Monika Piebrock
Settings by Barbara Barron
Costumes by Heidi Grosowski
Photographs by Anne Wordsworth
Nellie McClung — Diane Grant
E. Cora Hind — Francine Volker
Frances Beynon — Jacquie Presly
Lillian Beynon Thomas — Elizabeth Murphy
Sir Rodmond Roblin — Geoffrey Saville-Read
P.T.Fletcher — Paul Brown

Original
production
notes

Casting

In the original production, actors doubled roles. E. Cora Hind
doubled as a factory woman, Adelaide, and Evelyn. Lillian doubled
as a factory woman and as Millicent.

One actor played Sir Rodmond Roblin and all other male roles
were taken by the second actor.

An actor's change from one character to another was accomplished
by a Brechtian technique using a change of hat, vest or veil. No
attempt was made to disguise the actor, and sometimes the trans-
formation was made onstage. However, there is no reason why a
different actor cannot be used for each role.

The members of the Legislative Assembly and the Mock Parliament
were represented by balloons which were used to suggest a large
number of anonymous and obedient government backbenchers.
This effect could also be achieved by using several actors dressed
alike.

Staging

Although the play works equally well on a thrust stage or in the
round, the first production was blocked for the proscenium. Minimal hand props, seven chairs and three moveable desks denoted
different objects and places.

Lighting

The stage was divided into six lighting areas and actors changed

E4

scenes by moving themselves and the furniture from one area to another.

A follow spot is suggested for several of the scenes.

There is a diagram of lighting areas on page E79.

Music
In the original production, one violin provided musical accompaniment, but any other instrument or instrumental group is possible if it evokes the "ladies' musical social" atmosphere.

Cast of characters
Sir Rodmond Roblin, the Premier of Manitoba; a portly, dignified man in his early sixties
P.T.Fletcher, the parliamentary secretary to Sir Rodmond Roblin
Nellie McClung, a social reformer, novelist and suffragist; an attractive woman in her thirties
Frances Beynon, a journalist and suffragist
Lillian Beynon Thomas, a journalist and suffragist, Frances' sister
E. Cora Hind, an agriculture expert and journalist; a forceful woman in her early fifties
Mr. Wilson, a rancher from Calgary, Alberta
Gerry, an insurance clerk
Mr. Black, the boss to Gerry
Adelaide Roblin, the wife to Sir Rodmond Roblin
Mr. Ackroyd, a factory owner
Two factory women, employees of Mr. Ackroyd's
C.P.Walker, a theatre magnate
A man, a petitioner for male suffrage
A charwoman
Evelyn, an eastern woman
Millicent, sister to Evelyn
Tobias Crawford Norris, leader of the Liberal Party; a man in his early fifties
Various members of the Legislative Assembly, male cast members
Various members of the Mock Parliament, female cast members

General setting The play is set in Winnipeg, Manitoba

Time Between 1912 and 1916

Act one *In area 1 there are three chairs facing front, set diagonally from right to left. In area 3 there are two chairs facing front, set diagonally from left to right. In area 6 there is one chair facing front.*

The actors and musician enter in black. The musician turns on the Tiffany lamp above her head. The lights in area 6 are turned up low. The musician tunes her violin. In the darkness, we hear the voices of Roblin and Fletcher.

Roblin: No woman, idiot, lunatic or criminal shall vote.

Fletcher: Elections Act, Dominion of Canada.

(A spot comes up on Nellie, facing front, centre stage.)

Scene **Nellie:** People still speak of womanhood as if it were a disease. They may be somewhat prejudiced. If prejudices belonged to the vegetable world, they would be described under the general heading of: Hardy Perennials — will grow in any soil, bloom without ceasing, require no cultivation; will do better if left alone. In regard to tenacity of life, no yellow old cat has anything on a prejudice. You may kill it with your own hands, bury it deep and sit on the grave and behold, the next day, it will walk in at the back door, purring. Take some of the prejudices regarding women that have been exploded and blown to pieces many, many times and yet walk among us today in the fullness of life and vigour. One of the oldest and falsest of our beliefs regarding women is that they are protected — that some way in the battle of life, they get the best of it. People talk of men's chivalry, that vague, indefinite quality which is supposed to transmute the common clay of life into gold. Chivalry is a magic word. It seems to breathe of foreign strands and moonlit groves and silver sands and knights and kings; it seems to tell of glorious deeds and waving plumes and prancing steeds and belted earls and things. People tell us of the good old days of chivalry when womanhood was really respected and reverenced, when brave knight rode forth to die for his lady love. But, in order to be really loved and respected, there was one hard and fast condition laid down, to which all women must conform. They must be beautiful — no getting out of that. They simply had to have starry eyes and golden hair, or pale, white and haughty brow and a laugh like a ripple of magic. Then they were alright and armoured knights would die for them quick as a wink. The homely women were all witches, dreadful witches, and they drowned them on public holidays, in the mill pond.

E7

(Applause. Areas 1 and 2 come up as spot goes out. Lillian, Frances and Cora are seated, facing front — stage right. The women move down to area 2 which stays up as the musician plays the introduction to "Win Them, Win Them, One By One". Area 1 fades to black. They sing the song . . . .)

Women: Win new members day by day
        We'll help win them, here's the way.
        Just one way can this be done
        We must win them, one by one.

        So you win the one next to you
        And I'll win the one next to me,
        In all kinds of weather
        We'll all work together
        To see what can be done.

        If you win the one next to you
        And I win the one next to me,
        In no time at all
        We'll have them all
        So win them, win them, one by one.

(In areas 3, 4, and 5, lights come up.)

Frances: Congratulations, Nellie.

Nellie: Thank you.

Cora: First class speech. I enjoyed it immensely.

(Cora exits upstage right.)

Nellie: Thank you, Cora.

Lillian: What's your next stop?

(Lillian moves one of stage right chairs to area 4.)

Nellie: Moosamin.

Frances: Will you be seeing Mrs. Burritt in Sturgeon River? She's asked for fifty petition forms.

(Frances moves one of stage right chairs to area 5. She exits upstage left.)

Nellie: Really.

Lillian: That's 1,500 signatures.

Nellie: I'll have to see if they'll fit in my suitcase.

(Nellie exits downstage right.)

Lillian: How many people are there in Sturgeon River, Cora?

Cora *(entering upstage right, with pamphlets)*: Eight hundred and seventy-five. Nellie, how old is Mrs. Burritt?

Nellie *(entering with suitcase, downstage right)*: Ninety-one.

Frances *(entering with petition forms, downstage left)*: Good night! *(Gives forms to Nellie)* I must make a note to order some more forms. We're running out of them already.

Lillian: That's wonderful.

(Lillian exits upstage right.)

Cora: Do include my Lucy Stone pamphlet, Nellie. I think it's rather good.

Nellie *(takes pamphlets)*: I wouldn't dream of leaving it out.

(Nellie puts petition forms and pamphlets in suitcase.)

Lillian *(entering with basket, downstage right)*: Here's a treat for the train.

Nellie: Oh, how nice, Lillian. Thank you. *(Takes basket from Lillian.)*

Lillian: Who are you staying with in Moosamin, Nellie?

Nellie: The MacMillans.

Cora: You lucky thing. Doesn't she set a generous table?

E9

Nellie: She certainly does. Those lemon biscuits. Aren't they good, Cora?

Cora: "You need five cents worth of oil of lemon and five cents worth of citrate of ammonia. Otherwise, it's just a *(Cora and Nellie in unison)* plain beaten biscuit."

Nellie: I must run. I have to pick up my tickets.

Lillian: Oh, that reminds me. Did you get the tickets for "Ben Hur" tonight?

Frances: Yes, I did. *(To Cora)* Aunt Alice is coming, isn't she?

Lillian *(to Nellie)*: I'm sorry you'll miss it.

Nellie: Well, duty calls.

Cora: "And no one shall work for money and no one shall work for fame, but each for the joy of working . . . ." That's . . . .

Nellie: Kipling, you know.

(The women laugh. Nellie takes Cora's arm. A chorus of, "Goodbye", "Have a good trip", "Good luck". Frances and Lillian exit downstage right, and Fletcher enters upstage left, carrying a brown paper bag. He passes Nellie and Cora who are exiting upstage left.)

Fletcher *(without pleasure)*: Morning.

Nellie & Cora: Good morning.

Scene   In The Park *(Sir Rodmond Roblin enters from upstage right.)*

Fletcher: Good morning, Mr. Premier.

Roblin: Morning, Fletcher. Nice day.

Fletcher: Yes, sir.

(Roblin mimes taking seed from Fletcher's paper bag and begins to mime feeding pigeons.)

Roblin *(pointing to pigeon)*: I think old Ferguson is getting a

E10

little fat, don't you?

Fletcher: Yes, sir.

Roblin: Fletcher?

Fletcher *(brushing off pigeon)*: Shoo. Shoo. Yes, sir?

Roblin: There aren't many men who would cheat their wives out of their share of the property, are there?

Fletcher: Course not, sir.

Roblin: My God, a man is forced to support his wife, isn't he? What more does she want?

Fletcher: Trouble at home, sir?

Roblin: Runny poached eggs.

Fletcher: What?

Roblin: Adelaide. She's taken to reading the Free Press . . . . She's been burning the toast as well. It's all this suffragist business. *(Pause. Roblin takes a pamphlet from his pocket)* She got this pamphlet in the mail from the Political Equality League. I confiscated it. *(Fletcher nods wisely)* You know, I really think she's on their side.

Fletcher: So is Norris, sir. He had the whole gaggle of them down to the Liberal convention last week.

Roblin: That damned opportunist. He'll do anything to win the next election.

Fletcher *(sardonically)*: He says he thinks they're right.

Roblin: Right? Of course, they're not right. The man's a bachelor. What does he know? "Wives submit yourselves unto your own husbands, as unto the Lord." That's damn well right. "For the husband is the head of the wife, even as Christ is the head of the Church." Paul to the Ephesians, Chapter 5, Verse 22.

Fletcher: Harmony . . . a house needs harmony.

E11

Roblin: "Unto the woman he said, 'I will greatly multiply thy sorrow and thy conception; in sorrow thou shalt bring forth children and thy desire shall be to thy husband, and he shall rule over thee'."

Fletcher: Amen. *(Pause. Roblin resumes feeding pigeons.)*

Roblin: Here, Fergie.

Fletcher: You know, their heads are smaller. Their brains are probably smaller, too. Do you think they're smart enough to vote?

(Nellie enters downstage right, carrying suitcase.)

Roblin *(lifts his hat)*: Good day to you, madam.

Nellie: Good day to you, sir. *(She continues walking, stops, and looks back)* Lovely day.

Roblin & Fletcher: Lovely day.

(Nellie exits upstage left. The men watch her leave.)

Roblin *(ruminatively)*: You know, Fletcher. I believe you're right. Their heads are smaller.

(Roblin and Fletcher exit upstage left. Music: "Victory Bells" is playing as Frances enters from downstage right, wheeling on a desk. On the desk are a typewriter and a telephone. She wheels it into area 1 — lights stay up. Areas 2, 3, 4, and 5 — lights fade. She sits and begins to type as Al enters from upstage left. Al is a snappy dresser, a fast talker and he is chewing on a toothpick. He is a salesman for Purity Flour. Frances continues typing as "Victory Bells" fades and Al approaches her.)

Scene   **Frances**

Al *(brightly)*: Good morning, is this the Grain Grower's Guide?

Frances: Yes, it is. May I help you?

Al: Who is the editor of the women's page?

Frances: Why, that would be Frances Marion Beynon.

E12

(Al takes chair from area 4, places it next to Frances and sits.)

Al: Tell him I'm here.

Frances: I'm Frances Marion Beynon.

Al *(unfazed)*: How do you do? Well, I won't waste your time, Mrs. Beynon.

Frances: Miss.

Al: Yes. I'm here on behalf of Purity Flour. Now, have you seen our latest advertising poster? *(Unrolls a large poster featuring a girl with pies, breads and cakes)* There she is. Miss Purity. Isn't she a peach?

Frances: Well, actually, we use your advertising regularly, Mr. . . . .

Al *(moving in)*: You can call me Al. Yes, I know you do and that's why I'm here. Frankly, Miss Beynon, I find your column distressing. Too many articles on politics, prohibition, child welfare. Where are the recipes?

Frances: But we just published a lovely recipe for prune aspic.

Al: Prune aspic. Where are the cakes, the pies, the tortes? What would life be like without blueberry turnovers?

Frances: Infinitely impoverished.

Al: Miss Beynon — Frances — you have a wonderful sense of humour but no sense of proportion. Your column is encouraging women to leave the kitchen. They'll join clubs. They'll go to meetings. *(Intimately)* Do you have any idea of what goes on in those meetings?

Frances: As a matter of fact, I do. I'm a member of the Political Equality League.

Al: Oh. *(Pause)* What does go on in those meetings?

Frances: We like to discuss ideas of importance in the world, such as woman suffrage. Are you interested in women getting the vote?

Al: Oh, no. Oh, no. Think of the consequences, Miss Beynon. Women will go out into the world, that dangerous, dirty world.

E14

Frances: But Al, charwomen have been cleaning up that dirty world for years . . . going abroad at 5:30 in the morning.

Al *(emphatically)*: Well, that's fine. They're used to it. What I'm talking about is commerce, science, politics, engineering.

Frances: Oh, you mean it's the clean professions women should stay away from.

Al *(angrily)*: No, I mean they should stay in the kitchen. That's their proper sphere.

Frances: Well then, you may be interested in this. I just received a report that Cornell University has just enrolled twelve men in domestic science. They seem to have a natural aptitude for it.

Al: Sissies.

Frances: Oh, I don't think so. It says here that one is a member of the Varsity baseball team and one is in the glee club.

Al: Ah hah.

Frances: The point is that labour is sexless.

Al *(infuriated)*: That's not the point. *(Regains composure)* And that's not the issue. The issue here is flour. Pastry that appeals.

Frances: Oh, I see. *(She stands up and wheels desk upstage to area 4. Crossfade to area 4)* Al, I don't think you quite understand the kind of thing I want to get into my column.

(Al picks up the chair on which Frances has been sitting and follows her with it.)

Al: I want you to think about this recipe for orange torte. *(He attempts to slide chair under Frances as she pauses behind desk, which she leaves in area 4)* This'll make your mouth water. *(Frances continues moving into area 2. Area 2 comes up as she moves into it. Al leaves chair behind desk and pursues Frances)* You take two cups of flour.

(Lillian enters from downstage left. She meets Frances and Al in area 2.)

Lillian: Hello.

E15

Al: How do you do?

Frances: May I present Mr. . . . .

Al: You can call me Al.

Frances: Al. My sister, Lillian Thomas.

Al: Charmed, Miss Thomas.

Lillian: Mrs.

Al: Of course.

Frances *(to Lillian)*: Will you be at the lecture next week?

Lillian: Yes, I will. *(The phone rings in area 4)* I must run.

Frances: See you then. 'Bye. *(The phone rings again.)*

Lillian: Goodbye.

Al: As I was saying, the secret's in the flour . . . *(Al and Frances exit downstage left, Al hot on Frances' heels. The phone rings and Lillian picks it up . . . .)*

Scene   Lillian

Lillian: Manitoba Free Press. Lillian Beynon Thomas. Yes. My mail is still on my desk. I haven't opened it yet. Mrs. McKenna, I'm a journalist, not a lawyer. Uh huh. The Political Equality League has a pamphlet out on the Legal Status of Women. I'd be happy to send you one. Uh huh. Mrs. Ruth McKenna, R.R. 3, Fort Rouge. Fine. I'll send it right away. 'Bye. *(She hangs up phone and sorts through the mail)* Mrs. McKenna, Mrs. McKenna. *(She opens the letters and reads)* "Dear Mrs. Thomas, I read your column on Court Protection for women and I'm wondering if I could get it. I have been married for seventeen years. Everything was fine until about five years ago. We lost quite a bit of money and my husband started drinking all the time. We have one girl at home. She's ten, and when he gets drunk, he beats her up, too. I don't care so much about myself anymore, but I'm worried about Janet. What do you think I should do? Mrs. Ruth McKenna." *(She picks up phone)* Operator, a Mrs. Ruth McKenna, Fort Rouge. *(Crossfade to area*

E16

3 as Roblin enters from downstage left and sits on chair. He is reading the pamphlet which he confiscated from Adelaide. Lillian picks up pamphlet from desk — crossfade to area 4) Hello. Lillian Thomas here. I just read your letter, Mrs. McKenna. Yes, I think that you should apply for Court Protection right away. You are eligible, I'm quite sure. *(Finds section in pamphlet)* Here it is. The Married Woman's Protection Act. Section Two.

(Crossfade to area 3.)

Roblin: A married woman may apply to a county court judge for an order of protection in case of . . . assault . . . desertion . . . persistent cruelty . . . habitual drunkeness . . . or wilful neglect of children.

(Crossfade to area 4.)

Lillian: Section Three. A married woman who has committed an act of adultery cannot obtain an order of protection under this Act. Section Four . . . . I beg your pardon? Of course. Section Three . . . .

(Crossfade to area 3.)

Roblin: A married woman who has committed an act of adultery cannot obtain an order of protection under this Act. Hmm.

(Crossfade to area 4.)

Lillian: Mrs. McKenna? Are you still there? Mrs. McKenna? *(Pause. She hangs up the phone)* Hmm.

(Lillian wheels desk to area 5 as Roblin exits. Crossfade to area 5. E. Cora Hind enters from downstage right, galley proof in hand. She is in high dudgeon. She walks briskly into area 5.)

Scene   Cora

Cora: Blast it, blast it, blast it! They've signed it E. C. Hind again. It's E. Cora Hind! This column is written by a woman and I want everyone to know it. *(Sees Lillian)* Lillian, what are you doing here?

Lillian *(agitated)*: Who do you know in Fort Rouge?

Cora *(busy with proof)*: Fort Rouge. There's Helen and Bertha Wood. You met them last summer. There's Reverend Braden . . . .

E17

Lillian: Reverend Braden. He's the one. I'll ask him to call on her. *(She starts to exit.)*

Cora *(still busy with proof)*: Call on who?

Lillian *(over her shoulder)*: Mrs. McKenna.

(Lillian exits downstage left. The telephone rings as Frances enters from upstage left.)

Cora *(picks up phone)*: Agriculture. Miss Hind. Ask him to come right up. *(Hangs up phone)* Good morning, Frances.

Frances: Good night, your office is a shambles. Are you ready for the lecture this afternoon?

Cora *(shuffles through papers on her desk)*: I have my notes here somewhere . . . weekly market report for the cheese factories . . . weekly market report for the creameries . . . last year's wheat crop estimates . . . last year's . . . ! *(Looks up, delighted)* An invitation to the Stampede . . . !

(Mr. Wilson enters from downstage left. He is a rancher from Alberta.)

Mr. Wilson: I hope you're going to be there, Miss Hind. We're looking forward to seeing you down our way.

Cora: I've already laid out my riding boots and breeches. *(To Frances)* Frances, meet Mr. Wilson from Calgary. Mr. Wilson . . . Miss Beynon. *(They nod)* How's the ranch?

Mr. Wilson: Fine, Miss Hind. You know, though, I might'a got stuck with some questionable bulls.

Cora: What's the trouble?

Mr. Wilson *(scratches head)*: Well, I only had a conception rate of forty-eight percent on eleven bulls this year.

Frances: Cora, I think I'll . . . .

Cora: I hope you checked the semen quality.

Mr. Wilson: Oh, yah . . . seems pretty good.

E19

Cora: Any cryptochordism?

Frances: Cora, I . . . .

Cora *(to Frances)*: That's when one or both of the testicles haven't descended into the scrotal sac.

Mr. Wilson: Nope. They've all dropped down. I mean, both dropped down on all of 'em. You see what I mean.

Cora: I don't know what the problem could be.

Mr. Wilson: Yah, it's ticklish. *(Turns to go)* Well, I won't keep you, Miss Hind. Just came in to chew the fat.

(Cora watches him go, smiling. Mr. Wilson exits downstage left. Pause.)

Cora: Lovely man.

Frances *(faintly)*: I think I need a cup of tea.

Cora *(briskly)*: Now, Frances, that's what's the matter with you women today. Forever nibbling on cinnamon toast and drinking tea. What you need to build you up is a nice juicy beefsteak.

(Frances exits downstage right. Cora wheels her desk off upstage right, as Gerry enters downstage right, wheeling in desk on which there is a sign saying "Neepawa Insurance Agency". He wheels it into area 3. Nellie enters from downstage right. Crossfade from area 5 to area 3. Gerry is a young man whose voice is still not firmly placed. He enjoys his work.)

Scene   **The Insurance Policy**

Nellie *(places suitcase on desk)*: Good afternoon, Gerry.

Gerry: Oh, hi, Mrs. McClung. How's things?

Nellie: Just fine, Gerry.

Gerry: What'll it be today?

Nellie: The usual.

E20

Gerry: Ten days coverage for two dollars. Right? *(Takes pen and Accident Insurance Policy from drawer of desk)* There you go. Just sign on the bottom line.

Nellie *(takes pen and policy and signs)*: Thank you, Gerry. There you are.

Gerry *(putting pen away)*: Where are you off to today?

Nellie: Moosamin.

(Nellie begins to read the Accident Insurance Policy.)

Gerry: It's nice there this time of year.

Nellie *(reading)*: Yes. The lilacs are in bloom.

Gerry: Oh, that's nice. Say, how's Wes and the kids?

Nellie *(still reading)*: They're fine. Jack has a cold. Runs right through the family.

Gerry: Colds are awful. I hate to get them. *(Suddenly)* Did you say Moosamin? You'd better hurry. The train leaves in four minutes.

Nellie *(startled)*: Four minutes! Thank you. *(She picks up suitcase and begins to exit downstage right)* Have a good day, Gerry.

(Nellie walks away, continuing to read policy. She turns it over.)

Gerry: 'Bye, Mrs. McClung.

(Nellie stops suddenly and turns back.)

Nellie: Gerry!

Gerry *(surprised)*: Oh, hi, Mrs. McClung. Short trip.

Nellie: Gerry, I've been buying this Accident Insurance Policy for a year and a half and I just read it. I'm not covered. Have you read it?

Gerry: No, I don't read them. I just sell them.

Nellie *(shows him the back of the policy)*: Look at that.

E21

Gerry *(peers closely at paper)*: Gee, that's written kind of small, isn't it? Would you like to speak to someone who knows something about it?

Nellie: Yes, I would, Gerry. Thank you.

(As Nellie waits, the lights dim and Gerry puts on a coat and glasses, transforming himself into Mr. Black. Mr. Black is an older man who has been in the insurance game for many years. The lights come up.)

Mr. Black: Sit down, sit down. Mrs. McClung?

Nellie: Yes.

Mr. Black: Mr. Black. Problem?

Nellie: I have only three minutes to catch my train, so I'll be brief.

Mr. Black: I'm a busy man myself.

Nellie *(firmly)*: I'd like to read this to you. "If the insured be a male, he will be paid the full principal sum for the loss of both hands or both feet or the sight of both eyes. . . . If the insured be a male, he will be paid the full principal sum for the loss of one hand or one foot or the sight of one eye. . . . If the insured be a male, etc. etc. . . loss shall mean with regard to hands and feet, actual severance above or through the wrist . . . ."

Mr. Black *(sharply)*: I'm quite aware of what's in the policy, Mrs. McClung.

Nellie: Then you know what's on the back. In the black border.

Mr. Black: Yes.

Nellie: Females are insured against death only.

Mr. Black: Surely you know why, Mrs. McClung.

Nellie: No, I don't, Mr. Black.

Mr. Black: Women are too sensitive to be trusted. They are victims of pure nerves in an accident. I remember one case . . . an hysterical

E22

woman who claimed that she was in shock after a minor collision in Moos . . . Moos . . . Moos . . .

Nellie: Moosamin?

Mr. Black: Whatever. Do you know what she was, Mrs. McClung? *(Pause)* Pregnant. Yes, pregnant. No, no. There'd be no end of trouble. They'd imagine they were hurt and it'd be impossible to tell.

Nellie: But surely, Mr. Black, you could check to see if they imagined they'd lost a foot or had a hand cut off.

Mr. Black *(pause)*: Is there anything else I can do for you, Mrs. McClung?

Nellie: Yes, I'd like my two dollars back.

Mr. Black: Certainly. *(Takes form from drawer)* Just fill in this form and your money will be mailed to you in ten days in postage stamps.

Nellie *(filling in form)*: Thank you for your time, Mr. Black. I hope to have the opportunity of bringing this matter before the next convention of insurance men.

Mr. Black: The insurance men have invited you to speak to them?

Nellie: Not yet. But they will.

(Nellie exits downstage right. Mr. Black exits downstage left, taking the sign "Neepawa Insurance Agency" with him. He leaves the desk in area 3. Crossfade — lights come up in areas 2, 4, and 5 as they go down in area 3, and Lillian and Frances enter from upstage right.)

Scene **The Temperance Lecture**

Lillian *(sitting, facing front in area 4)*: It looks like everyone's here. What a good crowd.

Frances *(moving downstage into area 2)*: We are proud to have with us today Miss E. Cora Hind, the Agricultural Editor of the Winnipeg Free Press. Miss Hind. *(Cora enters from upstage left, carrying an easel and a number of large white cards. To Cora)* May I help you?

(Frances takes a chair from area 1, places it in area 2 beside the

E23

easel which Cora sets up. Cora hands Frances the white cards.)

Cora: Thank you. *(Cora faces audience in area 2. Frances sits, facing front)* Good afternoon. Have you ever seen a spider entice a silly fly into its cobweb? Have you ever watched as it drained the last drop of blood from its victim? Just so does alcohol lure its victim. Just so does the drink traffic drain the lifeblood of the nation. It is the moral sepulchre in which are buried some of the most promising beginners in life's battles. Let me quote to you from a report of a special committee of the Legislative Assembly of Canada. This survey is based on one hundred families studied over a five year period. Number of drunks in one hundred families . . . .

Frances: Two hundred and fourteen. *(She places a card which reads 214 on the easel.)*

Cora: Number of widows left . . . .

Frances: Forty-six. *(She places a card which reads 46 on the easel.)*

Cora: Number of orphans . . . .

Frances: Two hundred and thirty-five. *(She places a card which reads 235 on the easel.)*

Cora: Number of premature deaths due to drunkeness . . . .

Frances: Two hundred and three. *(She places a card which reads 203 on the easel.)*

Cora: Number of years of human life lost through drunkenness . . . .

Frances: One thousand, nine hundred and fifteen. *(She places a card which reads 1,915 on the easel.)*

Cora: These are not just idle numbers on a card. I have travelled throughout the west and I have seen the defeated men, the broken families, the abandoned farms and the battered women and children. It is the women who suffer the most. Without property rights, they cannot protect their farms. Without guardianship rights, they cannot protect their children. Let us pray that when women get the vote, which they will, they will use it as a weapon and cast their votes for prohibition. *(Frances places the card "Prohibition" on the easel)* Prohibition! It's a hard sounding word, hard as a locked door. But

E24

the drink traffic is always with us. It stalks our streets. It throws its challenge in our faces. In order that we may go forward into the glorious future that Canada holds out to us, we must accept this challenge. When science discovered the relationship between the housefly and typhoid, the mosquito and yellow fever, the breeding places of these insects were wiped out. Now, these epidemics are almost unknown. Alcohol is an epidemic. Every man, woman and child here today must ask himself, "Am I part of the world's disease, or am I part of the world's cure?" Thank you.

Frances: Thank you, Miss Hind. That was a fine speech, indeed. And now, we would like to render for you one of our most popular numbers. Page forty-nine in your songbooks. Please omit verse three.

(Lillian, Frances and Cora move downstage centre and sing. Areas 2, 4, and 5 fade to darkness — spot comes up on women, centre. The song is "Going Dry".)

Women: Hearken brave crusaders to the message cheering
Temperance waves are rising round us mountain high.
Over all the land, saloons are disappearing
Cities, towns and hamlets all are going dry.

Carman's going dry
Sperling's going dry
Pass along the watchword
Brandon's going dry.

Carman's going dry
Sperling's going dry
Pass along the watchword
Brandon's going dry.

To the front, crusaders, where the fight is waging
For the liquor traffic has been doomed to die.
Gird you on the armour and the foe engaging
Pass along the watchword, your town's going dry.

Carman's going dry
Sperling's going dry
Pass along the watchword
Brandon's going dry.

E25

Carman's going dry
Sperling's going dry
Pass along the watchword
Brandon's going dry.

*(Spot out. Lillian and Cora exit upstage right in black. Cora strikes
the easel. Frances places chair in area 5 and sits as Nellie enters area 1
and sits. Roblin enters area 3 as area 3 lights come up. He is smoking
a big cigar and carrying a Union Jack which he places on the desk.
Fletcher follows, carrying an ashtray and some papers. He gives the
papers to Roblin and Roblin begins to look them over.)*

Scene   **Who Is This Nellie McClung?**

Roblin: Who is this Nellie McClung?

Fletcher: Oh, you know, sir. She's that madwoman. "Drink Is The
Devil's Brew." "Stampede For Suffrage." She writes those trashy novels,
too.

Roblin: Trashy, eh? *(Smiling)* Somewhat prurient, Fletcher?

Fletcher: No, no. They're temperance tracts in disguise. I read one of
them. All about an Irish family that didn't drink. Hah. "Sowing Seeds in
Danny", it was called.

Roblin: "Sowing Seeds in Danny!" Adelaide reads that.

Fletcher: Poison her mind.

Roblin: What does she want to see me for?

Fletcher: Mrs. McClung, sir?

Roblin: What the deuce, Fletcher. She phoned me up. Wants me to see
some damned fool factory or other. I mean, Fletcher, that's not my
job.

Fletcher: Quite right, sir.

Roblin: And what's all this about a female factory inspector? What do
they want a woman in there for?

Fletcher: I dunno, sir. I'll take care of it. No need to bother yourself

E26

with such a small matter. *(Pause)* Course, if you don't go, they'll undoubtedly persuade Norris to. He's such an opportunist. *(Pause.)*

Roblin: You know, Fletcher. I think the fresh air will probably do me good. Besides, I'd like to meet this McClung woman.

(Blackout. Roblin remains seated onstage and Fletcher exits downstage left. Fletcher strikes the Union Jack and papers. Nellie enters upstage left. Frances enters upstage right. Lights full up suddenly in areas 2, 4, and 5. Nellie is standing, chair in hand and talking across the stage to Frances, who is also standing, chair in hand.)

Scene   The Ride To The Factory

Nellie: What a lovely car.

Frances: So roomy.

(Roblin, chair in hand, walks into area 2, from area 3. During Roblin's next speech, Frances and Nellie place their chairs side by side diagonally, facing downstage left — Nellie's chair slightly upstage of Frances' chair. Roblin places his chair a few feet in front of the two behind, slightly to the left of Nellie's to suggest a car. Music plays "Rondino" softly under the following scene.)

Roblin: This, madam, is a Pierce Arrow. I had it made to my own specifications. *(He opens door and Frances and Nellie get into car. Frances sits stage right and Nellie sits stage left)* Twelve cylinders. Very powerful. *(Roblin pokes his head through the window)* You'd be wise to hold on to the straps. *(He dashes to the front of the car and cranks it up. Shouting)* Teak dashboard, hand tooled leather. It's one of the rewards of hard work.

Nellie *(to Frances)*: I've never seen cut glass vases in a car before.

Frances *(leaning out of window and shouting to Roblin)*: I love the smell of carnations.

(The car starts. Roblin gets into the driver's seat. Nellie and Frances jiggle as the car idles.)

Roblin: I have them picked fresh every day. *(He releases the hand brake and puts car into gear)* They were my mother's favourite. *(The car lurches forward, pitching the women forward with it)* Sorry.

E27

Nellie *(jolted)*: Not at all.

Roblin: Yes, I believe in hard work. My mother worked from dawn to dusk and never seemed to complain. *(He beeps the klaxon — horn sound offstage)* Damned dogs. *(Nellie looks out window at disappearing dog)* Even used to make her own soap. Now you can buy it at the corner store. You modern young women have all these new-fangled gadgets — electricity, wringer washers, Hoovers. *(He makes a left turn, leaning into the turn. The women follow Roblin's lead, and lean to the left)* Hard day's work never hurt anyone. As a boy, I was up at sunrise and before. Happiest days of my life, running barefoot through the apple trees. *(The car leaps over a bump in the road, jostling the women)* Sorry.

Nellie: Not at all.

Roblin: Women's hearts are often too kind. Perhaps you're a little oversentimental about factory conditions. Most of these young factory girls just want to get out of the house and earn a little pin money.

Nellie: They certainly don't make enough to live on.

Roblin: Well, most of them are foreigners anyway. They were used to hard work over there, and don't expect to be lifted to the skies on a flowery bed of ease. *(Turns to talk over his shoulder)* Madam, extravagant women are the curse of the age.

(Frances sees the factory approaching rapidly.)

Frances *(alarmed)*: Here we are, sir. *(Roblin slams his foot on the brakes and honks the klaxon frantically — horn sound from offstage. Violin sounds a long note)* Oh, oh, oh, oh.

(Frances and Nellie brace themselves. The car stops and Roblin and Frances are thrown forward and back against the seats. Nellie falls off the seat. Roblin looks back and cannot see Nellie.)

Roblin: Mrs. McClung? *(Frances helps Nellie up)* Mrs. McClung! *(Roblin opens door, gets out of driver's seat and rushes to open door beside Nellie. He helps her out of the car)* Sorry.

Nellie: Not at all.

(Roblin, Nellie and Frances destroy the illusion of the car by placing

E29

a chair each upstage centre, facing front and side by side, as Mr. Ackroyd enters from downstage left, carrying a kerosene lantern. He places the lantern on the desk in area 3 and continues into area 2.)

Scene   **The Factory**

Mr. Ackroyd: Mr. Premier.

Nellie: Good morning, Mr. Ackroyd.

Mr. Ackroyd *(ignoring Nellie)*: Good day, Mr. Premier. So good to see you. We are honoured to have you visit Ackroyd, Acme and Associates.

Roblin: My pleasure.

Mr. Ackroyd *(takes oratorical stance)*: I am pleased and happy, and I'm sure that the late Mr. Acme would also be pleased and happy, to welcome you to our factory. I would like to present you with this miniature tractor as a momento of this auspicious occasion.

(Frances and Nellie applaud.)

Roblin: Thank you, Mr. Ackroyd. Ladies. I am sure that my grandson will while away many happy hours with this, plowing through Mrs. Roblin's gladiolas. *(Mr. Ackroyd, Nellie and Frances laugh politely. Pause)* Shall we begin, Mr. Ackroyd?

Mr. Ackroyd: Certainly. But before we move off, one word of caution. There is a lot of noise and we shall have to stick together for safety's sake.

Roblin *(gallantly)*: The ladies shall be my special charge.

Mr. Ackroyd: This way.

(Ackroyd, followed by Frances, Nellie and Roblin, moves downstage left into area 3. Crossfade from areas 2, 4, and 5 to area 3. Ackroyd lights lantern.)

Frances: All the modern conveniences, eh, Mr. Ackroyd?

Mr. Ackroyd *(the irony is lost on him)*: Yes.

E30

(Mr. Ackroyd, followed by Roblin, Nellie and Frances, moves around desk to stage left. Area 3 starts to fade. They move upstage as if along a narrow passageway and the lantern provides the only light. The factory workers enter area 2 in black and begin to create an industrial machine. They do this using rods, chains, blocks, etc. — any material or object which suggests violent sound and motion. In this scene, the advantage of using extra players is obvious.)

Frances: My, it certainly is dark in here.

Nellie: And damp.

Mr. Ackroyd: Renovations.

Frances: Temporary inconvenience.

(When Mr. Ackroyd, Roblin, Nellie and Frances are in line with the three upstage chairs, the factory specials come up, backlighting areas 2, 4, and 5. Mr. Ackroyd climbs up on the first chair and walks across the chairs, crouched down, as if he were in a low tunnel. The other three follow. Mr. Ackroyd steps off the third chair into area 4. He ducks his head. Roblin steps off, and mimes bumping his head.)

Mr. Ackroyd: Watch your head.

(The noise of the factory is deafening and everyone shouts. Roblin slips on the floor.)

Roblin: Doesn't anyone ever sweep this floor?

(Mr. Ackroyd doesn't hear the question and smiles.)

Nellie: They don't have time. They're on piece work.

Roblin: Pardon?

Nellie: They're on piece work.

Roblin: What?

Frances: They're paid by the piece.

(Roblin strains to hear and does not watch where he is going. The nature of the machine will determine the next action but Roblin is

E31

either caught in the machine or hit by it. He narrowly misses a serious accident.)

Roblin *(shouting desperately)*: Ackroyd, Ackroyd, Ackroyd!

(Ackroyd, Nellie and Frances stop moving.)

Mr. Ackroyd: Stop the machine!

(The machine stops. There is great noise and confusion and everyone speaks at once.)

Mr. Ackroyd: Are you alright, sir?

Roblin: Yes.

Mr. Ackroyd *(to workers)*: You'll be fired for this. This is all your fault, you clumsy idiots.

Girl 1: You can't do that. It was her fault.

Girl 2: It wasn't my fault. It was his fault. Why didn't he look where he was going? Tell me that.

Girl 1: Tell me that. Why didn't he look where he was going?

Frances: Are you alright, Sir Rodmond?

Roblin: Yes, thank you.

Nellie: Are you alright?

Roblin: Yes, yes, yes! *(Mr. Ackroyd starts to exit upstage right. Roblin shouts above the noise)* Ackroyd!

Mr. Ackroyd: Yes, sir?

Roblin: I want these factories cleaned up.

Mr. Ackroyd: Right away, sir.

(Mr. Ackroyd exits upstage right. Roblin moves into area 3, followed by Nellie and Frances. Area 3 comes up.)

Roblin: Why do you women bother yourselves with these things?

Nellie: Somebody has to.

Frances: Your factory inspectors don't do their jobs. Perhaps a woman would be more conscientious.

Roblin: What the deuce, madam. What on earth could a woman do?

Nellie: She could begin by taking the Premier on a factory inspection tour.

Frances *(consulting her notebook)*: Ferguson and Sons. 10:15 a.m.

Roblin: Thank you, ladies. I've seen enough. I'll admit I'm shocked and I'll speak to Fletcher first thing in the morning.

(Roblin, Nellie and Frances exit downstage left. Ackroyd enters upstage left and throws a broom at the factory workers.)

Mr. Ackroyd: Sweep up this floor.

(Ackroyd exits downstage right. The workers move into area 2, desultorily sweeping.)

Girl 1 *(bursting into tears)*: I can't lose this job. I can't.

Girl 2 *(stopping sweeping)*: But, why?

Girl 1 *(wailing)*: Listen. *(Music: Intro to "Father's A Drunkard, And Mother Is Dead". The factory specials go out and a spot focuses on workers. Girl 1 sings the verses. Girl 2 joins in on the chorus)*
>We were all so happy till Father drank rum
>Then all our sorrow and trouble begun;
>Mother grew paler and wept every day,
>Baby and I were too hungry to play.
>Slowly they faded, and one summer's night
>Found their dear faces all silent and white;
>Then with big tears slowly dropping, I said:
>Father's a drunkard, and Mother is dead!
>
>Mother, oh! Why did you leave me alone,
>With no one to love me, no friends and no home?

E33

Dark is the night, and the storm rages wild,
God pity Bessie, the drunkard's lone child!

Oh! If the "Temp'rance men" only could find
Poor, wretched Father, and talk very kind.
If they could stop him from drinking, why, then
I should be so very happy again!
Is it too late? "Men of Temp'rance" please try.
Or poor little Bessie may soon starve and die.
All the day long I've been begging for bread—
Father's a drunkard, and Mother is dead!

Mother, oh! Why did you leave me alone,
With no one to love me, no friends and no home?
Dark is the night, and the storm rages wild,
God pity Bessie, the drunkard's lone child!

(Spot out. Factory workers exit upstage right, striking whatever material has been used for industrial machine. Nellie enters from upstage left and walks into area 2. Area 2 — lights up.)

Scene   The Convention of Insurance Men

Nellie: I would like to thank the Registered Insurance Agents of Manitoba for inviting me to speak to them today. I would like to say a few words about the Elections Act. A lunatic may regain his reason and be given his vote back. A criminal may vote again after he's let out of prison, and isn't it strange how the government manages to let him out just before an election? *(Applause from offstage)* On the other hand, if a man becomes an idiot, his vote is taken away. *(Applause from offstage)* A woman can't lose what she's never had. Thank God for small mercies. *(Applause from offstage.)*

(Blackout. Nellie exits downstage left. Roblin enters area 4. Lights come up in area 4. Roblin is wearing a carnation in his buttonhole.)

Scene   Breakfast With Adelaide

Roblin: Adelaide, have you seen my homburg?

(Adelaide enters from downstage right, carrying a homburg and two books. She is wearing a frilly breakfast cap.)

E34

Adelaide: I have it right here, dear. I was just giving it a brush.

Roblin: Thank you. *(He puts hat on at a jaunty angle and straightens his tie.)*

Adelaide: You look very spruce, Roddy.

Roblin: Thank you.

Adelaide: You're certainly in a hurry. You didn't even eat your egg.

Roblin: Pressing affairs of state, my dear. *(He whistles a few bars of "The Maple Leaf Forever" and fixes carnation in buttonhole.)*

Adelaide: They say that Mrs. McClung is a most attractive woman.

Roblin *(noncommital)*: Indeed?

Adelaide: And terribly charming.

Roblin: We'll see. *(Adelaide holds out the two books, "Sowing Seeds in Danny", for Roblin)* Adelaide. No!

Adelaide: Oh, please, dear. Just two tiny autographs. I promised Hettie Ferguson one, and one for myself. I'm sure Mrs. McClung won't mind.

Roblin: I mind, Adelaide.

Adelaide: Hettie will be so angry if I don't get her one. Please, Roddy, please.

Roblin *(takes books)*: Suffering peanuts.

(Crossfade area 4 to area 3. Roblin crosses downstage into area 3. Music: "The Maple Leaf Forever". Fletcher pushes a tea tray into area 3 on which there are two teacups and saucers, a milk pitcher, sugar bowl and sugar tongs, a plate with slices of lemon, and the Union Jack. He puts the Union Jack on the desk.)

Scene   The Second Meeting With Roblin

Roblin: You may show in Mrs. McClung, Fletcher. *(Fletcher hesitates)* Something troubling you, Fletcher?

E36

Fletcher: If you don't mind my saying so sir, she has no business in the building.

Roblin: For God's sake, Fletcher. Where's your sense of chivalry? It's just this once.

Fletcher *(quietly)*: If you let one in, you let them all in.

Roblin: What's that?

Fletcher: Nothing, Mr. Premier. This way, Mrs. McClung.

(Nellie enters from downstage right. She shakes hands with Roblin.)

Nellie: Sir Rodmond, I've come here today to speak to the cabinet.

Roblin *(taken aback)*: The cabinet.

Nellie: Yes.

Roblin: What a charming idea. *(Laughs)* Will you take tea?

Nellie: Yes, thank you.

(Fletcher places chair behind Nellie and she sits stage right of Roblin. Fletcher then begins to pour the tea. Roblin taps the books.)

Roblin *(takes pen from desk drawer)*: I wonder if you'd . . . uh . . . mind . . . uh . . . .

Nellie *(takes pen and books and signs)*: Not at all.

(Fletcher holds up the milk pitcher and looks inquiringly at Roblin. Nellie looks up.)

Roblin: Lemon or milk?

Nellie: Milk, please. *(Roblin nods to Fletcher who pours the milk into the cup. Roblin smiles at Nellie encouragingly)* You see, I don't think the cabinet realizes how unfair the laws are to women.

(Fletcher lifts sugar tongs and pauses, catches Roblin's eye.)

Roblin: Sugar?

E37

Nellie: Yes, thank you. *(Leaning in)* It occurred to me that if I could make it aware of the injustices, it would want to rectify the situation.

(Fletcher whispers in Roblin's ear.)

Roblin: One lump or two?

Nellie: Two.

(Pause. Fletcher proceeds to pour tea, then hands Nellie and Roblin the tea and they sip.)

Roblin: And how long do you think this interview will take, Mrs. McClung?

Nellie *(smiles)*: Oh, I wouldn't want to take up too much of their time.

Roblin: What makes you think that the cabinet will listen to you?

Nellie: I'm not that hard to listen to. Might brighten up their day.

Roblin *(unamused)*: Thank you, Fletcher. That will be all. *(Fletcher exits downstage left, after giving Nellie a malevolent look. Roblin is determined to be charming)* Mrs. McClung, I believe in leaving well enough alone. All these new-fangled ideas only lead to dissension and argument.

Nellie: But . . . .

Roblin: You take the Indians, for example. Before the white man came along, they were happy eating muskrat and the bark of trees. Now they've lost their good old-fashioned ways.

Nellie: Yes, but . . . .

Roblin: Now, you forget all this nonsense about women voting. Take it from me. *(Intimately)* Nice women don't want the vote.

Nellie: But they do, Mr. Premier, and I think I could make the cabinet understand why.

Roblin *(forcefully)*: Just a minute, Mrs. McClung. Enough's enough. I have no intention of allowing you to speak to the cabinet. *(Stands)*

E38

If you'll excuse me. It's been pleasant but I have a lot of work to do.

Nellie *(intensely)*: If you don't listen to me now, you'll be sending away the best advisor you ever had.

Roblin *(heatedly)*: What if I told you I didn't need your advice. *(Regains composure)* Mrs. McClung, you've had a little bit of success at country schoolhouse entertainments, and the applause has gone to your head. *(Nellie stands)* Madam, the rights of women is a very minor issue.

Nellie: Sir Rodmond, by the time the next election rolls around, the rights of women will be a very major issue.

Roblin *(smiles)*: Is that a threat?

Nellie *(serious)*: No. It's a prophecy.

(Roblin and Nellie shake hands. Lights fade on area 3 to black. Music: Last bar of "Victory Bells". Roblin and Nellie exit downstage left.)

Act two *In area 1, the two small desks are pushed together and surrounded by four chairs. Area 3 contains the large desk with a chair upstage right of it and one downstage left. The phone rings in black. It rings again as lights come up in area 1, and Frances enters from upstage right.*

Scene **Lillian's Idea**

Frances *(picks up phone)*: Hello, Political Equality League. Yes, we do have suffrage petitions. No, they're free of charge. Alright. Thank you for calling.

(Frances hangs up phone and sits down at typewriter. She puts paper in machine and begins to type briskly. She is tired. Lillian enters downstage right.)

Lillian: Frances, dear. How good to see you.

Frances: Hello, Lillian. *(Stops typing)* How was Vancouver?

E39

Lillian *(excitedly)*: It was just wonderful. We went walking in Stanley Park every day. We played tennis. I even went skiing. I hope you weren't too rushed off your feet.

Frances: It's been . . . .

Lillian: The University Women's Club gave me the royal treatment. They're very impressed with the work we are doing. How are the plans for the delegation to Premier Roblin coming along?

Frances: Fairly well. I . . . .

Lillian: Oh. I forgot to tell you. I saw the most marvellous play. It was called "A Mock Parliament", and in it all the women had the vote and the men had to beg for it. *(Laughing)* Can you imagine? I really enjoyed it.

Frances: I'm glad you had a nice time, Lillian, but I hope you realize that January 27th is exactly two weeks away.

Lillian: We've got to get busy.

Frances *(exasperated)*: I have been busy. I've been writing and organizing and knocking on doors. Nellie's in Brandon, you were in Vancouver and Cora's been off, heaven knows, in a field of wheat somewhere.

Lillian *(sits)*: Oh, I am sorry. We have left you to it.

Frances: Now I've got one hundred and twenty-five delegates ready to troop into the Legislative Assembly just to hear Sir Rodmond say no.

Lillian: Frances, you're overtired. What you need is a good strong cup of tea and some cinnamon toast to perk you up.

Frances: What we need is a lot more money and a few more ideas. Sometimes, I wonder about our sanity. We've been going through all this for years, and every time we know we're going to be turned down flat.

(Lillian sighs. Frances resumes typing. Pause. Lillian laughs suddenly.)

Lillian: Isn't that marvellous!

E42

Frances *(stops typing)*: What?

Lillian: We know we're going to be turned down flat.

Frances: What are you talking about?

Lillian: We could put on our own Women's Parliament right after the delegation — right after Sir Rodmond turns us down. What an opportunity for satire! Think of the publicity. And the money we'll make. It'll be a gala night at the Walker Theatre. I hope the theatre's not all booked up.

(Crossfade from area 1 to areas 2, 4, and 5. Cora enters from upstage right, carrying ice skates. C. P. Walker enters from downstage left, smoking a cigar.)

Scene   **Booking The Theatre**

Cora: Mr. Walker, Mr. Walker. Just the man I wanted to see.

Walker: Hello, Miss Hind. Skating?

Cora: I'm off to the rink. Care to join me?

Walker: No, thank you. I'm on my way to the theatre.

(They begin strolling along together.)

Cora: Mr. Walker, we had such a good time at "Ben Hur" last year. The chariot race was so exciting. Aunt Alice and I were clutching each other in delight.

Walker: Well, if you enjoyed last year's season, wait 'til you see what I've got lined up this year. Do you know I've booked George Arliss in "Disraeli"!

Cora *(stops)*:
>"For he must blaze a nation's ways
>   With hatchet and with brand
>   'Til on his last won wilderness,
>   An Empire's bulwarks stand."

Walker: Hmmm. Kipling.

E43

Cora: Yes.

(They begin to walk.)

Walker: And do you know who else I've got booked? Mrs. Schumann-Heink.

Cora *(stops)*: What a great voice. I'll never forget her, standing on your stage, singing "Tristan and Isolde". I imagined her in a great field of wheat, lifting her voice up to heaven. She and Mrs. Walker are great friends, aren't they?

Walker: Yes. She's such a jolly woman. What a sense of humour she has. There's a story that when she played Washington, or Vashington as she calls it, she said, "I love to play Vinnipeg the best because my friend, Mrs. Valker, always brings me the beer". *(Walker has forgotten that Cora is a member of the W.C.T.U. Pause)* Lovely woman.

Cora: Lovely voice. *(Stops)* Mr. Walker, is the theatre booked for January the 28th?

Walker: No, I don't think so, Cora. Why?

Cora: Well, I'm here on behalf of the Political Equality League, and we want to put on a wonderful political burlesque.

(They resume walking.)

Walker: A burlesque? But Cora, you don't sing. You don't dance.

Cora: Mr. Walker, it's not that kind of a play.

Walker: Oh, I see. What kind of a play is it, then? Who wrote it?

Cora: Why, we did. We all did.

Walker *(stops)*: A Canadian play?

(Blackout. Cora and Walker exit downstage left. Music: "The Maple Leaf Forever" throughout the following scene change. Lights slowly up in all areas. Frances enters from upstage left, crosses to area 1 and strikes small desk with typewriter downstage right. Lillian enters from upstage right, wheels second desk from area 1 into area 5, upstage right of large desk in area 3. Nellie enters from downstage left, crosses

to area 1. Nellie and Frances take the four chairs in area 1 and arrange them diagonally from right to left, side by side in areas 1 and 4. Lillian takes chair upstage right of large desk and places it behind small desk. She places chair downstage left behind large desk. Cora enters from upstage left with "Vote With Women" banners which she distributes. The women put them on and stand in front of stage right chairs, Nellie in front of upstage chairs, next Cora, Lillian and Frances, respectively. Roblin, carrying Union Jack, enters from downstage left, followed by Fletcher carrying balloons. The men cross upstage centre, then left. Fletcher stands behind the small desk, still carrying balloons. Roblin crosses to large desk and sits. Fletcher and the women sit.)

Scene   **The Delegation**

Roblin *(sotto voce)*: Are the boys all here, Fletcher?

Fletcher: Yes, Mr. Premier.

Roblin *(stands)*: Members of the Committee. We are pleased to have with us today the charming members of the Political Equality League, who are here to petition for suffrage. The first spokesman — uh — spokeswoman will be Mrs. Nellie McClung. Mrs. McClung.

Fletcher: Here, here.

Nellie *(stands)*: I want to thank you for your gracious reception of our delegation. *(Applause from the women. Roblin nods graciously)* We are not here to ask for mercy but for justice. Do we not have brains to think, hands to work, hearts to feel and lives to live? Do we not bear our part in citizenship? Do we not help to build the empire? We want the women's point of view represented in our legislation. How would you, Sir Rodmond, like to be governed by a parliament of women?

Roblin: I have a good wife. She governs me well enough.

(Fletcher laughs.)

Nellie: The Premier has a good wife. He, at least, is not afraid to trust the women with the franchise. *(The women laugh)* However, there are some who say that the government is afraid to give us the vote.

E45

Women: Here, here. True, true. Go on.

Roblin: Some people will say anything.

Nellie: Indeed, they will. Some even say that politics is too corrupt for women. But why should politics be corrupt? There is nothing inherently vicious about politics, and the politician who says it is corrupt is admitting one of two things — either that he is a party to that corruption, or that he is unable to prevent it.

(The women applaud.)

Women: Here, here. True, true. Go on.

Nellie: In either case, he is sounding the alarm and we are willing, even anxious to come to the rescue.

(The women laugh and applaud. Roblin rises in anger and interjects.)

Roblin (shouting): When you say things are corrupt, it is only the imaginings of a vile and wicked mind.

(Fletcher pounds his desk.)

Women: No, no. Shame, shame. Go on, Nellie, go on.

Roblin: I did not dispute you when you were speaking. You will be good enough to listen to my reply. (Nellie sits down. Roblin regains composure) Now. The question raised today is not a new one, and it is not confined to Manitoba, for the claim of women for equal suffrage is being made in a great many civilized countries, mostly English-speaking ones.

Fletcher: Here, here.

Roblin: As you know, we draw our inspiration in legislation, theology, art and sicence from the motherland. Now, that being a fact that none will deny, can you, can anyone, say with confidence that what we have today will be preserved and not destroyed? So surely as the sun arose today in the east and will set in the west, so surely, if you are right, the franchise will come. But, consider the example of England. There, when Mrs. Pankhurst and her militant supporters were briefly disappointed in their cause, they became hysterical, endangered life, and destroyed millions of dollars worth of property. As I have listened, I

E47

have thought how delighted Lloyd George, Asquith, and other British statesmen would have been if they had been approached in the same ladylike manner as I have been today. A mother has a hundredfold more influence in shaping public opinion around her dinner table than she would have in the market place, hurling her eloquent phrases to the multitude. I believe that woman suffrage would break up the home. It would throw the children into the arms of the servant girls! *(The women stand, applauding vigorously. Fletcher applauds and then, hearing the applause, stops, perplexedly. Roblin turns and stares at the women. He turns to Fletcher)* Come on, boys.

(Music: "The Maple Leaf Forever". Lights slowly fade. Roblin and Fletcher, with balloons, exit downstage right, followed by Nellie, Cora, Lillian and Frances respectively. Nellie carries with her the Union Jack. Violinist begins to tune in black. Lights come up slowly in all areas.)

Scene   **The Walker Theatre**

Nellie *(entering from upstage right, carrying bunting)*: I've got the bunting.

(Nellie crosses to large desk in area 3. Frances enters from downstage right, carrying newspaper. She crosses to area 3, and gives newspaper to Nellie. Nellie and Frances move large desk upstage centre. Lillian enters from downstage right.)

Lillian: I want to talk to Mr. Walker. Won't be a moment.

(Lillian crosses to small desk in area 5, wheels it out upstage left. Nellie puts newspaper on chair upstage right, and drapes bunting on large desk. Frances, facing front, talks out.)

Frances: Frank? May I please see the spotlight for the last speech?

(Blackout. Spot up, which wavers about. Cora enters from upstage right and is hit by the spot. She is carrying the balloons.)

Cora: What is going on? I can't see a blasted thing. And where is Lillian?

(The spot continues to wander about the stage. Lillian enters from upstage left with mace. Cora places balloons on stage right chairs, except for first chair, downstage right.)

Lillian: I can't find Mr. Walker. We've only got five minutes.

(She crosses upstage centre and places mace on large desk. Lillian exits downstage right.)

Frances: Oh, Frank. That will never do.

(Blackout.)

Lillian *(offstage right)*: Frances, your hat is here. Come and put it on.

Frances: Coming, Lillian. For heaven's sake, Frank. Turn something on.

(Frances exits downstage left. All areas come up. Lillian enters from downstage right, carrying hat.)

Lillian: Where's Frances?

Nellie: Trying on her hat.

(Lillian puts the hat on the large desk. Frances enters from downstage left.)

Frances: Wonderful news. We're all sold out.

All *(simultaneously)*: Marvellous. Isn't that splendid! Hurray!

(Blackout. Nellie moves downstage centre into area 2. Cora stands in front of chair, downstage right. Lillian stands in front of chair, downstage left. Frances crosses upstage centre, puts on hat and picks up mace.)

Cora *(whispers)*: Good luck, everybody.

(Spot up on Nellie. All areas come up slowly.)

Nellie: Ladies and gentlemen, may I remind you that for the next short while, positions in society will be reversed. The women will have the vote and the men will have to beg for it.

(Spot out. All areas are up. Nellie crosses to upstage left chair and stands in front of it.)

Frances *(Speaker of the House)*: No idiot, lunatic, criminal or man

E49

shall vote. *(Raps mace three times)* I hereby declare this parliament in session.

(All converge centre stage and talk at once, as follows.)

Nellie: I just adore that mace. It's the prettiest thing.

Frances: Thank you. I love your hat.

Nellie: This old thing?

Lillian: Did you hear that Mrs. Armstrong had a boy?

Frances: Order, order, ladies.

Cora: A boy? She must be so disappointed.

Nellie: That makes five boys. Tsk, tsk.

Frances: Order, order, ladies.

Lillian: Five!

Cora: Have you seen that new Sears catalogue?

Nellie: Aren't the short skirts ghastly?

Frances: *(raising her voice)*: Order! *(Silence. Nellie, Cora and Lillian sit down. Frances, sweetly—)* Shall we begin, ladies? *(Pause)* The first item on the agenda is the question of the franchise for men.

Lillian *(as Government, stands)*: Madame Speaker. It's a well-known fact, and I speak as a mother, that the male child is more difficult to toilet train than the female child, and the same would undoubtedly hold true when training men in parliamentary procedures. *(Sits.)*

Cora *(as Opposition, stands)*: Red herring. Red herring.

Frances *(Speaker)*: Order. Order. I recognize the Honourable Leader of the Opposition.

Cora *(Opposition)*: Speaking as one who is rather keen on men, I submit that it is poppycock to shut out half of the world's population simply because of a minor biological difference. *(Sits.)*

E50

Lillian *(as Government, stands)*: Madame Speaker, may I retort?

Cora *(as Opposition, stands)*: That's a nickel word.

Frances *(Speaker)*: Order. Order. Perhaps the Honourable member of the Opposition will allow the Honourable member from Brandon-Souris to reply.

Cora *(Opposition)*: Don't you mean retort?

Frances *(Speaker)*: Order!

(Cora — the Opposition — sits.)

Lillian *(Government)*: This difference. A minor one, you say? Let me appeal to your finer sensibilities, woman to woman. Would you want this room, this very room, filled with the reek of cigar smoke? Would you want to hear the clink of brandy glasses in caucus? Would you want the halls festooned with spitoons, echoing with ribald laughter? Think. Can you, in all honesty, still say a minor difference?

Cora *(Opposition)*: Balderdash. Poppycock. Emotional hogwash.

Frances *(Speaker)*: Order. Order. Time has expired. Chair recognises the . . . .

Lillian *(Government)*: And have you considered the suggestive nature of male attire — the coloured waist-coats, the embroidered suspenders, the bay rum behind the ears, the waxed ends of moustaches and the tight trousers? *(Sits.)*

Cora *(Opposition)*: Yes, yes, yes.

Frances *(Speaker, rapping mace)*: May I have order! We have reached the end of the question period.

Cora *(as Opposition, stands)*: I would like to address . . . .

Frances *(Speaker)*: I gather that the Honourable Leader of the Opposition has a supplementary question.

Cora *(Opposition)*: I address my question to the Honourable member from Brandon-Souris. I speak on behalf of the fathers of Manitoba. Should they not have legal guardianship rights over their children?

E51

They plant the seed, should they not have a share in the harvest? *(Sits.)*

Lillian *(as Government, stands)*: Who brings the child forth in pain and travail? The mother. Who nurtures it at her breast? The mother. Who teaches it to walk, talk and sing?

All *(sing together)*: Put them all together, they spell "Mother".

(Cora — the Opposition, and Lillian — the Government, speak together, neither listening to the other. They are face to face.)

Cora *(Opposition)*: Furthermore, I find it disgusting that you should use this important question as an opportunity for oratory.

Lillian *(Government)*: My husband doesn't want the vote. He's the power behind the throne. That's good enough for him.

(As they argue, a man enters from upstage left. He is wearing a banner which says "Votes For Men". He crosses downstage right and attempts to get past Lillian and Cora. They pay no attention to him. The Speaker attempts to restore order as he pushes through the two women and stands downstage right. He, the delegate, is a timid soul but he knows that right is on his side.)

Frances *(Speaker)*: Order! *(Silence. Cora and Lillian sit. Frances, sweetly—)* The chair recognizes the delegate from the Franchise for Fellows Society.

Delegate: Ladies and . . . ladies. I am here on behalf of the Franchise for Fellows Society to ask, nay to beg for the vote.
> We have been shut out too long and we're
> knocking at the door.
> We bring home the bacon, may we not cook it?
> We lie in the beds, may we not make them?
> We have one less rib, why not one more
> privilege?
> We have the brains, why not the vote?

(Pause. All look at Nellie who is hidden behind the newspaper. She slowly lowers newspaper, looks around and gets to her feet.)

Nellie *(The Premier)*: We wish to compliment the delegation on its splendid gentlemanly appearance. *(All whistle a wolf whistle)* If, with-

E52

out exercising the vote, such splendid specimens of manhood can exist, such a system of affairs should not be interfered with. If the leader of the delegation is as intelligent as he is attractive, we should have no problem. As I have listened, I have thought how delighted Lady Lloyd George, Queen Mary, and other British stateswomen would have been if they had been approached in as gentlemanly a manner as I have been today. As to the work of woman, woman has toiled early and woman has toiled late so that the idol of her heart might have the culture and accomplishment that we see here in this man today. So surely as the sun arose today in the east and will set in the west, so surely, if we extend the vote to men, they will take a backward step — and fall off their pedestals. Why upset yourselves? Politics is an unsettling business, and unsettled men mean unsettled bills, broken furniture, broken vows and divorce! *(The women and the delegate gasp in horror)* Come on, girls.

(Nellie exits downstage left, followed by Lillian, Frances, and Cora, who picks up balloons and carries them out. Areas 2, 3, 4, and 5 fade to black, leaving man in area 1. Music: "Meditation From Thais" Spot up on large desk in areas 4 and 5. Man dejectedly takes off "Votes For Men" banner and walks out of area 1, which fades to black. Man crosses upstage centre into spot and whips bunting off the desk. He puts the bunting over his arm, takes area 4 chair and places it at the stage right end of desk. He crosses to upstage left chair and places it at the stage left end of desk. He takes a spoon and knife out of coat pocket and lays the table. Then, he takes an eggcup from another pocket, puts it on the table, takes an egg out of another pocket and puts it in the eggcup. He waits impassively at the stage left end of table as Roblin, on the last bars of the music, enters from downstage left. Roblin crosses into spot and sits in the stage left chair. Man exits downstage left. Lights come up in areas 4 and 5. Spot out. Roblin takes napkin off table and spreads it in lap. He looks about for his paper.)

Scene   Reading The Reviews

Roblin *(calling)*: Adelaide, have you seen my Telegram?

(Adelaide enters from upstage right, carrying two newspapers under her arm. She is wearing her frilly breakfast cap.)

Adelaide: I have it right here, dear. I want to read the reviews. *(Sits in stage right chair and opens newspaper)* Oh, I do wish I'd been there. *(Scanning paper)* I can never find anything in this . . .

oh, here it is. It says here: "From the standpoint of entertainment, it was excellent and few burlesques have ever met with a heartier response than last night's satire on the system of the government as it exists today." *(She hands the newspaper to Roblin which he straightens out and begins to read. Adelaide opens the other paper)* Hettie Ferguson went and she bought a new hat for it — blue with maribou . . . . I wonder what Frances Beynon has to say in the Grain Grower's Guide? "That in presenting this entertainment the Political Equality League has covered itself in glory is generally admitted throughout the city." *(Roblin puts down his paper, preparatory to eating his egg, and picks up his knife)* Oh. This would be of interest to you, dear. "Mrs. Nellie McClung, as Premier . . . as Premier," *(laughs)* . . . isn't that delightful . . . *(Roblin picks up his paper again)* "gave a hard, relentless and absolutely final negative. The arguments were so delightfully reminiscent of the speech addressed to the women recently by *(she looks up — Roblin lowers newspaper slightly)* one high in authority *(her voice trails off)* that the audience was convulsed in laughter." *(Adelaide pats Roblin's hand)* Oh. Oh. Never mind, dear. *(Roblin coughs softly from behind newspaper. Pause. Absentmindedly—)* Still, this might make all the difference. We might get the vote after all.

Roblin *(looking over paper)*: What do you mean, "we"?

(Adelaide rises hurriedly.)

Adelaide: I'll just get your coffee. Won't be a minute.

(Adelaide exits upstage right. Roblin watches her go. He picks up knife and cracks egg. He looks at it despondently.)

Roblin *(standing and calling)*: Adelaide. This egg is runny!

(Blackout. Fletcher enters from downstage right, carrying balloons. Roblin crosses downstage centre to area 2. Crossfade from areas 4 and 5 to area 2.)

Scene   **Taking The Vote**

Fletcher: Therefore, let it be resolved, that in the opinion of the House, such amendments should be made to the Manitoba Elections Act as will enable women to vote at elections for Members of the Legislative Assembly.

Roblin: Boys. I would consider the passage of this legislation a want

E55

of confidence in this government.

Fletcher: Let the roll be called.

(Throughout the calling of the roll, Fletcher manipulates the balloons so that, in turn, each one bounces.)

Roblin: Armstrong.

Fletcher: Nay.

Roblin: Argue.

Fletcher: Nay.

Roblin: Bernier.

Fletcher: Nay.

Roblin: Caldwell.

Fletcher: Nay.

Roblin: Ferguson. *(Pause. Both Roblin and Fletcher look at one balloon)* Ferguson.

(The balloon bounces.)

Fletcher: Nay.

(Roblin speeds up the roll call. The balloons bounce in a frenetic fashion and Fletcher continues to interject, "Nay".)

Roblin: Harvey, Howden, Hughes, Lawrence, Lyons, Lyle, McFadden, McMeans, Montague, Orok, Prefontaine, Reid, Reilly, Steel, Taylor.

Fletcher: The amendment is hereby defeated, thirty-two to twelve.

(Fletcher hands the balloons to Roblin.)

Roblin: Thank you, boys.

(Roblin exits downstage left, carrying balloons. Exit music is "The Maple Leaf Forever". Fletcher turns to exit upstage. Spot on Fletcher.

E58

He turns and strikes a pose. As he recites the following poem, a char-woman resets the stage. Fletcher attempts to ignore her. Charwoman enters from upstage right, wheeling on small desk. She crosses to area 1, leaves desk and exits downstage left. She enters from downstage left, wheeling on small desk with typewriter and telephone, pushes the two desks together and dusts them off with a feather duster. She places the stage right chairs around the desks. She crosses upstage centre and dusts Fletcher off as she passes him. He pauses, then continues. She wheels large desk into area 3, takes two stage left chairs and puts once behind large desk and one stage left of it. She picks up eggcup and silverware, then drops silverware at the end of the poem.)

Fletcher: A poem.

> She is not old, she is not young
> But a brave Irish lass is Nellie McClung
> With a tongue that would soothe the birds off the trees
> And bright sparkling eyes that show she's a tease.
> The ladies all love her, the men on her dote
> But what's riling Miss Nellie is they won't let her vote.

> Besides we all know, and the truth must be told
> Woman's sphere is the home, not out in the cold.
> She's too tender and fragile to mix with the gang
> Of Roblin's home guard, who sometimes use slang.
> So while we are sorry, it cannot be done
> Votes are for "Men Only" not Nellie McClung.

(The silverware crashes to the desk. Fletcher turns and glares at the charwoman.)

Fletcher: Thank you.

(Blackout. Fletcher and charwoman exit downstage left. The phone rings. Area 1 up. Cora enters from downstage right.)

Scene **Election Preparations — The Opposition**

Cora *(picks up phone)*: E. Cora Hind speaking. Yes. *(Calling)* Frances. Telephone. *(Frances enters from downstage right and takes phone from Cora. Meaningfully—)* I think it's someone special.

Frances: Frances Beynon speaking. Oh. Hello, Frank. Oh, thank you. I'm so glad you enjoyed it. Did you really think so? Well, thank you.

E59

Nellie was pretty good, too, didn't you think? Oh, uh huh. That would be fine. 'Bye, Frank. *(Hangs up the phone)* That was Frank.

Cora *(reading a letter)*: T. C. Norris wants Nellie to speak at a Liberal rally the night before the election.

Frances: Good. *(Looks at book on desk)* June is almost completely booked up. Binscarth on the eleventh, Russell on the thirteenth, Birtle on the fourteenth . . . .

(Lillian enters from downstage left. She is carrying a box of leaflets and a newspaper.)

Lillian: They burned Nellie in effigy last night.

Frances: Good night.

Cora: Where?

Lillian: In Brandon. An effigy with "Windy Nellie" on it was set on fire. Nobody knows who's responsible. *(Hands Cora a newspaper)* The government's issued an apology.

Cora *(reading)*: "No sane, sensible element in any party could so far forget the ordinary chivalry of manhood, to say nothing of common sense, as to burn in effigy a citizen who enjoys the respect of the entire province, irrespective of party. This incident may be attributed wholly to a hoodlum element."

Frances *(looking at leaflets)*: "Vote Sobriety, Vote Female Suffrage, Vote Liberal on July the 10th." Very nice.

Lillian *(takes box from Frances)*: We'd better get going, Cora. There are two hundred in here.

(Nellie enters from upstage right, as Cora and Lillian start to exit downstage left. They meet in area 2 which comes up.)

Nellie: Hello, everybody.

Frances: Are you alright?

Nellie *(laughs)*: It was an effigy they burned, not me.

E60

Cora *(starts to exit, pats Nellie's shoulder)*: Rowdies and drunken louts. Take no notice.

Lillian: We're off to knock on doors. See you later.

Nellie: 'Bye.

(Nellie sits stage left of desk. Cora and Lillian exit downstage left. Area 2 out.)

Frances: How are the children?

Nellie: Full of beans. Do you know that Jack has taught Mark to say, "I'm only a suffragist's child and I've never known a mother's love"?

Frances: One of them is sure to end up on the stage.

Nellie: I wouldn't be surprised. *(Sighs)* It's not the speaking that's exhausting, it's the travelling.

Frances: Speaking of travelling, there's been a new development. You remember you were to speak in Gimli on the twentieth?

Nellie: Yes.

Frances: Well, Mr. Skinner called and it seems that somewhere our wires got crossed. Now they want you to speak on the fourth.

Nellie: Today's the third.

Frances: Yes.

(Crossfade from area 1 to areas 4 and 5. Frances exits downstage right. Nellie takes chair and moves into area 4. Fletcher enters from upstage right, takes chair from area 1 and moves into area 4. Millicent and Evelyn, carrying newspapers, enter from upstage left and pick up chairs from area 3. They move into area 5. Fletcher and Nellie place their chairs back to back, Nellie's facing stage right and slightly upstage; Fletcher's facing stage left and slightly downstage. Millicent and Evelyn place their chairs side by side, a few feet downstage of, and facing, Fletcher's. The four chairs suggest a train. All sit simultaneously, and as they do, they begin to move as if they were on a train. All speak as they move into position, during the crossfade, as follows.)

E61

Scene   Encounter On A Train

Millicent: Now, Evelyn, I want the seat next to the window. You know I always get sick if I don't sit next to the window.

Evelyn: I'm so glad I bought these papers. I'll have something to read on the train.

(Fletcher hums the "Maple Leaf Forever".)

Nellie: Oh, well. I can have a nap on the train and put my feet up. That's small consolation, but it'll have to do.

(The train begins to move.)

Man *(offstage voice)*: First call to dinner. First call to dinner.

Millicent *(looking out of window)*: Just look, Evelyn, you can see for miles and miles.

Evelyn *(opening up a newspaper)*: I do like the political reports. All this election news is so exciting.

Millicent: It's not all that flat, though. Look, there's a hill.

Evelyn: That's nice, dear. How interesting. Here's another article about that McClung woman.

(Fletcher listens in.)

Millicent: Who?

Evelyn: Nellie McClung. She's speaking in Brandon tonight.

(Nellie hears her name and smiles.)

Fletcher *(raises hat)*: Pardon me, ladies. May I introduce myself. My name is P. T. Fletcher. I couldn't help overhearing you mention Nellie McClung.

Evelyn: Yes?

Millicent: You know her, sir?

E63

Fletcher: Everybody knows Windy Nellie.

(Nellie listens.)

Evelyn: She seems to have created quite a stir. It says here the Liberals are getting on her bandwagon.

Fletcher: Tempest in a teapot, madam. Our beloved Premier is unbeatable. She thinks she's so smart. The Liberals are just using her. *(Intimately)* She's on their payroll.

Evelyn: Indeed?

Fletcher: She gets twenty-five dollars a day to do their dirty work. Norris wants to be Premier so badly he'll do anything to win the election.

Millicent: Oh, shocking.

Fletcher: She's shanty Irish, you know. Red face, big hands, big feet feet. Atrocious dresser. Horrible hats.

Evelyn: But Mr. Fletcher, there's a picture of her in here and she appears quite respectable to me.

Fletcher: Respectable? Her children run wild. She has seven or eight of them. My sister lives on her block and she often gives them clothes and feeds them. Bless her heart.

Evelyn: You paint a black picture. Surely, you exaggerate.

Fletcher: The truth is not always pleasant, madam.

Millicent: She sounds terribly wicked, Evelyn. Shall we stop over in Brandon tonight? I'd love to hear her speak.

Evelyn: What a good idea. And now, I'd like some dinner. *(Rising)* Good day, sir.

(Fletcher rises and tips his hat. Evelyn and Millicent exit upstage left. Fletcher is about to sit when he hears Nellie's voice behind him. He turns around.)

Nellie *(stands)*: Why, Mr. Fletcher. *(Shakes Fletcher's hand)* How do you do? I can't thank you enough for drumming up business for me. You must thank your sister for all her kindnesses to my children. I didn't know you had a sister. Such an angel of mercy. *(Nellie turns to exit upstage right and then turns back)* You know, I'm rather fond of this hat.

(Blackout. Fletcher and Nellie turn their chairs around and sit, facing us. Lillian and Cora enter from upstage left, turn the stage left chairs around and sit, facing upstage. Roblin enters from upstage right, crosses to centre, upstage of chairs. Lights up in areas 4 and 5.)

Scene   **Election Preparations — The Government**

Roblin: We are confident that we will sweep the province. *(Fletcher applauds)* I would like to thank *(slight pause)* all of you for turning out this afternoon. Let me just say this. Although we appreciate the innocent faith expressed by Mrs. McClung in the good intentions of the Liberals, we cannot share that faith. Furthermore, although we honour the woman, however innocent, who enters the arena of politics with good intentions, it is the woman who right nobly does a woman's work to whom we give all honour. *(Cora stands and exits upstage left. Roblin raises his voice)* We know that there are women who claim a share in the arduous task of government, thereby sacrificing the best traditions of civilized humanity . . . . *(Nellie stands, picks up chair, crosses to area 1, leaves chair and exits upstage right)* But, it is precisely the best women who will not sell their birthright — which may be said to be embodied in the popular proverb: "The woman who rocks the cradle rules the world."

(Lillian stands, picks up chair, crosses to area 1, leaves chair, and exits downstage right. Fletcher turns in his chair and he and Roblin watch her go. Fletcher stands, picks up chair. Roblin takes the remaining chair and walks with Fletcher into area 3. Crossfade areas 4 and 5 to area 3.)

Roblin: What you need is a drink.

Fletcher: No. Slows me down.

Roblin: Ah, the campaign trail is not what it used to be.

Fletcher: They're winning the support of more and more of the men.

Roblin: Yes, yes, I know. Why is that, Fletcher?

E65

Fletcher *(pause)*: Do you suppose they're withholding their conjugal rights?

Roblin *(pause)*: No, I don't think so, Fletcher.

(Roblin takes two glasses and a whisky bottle out of his desk drawer. He pours himself one. Fletcher shakes his head "no".)

Fletcher *(eagerly)*: Maybe we could make a deal with this McClung creature.

Roblin *(drinks)*: No, I don't think so, Fletcher.

Fletcher *(intensely)*: Norris has promised them the vote. The Grain Growers Association has thrown its weight behind them. The United Farm Workers . . . .

Roblin: I know. The farmer needs a wife, not a business partner.

Fletcher: Well, what are we going to do?

(Pause. Roblin cannot come to grips with the new political picture. He pours himself another drink.)

Roblin: I'm going to stand on my record. Thirty-five years in the public service must mean something. I am the Premier of the Province.

Fletcher *(desperately)*: But sir, you can't hide behind the office.

Roblin *(firmly)*: Fletcher, I intend to stand on my record. *(Fletcher gives up trying to reach Roblin and pours himself a drink. Convincing himself)* Deuce it, man. I know what this country needs. I was here at the beginning when Portage was a sea of mud on the edge of the western frontier. *(Pause)* Did I ever tell you about the time I was in the cheese exporting business?

Fletcher: Yes, sir. You did.

Roblin: Oh. *(Pause)* You know, Fletcher, they used to call Manitoba the postage stamp province. It took a hell of a lot of work to extend that boundary to the sea. Now Winnipeg is the grain capital of the world. *(Drinks.)*

Fletcher *(automatically)*: That's right.

E66

Roblin: Hundreds of outlying districts now have railways, roads, telephones.

(Roblin pours another drink for himself and Fletcher.)

Fletcher: That's true, sir.

Roblin: Damned Bell Telephone system has no imagination. Eyes always on the profit margin, never on public convenience. *(He raises his glass)* Fletcher, I give you the Manitoba Government Telephone system. *(Fletcher raises his glass. Roblin drinks)* I put the British flag on every schoolhouse in Manitoba.

Fletcher *(sardonically)*: The King.

Roblin *(reverently)*: The King. *(Now lost in the past)* I built the first agricultural college in Manitoba.

Fletcher *(drinks)*: The finest in the world.

Roblin: The finest in the world.

Fletcher: That's what I said.

Roblin: I provided a reasonable, workable, popular and satisfactory Workmen's Compensation Act.

Fletcher: Truly visionary.

(Pause.)

Roblin: Dreams, dreams . . . a man must have dreams. *(To Fletcher)* Sometimes, my boy, when the world has brought me low, I give reign to my wildest fancies. I see myself in flowing robe, galloping across the white hot sands. Fletcher, beneath this breast beats the heart of a son of the desert. *(Music: Introduction to "A Son Of The Desert Am I". Roblin looks tipsily at the musician)* Thank you, my dear. *(Follow spot up. Roblin sings, moving freely about the stage. Fletcher eventually joins in. They improvise steps together. Spot follows them and area 3 dims down)*

> A son of the desert am I,
> The iron clad hoofs of my horse spurn the sand.
> The wide spreading desert is peaceful and grand
> My good lance at rest, at my side hangs my brand.

My brave Arab comrades come at my command,
For a son of the desert am I.

None so dauntless and free on land or on sea,
For a son of the desert am I,
None so dauntless and free on land or on sea,
For a son of the desert am I.

I scoff at the sybarite's case so secure,
Luxurious life I could never endure:
'Tis freedom I love, though the world be obscure.
The desert's wild grandeur alone can allure,
For a son of the desert am I.

None so dauntless and free on land or on sea,
For a son of the desert am I,
None so dauntless and free on land or on sea,
For a son of the desert am I.

And I know that Zulica awaits in her tent,
The fairest in all the sunkiss'd Orient;
Whose form has the grace of the palm heaven-sent,
She will welcome her love when the storm cloud is spent,
For a son of the desert am I.

None so dauntless and free on land or on sea,
For a son of the desert am I,
None so dauntless and free on land or on sea,
For a son of the desert am I.

(Spot out. Roblin and Fletcher exit upstage right. Area 1 up as Lillian, Cora and Frances enter from upstage right.)

Scene **After The Election**

Lillian: Well, we won in Souris. They've never gone Liberal before. I do hope the northern ridings go Liberal.

Frances: They always go Conservative, Lillian. You know that.

Lillian: Anything can happen in this election. We've made a gain of nine seats. That's unprecedented.

Cora: It's wonderful. We've got twenty-one seats.

E68

Frances: And the Conservatives have twenty-five.

Lillian: That's hardly a landslide.

(Frances paces in the office.)

Cora: Valentine Winkler's in again.

Lillian *(to Frances)*: Tom Johnson . . . .

Cora *(to Frances)*: And Mr. Hudson.

(The phone rings. Frances hurriedly picks it up.)

Frances: Hello. Yes. *(Pause)* Oh. Thank you for calling.

(She slowly hangs up the phone. Pause.)

Cora: Well?

Frances: All three northern ridings went Conservative.

(Pause.)

Lillian: Three more for Sir Rodmond. *(Pause. Ironically—)* Who said, "If they beat us on the tenth, we'll be up on our feet on the eleventh"?

Cora: Who did say that?

Lillian *(smiling)*: Must have been that McClung woman.

(Crossfade to dim in area 1, up in area 3. A dishevelled Roblin is at his desk, trying to read some papers.)

Roblin *(muttering)*: Damned woman.

(Frances types . . . stops.)

Cora: Telephone scandal.

Roblin *(seems to hear a voice)*: What?

(Frances types . . . stops.)

E70

Lillian: Elevator scandal.

Roblin: Hmmm?

(Frances types . . . stops.)

Frances: University site scandal.

Roblin *(to himself)*: No. That was the best place for the university. Costs a little more but you pay for what you get.

Frances: Do you know who got the contract for the law school? Thomas Kelly and Sons.

Cora: And at what a price.

Roblin *(stands, as if making a speech)*: Dr. Montague tells me that Thomas Kelly and Sons is one of the finest contract engineers in Manitoba. Isn't that so, Montague. *(Pause)* Montague?

Lillian: And do you know who has the contract for the new parliament buildings? Thomas Kelly and Sons.

Roblin: We are erecting a building that we hope will stand the test of time. When future generations have passed into history, Manitoba's provincial capital will remain standing, a credit to our city and our province.

Frances: The government's been charged with robbing the public purse of two million dollars; of conspiring with Thomas Kelly and Sons.

Roblin: But we all wanted it to be first class. Kelly had to change his plans. Simon told me so himself. Didn't you, Simon? *(Pause)* Simon? *(He looks for Simon who has deserted him)* Ferguson, where is Simon? *(He waits for Ferguson to answer. Ferguson has deserted him)* Fletcher, where is Ferguson? *(Pause)* Fletcher, Fletcher?

(Roblin exits upstage left, calling "Fletcher". Crossfade from area 3 to area 1. Nellie enters from downstage right, carrying newspapers.)

Nellie *(excitedly)*: The papers are all out.

All *(together)*: Give me one, Nellie. Thank you. I'll take that.

E71

(They all read the newspapers. Pause.)

Nellie: Listen to this. Mr. P. T. Fletcher, Roblin's long-time parliamentary assistant, today denied any knowledge of the parliament buildings affair.

Lillian: The wretch.

Frances: Mr. Horwood has admitted that he has committed perjury, forgery, utterance, false pretenses, theft and falsifying public accounts. Good night.

Cora: How delicious. Kelly was overpaid by seven hundred and one thousand ninety-three dollars and fifty-nine cents. Oh, and his son's been overpaid, too.

Nellie: They got Dr. Simpson. Good. I almost hit that man over the head with my umbrella once.

Lillian: Nellie. I think they've had enough. The Conservatives are through in Manitoba.

All *(together, throwing their newspaper in the air)*: Hooray!

(Music: "Victory Bells". Area 1 out. Spot up on women as they sing.)

Women: Victory bells are ringing over the land we love,
Jubilant voices singing praises to God above.
Vigilant hosts are marching forward to meet the foe
Fighting to get the ballot, we'll win, we know.

Victory bells, victory bells, ringing all over the land,
Victory bells, victory bells, hailing a triumph grand.
Votes for women! Votes for women!
Shout the battle cry.
Votes for women! Votes for women!
Victory draweth nigh.

(Blackout. Area 2 up. Roblin enters from upstage left, carrying the Union Jack.)

E72

Scene   Roblin's Resignation Speech

Roblin: Mr. Speaker, at the last session of the Legislature, certain serious statements were made, alleging overpayments in connection with the construction of the new parliament buildings. A Royal Commission was appointed to inquire into the whole matter. The authority or jurisdiction of the Commission is now challenged. This means considerable delay before that point can be determined by the courts. The government believes such delay is undesirable and contrary to public policy. That government also realized that, constitutionally, they were responsible for the acts of their officials. For these reasons, I have tendered my resignation to his Honour, the Lieutenant-Governor with the recommendation that he call upon T. C. Norris, Leader of the Opposition, to form a new government. I do not hesitate to say that my decision in this matter has been influenced to no small amount by the results of the general election of July, 1914. Upon that occasion, certain questions, which need not be considered now, led a large number of my former friends to withdraw their support. For my successor, I have nothing but the most kindly feelings and I trust that under his leadership, the province may enjoy a measure of prosperity and development as great as or greater than that which has marked the period during which I have had the honour to be Premier. "The old order changeth, yielding place to new, and God fulfills himself in many ways, lest one good custom should corrupt the world."

(Music: "The Maple Leaf Forever". Tobias Norris enters from down-stage right and meets Roblin centre stage. Norris is carrying a Canadian Ensign flag. Roblin and Norris exchange flags. Roblin exits downstage right . . . . Offstage are shouts of hooray, and applause.)

Scene   The End

Norris: Mr. Speaker, Honourable Members, Honoured Guests, thank you. The Liberal party is proud to have won the overwhelming mandate of the people *(cheers from offstage)* and I, as Premier of the province, am especially proud that, for the first time in history, the women of Manitoba will take their place in the Legislative Assembly. *(Cheers from offstage)* Today, January 27, 1916, the Elections Act of Manitoba has been amended to extend the franchise to women. *(Cheers and applause from offstage.)*

(Music: "Win Them, Win Them, One By One". The women enter on the introduction, Lillian and Frances from upstage left, Nellie and

Cora from upstage right. They take Norris by the arm and move downstage centre, singing. Spot up. Area 2 out.)

Women: Win new members, day by day
We'll help win them, here's the way
Just one way can this be done
We must win them, one by one.

So you win the one next to you
And I'll win the one next to me
In all kinds of weather, we'll all work together
To see what can be done.

(Roblin enters from upstage left and joins in.)

If you win the one next to you
And I win the one next to me
In no time at all, we'll have them all
So win them, win them, one by one.

(Spot focuses in on Nellie.)

Nellie: Never retract, never explain. Get the thing done and let them howl.

(Blackout.)

The end

Costumes   **Act one**
Two bowler hats

Red bow tie

Mr. Black's jacket

Two aprons - factory workers
Two scarves - factory workers

Breakfast cap - Adelaide
Homburg

Act two
Fur coat - Lillian
Man's overcoat, gloves, scarf, hat - Walker
White toque - Cora
White gloves - Cora
Ice skates - Cora

Mauve hat with feathers - Frances

Breakfast cap - Adelaide

One headscarf - Charwoman

Two pair black gloves — Millicent and Evelyn
Two black veils — Millicent and Evelyn

E76

Props   **Set**

One small desk with
mailing basket
One small desk
One typewriter
One telephone
Telephone bell and batteries
One large desk
Seven chairs
One Tiffany lamp

Act one

Basket and checkered cloth
Lucy Stone pamphlet
Petition forms
Nellie's suitcase

Birdseed bag
Legal Status Of Women pamphlet

Cornell press release
Toothpick
Miss Purity poster

Lillian's mail
Pencils and pens
Mrs. Ruth McKenna's letter
Legal Status Of Women pamphlet

Cora's reports
Galley proof

Neepawa insurance policy
Request for refund form
Nib pens

Temperance lecture cards
Temperance lecture stand

Metal ashtray
Governmental papers
Cigars
Safety matches
Union Jack on stand

E77

Klaxon horn
Miniature tractor
Kerosene lamp
Safety matches
Broom

Two novels - Sowing Seeds In Danny

Two spoons
Two cups and saucers
Sliced lemon
Tea service - pot, sugar bowl, creamer
Tea cloth

Act two
Cigar

Four "Votes For Women" banners
Balloons (approx. 20)

Bunting
Newspaper
Mace
One "Votes For Men" banner
Balloons

One eggcup
One spoon
One knife
One napkin
One Winnipeg Telegram
One Grain Growers' Guide
Egg

Newspapers

Two shot glasses
One whisky bottle

Newspapers

Union Jack
Canadian Ensign

E78

LIGHTING AREAS

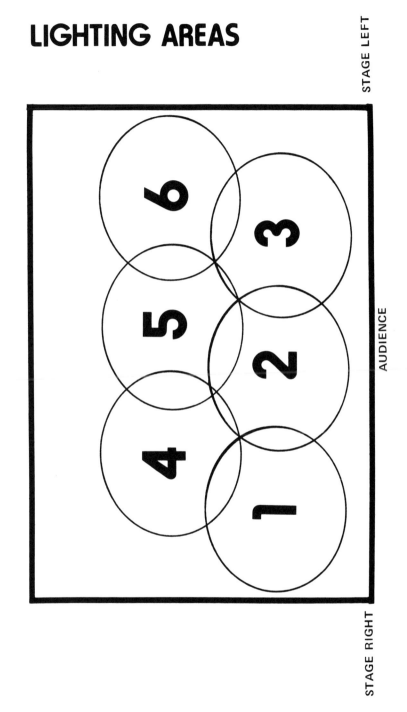

AUDIENCE

Song titles	WIN THEM ONE BY ONE — Nellie, Frances, Lillian, Cora
	GOING DRY — Lillian, Frances, Cora

Song titles

WIN THEM ONE BY ONE — Nellie, Frances, Lillian, Cora
GOING DRY — Lillian, Frances, Cora
FATHER'S A DRUNKARD, AND MOTHER IS DEAD — Two factory girls (Cora and Lillian)
A SON OF THE DESERT AM I — Roblin, Fletcher
VICTORY BELLS — Nellie, Frances, Lillian, Cora
WIN THEM ONE BY ONE REPRISE — Nellie, Frances, Lillian, Cora, Norris, Roblin
(Production music available upon application to Simon & Pierre Publishing Company Limited. See Copyright on page E2.)

Summary of music credits

"WIN THEM ONE BY ONE" by C. Austin Miles, from "THE VOICE OF SONG", published by the Woman's Christian Temperance Union, Evanston, Illinois, U.S.A.
"GOING DRY", words by Elisha A. Hoffman, music by George A. Minor, from "PROHIBITION SONGS", edited by Elisha A. Hoffman, published by the Ontario Woman's Christian Temperance Union, Toronto Ontario, Canada
"RONDINO ON A THEME" by Beethoven, published by Foley Limited, a subsidiary of Carl Fischer Co. Ltd., New York, N.Y., U.S.A.
"THE MAPLE LEAF FOREVER" by Alexander Muir, from "PROHI-BITION SONGS", edited by Elisha A. Hoffman, published by the Ontario Woman's Christian Temperance Union, Toronto, Ontario, Canada
"FATHER'S A DRUNKARD, AND MOTHER IS DEAD", words by "Stella" (of Washington), music by Mrs. E.A.Parkhurst
"MEDITATION FROM THAIS" by Jules Massenet, published by United Music Publishing Co. Ltd., London, England
"A SON OF THE DESERT AM I", words by John P. Wilson, music by Walter A. Phillips
"VICTORY BELLS", words by E.E.Hewitt, music by Charles H. Gabriel, from "PROHIBITION SONGS", edited by Elisha A. Hoffman, published by the Ontario Woman's Christian Temperance Union, Toronto Ontario, Canada.